Mathematical Ideas
for BMCC

This book belongs to ....

Charles D. Miller

Vern E. Heeren
American River College

E. John Hornsby, Jr.
University of New Orleans

▲ **ADDISON-WESLEY**

An imprint of Addison Wesley Longman, Inc.

Reading, Massachusetts • Menlo Park, California • New York • Harlow, England
Don Mills, Ontario • Sydney • Mexico City • Madrid • Amsterdam

Manager of Addison Wesley Longman Custom Publishing: Lynn Colgin
Production Administrator: Rohnda Barnes

Mathematical Ideas for BMCC includes selected sections from *Mathematical Ideas,* Seventh Edition (0-673-46738-4) by Charles D. Miller, Vern E. Heeren, and E. John Hornsby.

Mathematical Ideas for BMCC

ISBN: 0-201-43494-6

1 2 3 4 5 6 7 8 9—CCI—01 00 99 98

Contents

CHAPTER 1 *Sets*

The human mind likes to create collections. Instead of seeing a group of five stars as five separate items, people tend to see them as one group of stars. The mind tries to find order and patterns.

In mathematics this tendency to create collections is represented with the idea of a *set.* A set is a collection of objects. Sets occur in mathematics in many ways, for example when we group together all the solutions to a given problem, or perhaps all the numbers that have a meaning in a given situation.

The basic ideas of set theory were developed by the German mathematician Georg Cantor (1845–1918) in about 1875. Some of the things he proved flew in the face of accepted mathematical beliefs of the times. Controversial ideas are seldom well received, and this was especially so in the 1870s. Cantor's ideas are discussed in more detail in Section 5.

1 Basic Concepts

A *set* was described above as a "collection of objects." The idea of set, or collection, is also conveyed by many other words, such as *group* and *assemblage.* The objects belonging to the set are called the **elements,** or **members,** of the set. Sets are designated in at least the following three ways: by (1) *word description,* (2) the *listing method,* and (3) *set-builder notation.* A given set may be more conveniently denoted by one method rather than another, but most sets can be given in any of the three ways. For example, here is a word description:

the set of even counting numbers less than ten.

This same set can be expressed by listing:

$$\{2, 4, 6, 8\},$$

or by set-builder notation:

$$\{x \mid x \text{ is an even counting number less than 10}\}.$$

In the listing and set-builder notations, the braces at the beginning and ending indicate that we are thinking of a set. Other grouping symbols, such as parentheses or square brackets, are *not* used in set notation. Also, in the listing method, the commas are essential. Other separators, such as semicolons or colons, are *not* used. The set-builder notation utilizes the algebraic idea of a variable. (Any symbol would do, but just as in other algebraic applications, the letter x is a common choice.) Before the vertical line we give the variable, which represents an element in general, and after the vertical line we state the criteria by which an element qualifies for membership in the set. By including *all* objects that meet the stated criteria, we generate the entire set. (Set-builder notation is sometimes called *set-generator* notation.)

Sets are commonly given names (usually capital letters) so that they can be easily referred to later in the discussion. If E is selected as a name for the set of all letters of the English alphabet, then we can write

$$E = \{a, b, c, d, e, f, g, h, i, j, k, l, m, n, o, p, q, r, s, t, u, v, w, x, y, z\}.$$

In many cases, the listing notation can be shortened by clearly establishing the pattern of elements included, and using an ellipsis (three dots) to indicate a continuation of the pattern. Thus, for example,

$$E = \{a, b, c, d, \ldots, x, y, z\}$$

or

$$E = \{a, b, c, d, e, \ldots, z\}.$$

EXAMPLE 1   Give a complete listing of all the elements of each of the following sets.

(a) the set of counting numbers between six and twelve

This set can be denoted $\{7, 8, 9, 10, 11\}$. (Notice that the word *between* excludes the endpoint values.)

(b) $\{5, 6, 7, \ldots, 14\}$

This set begins with the element 5, then 6, then 7, and so on, with each element obtained by adding 1 to the previous element in the list. This pattern stops at 14, so a complete listing is

$$\{5, 6, 7, 8, 9, 10, 11, 12, 13, 14\}.$$

(c) $\{x \mid x$ is a counting number between 8 and 9$\}$

After a little thought, we realize that there are no counting numbers between 8 and 9, so the listing for this set will contain no elements at all. We can write the set as

$$\{ \ \} \text{ or } \varnothing. \ \bullet$$

A set containing no elements, such as the set in Example 1(c), is called the **empty set,** or **null set.** The special symbol $\varnothing$ is often used to denote the empty set, so that $\varnothing$ and $\{ \ \}$ have the same meaning. We do *not* denote the empty set with the symbol $\{\varnothing\}$, since this notation represents a set with one element (that element being the empty set).

Example 1 above referred to counting numbers (or natural numbers). Other important categories of numbers are summarized below.

Empty Set Some Zen Buddhists meditate facing a blank wall, symbol of the universal void.

Infinite Pains Georg Cantor created a new field of theory and at the same time continued the long debate over infinity that began in ancient times. Cantor developed counting by one-to-one correspondence to determine how many objects are contained in a

---

Important Number Sets

Natural or counting numbers $\{1, 2, 3, 4, \ldots\}$
Whole numbers $\{0, 1, 2, 3, 4, \ldots\}$
Integers $\{\ldots, -3, -2, -1, 0, 1, 2, 3, \ldots\}$
Rational numbers $\{p/q \mid p$ and q are integers, and $q \neq 0\}$
(Some examples of rational numbers are 3/5, −7/9, 5, and 0. Any rational number may be written as a terminating decimal number, like 0.25, or a repeating decimal number, like 0.666. . . .)
Real numbers $\{x \mid x$ is a number that may be written as a decimal$\}$
Irrational numbers $\{x \mid x$ is a real number and x cannot be written as a quotient of integers$\}$
(Some examples of irrational numbers are $\sqrt{2}$, $\sqrt[3]{4}$, and π. A characteristic of irrational numbers is that their decimal representations never terminate and never repeat, that is, they never reach a point where a given pattern of digits repeats from that point on.)

set (see Section 5). Infinite sets differ from finite sets by not obeying the familiar law that the whole is greater than any of its parts.

Cantor's teacher had been the mathematician Leopold Kronecker, who denied Cantor's "transfinite" numbers. Kronecker believed that all numbers could be expressed as combinations of integers.

The number of elements in a set is called the **cardinal number** of the set. The symbol $n(A)$, which is read "n of A," represents the cardinal number of set A.

If elements are repeated in a set listing, they should not be counted more than once when determining the cardinal number of the set. For example, the set $B = \{1, 1, 2, 2, 3\}$ has only three distinct elements, and so $n(B) = 3$.

EXAMPLE 2   Find the cardinal number of each of the following sets.

(a) $K = \{10, 12, 14, 16\}$
Set K contains four elements, so the cardinal number of set K is 4, and $n(K) = 4$.

(b) $M = \{0\}$
Set M contains only one element, zero, so $n(M) = 1$.

(c) $R = \{3, 4, 5, \ldots, 11, 12\}$
There are only five elements listed, but the ellipsis indicates that there are other elements in the set. Counting them, we find that there are ten elements, so $n(R) = 10$.

(d) The empty set, $\varnothing$, contains no elements, and $n(\varnothing) = 0$. ●

If the cardinal number of a set is a particular whole number (0 or a counting number), as in all parts of Example 2 above, we call that set a **finite set.** Given enough time, we could finish counting all the elements of any finite set and arrive at its cardinal number. Some sets, however, are so large that we could never finish the counting process. The counting numbers themselves are such a set. Whenever a set is so large that its cardinal number is not found among the whole numbers, we call that set an **infinite set.** Cardinal numbers of infinite sets will be discussed in Section 5. Infinite sets can also be designated using the three methods already mentioned.

Infinity Close-up of a camera lens shows the infinity sign ∞, defined as any distance greater than 1,000 times the focal length of a lens.

The sign was invented by the mathematician John Wallis in 1655. Wallis used 1/∞ to represent an infinitely small quantity. The philosopher Voltaire described the ∞ as a loveknot, and he was skeptical about the sign making the idea of infinity any clearer.

EXAMPLE 3   Designate all odd counting numbers by the three common methods of set notation.

1. word description

The set of all odd counting numbers

2. listing

$$\{1, 3, 5, 7, 9, \ldots\}$$

Notice that the ellipsis is utilized, but that there is no final element given. The listing goes on forever.

3. set-builder

$$\{x \mid x \text{ is an odd counting number}\} \quad ●$$

For a set to be useful, it must be **well defined.** This means that if a particular set and some particular element are given, it must be possible to tell whether or not the element belongs to the set. For example, the preceding set E of the letters of the English alphabet is well defined. If someone gives us the letter q, we know that q is an element of E. If someone gives us the Greek letter θ (theta), we know that it is not an element of set E.

However, given the set C of all fat chickens, and a particular chicken, Herman, it is not possible to say whether

Herman is an element of C

or

Herman is *not* an element of C.

The problem is the word "fat"; how fat is fat? Since we cannot necessarily decide whether or not a given chicken belongs to set C, set C is not well defined.

The letter q is an element of set E, where E is the set of all the letters of the English alphabet. To show this, $\in$ is used to replace the words "is an element of," or

$$q \in E,$$

which is read "q is an element of set E." The letter θ is not an element of E; write this with $\in$ and a slash mark:

$$\theta \notin E.$$

This is read "θ is not an element of set E."

EXAMPLE 4   Decide whether each statement is *true* or *false*.

(a) $3 \in \{-3, -1, 5, 9, 13\}$

The statement claims that the number 3 is an element of the set $\{-3, -1, 5, 9, 13\}$, which is false.

(b) $0 \in \{-3, -2, 0, 1, 2, 3\}$

Since 0 is indeed an element of the set $\{-3, -2, 0, 1, 2, 3\}$, the statement is true.

(c) $1/5 \notin \{1/3, 1/4, 1/6\}$

This statement says that 1/5 is not an element of the set $\{1/3, 1/4, 1/6\}$, which is true. ●

We now consider the concept of set equality.

Set Equality

Set A is **equal** to set B provided the following two conditions are met:

1. every element of A is an element of B, and
2. every element of B is an element of A.

In practice, a less formal idea may be used to determine if two sets are equal. Two sets are equal if they contain exactly the same elements, regardless of order. For example,

$$\{a, b, c, d\} = \{a, c, d, b\}$$

since both sets contain exactly the same elements.

Since repetition of elements in a set listing does not add new elements, we can say that

$$\{1, 0, 1, 2, 3, 3\} = \{0, 1, 2, 3\},$$

since these sets contain exactly the same elements.

EXAMPLE 5   Are $\{-4, 3, 2, 5\}$ and $\{-4, 0, 3, 2, 5\}$ equal sets?

Every element of the first set is an element of the second; however, 0 is an element of the second and not the first. In other words, the sets do not contain exactly the same elements, so they are not equal:

$$\{-4, 3, 2, 5\} \neq \{-4, 0, 3, 2, 5\}. \quad \bullet$$

Although any of the three notations can designate a given set, sometimes one will be clearer than another. For example

$$\{x \mid x \text{ is an odd counting number between 2 and 810}\}$$

may be preferable to

$$\{3, 5, 7, 9, \ldots, 809\},$$

since it clearly states the common property that identifies all elements of the set. When working with sets, it is necessary to be able to translate from one notation to another to have a clear understanding of the sets involved.

EXAMPLE 6   Decide whether each statement is true or false.

(a) $\{3\} = \{x \mid x \text{ is a counting number between 1 and 5}\}$

The set on the right contains *all* counting numbers between 1 and 5, namely 2, 3, and 4, while the set on the left contains *only* the number 3. Since the sets do not contain the exact same elements, they are not equal. The statement is false.

(b) $\{x \mid x \text{ is a math class that requires no thinking}\} = \{y \mid y \text{ is a living tree with no roots}\}$.

Since each set is the empty set, the sets are equal. The statement is true. $\bullet$

---

1 EXERCISES

List all the elements of each set.

1. the set of all counting numbers less than 5
2. the set of all whole numbers greater than 8 and less than 16
3. the set of all whole numbers not greater than 6
4. the set of all counting numbers between 2 and 12
5. $\{6, 7, 8, \ldots, 14\}$
6. $\{3, 6, 9, 12, \ldots, 30\}$
7. $\{-15, -13, -11, \ldots, -1\}$
8. $\{-4, -3, -2, \ldots, 4\}$
9. $\{2, 4, 8, \ldots, 256\}$
10. $\{90, 87, 84, \ldots, 54\}$
11. $\{1, 1/3, 1/9, \ldots, 1/243\}$
12. $\{1/2, 1/4, 1/6, \ldots, 1/20\}$
13. $\{x \mid x \text{ is an even whole number less than 15}\}$
14. $\{x \mid x \text{ is an odd integer between } -8 \text{ and 5}\}$

Denote each set by the listing method. There may be more than one correct answer.

15. the set of all counting numbers greater than 20   **16.** the set of all integers between −200 and 500

17. the set of traditional major political parties in the United States

18. the set of all persons living on February 1, 1992, who had been President of the United States

19. {x | x is a positive multiple of 4}   **20.** {x | x is a negative multiple of 7}

21. {x | x is the reciprocal of a natural number}   **22.** {x | x is a positive integer power of 3}

Denote each set by set-builder notation, using x *as the variable. There may be more than one correct answer.*

23. the set of all rational numbers   **24.** the set of all even counting numbers

25. the set of all movies released this year   **26.** the set of all multinational corporations

27. {1, 3, 5, . . . , 99}   **28.** {35, 40, 45, . . . , 995}

Identify each set as finite *or* infinite.

29. {2, 4, 6, . . . , 28}   **30.** {6, 12, 18, . . .}

31. {1/2, 2/3, 3/4, . . . , 99/100}   **32.** {−10, −8, −6, . . . , 0}

33. {x | x is a counting number greater than 30}   **34.** {x | x is a counting number less than 30}

35. {x | x is a rational number}   **36.** {x | x is a rational number between 0 and 1}

Find n(A) for each set.

37. A = {0, 1, 2, 3, 4, 5, 6}   **38.** A = {−3, −2, −1, 0, 1, 2}

39. A = {2, 4, 6, . . . , 1000}   **40.** A = {0, 1, 2, 3, . . . , 3000}

41. A = {a, b, c, . . . , z}   **42.** A = {x | x is a vowel in the English alphabet}

43. A = the set of integers between −10 and 10   **44.** A = the set of current U.S. senators

45. A = {1/3, 2/4, 3/5, 4/6, . . . , 27/29, 28/30}   **46.** A = {1/2, −1/2, 1/3, −1/3, . . . , 1/10, −1/10}

Identify each set as well defined *or* not well defined.

47. {x | x is a real number}   **48.** {x | x is a negative number}

49. {x | x is a good singer}   **50.** {x | x is a skillful actor}

51. {x | x is a difficult class}   **52.** {x | x is a counting number less than 1}

Fill each blank with either ∈ *or* ∉ *to make the following statements true.*

53. 5 ——— {2, 4, 5, 6}   **54.** 8 ——— {3, −2, 5, 9, 8}

55. −4 ——— {4, 7, 9, 12}   **56.** −12 ——— {3, 8, 12, 16}

57. 0 ——— {−2, 0, 5, 7}   **58.** 0 ——— {3, 4, 7, 8, 10}

59. {3} ——— {2, 3, 4, 5}   **60.** {5} ——— {3, 4, 5, 6, 7}

Write true *or* false *for each of the following statements.*

61. $3 \in \{2, 5, 6, 8\}$

62. $6 \in \{-2, 5, 8, 9\}$

63. $b \in \{h, c, d, a, b\}$

64. $m \in \{l, m, n, o, p\}$

65. $9 \notin \{6, 3, 4, 8\}$

66. $2 \notin \{7, 6, 5, 4\}$

67. $\{k, c, r, a\} = \{k, c, a, r\}$

68. $\{e, h, a, n\} = \{a, h, e, n\}$

69. $\{5, 8, 9\} = \{5, 8, 9, 0\}$

70. $\{3, 7, 12, 14\} = \{3, 7, 12, 14, 0\}$

71. $\{d, x, m, x, d\} = \{m, d, x\}$

72. $\{u, v, u, v\} = \{u, v\}$

73. $\{x \mid x \text{ is a counting number less than } 3\} = \{1, 2\}$

74. $\{x \mid x \text{ is a counting number greater than } 10\} = \{11, 12, 13, \ldots\}$

Write true *or* false *for each of the following statements.*

$$\text{Let} \quad A = \{2, 4, 6, 8, 10, 12\}$$
$$B = \{2, 4, 8, 10\}$$
$$C = \{4, 10, 12\}.$$

75. $4 \in A$ **76.** $8 \in B$ **77.** $4 \notin C$ **78.** $8 \notin B$ **79.** $10 \notin A$ **80.** $6 \notin A$

81. Every element of C is also an element of A.

82. Every element of C is also an element of B.

83. This chapter opened with the statement, "The human mind likes to create collections." Why do you suppose this is so? In explaining your thoughts, utilize one or more particular "collections," mathematical or otherwise.

84. Explain the difference between a well defined set and a not well defined set. Give examples and utilize terms introduced in this section.

Recall that two sets are called equal *if they contain identical elements. On the other hand, two sets are called* equivalent *if they contain the same number of elements (but not necessarily the same elements). For each of the following conditions, give an example or explain why it is impossible.*

85. two sets that are neither equal nor equivalent

86. two sets that are equal but not equivalent

87. two sets that are equivalent but not equal

88. two sets that are both equal and equivalent

89. Joan McKee is health conscious, but she does like a certain kind of chocolate bar, each of which contains 220 calories. In order to burn off unwanted calories, Joan participates in her favorite activities, shown below, in increments of one hour and never repeats a given activity on a given day.

Activity	Symbol	Calories Burned per Hour
Volleyball	v	160
Golf	g	260
Canoeing	c	340
Swimming	s	410
Running	r	680

(a) On Monday, Joan has time for no more than two hours of activities. List all possible sets of activities that would burn off at least the number of calories obtained from three chocolate bars.

(b) Assume that Joan can afford up to three hours of time for activities on Saturday. List all sets of activities that would burn off at least the number of calories in five chocolate bars.

90. The table below categorizes municipal solid waste generated in the United States.

Category	Symbol	Percentage
Food wastes	*F*	7
Yard wastes	*Y*	18
Metals	*M*	8
Glass	*G*	7
Plastics	*L*	8
Paper	*P*	40
Rubber, leather, textile, wood, other	*R*	12

Using the given symbols, list the elements of the following sets.
(a) $\{x \mid x$ is a category accounting for more than 15% of the wastes$\}$
(b) $\{x \mid x$ is a category accounting for less than 10% of the wastes$\}$

2

Venn Diagrams and Subsets

When working a problem, we can usually expect a certain type of answer. For example, a problem about money should give an answer in dollars and cents. The answer probably would not involve names, animals, or pencils.

In every problem there is either a stated or implied **universe of discourse.** The universe of discourse includes all things under discussion at a given time. For example, in studying reactions to a proposal that a certain campus raise the minimum age of individuals to whom beer may be sold, the universe of discourse might be all the students at the school, the nearby members of the public, the board of trustees of the school, or perhaps all of these groups of people.

In the mathematical theory of sets, the universe of discourse is called the **universal set.** The letter *U* is typically used for the universal set. The universal set might well change from problem to problem. In one problem the universal set might be the set of all natural numbers, while in another problem the universal set might be the set of all females over twenty-five years of age who have two or more children.

In most all areas of mathematics, our reasoning can be aided and clarified by utilizing various kinds of drawings and diagrams. In set theory, we commonly use **Venn diagrams,** developed by the logician John Venn (1834–1923). In these diagrams, the universal set is represented by a rectangle, and other sets of interest within the universal set are depicted by oval regions, or sometimes by circles or other shapes. We will use Venn diagrams to illustrate many concepts throughout the remainder of this chapter. In the Venn diagram of Figure 1, the entire region bounded by the rectangle represents the universal set *U*, while the portion bounded by the oval represents set *A*. (The size of the oval representing *A* is irrelevant.) Notice also in the figure that the shaded region inside *U* and outside the oval is labeled *A'* (read "*A* prime"). This set, called the *complement* of *A,* contains all elements that are contained in *U* but not contained in *A*.

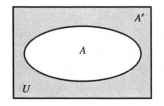

FIGURE 1

The Complement of a Set

For any set *A* within the universal set *U*, the **complement** of *A*, written *A'*, is the set of elements of *U* that are not elements of *A*. That is

$$A' = \{x \mid x \in U \text{ and } x \notin A\}.$$

EXAMPLE 1	Let	$U = \{a, b, c, d, e, f, g, h\}$
		$M = \{a, b, e, f\}$
		$N = \{b, d, e, g, h\}.$

Find each of the following sets.

(a) M'

Set M' contains all the elements of set U that are not in set M. Since set M contains the elements a, b, e, and f, these elements will be disqualified from belonging to set M', and consequently set M' will contain c, d, g, and h, or

$$M' = \{c, d, g, h\}.$$

(b) N'

Set N' contains all the elements of U that are not in set N, so $N' = \{a, c, f\}$. ●

Consider the complement of the universal set, U'. The set U' is found by selecting all the elements of U that do not belong to U. There are no such elements, so there can be no elements in set U'. This means that

$$U' = \emptyset$$

for any universal set U.

Now consider the complement of the empty set, $\emptyset'$. Since $\emptyset' = \{x \mid x \in U$ and $x \notin \emptyset\}$ and set $\emptyset$ contains no elements, every member of the universal set U satisfies this definition. Therefore

$$\emptyset' = U$$

for any universal set U.

Suppose that in a particular discussion, the universal set is $U = \{1, 2, 3, 4, 5\}$, while one of the sets under discussion is $A = \{1, 2, 3\}$. Every element of set A is also an element of set U. Because of this, set A is called a *subset* of set U, written

$$A \subseteq U.$$

("A is not a subset of set U" would be written $A \nsubseteq U$.) A Venn diagram showing that set M is a subset of set N is shown in Figure 2.

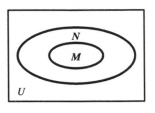

FIGURE 2

Subset of a Set

Set A is a **subset** of set B if every element of A is also an element of B.
In symbols,

$$A \subseteq B.$$

| **EXAMPLE 2** | Write $\subseteq$ or $\nsubseteq$ in each blank to make a true statement. |

(a) $\{3, 4, 5, 6\}$  $\{3, 4, 5, 6, 8\}$

Since every element of $\{3, 4, 5, 6\}$ is also an element of $\{3, 4, 5, 6, 8\}$, the first set is a subset of the second, so $\subseteq$ goes in the blank.

(b) $\{1, 2, 3\}$ _____ $\{2, 4, 6, 8\}$

The element 1 belongs to $\{1, 2, 3\}$ but not to $\{2, 4, 6, 8\}$. Place $\nsubseteq$ in the blank.

(c) $\{5, 6, 7, 8\}$ _____ $\{5, 6, 7, 8\}$

Every element of $\{5, 6, 7, 8\}$ is also an element of $\{5, 6, 7, 8\}$. Place $\subseteq$ in the blank. ●

As Example 2(c) suggests, every set is a subset of itself:

$$B \subseteq B \quad \text{for any set } B.$$

When studying subsets of a set B, it is common to look at subsets other than set B itself. Suppose that $B = \{5, 6, 7, 8\}$ and $A = \{6, 7\}$. A is a subset of B, but A is not all of B; there is at least one element in B that is not in A. (Actually, in this case there are two such elements, 5 and 8.) In this situation, A is called a *proper subset* of B. To indicate that A is a proper subset of B, write $A \subset B$.

Proper Subset of a Set

Set A is a **proper subset** of set B if $A \subseteq B$ and $A \neq B$. In symbols,

$$A \subset B.$$

(Notice the similarity of the subset symbols, $\subset$ and $\subseteq$, to the inequality symbols from algebra, $<$ and $\leq$.)

EXAMPLE 3　　Decide whether $\subset$, $\subseteq$, or both could be placed in each blank to make a true statement.

(a) $\{5, 6, 7\}$ ——— $\{5, 6, 7, 8\}$

Every element of $\{5, 6, 7\}$ is contained in $\{5, 6, 7, 8\}$, so $\subseteq$ could be placed in the blank. Also, the element 8 belongs to $\{5, 6, 7, 8\}$ but not to $\{5, 6, 7\}$, making $\{5, 6, 7\}$ a proper subset of $\{5, 6, 7, 8\}$. This means that $\subset$ could also be placed in the blank.

(b) $\{a, b, c\}$ ——— $\{a, b, c\}$

The set $\{a, b, c\}$ is a subset of $\{a, b, c\}$. Since the two sets are equal, $\{a, b, c\}$ is not a proper subset of $\{a, b, c\}$. Only $\subseteq$ may be placed in the blank. ●

Set A is a subset of set B if every element of set A is also an element of set B. This definition can be reworded by saying that set A is a subset of set B if there are no elements of A that are not also elements of B. This second form of the definition shows that the empty set is a subset of any set, or

$$\varnothing \subseteq B \quad \text{for any set } B.$$

This is true since it is not possible to find any elements of $\varnothing$ that are not also in B. (There are no elements in $\varnothing$.) The empty set $\varnothing$ is a proper subset of every set except itself:

$$\varnothing \subset B \text{ if } B \text{ is any set other than } \varnothing.$$

Every set (except $\varnothing$) has at least two subsets, $\varnothing$ and the set itself. Let us find a rule to tell *how many subsets* a given set has. The next example provides a starting point.

EXAMPLE 4   Find all possible subsets of each set.

(a) {7, 8}

By trial and error, the set {7, 8} has four subsets:

$$\varnothing, \quad \{7\}, \quad \{8\}, \quad \{7, 8\}.$$

(b) {a, b, c}

Here trial and error leads to 8 subsets for {a, b, c}:

$$\varnothing, \quad \{a\}, \quad \{b\}, \quad \{c\}, \quad \{a, b\}, \quad \{a, c\}, \quad \{b, c\}, \quad \{a, b, c\}. \quad \blacklozenge$$

In Example 4 the subsets of {7, 8} and the subsets of {a, b, c} were found by trial and error. An alternative method involves drawing a **tree diagram,** a systematic way of listing all the subsets of a given set. Figures 3(a) and (b) show tree diagrams for {7, 8} and {a, b, c}.

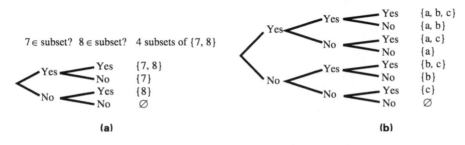

(a)   **(b)**

FIGURE   3

In Example 4, we determined the number of subsets of a given set by exhibiting a list of all such subsets and then counting them. The tree diagram method also produced a list of all possible subsets in each case. In many applications, we don't need to display all the subsets but simply determine how many there would be. Furthermore, the trial and error method and the tree diagram method would both involve far too much work if the original set had a very large number of elements. For these reasons, it is desirable to have a formula for the number of subsets. To obtain such a formula, we can use the technique of inductive reasoning. That is, we observe particular cases to try to discover a general pattern. Begin with the set containing the least number of elements possible—the empty set. This set, $\varnothing$, has only one subset, $\varnothing$ itself. Next, a set with one element has only two subsets, itself and $\varnothing$. These facts, together with those obtained above for sets with two and three elements, are summarized here.

Number of elements	0	1	2	3
Number of subsets	1	2	4	8

This chart suggests that as the number of elements of the set increases by one, the number of subsets doubles. This suggests that the number of subsets in each case might be a power of 2. Every number in the second row of the chart is indeed a power of 2. Add this information to the chart.

Number of elements	0	1	2	3
Number of subsets	$1 = 2^0$	$2 = 2^1$	$4 = 2^2$	$8 = 2^3$

This chart shows that the number of elements in each case is the same as the exponent on the 2. Inductive reasoning gives us the following generalization.

Number of Subsets

The number of subsets of a set with n elements is 2^n.

Powers of 2

$2^0 = 1$
$2^1 = 2$
$2^2 = 2 \times 2 = 4$
$2^3 = 2 \times 2 \times 2 = 8$
$2^4 = 2 \times 2 \times 2 \times 2 = 16$
$2^5 = 32$
$2^6 = 64$
$2^7 = 128$
$2^8 = 256$
$2^9 = 512$
$2^{10} = 1,024$
$2^{11} = 2,048$
$2^{12} = 4,096$
$2^{15} = 32,768$
$2^{20} = 1,048,576$
$2^{25} = 33,554,432$
$2^{30} = 1,073,741,824$

The small numbers at the upper right are called *exponents*. Here the *base* is 2. Notice how quickly the values grow; this is the origin of the phrase *exponential growth*.

Since the value 2^n includes the set itself, we must subtract 1 from this value to obtain the number of proper subsets of a set containing n elements. Here is another generalization.

Number of Proper Subsets

The number of proper subsets of a set with n elements is $2^n - 1$.

Although inductive reasoning is a good way of *discovering* principles, or arriving at a *conjecture,* it does not provide a proof that the conjecture is true in general. A proof must be provided by other means. The two formulas above are true, by observation, for $n = 0$, 1, 2, or 3. (For a general proof, see Exercise 66 at the end of this section.) To illustrate the use of these formulas, we consider the set {3, 8, 11, 17, 20, 25, 28}. Since this set has 7 elements (by counting), it must have $2^7 = 128$ subsets, of which $2^7 - 1 = 128 - 1 = 127$ are proper subsets.

EXAMPLE 5   Find the number of subsets and the number of proper subsets of each set.

(a) {3, 4, 5, 6, 7}
This set has 5 elements and $2^5 = 2 \times 2 \times 2 \times 2 \times 2 = 32$ subsets. Of these, 31 are proper subsets.

(b) {1, 2, 3, 4, 5, 9, 12, 14}
The set {1, 2, 3, 4, 5, 9, 12, 14} has 8 elements. There are $2^8 = 256$ subsets and 255 proper subsets.   ●

In a similar way, a set with 100 elements has 2^{100} subsets. Using more extensive mathematical tables,

$$2^{100} = 1,267,650,600,228,229,401,496,703,205,376.$$

2 EXERCISES

Insert ⊆ *or* ⊄ *in each blank so that the resulting statement is true.*

1. $\{-2, 0, 2\}$ —— $\{-2, -1, 1, 2\}$
2. {Monday, Wednesday, Friday} —— {Sunday, Monday, Tuesday, Wednesday, Thursday}
3. $\{2, 5\}$ —— $\{0, 1, 5, 3, 4, 2\}$ 4. {a, n, d} —— {r, a, n, d, y}
5. $\varnothing$ —— {a, b, c, d, e}   6. $\varnothing$ —— $\varnothing$
7. $\{-7, 4, 9\}$ —— $\{x \mid x$ is an odd integer$\}$ 8. $\{2, 1/3, 5/9\}$ —— the set of rational numbers

Decide whether ⊂, *or* ⊆, *or both, or neither can be placed in the blank to make the statement true.*

9. {B, C, D} —— {B, C, D, F}
10. {red, green, blue, yellow} —— {green, yellow, blue, red}
11. $\{9, 1, 7, 3, 5\}$ —— $\{1, 3, 5, 7, 9\}$ 12. {S, M, T, W, Th} —— {M, W, Th, S}
13. $\varnothing$ —— $\{0\}$ 14. $\varnothing$ —— $\varnothing$
15. $\{-1, 0, 1, 2, 3\}$ —— $\{0, 1, 2, 3, 4\}$ 16. $\{5/6, 9/8\}$ —— $\{6/5, 8/9\}$

For Exercises 17–38, tell whether each statement is true *or* false.

Let $U = \{a, b, c, d, e, f, g\}$
$A = \{a, e\}$
$B = \{a, b, e, f, g\}$
$C = \{b, f, g\}$
$D = \{d, e\}$.

17. $A \subset U$ 18. $C \subset U$ 19. $D \subseteq B$ 20. $D \subseteq A$
21. $A \subset B$ 22. $B \subseteq C$ 23. $\varnothing \subset A$ 24. $\varnothing \subseteq D$
25. $\varnothing \subseteq \varnothing$ 26. $D \subset B$ 27. $\{g, f, b\} \subset B$ 28. $\{0\} \subset D$
29. $D \nsubseteq B$ 30. $A \nsubseteq B$
31. There are exactly 6 subsets of C.   32. There are exactly 31 subsets of B.
33. There are exactly 3 subsets of A.   34. There are exactly 4 subsets of D.
35. There is exactly one subset of $\varnothing$.   36. There are exactly 127 proper subsets of U.
37. The drawing below correctly represents the relationship among sets A, C, and U.   38. The drawing below correctly represents the relationship among sets B, C, and U.

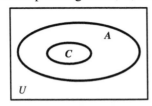   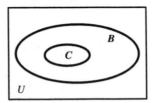

Find the number of subsets and the number of proper subsets of each of the following sets.

39. $\{1, 3, 5\}$ 40. $\{-8, -6, -4, -2\}$
41. $\{a, b, c, d, e, f\}$ 42. the set of days of the week
43. $\{x \mid x$ is an odd integer between -4 and $6\}$ 44. $\{x \mid x$ is an even whole number less than 3$\}$

Let $U = \{1, 2, 3, 4, 5, 6, 7, 8, 9, 10\}$ *and find the complement of each of the following sets.*

45. $\{1, 4, 6, 8\}$ 46. $\{2, 5, 7, 9, 10\}$ 47. $\{1, 3, 4, 5, 6, 7, 8, 9, 10\}$
48. $\{3, 5, 7, 9\}$ 49. $\varnothing$ 50. U

51. Greg Odjakjian and his family, wishing to see a movie this evening, have made up the following lists of characteristics for their two main options.

Go to a Movie Theater	Rent a Home Video
High cost	Low cost
Entertaining	Entertaining
Fixed schedule	Flexible schedule
Current films	Older films

Find the smallest universal set U that contains all listed characteristics of both options.

Let T represent the set of characteristics of the movie theater option, and let V represent the set of characteristics of the home video option. Using the universal set from Exercise 51, find each of the following.

52. T' **53.** V'

Find the set of elements common to both of the sets in Exercises 54–57, where T and V are defined as above.

54. T and V **55.** T' and V **56.** T and V' **57.** T' and V'

Anita Virgilio, Brett Sullivan, Curt Reynolds, Debbie Roper, and Elizabeth Miller plan to meet in the hospitality suite at a sales convention to compare notes. Denoting these five people by A, B, C, D, and E, list all the possible ways that the given number of them can gather in the suite.

58. 5   **59.** 4   **60.** 3

61. 2   **62.** 1   **63.** 0

64. Find the total number of ways that members of this group can gather in the suite. (*Hint:* Add your answers to Exercises 58–63.)

65. How does your answer in Exercise 64 compare with the number of subsets of a set of 5 elements? How can you interpret the answer to Exercise 64 in terms of subsets?

66. In discovering the formula (2^n) for the number of subsets of a set with n elements, we observed that for the first few values of n, increasing the number of elements by one doubles the number of subsets. Here, you can prove the formula in general by showing that the same is true for any value of n. Assume set A has n elements and s subsets. Now add one additional element, say e, to the set A. (We now have a new set, say B, with $n + 1$ elements.) Divide the subsets of B into those that do not contain e and those that do.
   (a) How many subsets of B do not contain e? (*Hint:* Each of these is a subset of the original set A.)
   (b) How many subsets of B do contain e? (*Hint:* Each of these would be a subset of the original set A, with the element e thrown in.)
   (c) What is the total number of subsets of B?
   (d) What do you conclude?

67. Suppose you have available the bills shown here.

   (a) If you must select at least one bill, and you may select up to all of the bills, how many different sums of money could you make?
   (b) In part (a), remove the condition "you must select at least one bill." Now, how many sums are possible?

68. Some commonly available U.S. coins are shown below.

(a) Suppose that you have one of each in your pocket and you wish to leave a tip for a waitress. Since you must select at least one coin, and you may select up through all of the coins, how many different sums of money could she receive?

(b) In part (a), remove the condition "you must select at least one coin." How many sums are possible now?

3

Operations with Sets

After comparing the campaign promises of two candidates for sheriff, a voter came up with the following list of promises made by the people running for office. Each promise is given a code letter.

Honest John Lenchek	**Learned Louise Howe**
Spend less money, m	Spend less money, m
Emphasize traffic law enforcement, t	Crack down on crooked politicians, p
Increase service to suburban areas, s	Increase service to the city, c

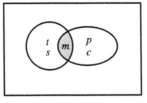

The only promise common to both candidates is promise m, to spend less money. Suppose we take each candidate's promises to be a set. The promises of candidate Lencheck give the set $\{m, t, s\}$, while the promises of Howe give $\{m, p, c\}$. The only element common to both sets is m; this element belongs to the *intersection* of the two sets $\{m, t, s\}$ and $\{m, p, c\}$, as shown by shading in the Venn diagram in Figure 4. In symbols,

FIGURE 4

$$\{m, t, s\} \cap \{m, p, c\} = \{m\},$$

where the cap-shaped symbol $\cap$ represents intersection. Notice that the intersection of two sets is itself a set.

Intersection of Sets

The **intersection** of sets A and B, written $A \cap B$, is the set of elements common to both A and B, or

$$A \cap B = \{x \mid x \in A \text{ and } x \in B\}.$$

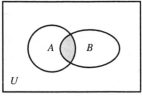

$A \cap B$

FIGURE 5

Form the intersection of sets A and B by taking all the elements included in both sets, as shown by shading in Figure 5.

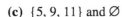 **EXAMPLE 1**   Find the intersection of the given sets.

(a) $\{3, 4, 5, 6, 7\}$ and $\{4, 6, 8, 10\}$
Since the elements common to both sets are 4 and 6,

$$\{3, 4, 5, 6, 7\} \cap \{4, 6, 8, 10\} = \{4, 6\}.$$

(b) $\{9, 14, 25, 30\}$ and $\{10, 17, 19, 38, 52\}$
These two sets have no elements in common, so

$$\{9, 14, 25, 30\} \cap \{10, 17, 19, 38, 52\} = \varnothing.$$

(c) $\{5, 9, 11\}$ and $\varnothing$
There are no elements in $\varnothing$, so there can be no elements belonging to both $\{5, 9, 11\}$ and $\varnothing$. Because of this,

$$\{5, 9, 11\} \cap \varnothing = \varnothing. \quad \bullet$$

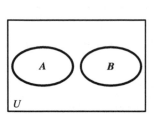

Disjoint sets

FIGURE 6

Examples 1(b) and 1(c) showed two sets that have no elements in common. Sets with no elements in common are called **disjoint sets.** A set of men and a set of women would be disjoint sets. In mathematical language, sets A and B are disjoint if $A \cap B = \varnothing$. Two disjoint sets A and B are shown in Figure 6.

FOR FURTHER THOUGHT

The arithmetic operations of addition and multiplication, when applied to numbers, have some familiar properties. If *a, b* and *c* are real numbers, then the **commutative property of addition** says that the order of the numbers being added makes no difference: $a + b = b + a$. (Is there a commutative property of multiplication?) The **associative property of addition** says that when three numbers are added, the grouping used makes no difference: $(a + b) + c = a + (b + c)$. (Is there an associative property of multiplication?) The number 0 is called the **identity element for addition** since adding it to any number does not change that number: $a + 0 = a$. (What is the **identity element for multiplication**?) Finally, the **distributive property of multiplication over addition** says that $a(b + c) = ab + ac$. (Is there a **distributive property of addition over multiplication**?)

For Group Discussion Now consider the operations of union and intersection, applied to sets. By recalling definitions, or by trying examples, try to answer the following questions.

1. Is set union commutative? How about set intersection?
2. Is set union associative? How about set intersection?
3. Is there an identity element for set union? If so, what is it? How about set intersection?
4. Is set intersection distributive over set union? Is set union distributive over set intersection?

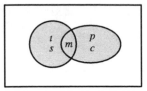

FIGURE 7

At the beginning of this section, we showed lists of campaign promises of two candidates running for sheriff. The intersection of those lists was found above. Suppose a student in a political science class must write a paper on the types of promises made by candidates for public office. The student would need to study *all* the promises made by *either* candidate, or the set

$$\{m, t, s, p, c\},$$

the *union* of the sets of promises made by the two candidates, as shown shaded in the Venn diagram in Figure 7. In symbols,

$$\{m, t, s\} \cup \{m, p, c\} = \{m, t, s, p, c\},$$

where the cup-shaped symbol $\cup$ denotes set union. Be careful not to confuse this symbol with the universal set U. Again, the union of two sets is a set.

Union of Sets

The **union** of sets A and B, written $A \cup B$, is the set of all elements belonging to either of the sets, or

$$A \cup B = \{x \mid x \in A \text{ or } x \in B\}.$$

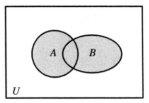

$A \cup B$

FIGURE 8

Form the union of sets A and B by taking all the elements of set A and then including the elements of set B that are not already listed, as shown shaded in Figure 8.

EXAMPLE 2   Find the union of the given sets.

(a) $\{2, 4, 6\}$ and $\{4, 6, 8, 10, 12\}$

Start by listing all the elements from the first set, 2, 4, and 6. Then list all the elements from the second set that are not in the first set, or 8, 10, and 12. The union is made up of all these elements, or

$$\{2, 4, 6\} \cup \{4, 6, 8, 10, 12\} = \{2, 4, 6, 8, 10, 12\}.$$

(b) $\{a, b, d, f, g, h\}$ and $\{c, f, g, h, k\}$

The union of these sets is

$$\{a, b, d, f, g, h\} \cup \{c, f, g, h, k\} = \{a, b, c, d, f, g, h, k\}.$$

(c) $\{3, 4, 5\}$ and $\varnothing$

Since there are no elements in $\varnothing$, the union of $\{3, 4, 5\}$ and $\varnothing$ contains only the elements 3, 4, and 5, or

$$\{3, 4, 5\} \cup \varnothing = \{3, 4, 5\}. \quad \bullet$$

Recall from the previous section that A' represents the *complement* of set A. Set A' is formed by taking all the elements of the universal set U that are not in A. This idea is shown in the next example.

EXAMPLE 3   Let $U = \{1, 2, 3, 4, 5, 6, 9\}$
$A = \{1, 2, 3, 4\}$
$B = \{2, 4, 6\}$
$C = \{1, 3, 6, 9\}.$

Find each set.

(a) $A' \cap B$

First identify the elements of set A', the elements of U that are not in set A;

$$A' = \{5, 6, 9\}.$$

Now find $A' \cap B$, the set of elements belonging both to A' and to B:

$$A' \cap B = \{5, 6, 9\} \cap \{2, 4, 6\} = \{6\}.$$

(b) $B' \cup C' = \{1, 3, 5, 9\} \cup \{2, 4, 5\} = \{1, 2, 3, 4, 5, 9\}.$

(c) $A \cap (B \cup C')$

First find the set inside the parentheses:

$$B \cup C' = \{2, 4, 6\} \cup \{2, 4, 5\} = \{2, 4, 5, 6\}.$$

Now finish the problem:

$$
\begin{aligned}
A \cap (B \cup C') &= A \cap \{2, 4, 5, 6\} \\
&= \{1, 2, 3, 4\} \cap \{2, 4, 5, 6\} \\
&= \{2, 4\}.
\end{aligned}
$$

(d) $(A' \cup C') \cap B'$

Set $A' = \{5, 6, 9\}$ and set $C' = \{2, 4, 5\}$, with

$$A' \cup C' = \{5, 6, 9\} \cup \{2, 4, 5\} = \{2, 4, 5, 6, 9\}.$$

Set B' is $\{1, 3, 5, 9\}$, so

$$(A' \cup C') \cap B' = \{2, 4, 5, 6, 9\} \cap \{1, 3, 5, 9\} = \{5, 9\}. \quad \blacklozenge$$

It is often said that mathematics is a "language." As such, it has the advantage of concise symbolism. For example, the set $(A \cap B)' \cup C$ is less easily expressed in words. One attempt is the following: "The set of all elements that are not in both A and B, or are in C."

EXAMPLE 4   Describe each of the following sets in words.

(a) $A \cap (B \cup C')$

This set might be described as "the set of all elements that are in A, and are in B or are not in C."

(b) $(A' \cup C') \cap B'$

One possibility is "the set of all elements that are not in A or not in C, and are not in B." $\quad \blacklozenge$

When we have specific sets, more complicated sets like those in Example 4 can be found by working first inside the parentheses as we will see in Example 5(c).

Another operation on sets is the *difference* of two sets. Suppose that $A = \{1, 2, 3, \ldots, 10\}$ and $B = \{2, 4, 6, 8, 10\}$. If the elements of B are excluded (or taken away) from A, the set $C = \{1, 3, 5, 7, 9\}$ is obtained. C is called the difference of sets A and B.

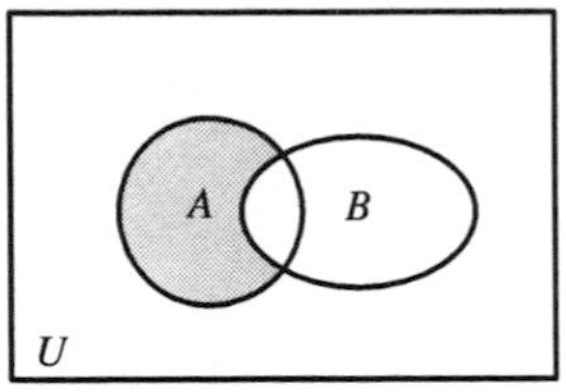

Difference of Sets

The **difference** of sets A and B, written $A - B$, is the set of all elements belonging to set A and not to set B, or

$$A - B = \{x \mid x \in A \text{ and } x \notin B\}.$$

$A - B$

FIGURE 9

Since $x \notin B$ has the same meaning as $x \in B'$, the set difference $A - B$ can also be described as $\{x \mid x \in A \text{ and } x \in B'\}$, or $A \cap B'$. Figure 9 illustrates the idea of set difference. The shaded region represents $A - B$.

EXAMPLE 5   Let $U = \{1, 2, 3, 4, 5, 6, 7\}$
$A = \{1, 2, 3, 4, 5, 6\}$
$B = \{2, 3, 6\}$
$C = \{3, 5, 7\}.$

Find each set.

(a) $A - B$

Begin with set A and exclude any elements found also in set B. So, $A - B = \{1, 2, 3, 4, 5, 6\} - \{2, 3, 6\} = \{1, 4, 5\}$.

(b) $B - A$

To be in $B - A$, an element must be in set B and not in set A. But all elements of B are also in A. Thus, $B - A = \varnothing$.

(c) $(A - B) \cup C'$

From part (a), $A - B = \{1, 4, 5\}$. Also, $C' = \{1, 2, 4, 6\}$, so

$$(A - B) \cup C' = \{1, 2, 4, 5, 6\}. \quad \blacklozenge$$

The results in Examples 5(a) and 5(b) illustrate that, in general,

$$A - B \neq B - A.$$

When writing a set that contains several elements, the order in which the elements appear is not relevant. For example, $\{1, 5\} = \{5, 1\}$. However, there are many instances in mathematics where, when two objects are paired, the order in which the objects are written is important. This leads to the idea of the *ordered pair*. When writing ordered pairs, use parentheses (as opposed to braces, which are reserved for writing sets).

Ordered Pairs

In the **ordered pair** *(a, b)*, *a* is called the **first component** and *b* is called the **second component.** In general, *(a, b)* ≠ *(b, a)*.

Two ordered pairs *(a, b)* and *(c, d)* are **equal** provided that their first components are equal and their second components are equal; that is, *(a, b)* = *(c, d)* if and only if *a = c* and *b = d*.

EXAMPLE 6   Decide whether each statement is *true* or *false*.

(a) $(3, 4) = (5 - 2, 1 + 3)$

Since $3 = 5 - 2$ and $4 = 1 + 3$, the ordered pairs are equal. The statement is true.

(b) $\{3, 4\} \neq \{4, 3\}$

Since these are sets and not ordered pairs, the order in which the elements are listed is not important. Since these sets are equal, the statement is false.

(c) $(7, 4) = (4, 7)$

These ordered pairs are not equal since they do not satisfy the requirements for equality of ordered pairs. The statement is false. ●

A set may contain ordered pairs as elements. If *A* and *B* are sets, then each element of *A* can be paired with each element of *B*, and the results can be written as ordered pairs. The set of all such ordered pairs is called the *Cartesian product* of *A* and *B*, written $A \times B$ and read "A cross B." The name comes from that of the French mathematician René Descartes.

Cartesian Product of Sets

The **Cartesian product** of sets *A* and *B*, written $A \times B$, is

$$A \times B = \{(a, b) \mid a \in A \text{ and } b \in B\}.$$

EXAMPLE 7   Let $A = \{1, 5, 9\}$ and $B = \{6, 7\}$. Find each set.

(a) $A \times B$

Pair each element of *A* with each element of *B*. Write the results as ordered pairs, with the element of *A* written first and the element of *B* written second. Write as a set.

$$A \times B = \{(1, 6), (1, 7), (5, 6), (5, 7), (9, 6), (9, 7)\}$$

(b) $B \times A$

Since B is listed first, this set will consist of ordered pairs that have their components interchanged when compared to those in part (a).

$$B \times A = \{(6, 1), (7, 1), (6, 5), (7, 5), (6, 9), (7, 9)\} \quad \bullet$$

It should be noted that the order in which the ordered pairs themselves are listed is not important. For example, another way to write $B \times A$ in Example 7 would be

$$\{(6, 1), (6, 5), (6, 9), (7, 1), (7, 5), (7, 9)\}.$$

EXAMPLE 8   Let $A = \{1, 2, 3, 4, 5, 6\}$. Find $A \times A$.

In this example we take the Cartesian product of a set with *itself*. By pairing 1 with each element in the set, 2 with each element, and so on, we obtain the following set:

$$\begin{aligned} A \times A = \{&(1, 1), (1, 2), (1, 3), (1, 4), (1, 5), (1, 6),\\ &(2, 1), (2, 2), (2, 3), (2, 4), (2, 5), (2, 6),\\ &(3, 1), (3, 2), (3, 3), (3, 4), (3, 5), (3, 6),\\ &(4, 1), (4, 2), (4, 3), (4, 4), (4, 5), (4, 6),\\ &(5, 1), (5, 2), (5, 3), (5, 4), (5, 5), (5, 6),\\ &(6, 1), (6, 2), (6, 3), (6, 4), (6, 5), (6, 6)\}. \quad \bullet \end{aligned}$$

It is not unusual to take the Cartesian product of a set with itself, as in Example 8. In fact, the Cartesian product in Example 8 represents all possible results that are obtained when two distinguishable dice are rolled. Determining this Cartesian product is important when studying certain problems in counting techniques and probability.

From Example 7 it can be seen that, in general, $A \times B \neq B \times A$, since they do not contain exactly the same ordered pairs. However, each set contains the same number of elements, 6. Furthermore, $n(A) = 3$, $n(B) = 2$, and $n(A \times B) = n(B \times A) = 6$. Since $3 \times 2 = 6$, you might conclude that the cardinal number of the Cartesian product of two sets is equal to the product of the cardinal numbers of the sets. In general, this conclusion is correct.

Cardinal Number of a Cartesian Product

If $n(A) = a$ and $n(B) = b$, then $n(A \times B) = n(B \times A) = n(A) \times n(B) = ab$.

EXAMPLE 9   Find $n(A \times B)$ and $n(B \times A)$ from the given information.

(a) $A = \{a, b, c, d, e, f, g\}$ and $B = \{2, 4, 6\}$

Since $n(A) = 7$ and $n(B) = 3$, $n(A \times B)$ and $n(B \times A)$ are both equal to 7×3, or 21.

(b) $n(A) = 24$ and $n(B) = 5$

$$n(A \times B) = n(B \times A) = 24 \times 5 = 120. \quad \bullet$$

Finding the intersections, unions, differences, Cartesian products, and complements of sets are examples of *set operations*. An **operation** is a rule or procedure by which one or more objects are used to obtain another object. The objects involved in an operation are usually sets or numbers. The most common operations on numbers are addition, subtraction, multiplication, and division. For example, starting with the numbers 5 and 7, the addition operation would produce the number $5 + 7 = 12$. With the same two numbers, 5 and 7, the multiplication operation would produce $5 \times 7 = 35$.

The most common operations on sets are summarized below, along with their Venn diagrams.

Common Set Operations

Let A and B be any sets, with U the universal set.

The **complement** of A, written A', is

$$A' = \{x \mid x \in U \text{ and } x \notin A\}.$$

The **intersection** of A and B is

$$A \cap B = \{x \mid x \in A \text{ and } x \in B\}.$$

The **union** of A and B is

$$A \cup B = \{x \mid x \in A \text{ or } x \in B\}.$$

The **difference** of A and B is

$$A - B = \{x \mid x \in A \text{ and } x \notin B\}.$$

The **Cartesian product** of A and B is

$$A \times B = \{(x, y) \mid x \in A \text{ and } y \in B\}.$$

When dealing with a single set, we can use a Venn diagram as seen in Figure 10. The universal set U is divided into two regions, one representing set A and the other representing set A'.

Two sets A and B within the universal set suggest a Venn diagram as seen in Figure 11, where the four resulting regions have been numbered to provide a convenient way to refer to them. (The numbering is arbitrary.) Region 1 includes those elements outside of both set A and set B. Region 2 includes the elements belonging to A but not to B. Region 3 includes those elements belonging to both A and B. How would you describe the elements of region 4?

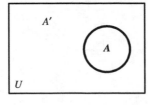

FIGURE   10

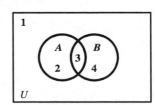

Numbering is arbitrary.

FIGURE   11

EXAMPLE 10   Draw a Venn diagram similar to Figure 11 and shade the region or regions representing the following sets.

(a) $A' \cap B$

Refer to the labeling in Figure 11. Set A' contains all the elements outside of set $A,$ in other words, the elements in regions 1 and 4. Set B is made up of the elements in regions 3 and 4. The intersection of sets A' and $B,$ the set $A' \cap B,$ is made up of the elements in the region common to 1 and 4 and 3 and 4, that is, region 4. Thus, $A' \cap B$ is represented by region 4, which is shaded in Figure 12. This region can also be described as $B - A.$

(b) $A' \cup B'$

Again, set A' is represented by regions 1 and 4, while B' is made up of regions 1 and 2. The union of A' and $B',$ the set $A' \cup B',$ is made up of the elements belonging either to regions 1 and 4 or to regions 1 and 2. This union is composed of regions 1, 2, and 4, which are shaded in Figure 13. ◆

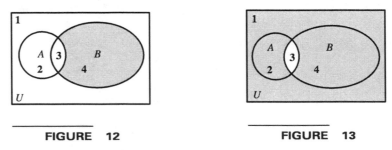

FIGURE 12   FIGURE 13

When the specific elements of sets A and B are known, it is sometimes useful to show where the various elements are located in the diagram.

EXAMPLE 11   Let $U = \{q, r, s, t, u, v, w, x, y, z\}$

$A = \{r, s, t, u, v\}$

$B = \{t, v, x\}.$

Place the elements of these sets in their proper locations on a Venn diagram.

Since $A \cap B = \{t, v\},$ elements t and v are placed in region 3 in Figure 14. The remaining elements of $A,$ that is r, s, and u, go in region 2. The figure shows the proper placement of all other elements. ◆

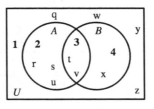

FIGURE 14

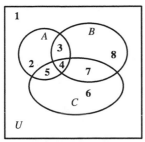

Numbering is arbitrary.

FIGURE 15

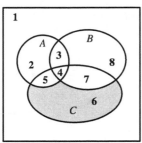

$(A' \cap B') \cap C$

FIGURE 16

To include three sets *A, B,* and *C* in a universal set, draw a Venn diagram as in Figure 15, where again an arbitrary numbering of the regions is shown.

EXAMPLE 12   Shade the set $(A' \cap B') \cap C$ in a Venn diagram similar to the one in Figure 15.

Work first inside the parentheses. As shown in Figure 16, set A' is made up of the regions outside set *A,* or regions 1, 6, 7, and 8. Set B' is made up of regions 1, 2, 5, and 6. The intersection of these sets is given by the overlap of regions 1, 6, 7, 8 and 1, 2, 5, 6, or regions 1 and 6. For the final Venn diagram, find the intersection of regions 1 and 6 with set *C.* As seen in Figure 16, set *C* is made up of regions 4, 5, 6, and 7. The overlap of regions 1, 6 and 4, 5, 6, 7 is region 6, the shaded region in Figure 16. ●

EXAMPLE 13   Is the statement

$$(A \cap B)' = A' \cup B'$$

true for every choice of sets *A* and *B?*

To help decide, use the regions labeled in Figure 11. Set $A \cap B$ is made up of region 3, so that $(A \cap B)'$ is made up of regions 1, 2, and 4. These regions are shaded in Figure 17(a).

To find a Venn diagram for set $A' \cup B'$, first check that A' is made up of regions 1 and 4, while set B' includes regions 1 and 2. Finally, $A' \cup B'$ is made up of regions 1 and 4, or 1 and 2; that is, regions 1, 2, and 4. These regions are shaded in Figure 17(b).

The fact that the same regions are shaded in both Venn diagrams suggests that

$$(A \cap B)' = A' \cup B'. \quad ●$$

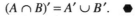

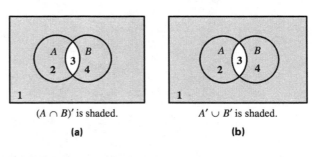

$(A \cap B)'$ is shaded. $A' \cup B'$ is shaded.

(a)   **(b)**

FIGURE 17

This result is one of De Morgan's laws, named after the British logician Augustus De Morgan (1806–1871). De Morgan's two laws for sets follow.

De Morgan's Laws

For any sets A and B,

$$(A \cap B)' = A' \cup B'$$

and

$$(A \cup B)' = A' \cap B'.$$

The Venn diagrams in Figure 17 strongly suggest the truth of the first of De Morgan's laws. They provide a *conjecture*. Actual proofs of De Morgan's laws would require methods used in more advanced courses on set theory.

An area in a Venn diagram (perhaps set off by being shaded) may be described using set operations. When doing this, it is a good idea to translate the region into words, remembering that intersection translates as "and," union translates as "or," and complement translates as "not." There are often several ways to describe a given region.

EXAMPLE 14   For each Venn diagram write a symbolic description of the shaded area, using A, B, C, $\cap$, $\cup$, $-$, and $'$ as necessary.

(a)

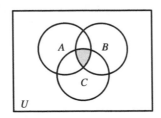

The shaded region belongs to all three sets, A and B and C. Therefore, the region corresponds to $A \cap B \cap C$.

(b)

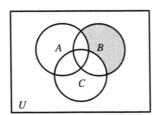

The shaded region is in set B and is not in A and is not in C. Since it is not in A, it is in A', and similarly it is in C'. The region is, therefore, in B and in A' and in C', and corresponds to $B \cap A' \cap C'$.

(c) Refer to the figure in part (b) and give two additional ways of describing the shaded region.

The shaded area includes all of B except for the regions belonging to either A or C. This suggests the idea of set difference. The region may be described as $B - (A \cup C)$, or equivalently, $B \cap (A \cup C)'$. ●

3 EXERCISES

Perform the indicated operations.

$$Let \quad U = \{a, b, c, d, e, f, g\}$$
$$X = \{a, c, e, g\}$$
$$Y = \{a, b, c\}$$
$$Z = \{b, c, d, e, f\}.$$

1. $X \cap Y$ **2.** $X \cup Y$ **3.** $Y \cup Z$ **4.** $Y \cap Z$

5. $X \cup U$ **6.** $Y \cap U$ **7.** X' **8.** Y'

9. $X' \cap Y'$ **10.** $X' \cap Z$ **11.** $Z' \cap \emptyset$ **12.** $Y' \cup \emptyset$

13. $X \cup (Y \cap Z)$ **14.** $Y \cap (X \cup Z)$ **15.** $(Y \cap Z') \cup X$ **16.** $(X' \cup Y') \cup Z$

17. $(Z \cup X')' \cap Y$ **18.** $(Y \cap X')' \cup Z'$ **19.** $X - Y$ **20.** $Y - X$

21. $X' - Y$ **22.** $Y' - X$ **23.** $X \cap (X - Y)$ **24.** $Y \cup (Y - X)$

Describe each set in words. (See Example 4.)

25. $A \cup (B' \cap C')$ **26.** $(A \cap B') \cup (B \cap A')$ **27.** $(C - B) \cup A$

28. $B \cap (A' - C)$ **29.** $(A - C) \cup (B - C)$ **30.** $(A' \cap B') \cup C$

31. The table lists some common adverse effects of prolonged tobacco and alcohol use.

Tobacco	Alcohol
Emphysema, *e*	Liver damage, *l*
Heart damage, *h*	Brain damage, *b*
Cancer, *c*	Heart damage, *h*

Find the smallest possible universal set U that includes all the effects listed.

Let T be the set of listed effects of tobacco and A be the set of listed effects of alcohol. (See Exercise 31.) Find each set.

32. A' **33.** T' **34.** $T \cap A$ **35.** $T \cup A$ **36.** $A \cap T'$

Describe in words each set in Exercises 37–42.

$$Let \quad U = \text{the set of all tax returns}$$
$$A = \text{the set of all tax returns with itemized deductions}$$
$$B = \text{the set of all tax returns showing business income}$$
$$C = \text{the set of all tax returns filed in 1994}$$
$$D = \text{the set of all tax returns selected for audit.}$$

37. $B \cup C$ **38.** $A \cap D$ **39.** $C - A$

40. $D \cup A'$ **41.** $(A \cup B) - D$ **42.** $(C \cap A) \cap B'$

Assuming that A and B represent any two sets, *identify each of the following statements as either* always true *or* not always true.

43. $A \subseteq (A \cup B)$ **44.** $A \subseteq (A \cap B)$ **45.** $(A \cap B) \subseteq A$ **46.** $(A \cup B) \subseteq A$

47. $n(A \cup B) = n(A) + n(B)$ **48.** $n(A \cap B) = n(A) - n(B)$

49. $n(A \cup B) = n(A) + n(B) - n(A \cap B)$ **50.** $n(A \cap B) = n(A) + n(B) - n(A \cup B)$

51. If $B \subseteq A$, $n(A) - n(B) = n(A - B)$ **52.** $n(A - B) = n(B - A)$

For Exercises 53–60,

$$Let \quad U = \{1, 2, 3, 4, 5\}$$
$$X = \{1, 3, 5\}$$
$$Y = \{1, 2, 3\}$$
$$Z = \{3, 4, 5\}.$$

In each case, state a general conjecture based on your observation.

53. (a) Find $X \cup Y$.　　**(b)** Find $Y \cup X$.　　**(c)** State a conjecture.

54. (a) Find $X \cap Y$.　　**(b)** Find $Y \cap X$.　　**(c)** State a conjecture.

55. (a) Find $X \cup (Y \cup Z)$.　　**(b)** Find $(X \cup Y) \cup Z$.　　**(c)** State a conjecture.

56. (a) Find $X \cap (Y \cap Z)$.　　**(b)** Find $(X \cap Y) \cap Z$.　　**(c)** State a conjecture.

57. (a) Find $(X \cup Y)'$.　　**(b)** Find $X' \cap Y'$.　　**(c)** State a conjecture.

58. (a) Find $(X \cap Y)'$.　　**(b)** Find $X' \cup Y'$.　　**(c)** State a conjecture.

59. (a) Find $X \cup \varnothing$.　　**(b)** State a conjecture.

60. (a) Find $X \cap \varnothing$.　　**(b)** State a conjecture.

Write true *or* false *for each of the following.*

61. $(3, 2) = (5 - 2, 1 + 1)$　　　**62.** $(10, 4) = (7 + 3, 5 - 1)$　　　**63.** $(4, 12) = (4, 3)$

64. $(5, 9) = (2, 9)$　　　**65.** $(6, 3) = (3, 6)$　　　**66.** $(2, 13) = (13, 2)$

67. $\{6, 3\} = \{3, 6\}$　　　**68.** $\{2, 13\} = \{13, 2\}$

69. $\{(1, 2), (3, 4)\} = \{(3, 4), (1, 2)\}$　　　**70.** $\{(5, 9), (4, 8), (4, 2)\} = \{(4, 8), (5, 9), (4, 2)\}$

Find $A \times B$ and $B \times A$, for A and B defined as follows.

71. $A = \{2, 8, 12\}, \quad B = \{4, 9\}$　　　**72.** $A = \{3, 6, 9, 12\}, \quad B = \{6, 8\}$

73. $A = \{d, o, g\}, \quad B = \{p, i, g\}$　　　**74.** $A = \{b, l, u, e\}, \quad B = \{r, e, d\}$

Use the given information to find $n(A \times B)$ and $n(B \times A)$ in Exercises 75–78.

75. The sets in Exercise 71　　　**76.** The sets in Exercise 73

77. $n(A) = 35$ and $n(B) = 6$　　　**78.** $n(A) = 13$ and $n(B) = 5$

79. If $n(A \times B) = 36$ and $n(A) = 12$, find $n(B)$.　　　**80.** If $n(A \times B) = 100$ and $n(B) = 4$, find $n(A)$.

Place the elements of these sets in the proper location on the given Venn diagram.

81. Let　$U = \{a, b, c, d, e, f, g\}$
$A = \{b, d, f, g\}$
$B = \{a, b, d, e, g\}$.

82. Let　$U = \{5, 6, 7, 8, 9, 10, 11, 12, 13\}$
$M = \{5, 8, 10, 11\}$
$N = \{5, 6, 7, 9, 10\}$.

Use a Venn diagram similar to the one shown here to shade each of the following sets.

83. $B \cap A'$　　　**84.** $A \cup B$　　　**85.** $A' \cup B$

86. $A' \cap B'$　　　**87.** $B' \cup A$　　　**88.** $A' \cup A$

89. $B' \cap B$　　　**90.** $A \cap B'$　　　**91.** $B' \cup (A' \cap B')$

92. $(A \cap B) \cup B$　　　**93.** U'　　　**94.** $\varnothing'$

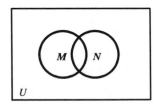

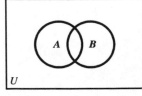

95. Let $U = \{m, n, o, p, q, r, s, t, u, v, w\}$
$A = \{m, n, p, q, r, t\}$
$B = \{m, o, p, q, s, u\}$
$C = \{m, o, p, r, s, t, u, v\}.$

Place the elements of these sets in the proper location on a Venn diagram similar to the one shown here.

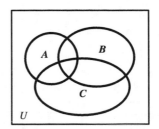

96. Let $U = \{1, 2, 3, 4, 5, 6, 7, 8, 9\}$
$A = \{1, 3, 5, 7\}$
$B = \{1, 3, 4, 6, 8\}$
$C = \{1, 4, 5, 6, 7, 9\}.$

Place the elements of these sets in the proper location on a Venn diagram.

Use a Venn diagram to shade each of the following sets.

97. $(A \cap B) \cap C$ **98.** $(A \cap C') \cup B$ **99.** $(A \cap B) \cup C'$ **100.** $(A' \cap B) \cap C$

101. $(A' \cap B') \cap C$ **102.** $(A \cup B) \cup C$ **103.** $(A \cap B') \cup C$ **104.** $(A \cap C') \cap B$

105. $(A \cap B') \cap C'$ **106.** $(A' \cap B') \cup C$ **107.** $(A' \cap B') \cup C'$ **108.** $(A \cap B)' \cup C$

Write a description of each shaded area. Use the symbols A, B, C, $\cap$, $\cup$, $-$, and $'$ as necessary. More than one answer may be possible.

109.

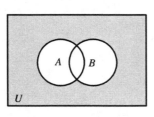

110.

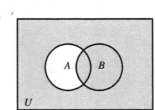

111.

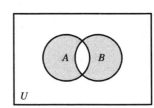

112.

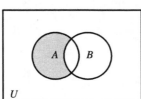

113.

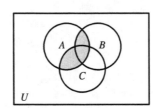

114.

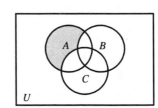

115.

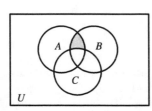

116.

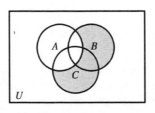

Suppose A and B are sets. Describe the conditions under which each of the following statements would be true.

117. $A = A - B$ **118.** $A = B - A$ **119.** $A = A - \varnothing$ **120.** $A = \varnothing - A$

121. $A \cup \varnothing = \varnothing$ **122.** $A \cap \varnothing = \varnothing$ **123.** $A \cap \varnothing = A$ **124.** $A \cup \varnothing = A$

125. $A \cup A = \varnothing$ **126.** $A \cap A = \varnothing$

127. Give examples of how the conciseness of the "language of mathematics" can be an advantage.

128. Give examples of how a language such as English, Spanish, Arabic, or Vietnamese can have an advantage over the symbolic language of mathematics.

129. If A and B are sets, is it necessarily true that $n(A - B) = n(A) - n(B)$? Explain.

130. If $Q = \{x \mid x \text{ is a rational number}\}$ and $H = \{x \mid x \text{ is an irrational number}\}$, describe each of the following sets.
  (a) $Q \cup H$ **(b)** $Q \cap H$

White light can be viewed as a blending of the three primary *colors red, green, and blue. Or, we can obtain a secondary color by blending any* two *primary colors. (For example, red and blue produce magenta.) For the following exercises, refer to the drawing shown here.*

131. Name all the secondary colors of light. For each one, give its primary components.

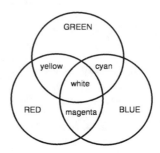

132. In terms of set operations, white light is the three-way "intersection" of red, green, and blue. What *other* three-way intersection would also produce white light?

133. Explain why scientists sometimes refer to yellow as "minus blue."

134. What color is obtained if red is filtered out of (or subtracted from) white light?

135. What must be filtered out of white light to obtain green light?

For each of the following exercises, draw two appropriate Venn diagrams to decide whether the given statement is always true *or* not always true.

136. $A \cap A' = \varnothing$ **137.** $A \cup A' = U$ **138.** $(A \cap B) \subseteq A$

139. $(A \cup B) \subseteq A$ **140.** If $A \subseteq B$, then $A \cup B = A$.   **141.** If $A \subseteq B$, then $A \cap B = B$.

142. $(A \cup B)' = A' \cap B'$ (De Morgan's second law)

143. George Owen plans to place several bets for the daily double at the horseracing track. For race 1 he will place a bet on horse 3 to win and will also place a second bet on horse 4 to win. For race 2 he will bet on horse 5 to win and also on horse 6 to win. Let
$$R1 = \{3, 4\} \quad \text{and} \quad R2 = \{5, 6\}.$$
  (a) Write out the Cartesian product $R1 \times R2$.
  (b) Explain what $R1 \times R2$ represents in terms of George's betting results.

4

Surveys and Cardinal Numbers

Many problems involving sets of people (or other objects) require analyzing known information about certain subsets to obtain cardinal numbers of other subsets. In this section we apply three useful problem solving techniques to such problems: Venn diagrams, cardinal number formulas, and tables. The "known information" is quite often (though not always) obtained by administering a survey.

Suppose a group of college students in Arizona are questioned about their favorite musical performers, and the following information is produced.

33 like Garth Brooks	15 like Garth and Tanya
32 like Wynonna Judd	14 like Wynonna and Tanya
28 like Tanya Tucker	5 like all three
11 like Garth and Wynonna	7 like none of these performers

To determine the total number of students surveyed, we cannot just add the eight numbers above since there is some overlapping. For example, in Figure 18, the 33 students who like Garth Brooks should not be positioned in region *b* but should be distributed among regions *b, c, d,* and *e,* in a way that is consistent with all of the given data. (Region *b* actually contains those students who like Garth but do not like Wynonna and do not like Tanya.)

Since, at the start, we do not know how to distribute the 33 who like Garth, we look first for some more manageable data. The smallest total listed, the 5 students who like all three singers, can be placed in region *d* (the intersection of the three sets). And the 7 who like none of the three must go into region *a*. Then, the 11 who like Garth and Wynonna must go into regions *d* and *e*. Since region *d* already contains 5 students, we must place $11 - 5 = 6$ in region *e*. Since 15 like Garth and Tanya (regions *c* and *d*), we place $15 - 5 = 10$ in region *c*. Now that regions *c, d,* and *e* contain 10, 5, and 6 students, respectively, region *b* receives $33 - 10 - 5 - 6 = 12$. By similar reasoning all regions are assigned their correct numbers, as shown in Figure 19.

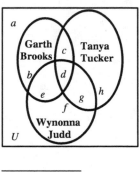

FIGURE 18

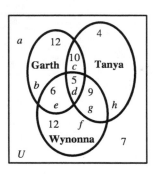

FIGURE 19

EXAMPLE 1   Using the survey data on student preferences for performers, as summarized in Figure 19, answer the following questions.

(a) How many students like Tanya Tucker only?

A student who likes Tanya only does not like Garth and does not like Wynonna. These students are inside the regions for Tanya and outside the regions for Garth and Wynonna. Region *h* is the necessary region in Figure 19, and we see that 4 students like Tanya only.

(b) How many students like exactly two performers?

The students in regions *c, e,* and *g* like exactly two performers. The total number of such students is $10 + 6 + 9 = 25$.

(c) How many students were surveyed?

Since each student surveyed has been placed in exactly one region of Figure 19, the total number surveyed is the sum of the numbers in all eight regions:

$$7 + 12 + 10 + 5 + 6 + 12 + 9 + 4 = 65. \quad \bullet$$

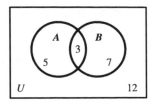

FIGURE 20

If the numbers shown in Figure 20 are the cardinal numbers of the individual regions, then $n(A) = 5 + 3 = 8$, $n(B) = 3 + 7 = 10$, $n(A \cap B) = 3$, and $n(A \cup B) = 5 + 3 + 7 = 15$. Notice that $n(A \cup B) = n(A) + n(B) - n(A \cap B)$ since $15 = 8 + 10 - 3$. This relationship is true for any two sets A and B.

Cardinal Number Formula

For any two sets A and B,

$$n(A \cup B) = n(A) + n(B) - n(A \cap B).$$

This formula can be rearranged to find any one of its four terms when the others are known.

EXAMPLE 2   Find $n(A)$ if $n(A \cup B) = 22$, $n(A \cap B) = 8$, and $n(B) = 12$.

Since the formula above can be rearranged as

$$n(A) = n(A \cup B) - n(B) + n(A \cap B),$$

we obtain $n(A) = 22 - 12 + 8 = 18$. ●

Sometimes, even when information is presented as in Example 2, it is more convenient to fit that information into a Venn diagram as in Example 1.

EXAMPLE 3   Bob Carlton is a section chief for an electric utility company. The employees in his section cut down tall trees, climb poles, and splice wire. Carlton recently submitted the following report to the management of the utility:

My section includes 100 employees,
T = the set of employees who can cut tall trees,
P = the set of employees who can climb poles,
W = the set of employees who can splice wire.

$n(T) = 45$	$n(P \cap W) = 20$
$n(P) = 50$	$n(T \cap W) = 25$
$n(W) = 57$	$n(T \cap P \cap W) = 11$
$n(T \cap P) = 28$	$n(T' \cap P' \cap W') = 9$

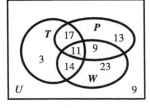

FIGURE 21

The data supplied by Carlton are reflected in Figure 21. The sum of the numbers in the diagram gives the total number of employees in the section:

$$9 + 3 + 14 + 23 + 11 + 9 + 17 + 13 = 99.$$

Carlton claimed to have 100 employees, but his data indicate only 99. The management decided that this error meant that Carlton did not qualify as section chief. He was reassigned as night-shift information operator at the North Pole. (The moral: he should have taken this course.) ●

Sometimes information appears in a table rather than a Venn diagram. But the basic ideas of union and intersection still apply.

EXAMPLE 4 The officer in charge of the cafeteria on a North Carolina military base wanted to know if the beverage that enlisted men and women preferred with lunch depended on their age. So on a given day she categorized her lunch patrons according to age and according to preferred beverage, recording the resulting numbers in a table as follows.

		Beverage			
		Cola (C)	Iced Tea (I)	Sweet Tea (S)	Totals
	18–25 (Y)	45	10	35	90
Age	26–33 (M)	20	25	30	75
	Over 33 (O)	5	30	20	55
	Totals	70	65	85	220

Using the letters in the table, find the number of people in each of the following sets.

(a) $Y \cap C$

The set Y includes all personnel represented across the top row of the table (90 in all), while C includes the 70 down the left column. The intersection of these two sets is just the upper left entry: 45 people.

(b) $O' \cup I$

The set O' excludes the bottom row, so it includes the first and second rows. The set I includes the middle column only. The union of the two sets represents

$$45 + 10 + 35 + 20 + 25 + 30 + 30 = 195 \text{ people.}$$ ●

---

4 EXERCISES

Use Venn diagrams to answer each of the following questions.

In one recent year, financial aid available to college students in the United States was nearly 30 billion dollars. (Much of it went unclaimed, mostly because qualified students were not aware of it, did not know how to obtain or fill out the required applications, or did not feel the results would be worth their effort.) The three major sources of aid are government grants, private scholarships, and the colleges themselves.

  1. William Young, Financial Aid Director of a small private Midwestern college, surveyed the records of 100 sophomores and found the following:

49 receive government grants
55 receive private scholarships
43 receive aid from the college
23 receive government grants and private scholarships

18 receive government grants and aid from the college
28 receive private scholarships and aid from the college
8 receive help from all three sources.

How many of the students in the survey:
(a) have a government grant only?
(b) have a private scholarship but not a government grant?
(c) receive financial aid from only one of these sources?
(d) receive aid from exactly two of these sources?
(e) receive no financial aid from any of these sources?
(f) receive no aid from the college or from the government?

2. At a Florida community college, half of the 48 mathematics majors were receiving federal financial aid. Of these:

> 5 had Pell Grants
> 14 participated in the College Work Study Program
> 4 had Stafford Loans
> 2 had Stafford Loans and participated in Work Study.

Those with Pell Grants had no other federal aid.

How many of the 48 math majors had:
(a) no federal aid?
(b) more than one of these three forms of aid?
(c) federal aid other than these three forms?
(d) a Stafford Loan or Work Study?

3. The following list shows the preferences of 102 people at a wine-tasting party:

> 99 like Spañada   94 like Ripple and Boone's
> 96 like Ripple   96 like Spañada and Boone's
> 99 like Boone's Farm Apple Wine   93 like all three.
> 95 like Spañada and Ripple

How many people like:
(a) none of the three?
(b) Spañada, but not Ripple?
(c) anything but Boone's Farm?
(d) only Ripple?
(e) exactly two kinds of wine?

4. Bob Carlton (Example 3 in the text) was again reassigned, this time to the home economics department of the electric utility. He interviewed 140 people in a suburban shopping center to find out some of their cooking habits. He obtained the following results. Should he be reassigned yet one more time?

58 use microwave ovens   17 use microwave ovens and gas ranges
63 use electric ranges   4 use both gas and electric ranges
58 use gas ranges   1 uses all three
19 use microwave ovens and electric ranges   2 cook only with solar energy.

5. A chicken farmer surveyed his flock with the following results. The farmer has:

> 9 fat red roosters   7 thin brown hens
> 2 fat red hens   18 thin brown roosters
> 26 fat roosters   6 thin red roosters
> 37 fat chickens   5 thin red hens.

Answer the following questions about the flock. [*Hint:* You need a Venn diagram with circles for fat, for male (a rooster is a male, a hen is a female) and for red (assume that brown and red are opposites in the chicken world).] How many chickens are:

(a) fat?

(b) red?

(c) male?

(d) fat, but not male?

(e) brown, but not fat?

(f) red and fat?

6. It was once said that Country-Western songs emphasize three basic themes: love, prison, and trucks. A survey of the local Country-Western radio station produced the following data:

12 songs about a truck driver who is in love while in prison

13 about a prisoner in love

28 about a person in love

18 about a truck driver in love

3 about a truck driver in prison who is not in love

2 about people in prison who are not in love and do not drive trucks

8 about people who are out of prison, are not in love, and do not drive a truck

16 about truck drivers who are not in prison.

(a) How many songs were surveyed?

Find the number of songs about:

(b) truck drivers

(c) prisoners

(d) truck drivers in prison

(e) people not in prison

(f) people not in love.

7. Lucinda Turley conducted a survey among 75 patients admitted to the cardiac unit of a Massachusetts hospital during a two-week period. Let

B = the set of patients with high blood pressure

C = the set of patients with high cholesterol levels

S = the set of patients who smoke cigarettes.

Lucinda's data are as follows:

$n(B) = 47$ $n(B \cap S) = 33$

$n(C) = 46$ $n(B \cap C) = 31$

$n(S) = 52$ $n(B \cap C \cap S) = 21$

$n[(B \cap C) \cup (B \cap S) \cup (C \cap S)] = 51$

Find the number of these patients who:

(a) had either high blood pressure or high cholesterol levels, but not both

(b) had fewer than two of the indications listed

(c) were smokers but had neither high blood pressure nor high cholesterol levels

(d) did not have exactly two of the indications listed.

8. Gail Taggart, who sells college textbooks, interviewed freshmen on a west coast campus to find out the main goals of today's students. Let

W = the set of those who want to become wealthy

F = the set of those who want to raise a family

E = the set of those who want to become experts in their field.

Gail's findings are summarized here:

$$n(W) = 160 \qquad n(E \cap F) = 90$$
$$n(F) = 140 \qquad n(W \cap F \cap E) = 80$$
$$n(E) = 130 \qquad n(E') = 95$$
$$n(W \cap F) = 95 \qquad n[(W \cup F \cup E)'] = 10.$$

Find the total number of students interviewed.

9. Dwaine Tomlinson runs a basketball program in Sacramento. On the first day of the season, 60 young men showed up and were categorized by age level and by preferred basketball position, as shown in the following table.

		Position			
		Guard (G)	Forward (F)	Center (N)	Totals
	Junior High (J)	9	6	4	19
Age	Senior High (S)	12	5	9	26
	College (C)	5	8	2	15
	Totals	26	19	15	60

Using the set labels (letters) in the table, find the number of players in each of the following sets.

(a) $J \cap G$ (b) $S \cap N$ (c) $N \cup (S \cap F)$

(d) $S' \cap (G \cup N)$ (e) $(S \cap N') \cup (C \cap G')$ (f) $N' \cap (S' \cap C')$

10. A study of U.S. Army housing trends categorized personnel as commissioned officers (C), warrant officers (W), or enlisted (E), and categorized their living facilities as on-base (B), rented off-base (R), or owned off-base (O). One survey yielded the following data.

		Facilities			
		B	R	O	Totals
	C	12	29	54	95
Personnel	W	4	5	6	15
	E	374	71	285	730
	Totals	390	105	345	840

Find the number of personnel in each of the following sets.

(a) $W \cap O$ (b) $C \cup B$ (c) $R' \cup W'$

(d) $(C \cup W) \cap (B \cup R)$ (e) $(C \cap B) \cup (E \cap O)$ (f) $B \cap (W \cup R)'$

In the following exercises, make use of an appropriate formula.

11. Evaluate $n(A \cup B)$ if $n(A) = 8$, $n(B) = 14$, and $n(A \cap B) = 5$.

12. Evaluate $n(A \cap B)$ if $n(A) = 15$, $n(B) = 12$, and $n(A \cup B) = 25$.

13. Evaluate $n(A)$ if $n(B) = 20$, $n(A \cap B) = 6$, and $n(A \cup B) = 30$.

14. Evaluate $n(B)$ if $n(A) = 35$, $n(A \cap B) = 15$, and $n(A \cup B) = 55$.

Draw an appropriate Venn diagram and use the given information to fill in the number of elements in each region.

15. $n(U) = 43$, $n(A) = 25$, $n(A \cap B) = 5$, $n(B') = 30$

16. $n(A) = 19$, $n(B) = 13$, $n(A \cup B) = 25$, $n(A') = 11$

17. $n(A \cup B) = 15, n(A \cap B) = 8, n(A) = 13, n(A' \cup B') = 11$

18. $n(A') = 25, n(B) = 28, n(A' \cup B') = 40, n(A \cap B) = 10$

19. $n(A) = 24, n(B) = 24, n(C) = 26, n(A \cap B) = 10, n(B \cap C) = 8, n(A \cap C) = 15,$
$n(A \cap B \cap C) = 6, n(U) = 50$

20. $n(A) = 57, n(A \cap B) = 35, n(A \cup B) = 81, n(A \cap B \cap C) = 15, n(A \cap C) = 21,$
$n(B \cap C) = 25, n(C) = 49, n(B') = 52$

21. $n(A \cap B) = 21, n(A \cap B \cap C) = 6, n(A \cap C) = 26, n(B \cap C) = 7, n(A \cap C') = 20,$
$n(B \cap C') = 25, n(C) = 40, n(A' \cap B' \cap C') = 2$

22. $n(A) = 15, n(A \cap B \cap C) = 5, n(A \cap C) = 13, n(A \cap B') = 9, n(B \cap C) = 8,$
$n(A' \cap B' \cap C') = 21, n(B \cap C') = 3, n(B \cup C) = 32$

23. Could the information of Example 4 have been presented in a Venn diagram similar to those in Examples 1 and 3? If so, construct such a diagram. Otherwise explain the essential difference of Example 4.

24. Explain how a cardinal number formula can be derived for the case where *three* sets occur. Specifically, give a formula relating $n(A \cup B \cup C)$ to $n(A), n(B), n(C),$ $n(A \cap B), n(A \cap C), n(B \cap C),$ and $n(A \cap B \cap C)$. Illustrate with a Venn diagram.

25. In Section 2, we looked at Venn diagrams containing one, two, or three sets.* Use this information to complete the following table. (*Hint:* Make a prediction for 4 sets from the pattern of 1, 2, and 3 sets.)

Number of sets	1	2	3	4
Number of regions dividing U	2	——	——	——

The figure below shows U divided into 16 regions by four sets, A, B, C, and D. Find the numbers of the regions belonging to each set in Exercises 26–29.

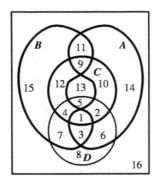

26. $A \cap B \cap C \cap D$ **27.** $A \cup B \cup C \cup D$

28. $(A \cap B) \cup (C \cap D)$ **29.** $(A' \cap B') \cap (C \cup D)$

30. If we placed 5 most generally related sets inside U, how many regions should result? Make a general formula. If n general sets are placed inside U, how many regions would result?

---

*For information on using more than four sets in a Venn diagram, see "The Construction of Venn Diagrams," by Branko Grünbaum, in *The College Mathematics Journal*, June 1984.

31. A survey of 130 television viewers revealed the following facts:

52 watch football	30 watch basketball and golf
56 watch basketball	21 watch tennis and golf
62 watch tennis	3 watch football, basketball, and tennis
60 watch golf	15 watch football, basketball, and golf
21 watch football and basketball	10 watch football, tennis, and golf
19 watch football and tennis	10 watch basketball, tennis, and golf
22 watch basketball and tennis	3 watch all four of these sports
27 watch football and golf	5 don't watch any of these four sports.

Use a Venn diagram with four sets like the one in Exercises 26–29 to answer the following questions.

(a) How many of these viewers watch football, basketball, and tennis, but not golf?

(b) How many watch exactly one of these four sports?

(c) How many watch exactly two of these four sports?

---

5   *Cardinal Numbers of Infinite Sets*

As mentioned at the beginning of this chapter, most of the early work in set theory was done by Georg Cantor. He devoted much of his life to a study of the cardinal numbers of sets. Recall that the *cardinal number* of a finite set is the number of elements that it contains. For example, the set {5, 9, 15} contains 3 elements and has a cardinal number of 3. The cardinal number of ∅ is 0.

Cantor proved many results about the cardinal numbers of infinite sets. The proofs of Cantor are quite different from the type of proofs you may have seen in an algebra or geometry course. Because of the novelty of Cantor's methods, they were not quickly accepted by the mathematicians of his day. (In fact, some other aspects of Cantor's theory lead to paradoxes.) The results we will discuss here, however, are commonly accepted today.

The idea of the cardinal number of an infinite set depends on the idea of one-to-one correspondence. For example, each of the sets {1, 2, 3, 4} and {9, 10, 11, 12} has four elements. Corresponding elements of the two sets could be paired off in the following manner (among many other ways):

$$\{1, \quad 2, \quad 3, \quad 4\}$$
$$\updownarrow \quad \updownarrow \quad \updownarrow \quad \updownarrow$$
$$\{9, \quad 10, \quad 11, \quad 12\}.$$

Such a pairing is a **one-to-one correspondence** between the two sets. The "one-to-one" refers to the fact that each element of the first set is paired with exactly one element of the second set and each element of the second set is paired with exactly one element of the first set.

Two sets A and B which may be put in a one-to-one correspondence are said to be **equivalent.** Symbolically, this is written $A \sim B$. Do you see that the two sets shown above are equivalent but not equal?

The following correspondence between sets {1, 8, 12} and {6, 11},

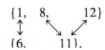

is not one-to-one since the elements 8 and 12 from the first set are both paired with the element 11 from the second set. These sets are not equivalent.

It seems reasonable to say that if two non-empty sets have the same cardinal number, then a one-to-one correspondence can be established between the two sets. Also, if a one-to-one correspondence can be established between two sets, then the two sets must have the same cardinal number. These two facts are fundamental in discussing the cardinal numbers of infinite sets.

FOR FURTHER THOUGHT

Paradox The word in Greek originally meant "wrong opinion" as opposed to orthodox, which meant "right opinion." Over the years, the word came to mean self-contradiction. An example is the statement "This sentence is false." By assuming it is true, we get a contradiction; likewise, by assuming it is false we get a contradiction. Thus, it's a paradox.

Before the twentieth century it was considered a paradox that any set could be placed into one-to-one correspondence with a proper subset of itself. This paradox, called Galileo's paradox, after the sixteenth-century mathematician and scientist Galileo (see the stamp at the right), is now explained by saying that the ability to make such a correspondence is how we distinguish infinite sets from finite sets. What is true for finite sets is not necessarily true for infinite sets.

Other paradoxes include the famous paradoxes of Zeno, born about 496 B.C. in southern Italy. Two of them claim to show that a faster runner cannot overtake a slower one, and that, in fact, motion itself cannot even occur.

For Group Discussion What is your explanation for the following two examples of Zeno's paradoxes?

1. Achilles, if he starts out behind a tortoise, can never overtake the tortoise even if he runs faster.

    Suppose Tortoise has a head start of one meter and goes one-tenth as fast as Achilles. When Achilles reaches the point where Tortoise started, Tortoise is then one-tenth meter ahead. When Achilles reaches *that* point, Tortoise is one-hundredth meter ahead. And so on. Achilles gets closer but can never catch up.

2. Motion itself cannot occur.

    You cannot travel one meter until after you have first gone a half meter. But you cannot go a half meter until after you have first gone a quarter meter. And so on. Even the tiniest motion cannot occur since a tinier motion would have to occur first.

The basic set used in discussing infinite sets is the set of counting numbers, $\{1, 2, 3, 4, 5, \ldots\}$. The set of counting numbers is said to have the infinite cardinal number $\aleph_0$ (the first Hebrew letter, aleph, with a zero subscript, read "aleph-null"). Think of $\aleph_0$ as being the "smallest" infinite cardinal number. To the question "How many counting numbers are there?" answer "There are $\aleph_0$ of them."

From the discussion above, any set that can be placed in a one-to-one correspondence with the counting numbers will have the same cardinal number as the set of counting numbers, or $\aleph_0$. It turns out that many sets of numbers have cardinal number $\aleph_0$.

The next few examples show some infinite sets that have the same cardinal number as the set of counting numbers.

EXAMPLE 1   Show that the set of whole numbers $\{0, 1, 2, 3, \ldots\}$ has cardinal number $\aleph_0$.

This problem is easily stated, but not quite so easily solved. All we really know about $\aleph_0$ is that it is the cardinal number of the set of counting numbers (by definition). To show that another set, such as the whole numbers, also has $\aleph_0$ as its cardinal number, we must apparently show that set to be equivalent to the set of counting numbers. And equivalence is established by a one-to-one correspondence between the two sets. This sequence of thoughts, involving just a few basic ideas, leads us to a plan: exhibit a one-to-one correspondence between the counting numbers and the whole numbers. Our strategy will be to sketch such a correspondence, showing exactly how each counting number is paired with a unique whole number. In the correspondence

$$
\begin{array}{ccccccccc}
\{1, & 2, & 3, & 4, & 5, & 6, & \ldots, & n, & \ldots\} \quad \text{Counting numbers} \\
\updownarrow & \updownarrow & \updownarrow & \updownarrow & \updownarrow & \updownarrow & & \updownarrow & \\
\{0, & 1, & 2, & 3, & 4, & 5, & \ldots, & n-1, & \ldots\} \quad \text{Whole numbers}
\end{array}
$$

the pairing of the counting number n with the whole number $n - 1$ continues indefinitely, with neither set containing any element not used up in the pairing process. So, even though the set of whole numbers has one more element (the number 0) than the set of counting numbers, and thus should have cardinal number $\aleph_0 + 1$, the above correspondence proves that both sets have the same cardinal number. That is,

$$\aleph_0 + 1 = \aleph_0. \quad \bullet$$

This result shows that intuition is a poor guide for dealing with infinite sets. Intuitively, it is "obvious" that there are more whole numbers than counting numbers. However, since the sets can be placed in a one-to-one correspondence, the two sets have the same cardinal number.

The set $\{5, 6, 7\}$ is a proper subset of the set $\{5, 6, 7, 8\}$, and there is no way to place these two sets in a one-to-one correspondence. On the other hand, the set of counting numbers is a proper subset of the set of whole numbers, and Example 1 showed that these two sets *can* be placed in a one-to-one correspondence. The only way a proper subset of a set can possibly be placed in a one-to-one correspondence with the set itself is if both sets are infinite. In fact, this important property is used as the definition of an infinite set.

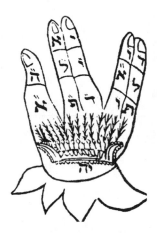

Number Lore of the Aleph-bet Aleph and other letters of the Hebrew alphabet are shown on a Kabbalistic diagram representing one of the ten emanations of God during Creation. Kabbalah, the ultra-mystical tradition within Judaism, arose in the fifth century and peaked in the sixteenth century in both Palestine and Poland.

 Kabbalists believed that the Bible held mysteries that could be discovered in permutations, combinations, and anagrams of its very letters. They also "read" the numerical value of letters in a word by the technique called Gematria (from geometry?). This was possible since each letter in the aleph-bet has a numerical value (aleph = 1), and thus a numeration system exists. The letter Y stands for 10, so 15 should be YH (10 + 5). However, YH is a form of the Holy Name, so instead TW (9 + 6) is the symbol.

Infinite Set

A set is **infinite** if it can be placed in a one-to-one correspondence with a proper subset of itself.

EXAMPLE 2 Show that the set of integers $\{\ldots, -3, -2, -1, 0, 1, 2, 3, \ldots\}$ has cardinal number $\aleph_0$.

Every counting number has a corresponding negative; the negative of 8, for example, is -8. Therefore, the cardinal number of the set of integers should be $\aleph_0 + \aleph_0$, or $2\aleph_0$. However, a one-to-one correspondence can be set up between the set of integers and the set of counting numbers, as follows:

$$\{1, \quad 2, \quad 3, \quad 4, \quad 5, \quad 6, \quad 7, \quad \ldots, \quad 2n, \quad 2n+1, \ldots\}$$
$$\updownarrow \quad \updownarrow \quad \updownarrow \quad \updownarrow \quad \updownarrow \quad \updownarrow \quad \updownarrow \qquad\quad \updownarrow \qquad \updownarrow$$
$$\{0, \quad 1, \quad -1, \quad 2, \quad -2, \quad 3, \quad -3, \quad \ldots, \quad n, \quad -n, \quad \ldots\}.$$

Because of this one-to-one correspondence, the cardinal number of the set of integers is the same as the cardinal number of the set of counting numbers, or

$$2\aleph_0 = \aleph_0. \quad \blacklozenge$$

Notice that the one-to-one correspondence of Example 2 also proves that the set of integers is infinite. The set of integers was placed in a one-to-one correspondence with a proper subset of itself.

As shown by Example 2, there are just as many integers as there are counting numbers. This result is not at all intuitive. However, the next result is even less intuitive. We know that there is an infinite number of fractions between any two counting numbers. For example, there is an infinite set of fractions, $\{1/2, 3/4, 7/8, 15/16, 31/32, \ldots\}$ between the counting numbers 0 and 1. This should imply that there are "more" fractions than counting numbers. It turns out, however, that there are just as many fractions as counting numbers, as shown by the next example.

EXAMPLE 3 Show that the cardinal number of the set of rational numbers is $\aleph_0$.

To show that the cardinal number of the set of rational numbers is $\aleph_0$, first show that a one-to-one correspondence may be set up between the set of nonnegative rational numbers and the counting numbers. This is done by the following ingenious scheme, devised by Georg Cantor. Look at Figure 22. The nonnegative rational numbers whose denominators are 1 are written in the first row; those whose denominators are 2 are written in the second row, and so on. Every nonnegative rational number appears in this list sooner or later. For example, 327/189 is in row 189 and column 327.

To set up a one-to-one correspondence between the set of nonnegative rationals and the set of counting numbers, follow the path drawn in Figure 22. Let 0/1 correspond to 1, let 1/1 correspond to 2, 2/1 to 3, 1/2 to 4 (skip 2/2, since 2/2 = 1/1), 1/3 to 5, 1/4 to 6, and so on. The numbers under the shaded disks are omitted, since they can be reduced to lower terms, and were thus included earlier in the listing.

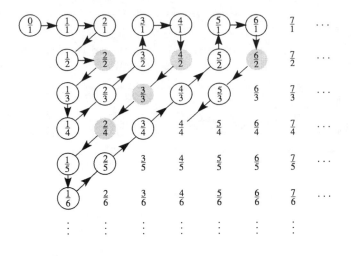

FIGURE 22

This procedure sets up a one-to-one correspondence between the set of non-negative rationals and the counting numbers, showing that both of these sets have the same cardinal number, $\aleph_0$. Now by using the method of Example 2, that is, letting each negative number follow its corresponding positive number, we can extend this correspondence to include negative rational numbers as well. Thus, the set of all rational numbers has cardinal number $\aleph_0$. ●

A set is called **countable** if it is finite, or if it has cardinal number $\aleph_0$. All the infinite sets of numbers discussed so far—the counting numbers, the whole numbers, the integers, and the rational numbers—are countable. It seems now that *every* set is countable, but this is not true. The next example shows that the set of real numbers is not countable.

EXAMPLE 4   Show that the set of all real numbers does not have cardinal number $\aleph_0$.

There are two possibilities:

1. The set of real numbers has cardinal number $\aleph_0$.
2. The set of real numbers does not have cardinal number $\aleph_0$.

Assume for the time being that the first statement is true. If the first statement is true, then a one-to-one correspondence can be set up between the set of real numbers and the set of counting numbers. We do not know what sort of correspondence this might be, but assume it can be done.

Every real number can be written as a decimal number (or simply "decimal"). Thus, in the one-to-one correspondence we are assuming, some decimal corresponds to the counting number 1, some decimal corresponds to 2, and so on. Suppose the correspondence is as follows:

$$1 \leftrightarrow .68458429006\ldots$$
$$2 \leftrightarrow .13479201038\ldots$$
$$3 \leftrightarrow .37291568341\ldots$$
$$4 \leftrightarrow .935223671611\ldots$$

and so on.

Assuming the existence of a one-to-one correspondence between the counting numbers and the real numbers means that every decimal is in the list above. Let's construct a new decimal K as follows. The first decimal in the above list has 6 as its first digit; let K start as $K = .4 \ldots$ We picked 4 since $4 \neq 6$; we could have used any other digit except 6. Since the second digit of the second decimal in the list is 3, we let $K = .45 \ldots$ (since $5 \neq 3$). The third digit of the third decimal is 2, so let $K = .457 \ldots$ (since $7 \neq 2$). The fourth digit of the fourth decimal is 2, so let $K = .4573 \ldots$ (since $3 \neq 2$). Continue K in this way.

Is K in the list that we assumed to contain all decimals? The first decimal in the list differs from K in at least the first position (K starts with 4, and the first decimal in the list starts with 6). The second decimal in the list differs from K in at least the second position, and the n-th decimal in the list differs from K in at least the n-th position. Every decimal in the list differs from K in at least one position, so that K cannot possibly be in the list. In summary:

> We assume every decimal is in the list above.
> The decimal K is not in the list.

Since these statements cannot both be true, the original assumption has led to a contradiction. This forces the acceptance of the only possible alternative to the original assumption: it is not possible to set up a one-to-one correspondence between the set of reals and the set of counting numbers; the cardinal number of the set of reals is not equal to $\aleph_0$. ●

The set of counting numbers is a proper subset of the set of real numbers. Because of this, it would seem reasonable to say that the cardinal number of the set of reals, commonly written c, is greater than $\aleph_0$. Other, even larger, infinite cardinal numbers can be constructed. For example, the set of all subsets of the set of real numbers has a cardinal number larger than c. Continuing this process of finding cardinal numbers of sets of subsets, more and more, larger and larger infinite cardinal numbers are produced.

We have seen that c is a larger cardinal number than $\aleph_0$. Is there a cardinal number between $\aleph_0$ and c? The person who began the study of set theory, Georg Cantor, did not think so, but he was unable to prove his guess. Cantor's *Hypothesis of the Continuum* was long considered one of the major unsolved problems of mathematics. However, in the early 1960s, the American mathematician Paul J. Cohen "solved" the problem in an unusual way. He showed the following: The assumption that no such cardinal number exists leads to a valid, consistent body of mathematical results, but the assumption that such a cardinal number does exist also leads to equally valid mathematical results. Thus, we could say that the existence of a cardinal number between $\aleph_0$ and c cannot be determined on the basis of today's mathematical knowledge. Some people, however, still hope for a more satisfying answer. For example, Rudy Rucker, in his book *Mind Tools*, suggests that a theory combining particle physics and information theory could possibly shed some light on the continuum problem.

The six most important infinite sets of numbers were listed in Section 1. All of them have been dealt with in this section except the irrational numbers. The irrationals have decimal representations, so they are all included among the real numbers. Since the irrationals are a subset of the reals, you might guess that the irra-

The Barber Paradox This is a version of a paradox of set theory that Bertrand Russell proposed in the early twentieth century.

(1) The men in a village are of two types: men who do not shave themselves and men who do.

(2) The village barber shaves all men who do not shave themselves and he shaves only those men.

But who shaves the barber? The barber cannot shave himself. If he did, he would fall into the category of men who shave themselves. However, (2) above states that the barber does not shave such men.

So the barber does not shave himself. But then he falls into the category of men who do not shave themselves. According to (2), the barber shaves all of these men; hence, the barber shaves himself too.

We find that the barber cannot shave himself, yet the barber does shave himself—a paradox.

tionals have cardinal number $\aleph_0$, just like the rationals. However, since the union of the rationals and the irrationals is all the reals, that would imply that $\aleph_0 + \aleph_0 = c$. That is, $2\aleph_0 = c$. But in Example 2 we showed that $2\aleph_0 = \aleph_0$. Hence, a better guess is that the cardinal number of the irrationals is c (the same as that of the reals). This is, in fact, true. The major infinite sets of numbers, with their cardinal numbers, are summarized below.

Cardinal Numbers of Infinite Number Sets

Infinite Set	Cardinal Number
Natural or counting numbers	$\aleph_0$
Whole numbers	$\aleph_0$
Integers	$\aleph_0$
Rational numbers	$\aleph_0$
Irrational numbers	c
Real numbers	c

5 EXERCISES

Place each pair of sets into a one-to-one correspondence, if possible.

1. {I, II, III} and {x, y, z}

2. {a, b, c, d} and {2, 4, 6}

3. {a, d, d, i, t, i, o, n} and {a, n, s, w, e, r}

4. {Reagan, Carter, Bush} and {Brown, Weinberger, Cheney}

Give the cardinal number of each set.

5. {a, b, c, d, . . . , k}

6. {9, 12, 15, . . . , 36}

7. { }

8. {0}

9. {300, 400, 500, . . .}

10. {−35, −28, −21, . . . , 56}

11. {−1/4, −1/8, −1/12, . . .}

12. {$x \mid x$ is an even integer}

13. {$x \mid x$ is an odd counting number}

14. {b, a, l, l, a, d}

15. {Jan, Feb, Mar, . . . , Dec}

16. {Alabama, Alaska, Arizona, . . . , Wisconsin, Wyoming}

17. Lew Lefton of the University of New Orleans has revised the old song "100 Bottles of Beer on the Wall" to illustrate a property of infinite cardinal numbers. Fill in the blank in the first line of Lefton's composition:

    "$\aleph_0$ bottles of beer on the wall, $\aleph_0$ bottles of beer, take one down and pass it around, ——— bottles of beer on the wall."

18. Two one-to-one correspondences are considered "different" if some elements are paired differently in one than in the other. For example:

    $$\{a, \quad b, \quad c\} \qquad \{a, \quad b, \quad c\}$$
    $$\updownarrow \quad \updownarrow \quad \updownarrow \ \text{and} \ \updownarrow \quad \updownarrow \quad \updownarrow \ \text{are different, while} \ \updownarrow \quad \updownarrow \quad \updownarrow \ \text{and} \ \updownarrow \quad \updownarrow \quad \updownarrow \ \text{are not.}$$
    $$\{a, \quad b, \quad c\} \qquad \{c, \quad b, \quad a\} \qquad\qquad \{a, \quad b, \quad c\} \qquad \{b, \quad c, \quad a\}$$
    $$\qquad\qquad\qquad\qquad\qquad\qquad\qquad\qquad\qquad\qquad \{c, \quad a, \quad b\} \qquad \{a, \quad b, \quad c\}$$

(a) How many *different* correspondences can be set up between the two sets

{George Burns, John Wayne, Chuck Norris}

and {Carlos Ray, Nathan Birnbaum, Marion Morrison}?

(b) Which one of these correspondences pairs each man with himself?

Determine whether the following pairs of sets are equal, equivalent, both, *or* neither.

19. {u, v, w}, {v, u, w}   **20.** {48, 6}, {4, 86}   **21.** {X, Y, Z}, {x, y, z}   **22.** {lea}, {ale}

23. {x | x is a positive real number}, {x | x is a negative real number}

24. {x | x is a positive rational number}, {x | x is a negative real number}

Show that each set has cardinal number $\aleph_0$ *by setting up a one-to-one correspondence between the given set and the set of counting numbers.*

25. the set of positive even numbers   **26.** {−10, −20, −30, −40, . . .}

27. {1,000,000, 2,000,000, 3,000,000, . . .}   **28.** the set of odd integers

29. {2, 4, 8, 16, 32, . . .} (*Hint:* $4 = 2^2$, $8 = 2^3$, $16 = 2^4$, and so on)

30. {−17, −22, −27, −32, . . .}

In each of Exercises 31–34, identify the given statement as always true *or* not always true. *If not always true, give an example.*

31. If A and B are infinite sets, then $A \sim B$.

32. If set A is an infinite set and set B can be put in a one-to-one correspondence with a proper subset of A, then B must be infinite.

33. If A is an infinite set and A is not equivalent to the set of counting numbers, then $n(A) = c$.

34. If A and B are both countably infinite sets, then $n(A \cup B) = \aleph_0$.

35. The set of real numbers can be represented by an infinite line, extending indefinitely in both directions. Each point on the line corresponds to a unique real number, and each real number corresponds to a unique point on the line.

(a) Use the figure below, where the line segment between 0 and 1 has been bent into a semicircle and positioned above the line, to prove that

{x | x is a real number between 0 and 1} $\sim$ {x | x is a real number}.

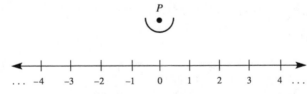

(b) What fact does part (a) establish about the set of real numbers?

36. Show that the two line segments shown here both have the same number of points.

Show that each of the following sets can be placed in a one-to-one correspondence with a proper subset of itself to prove that each set is infinite.

37. $\{3, 6, 9, 12, \ldots\}$

38. $\{4, 7, 10, 13, 16, \ldots\}$

39. $\{3/4, 3/8, 3/12, 3/16, \ldots\}$

40. $\{1, 4/3, 5/3, 2, \ldots\}$

41. $\{1/9, 1/18, 1/27, 1/36, \ldots\}$

42. $\{-3, -5, -9, -17, \ldots\}$

43. Describe the difference between *equal* and *equivalent* sets.

44. Explain how the correspondence suggested in Example 4 shows that the set of real numbers between 0 and 1 is not countable.

Find each infinite sum.

45. $\aleph_0 + \aleph_0 + \aleph_0 + \aleph_0$

46. $\aleph_0 + 6{,}000$

47. $c + 50{,}000$

48. $c + c + c$

49. $c + \aleph_0$

50. $100 + \aleph_0 + c$

CHAPTER SUMMARY

Symbols Used in This Chapter

Symbol	Meaning	Example
$\{\ \}$	Set braces	$\{3, 4, 5\}$ is a set
$\varnothing$	Empty set	The set of counting numbers less than 0
$n(A)$	Cardinal number of set A	$n(\{3, 4, 5, 6\}) = 4$
$\in$	Is an element of	$4 \in \{5, 6, 8, 4, 3\}$
$\{x \mid x \text{ has property } P\}$	Set-builder notation	$\{x \mid x \text{ is a counting number less than } 5\} = \{1, 2, 3, 4\}$
U	Universal set	
A'	Complement of set A	If $U = \{3, 6, 8, 9\}$ and $A = \{3, 9\}$, then $A' = \{6, 8\}$.
$\subseteq$	Is a subset of	$\{2, 4, 7\} \subseteq \{2, 3, 4, 5, 6, 7, 8\}$
$\subset$	Is a proper subset of	$\{d, f\} \subset \{b, d, f, h\}$
$\cap$	Intersection	$\{8, 9, 11, 12\} \cap \{7, 8, 10, 12\} = \{8, 12\}$
$\cup$	Union	$\{8, 9, 11, 12\} \cup \{7, 8, 10, 12\} = \{7, 8, 9, 10, 11, 12\}$
$-$	Set difference	$\{3, 4, 5, 6\} - \{4, 6, 8, 10\} = \{3, 5\}$
$=$	Set equality	$\{5, 2\} = \{6 - 4, 2 + 3\}$
$\sim$	Set equivalence	$\{a, b, c\} \sim \{1, 2, 3\}$
(a, b)	Ordered pair	$(4, 7)$ and $(7, 4)$ are different ordered pairs
$A \times B$	Cartesian product of A and B	If $A = \{1, 5\}$ and $B = \{6\}$, then $A \times B = \{(1, 6), (5, 6)\}$
$\aleph_0$	Cardinal number of the set of counting numbers	
c	Cardinal number of the set of real numbers	

1 Basic Concepts

Common Methods of Set Notation

Method	Example
1. Word description	The set of all students
2. Listing	$\{15, 25, 35, \ldots, 95\}$
3. Set-builder	$\{x \mid x \text{ is a rational number}\}$

Cardinal Number of a Set

$n(A)$ is the number of elements in set A *Example:* $n(\{2, 4, 6\}) = 3$

A is **finite** if $n(A) =$ a counting number.

Otherwise, A is **infinite.**

Set Equality

$A = B$ if A and B contain exactly the same elements.   *Example:* $\{a, b, c\} = \{c, a, b\}$

2   Venn Diagrams and Subsets

Universal Set (U)

Includes all things under discussion.

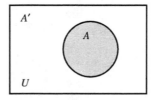

Complement of a Set

$A' = \{x \mid x \in U \text{ and } x \notin A\}$.

Subset of a Set

$A \subseteq B$ if B contains every element of A.

Proper Subset of a Set

$A \subset B$ if $A \subseteq B$ and $A \neq B$.

Number of Subsets (Formulas)

Any set with n elements has 2^n subsets and $2^n - 1$ proper subsets.

3   Operations with Sets

Common Set Operations

Let A and B be any sets, with U the universal set.

The **complement** of A, written A', is

$$A' = \{x \mid x \in U \text{ and } x \notin A\}.$$

The **intersection** of A and B is

$$A \cap B = \{x \mid x \in A \text{ and } x \in B\}.$$

The **union** of A and B is

$$A \cup B = \{x \mid x \in A \text{ or } x \in B\}.$$

The **difference** of A and B is

$$A - B = \{x \mid x \in A \text{ and } x \notin B\}.$$

The **Cartesian product** of A and B is

$$A \times B = \{(x, y) \mid x \in A \text{ and } y \in B\}.$$

Cardinal Number of a Cartesian Product (Formula)

If $n(A) = a$ and $n(B) = b$, then $n(A \times B) = ab$.

De Morgan's Laws

For any sets *A* and *B*,

$$(A \cap B)' = A' \cup B'$$

and $(A \cup B)' = A' \cap B'$.

4   Surveys and Cardinal Numbers

Cardinal Number Formula

For any sets *A* and *B*, $n(A \cup B) = n(A) + n(B) - n(A \cap B)$.

5   Cardinal Numbers of Infinite Sets

Two sets are **equivalent** ($A \sim B$) if they can be placed in a one-to-one correspondence. For example, *A* and *B* below are equivalent.

$$A = \{1, \quad 3, \quad 5, \quad 7, \quad 9\}$$
$$\updownarrow \quad \updownarrow \quad \updownarrow \quad \updownarrow \quad \updownarrow$$
$$B = \{a, \quad e, \quad i, \quad o, \quad u\}$$

Cardinal Numbers of Infinite Number Sets

Infinite Set	Cardinal Number
Natural or counting numbers	$\aleph_0$
Whole numbers	$\aleph_0$
Integers	$\aleph_0$
Rational numbers	$\aleph_0$
Irrational numbers	c
Real numbers	c

CHAPTER TEST

For Exercises 1–14,

$$\text{Let} \quad U = \{a, b, c, d, e, f, g, h\}$$
$$A = \{a, b, c, d\}$$
$$B = \{b, e, a, d\}$$
$$C = \{a, e\}.$$

Find each of the following sets.

1. $A \cup C$ **2.** $B \cap A$ **3.** B' **4.** $A - (B \cap C')$

Identify each of the following statements as true or false.

5. $b \in A$ **6.** $C \subseteq A$ **7.** $B \subset (A \cup C)$ **8.** $c \notin C$

9. $n[(A \cup B) - C] = 4$ **10.** $\varnothing \subset C$ **11.** $(A \cap B') \sim (B \cap A')$ **12.** $(A \cup B)' = A' \cap B'$

Find each of the following.

13. $n(A \times C)$ **14.** the number of proper subsets of *A*

Give a word description for each of the following sets.

15. $\{-3, -1, 1, 3, 5, 7, 9\}$ **16.** {January, February, March, . . . , December}

Express each of the following sets in set-builder notation.

17. $\{-1, -2, -3, -4, . . .\}$

18. $\{24, 32, 40, 48, . . . , 88\}$

Place, $\subset$, $\subseteq$, both, *or* neither *in each blank to make a true statement.*

19. $\varnothing$ ——— $\{x \mid x$ is a counting number between 17 and 18$\}$

20. $\{4, 9, 16\}$ ——— $\{4, 5, 6, 7, 8, 9, 10\}$

Shade each of the following sets in an appropriate Venn diagram.

21. $X \cup Y'$

22. $X' \cap Y'$

23. $(X \cup Y) - Z$

24. $[(X \cap Y) \cup (Y \cap Z) \cup (X \cap Z)] - (X \cap Y \cap Z)$

The following table lists ten inventions, important directly or indirectly in our lives, together with other pertinent data.

Invention	Date	Inventor	Nation
Adding machine	1642	Pascal	France
Barometer	1643	Torricelli	Italy
Electric razor	1917	Schick	U.S.
Fiber optics	1955	Kapany	England
Geiger counter	1913	Geiger	Germany
Pendulum clock	1657	Huygens	Holland
Radar	1940	Watson–Watt	Scotland
Telegraph	1837	Morse	U.S.
Thermometer	1593	Galileo	Italy
Zipper	1891	Judson	U.S.

Let U = the set of all ten inventions
A = the set of items invented in the United States
T = the set of items invented in the twentieth century

List the elements of each of the following sets.

25. $A \cap T$

26. $(A \cup T)'$

27. $A - T'$

28. State De Morgan's laws for sets in words rather than symbols.

29. Explain in your own words why, if A and B are any two non-empty sets, $A \times B \neq B \times A$ but $n(A \times B) = n(B \times A)$.

Sandra Miller, a psychology professor at a Southern California college, was planning a study of viewer responses to certain aspects of the movies Awakenings, Memphis Belle, *and* The Field. *Upon surveying her class of 55 students, she determined the following data:*

17 had seen Awakenings
17 had seen Memphis Belle
23 had seen The Field
6 had seen Awakenings *and* Memphis Belle
8 had seen Awakenings *and* The Field
10 had seen Memphis Belle *and* The Field
2 had seen all three of these movies.

How many students had seen

30. exactly two of these movies?

31. exactly one of these movies?

32. none of these movies?

33. *Awakenings* but neither of the others?

Gottfried Leibniz
(1646–1716) was a wide-ranging philosopher and a universalist who tried to patch up Catholic-Protestant conflicts. He promoted cultural exchange between Europe and the East. Chinese ideograms led him to search for a universal symbolism.

An early inventor of symbolic logic, Leibniz hoped to build a totally objective model for human reasoning and thus reduce all reasoning errors to minor calculational mistakes. His dream has so far proved futile.

Logic, logical thinking, and correct reasoning have wide applications in many fields, including law, psychology, rhetoric, science, and mathematics. While an interesting study can be made of logic in human lives, we shall restrict our attention mainly to logic as it is used in mathematics. This logic was first studied systematically by Aristotle (384 B.C.–322 B.C.). Aristotle and his followers studied patterns of correct and incorrect reasoning. Perhaps the most famous *syllogism* (pattern of logical reasoning) to come from Aristotle is the following:

> All men are mortal.
> Socrates is a man.
> _____
> Socrates is mortal.

The work of Aristotle was carried forward by medieval philosophers and theologians, who made an intimate study of logical arguments. A big advance in the study of mathematical logic came with the work of Gottfried Wilhelm von Leibniz (1646–1716), one of the inventors of calculus. Leibniz introduced *symbols* to represent ideas in logic—letters for statements and other symbols for the relations between statements. Leibniz hoped that logic would become a *universal characteristic* and unify all of mathematics.

For two hundred years after Leibniz, mathematicians had little interest in his universal characteristic. In fact, no further work in symbolic logic was done until George Boole (1815–1864) began his studies. Boole's major contribution came when he pointed out the connection between logic and sets. His rules for sets make up the subject of *Boolean algebra,* a key idea in the development of modern computers and calculators. Boole's work is summarized in his most famous book, *An Investigation of the Laws of Thought,* published in 1854.

Logic became a favorite subject of study by British mathematicians after Boole. John Venn (1834–1923) developed the Venn diagrams of Chapter 2. Augustus De Morgan (1806–1872) proved certain laws for both sets and logic. Charles Dodgson (1832–1898) wrote several popular textbooks on logic. Dodgson, a professor at Oxford University in England, wrote *Alice's Adventures in Wonderland* under the pen name Lewis Carroll. Some of his logic exercises are discussed in Section 6.

The work of all these mathematicians was summarized and expanded in *Principia Mathematica,* a 2,000-page three-volume work published between 1910 and 1913. The book begins with a small number of basic assumptions, or *axioms,* and a few undefined terms of logic. Then all the theory of arithmetic is developed in terms of the definitions and assumptions of logic. *Principia Mathematica* was written by Bertrand Russell (1872–1970) and Alfred North Whitehead (1861–1947).

1 Statements and Quantifiers

This section introduces the study of *symbolic logic,* which uses letters to represent statements, and symbols for words such as *and, or, not.* One of the main applications of logic is in the study of the *truth value* (that is, the truth or falsity) of statements with many parts. The truth value of these statements depends on the components that comprise them.

George Boole (1815–1864) grew up in poverty. His father, a London tradesman, gave him his first math lessons and taught him to make optical instruments. Boole was largely self-educated. At 16 he worked in an elementary school and by age 20 had opened his own school. He studied mathematics in his spare time. Lung disease killed him at age 49.

Boole's ideas have been used in the design of computers and telephone systems.

Many kinds of sentences occur in ordinary language, including factual statements, opinions, commands, and questions. Symbolic logic discusses only the first type of sentence, the kind that involves facts.

A **statement** is defined as a declarative sentence that is either true or false, but not both simultaneously. For example, both of the following are statements:

Radio provides a means of communication.
$2 + 1 = 6$

Each one is either true or false. However, the following sentences are not statements based on this definition:

Paint the wall.
How do you spell relief?
Michael Jordan is a better basketball player than Larry Bird.
This sentence is false.

These sentences cannot be identified as being either true or false. The first sentence is a command, and the second is a question. The third is an opinion. "This sentence is false" is a paradox; if we assume it is true, then it is false, and if we assume it is false, then it is true.

A **compound statement** may be formed by combining two or more statements. The statements making up the compound statements are called **component statements.** Various **logical connectives,** or simply **connectives,** can be used in forming compound statements. Words like *and, or, not,* and *if . . . then* are examples of connectives. (While a statement such as "Today is not Tuesday" does not consist of two component statements, for convenience it is considered compound, since its truth value is determined by noting the truth value of a different statement, "Today is Tuesday.")

Paradox A classic example is

A Cretan said,

"All Cretans are liars."

The source is found in St. Paul's Epistle to Titus. We read in the King James version of the Bible:

One of themselves, even a prophet of their own, said, The Cretians [sic] are always liars, evil beasts, slow bellies.

(Titus 1:12)

EXAMPLE 1　　Decide whether or not each statement is compound.

(a) Trey Yuen restaurant serves Peking duck and Pat O'Brien's serves drinks called Hurricanes.

This statement is compound, since it is made up of the component statements "Trey Yuen restaurant serves Peking duck" and "Pat O'Brien's serves drinks called Hurricanes." The connective is *and.*

(b) You can pay me now or you can pay me later.
The connective here is *or.* The statement is compound.

(c) If he said it, then it must be true.
The connective here is *if . . . then,* discussed in more detail in Section 3. The statement is compound.

(d) My pistol was made by Smith and Wesson.
While the word "and" is used in this statement, it is not used as a *logical* connective, since it is part of the name of the manufacturer. The statement is not compound. ●

Negations

The sentence "Tom Jones has a red car" is a statement; the **negation** of this statement is "Tom Jones does not have a red car." The negation of a true statement is false, and the negation of a false statement is true.

It would seem that a negation of "fat chance" is "slim chance." Then why do these two mean the same thing? And why do you drive on a parkway, and park in a driveway?

EXAMPLE 2   Form the negation of each statement.

(a) That state has a governor.

To negate this statement, we introduce *not* into the sentence: "That state does not have a governor."

(b) The sun is not a star.

Negation: "The sun is a star." ◉

One way to detect incorrect negations is to check the truth value. A negation must have the opposite truth value from the original statement.

The next example uses some of the following inequality symbols from algebra.

Symbolism	Meaning	Examples	
$a < b$	a is less than b	$4 < 9$	$\dfrac{1}{2} < \dfrac{3}{4}$
$a > b$	a is greater than b	$6 > 2$	$-5 > -11$
$a \le b$	a is less than or equal to b	$8 \le 10$	$3 \le 3$
$a \ge b$	a is greater than or equal to b	$-2 \ge -3$	$-5 \ge -5$

EXAMPLE 3   Give a negation of each inequality. Do *not* use a slash symbol.

(a) $p < 9$

The negation of "p is less than 9" is "p is *not* less than 9." Since we cannot use "not," which would require writing $p \not< 9$, phrase the negation as "p is greater than or equal to 9," or $p \ge 9$.

(b) $7x + 11y \ge 77$

The negation, with no slash, is $7x + 11y < 77$. ◉

Symbols

To simplify work with logic, symbols are used. Statements are represented with letters, such as *p*, *q*, or *r*, while several symbols for connectives are shown in the table. The table also gives the type of compound statement having the given connective.

Connective	Symbol	Type of Statement
and	$\wedge$	Conjunction
or	$\vee$	Disjunction
not	$\sim$	Negation

The symbol $\sim$ represents the connective *not*. If *p* represents the statement "Millard Fillmore was president in 1850" then $\sim p$ represents "Millard Fillmore was not president in 1850."

Aristotle, the first to systematize the logic we use in everyday life, appears above in a detail from the painting *The School of Athens,* by Raphael. He is shown debating a point with his teacher **Plato.** Aristotle's logic and analysis of how things work, many feel, is inseparably woven into the ways Westerners are taught to think.

Null-A (for "non-Aristotelian") refers to the many-valued logic of modern science versus the two-valued logic (*T* and *F*) of Aristotle. Null-A is featured in a pair of science-fiction novels by A. E. van Vogt, about Earth in the twenty-sixth century, when education is based on the null-A philosophy of General Semantics. Further reading: *The World of Null-A* and *The Players of Null-A,* both reprinted by Berkeley Publishing Company.

| **EXAMPLE 4** | Let p represent "It is 80° today," and let q represent "It is Tuesday." Write each symbolic statement in words.

(a) $p \vee q$

From the table, $\vee$ symbolizes *or;* thus, $p \vee q$ represents

It is 80° today or it is Tuesday.

(b) $\sim p \wedge q$

It is not 80° today and it is Tuesday.

(c) $\sim(p \vee q)$

It is not the case that it is 80° today or it is Tuesday.

(d) $\sim(p \wedge q)$

It is not the case that it is 80° today and it is Tuesday. ●

The statement in part (c) of Example 4 is usually translated in English as "Neither p nor q."

Quantifiers

The words *all, each, every,* and *no(ne)* are called **universal quantifiers,** while words and phrases like *some, there exists,* and *(for) at least one* are called **existential quantifiers.** Quantifiers are used extensively in mathematics to indicate *how many* cases of a particular situation exist. Be careful when forming the negation of a statement involving quantifiers.

The negation of a statement must be false if the given statement is true and must be true if the given statement is false, in all possible cases. Consider the statement

All girls in the group are named Mary.

Many people would write the negation of this statement as "No girls in the group are named Mary" or "All girls in the group are not named Mary." But this would not be correct. To see why, look at the three groups below.

Group I: Mary Jones, Mary Smith, Mary Jackson
Group II: Mary Johnson, Betty Parker, Margaret Boyle
Group III: Shannon Mulkey, Annie Ross, Patricia Gainey

These groups contain all possibilities that need to be considered. In Group I, *all* girls are named Mary; in Group II, *some* girls are named Mary (and some are not); and in Group III, *no* girls are named Mary. Look at the truth values in the chart and keep in mind that "some" means "at least one (and possibly all)."

Truth Value as Applied to:

	Group I	Group II	Group III
(1) All girls in the group are named Mary. **(Given)**	T	F	F
(2) No girls in the group are named Mary. **(Possible negation)**	F	F	T
(3) All girls in the group are not named Mary. **(Possible negation)**	F	F	T
(4) Some girls in the group are not named Mary. **(Possible negation)**	F	T	T

Negation

The negation of the given statement (1) must have opposite truth values in *all* cases. It can be seen that statements (2) and (3) do not satisfy this condition (for Group II), but statement (4) does. It may be concluded that the correct negation for "All girls in the group are named Mary" is "Some girls in the group are not named Mary." Other ways of stating the negation are:

> Not all girls in the group are named Mary.
> It is not the case that all girls in the group are named Mary.
> At least one girl in the group is not named Mary.

The following table can be used to generalize the method of finding the negation of a statement involving quantifiers.

Negations of Quantified Statements

Statement	Negation
All do.	Some do not. (Equivalently: Not all do.)
Some do.	None do. (Equivalently: All do not.)

The negation of the negation of a statement is simply the statement itself. For instance, the negations of the statements in the Negation column are simply the corresponding original statements in the Statement column. As an example, the negation of "Some do not" is "All do."

EXAMPLE 5   Write the negation of each statement.

(a) Some dogs have fleas.

Since *some* means "at least one," the statement "Some dogs have fleas" is really the same as "At least one dog has fleas." The negation of this is "No dog has fleas."

(b) Some dogs do not have fleas.

This statement claims that at least one dog, somewhere, does not have fleas. The negation of this is "All dogs have fleas."

(c) No dogs have fleas.

The negation is "Some dogs have fleas."   ◆

The many relationships among special sets of numbers can be expressed using universal and existential quantifiers. In the chapter on problem solving we introduced the counting or natural numbers, which form the "building blocks" of the real number system. Sets of real numbers are studied in algebra, and we summarize these in the box that follows.

Sets of Real Numbers

Natural or counting numbers $\{1, 2, 3, 4, \ldots\}$
Whole numbers $\{0, 1, 2, 3, 4, \ldots\}$
Integers $\{\ldots, -3, -2, -1, 0, 1, 2, 3, \ldots\}$
Rational numbers $\{p/q \mid p \text{ and } q \text{ are integers, and } q \neq 0\}$
(Some examples of rational numbers are 3/5, −7/9, 5, and 0. Any rational number may be written as a terminating decimal number, like 0.25, or a repeating decimal number, like 0.666. . . .)
Real numbers $\{x \mid x \text{ is a number which may be written as a decimal}\}$
Irrational numbers $\{x \mid x \text{ is a real number and } x \text{ cannot be written as a quotient of integers}\}$
(Some examples of irrational numbers are $\sqrt{2}$, $\sqrt[3]{4}$, and π.
A characteristic of irrational numbers is that their decimal representations never terminate and never repeat, that is, they never reach a point where a given pattern of digits repeats from that point on.)

EXAMPLE 6   Decide whether each of the following statements about sets of numbers involving a quantifier is *true* or *false*.

(a) There exists a whole number that is not a natural number.
   Because there is such a whole number (it is 0), this statement is true.

(b) Every integer is a natural number.
   This statement is false, because we can find at least one integer that is not a natural number. For example, −1 is an integer but is not a natural number. (There are infinitely many other choices we could have made.)

(c) Every natural number is a rational number.
   Since every natural number can be written as a fraction with denominator 1, this statement is true.

(d) There exists an irrational number that is not real.
   In order to be an irrational number, a number must first be real (see the box). Therefore, since we cannot give an irrational number that is not real, this statement is false. (Had we been able to find at least one, the statement would have then been true.)   ●

---

1 EXERCISES

Decide whether or not each of the following is a statement.

1. The area code for Jackson, Mississippi, is 601.

2. January 25, 1947, was a Tuesday.

3. This book has exactly 852 pages.

4. Stand up and be counted.

5. $8 + 15 = 23$

6. $9 - 4 = 5$ and $2 + 1 = 5$

7. Chester A. Arthur was president in 1882.

8. Not all numbers are positive.

9. Dancing is enjoyable.

10. Since 1950, more people have died in automobile accidents than of cancer.

11. Toyotas are better cars than Dodges.

12. Sit up and take notice.

13. One gallon of water weighs more than 5 pounds.

14. Kevin "Catfish" McCarthy once took a prolonged continuous shower for 340 hours, 40 minutes.

Decide whether each of the following statements is compound.

15. Some people have all the luck.

16. I read novels and I read newspapers.

17. Mary Kay Andrews is under 40 years of age, and so is Robert Andrews.

18. Yesterday was Friday.

19. $4 + 2 \neq 8$

20. $5 \neq 4 + 2$

21. If Buddy is a politician, then Eddie is a crook.

22. If Earl Karn sells his quota, then Pamela Fullerton will be happy.

Write a negation for each of the following statements.

23. The flowers must be watered.

24. Her aunt's name is Lucia.

25. No rain fell in southern California today.

26. Every dog has its day.

27. All students present will get another chance.

28. Some books are longer than this book.

29. Some people have all the luck.

30. No computer repairman can play blackjack.

31. Nobody doesn't like Sara Lee.

32. Everybody loves somebody sometime.

Give a negation of each inequality. Do not use a slash symbol.

33. $x > 3$

34. $y < -2$

35. $p \geq 4$

36. $q \leq 12$

37. Explain why the negation of "$r > 4$" is not "$r < 4$."

38. Try to negate the sentence "The exact number of words in this sentence is ten" and see what happens. Explain the problem that arises.

Let p represent the statement "She has blue eyes" *and let q represent the statement* "He is 43 years old." *Translate each symbolic compound statement into words.*

39. $\sim p$

40. $\sim q$

41. $p \wedge q$

42. $p \vee q$

43. $\sim p \vee q$

44. $p \wedge \sim q$

45. $\sim p \vee \sim q$

46. $\sim p \wedge \sim q$

47. $\sim(\sim p \wedge q)$

48. $\sim(p \vee \sim q)$

Let p represent the statement "Chris collects aluminum cans" *and let q represent the statement* "Jack is a catcher." *Convert each of the following compound statements into symbols.*

49. Chris collects aluminum cans and Jack is not a catcher.

50. Chris does not collect aluminum cans or Jack is not a catcher.

51. Chris does not collect aluminum cans or Jack is a catcher.

52. Jack is a catcher and Chris does not collect aluminum cans.

53. Neither Chris collects aluminum cans nor Jack is a catcher.

54. Either Jack is a catcher or Chris collects aluminum cans, and it is not the case that both Jack is a catcher and Chris collects aluminum cans.

55. Incorrect use of quantifiers is often heard in everyday language. Suppose you hear that a local electronics chain is having a 30% off sale, and the radio advertisement states "All items are not available in all stores." Do you think that, literally translated, the ad really means what it says? What do you think is really meant? Explain your answer.

56. Repeat Exercise 55 for the following: "All people don't have the time to devote to maintaining their cars properly."

Decide whether each statement involving a quantifier is true *or* false.

57. Every natural number is an integer.

58. Every whole number is an integer.

59. There exists an integer that is not a natural number.

60. There exists a rational number that is not an integer.

61. All irrational numbers are real numbers.

62. All rational numbers are real numbers.

63. Some whole numbers are not rational numbers.

64. Some rational numbers are not integers.

65. Each rational number is a positive number.

66. Each whole number is a positive number.

Refer to the sketches labeled A, B, and C, and identify the sketch (or sketches) that is (are) satisfied by the given statement involving a quantifier.

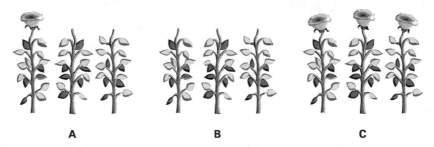

A	**B**	**C**

67. All plants have a flower.

69. No plant has a flower.

71. At least one plant does not have a flower.

73. Not every plant has a flower.

68. At least one plant has a flower.

70. All plants do not have a flower.

72. No plant does not have a flower.

74. Not every plant does not have a flower.

75. Explain the difference between the following statements:

> All students did not pass the test.
> Not all students passed the test.

76. Write the following statement using "every": There is no one here who has not done that at one time or another.

77. The statement "For some real number x, $x^2 \geq 0$" is true. However, your friend does not understand why, since he claims that $x^2 \geq 0$ for *all* real numbers x (and not *some*). How would you explain his misconception to him?

78. Only one of the following statements is true. Which one is it?

(a) For some real number x, $x \not< 0$.

(b) For all real numbers x, $x^3 > 0$.

(c) For all real numbers x less than 0, x^2 is also less than 0.

(d) For some real number x, $x^2 < 0$.

79. A newspaper headline reads "President Vetoes Bill to Repeal Law Against Capital Punishment." Does this headline indicate that action was taken for or against capital punishment?

80. A newspaper headline once read "Supreme Court refuses to hear challenge to lower court decision approving trial judge's refusal to allow defendant to refuse to speak." Can the defendant refuse to speak?

2	*Truth Tables*

In this section, the truth values of simple statements are used to find the truth values of compound statements. To begin, let us decide on the truth values of the **conjunction** *p and q,* symbolized $p \wedge q$. In everyday language, the connective *and* implies the idea of "both." The statement

> Monday immediately follows Sunday and March immediately follows February

is true, since each component statement is true. On the other hand, the statement

> Monday immediately follows Sunday and March immediately follows January

is false, even though part of the statement (Monday immediately follows Sunday) is true. For the conjunction $p \wedge q$ to be true, both p and q must be true. This result is summarized by a table, called a **truth table,** which shows all four of the possible combinations of truth values for the conjunction *p and q.* The truth table for *conjunction* is shown here.

Truth Table for the Conjunction p and q

p and q

p	q	$p \wedge q$
T	T	T
T	F	F
F	T	F
F	F	F

EXAMPLE 1 Let p represent "5 > 3" and let q represent "6 < 0." Find the truth value of $p \wedge q$.

Here p is true and q is false. Looking in the second row of the conjunction truth table shows that $p \wedge q$ is false. ◆

In some cases, the logical connective *but* is used in compound statements. For example, consider the statement

He wants to go to the mountains but she wants to go to the beach.

Here, *but* is used in place of *and* to give a different sort of emphasis to the statement. In such a case, we consider the statement as we would consider the conjunction using the word *and.* The truth table for the conjunction, given above, would apply.

In ordinary language, the word *or* can be ambiguous. The expression "this or that" can mean either "this or that or both," or "this or that but not both." For example the statement,

I will paint the wall or I will paint the ceiling

probably has the following meaning: "I will paint the wall or I will paint the ceiling or I will paint both." On the other hand, the statement

I will drive the Ford or the Datsun to the store

probably means "I will drive the Ford, or I will drive the Datsun, but I shall not drive both."

The symbol $\vee$ normally represents the first *or* described. That is, $p \vee q$ means "*p* or *q* or both." With this meaning of *or,* $p \vee q$ is called the *inclusive disjunction,* or just the **disjunction** of p and q.

In everyday language, the disjunction implies the idea of "either." For example, the disjunction

I have a quarter or I have a dime

is true whenever I have either a quarter, a dime or both. The only way this disjunction could be false would be if I had neither coin. A disjunction is false only if both component statements are false. The truth table for *disjunction* follows.

Truth Table for the Disjunction *p* or *q*

p or *q*

p	*q*	$p \vee q$
T	T	T
T	F	T
F	T	T
F	F	F

The inequality symbols ≤ and ≥ are examples of inclusive disjunction. For example, $x \leq 6$ is true if either $x < 6$ or $x = 6$.

EXAMPLE 2   The following list shows several statements and the reason that each is true.

Statement	Reason That It Is True
$8 \geq 8$	$8 = 8$
$3 \geq 1$	$3 > 1$
$-5 \leq -3$	$-5 < -3$
$-4 \leq -4$	$-4 = -4$

FOR FURTHER THOUGHT

Raymond Smullyan is one of today's foremost writers of logic puzzles. This multi-talented professor of mathematics and philosophy at City University of New York has written several books on recreational logic, including *The Lady or the Tiger?*, *What Is the Name of This Book?*, and *Alice in Puzzleland*. The title of the first of these is taken from the classic Frank Stockton short story, in which a prisoner must make a choice between two doors: behind one is a beautiful lady, and behind the other is a hungry tiger.

For Group Discussion Smullyan proposes the following: What if each door has a sign, and the man knows that only one sign is true? The sign on Door 1 reads:

> IN THIS ROOM THERE IS A LADY AND
> IN THE OTHER ROOM THERE IS A TIGER.

The sign on Door 2 reads:

> IN ONE OF THESE ROOMS THERE IS A LADY AND
> IN ONE OF THESE ROOMS THERE IS A TIGER.

With this information, the man is able to choose the correct door. Can you? (The answer is on the next page.)

The **negation** of a statement p, symbolized $\sim p$, must have the opposite truth value from the statement p itself. This leads to the truth table for the negation, shown here.

Truth Table for the Negation not p

not p

p	$\sim p$
T	F
F	T

EXAMPLE 3 Suppose p is false, q is true, and r is false. What is the truth value of the compound statement $\sim p \wedge (q \vee \sim r)$?

Here parentheses are used to group q and $\sim r$ together. Work first inside the parentheses. Since r is false, $\sim r$ will be true. Since $\sim r$ is true and q is true, find the truth value of $q \vee \sim r$ by looking in the first row of the *or* truth table. This row gives the result T. Since p is false, $\sim p$ is true, and the final truth value of $\sim p \wedge (q \vee \sim r)$ is found in the top row of the *and* truth table. From the *and* truth table, when $\sim p$ is true, and $q \vee \sim r$ is true, the statement $\sim p \wedge (q \vee \sim r)$ is true.

The paragraph above may be interpreted using a short-cut symbolic method, letting T represent a true statement and F represent a false statement:

$$\sim p \wedge (q \vee \sim r)$$
$$\sim F \wedge (T \vee \sim F)$$
$$T \wedge (T \vee T) \qquad \text{~F gives T.}$$
$$T \wedge T \qquad \text{T} \vee \text{T gives T.}$$
$$T. \qquad \text{T} \wedge \text{T gives T.}$$

The T in the final row indicates that the compound statement is true. ◆

The next two examples show the use of truth tables to decide on the truth values of algebraic statements.

EXAMPLE 4 Let p represent the statement $3 > 2$, q represent $5 < 4$, and r represent $3 < 8$. Decide whether the following statements are true or false.

(a) $\sim p \wedge \sim q$

Since p is true, $\sim p$ is false. By the *and* truth table, if one part of an "and" statement is false, the entire statement is false. This makes $\sim p \wedge \sim q$ false.

(b) $\sim (p \wedge q)$

First, work within the parentheses. Since p is true and q is false, $p \wedge q$ is false by the *and* truth table. Next, apply the negation. The negation of a false statement is true, making $\sim (p \wedge q)$ a true statement.

Answer to the Problem of
The Lady or the Tiger?
The lady is behind Door 2. Suppose that the sign on Door 1 is true. Then the sign on Door 2 would also be true, but this is impossible. So the sign on Door 2 must be true, making the sign on Door 1 false. Since the sign on Door 1 says the lady is in Room 1, and this is false, the lady must be behind Door 2.

(c) $(\sim p \wedge r) \vee (\sim q \wedge \sim p)$

Here p is true, q is false, and r is true. This makes $\sim p$ false and $\sim q$ true. By the *and* truth table, the statement $\sim p \wedge r$ is false, and the statement $\sim q \wedge \sim p$ is also false. Finally,

$$(\sim p \wedge r) \vee (\sim q \wedge \sim p)$$
$$\downarrow \qquad \qquad \downarrow$$
$$\text{F} \quad \vee \quad \text{F,}$$

which is false by the *or* truth table. (For an alternate solution, see Example 8(b).) ●

When a quantifier is used with a conjunction or a disjunction, we must be careful in determining the truth value, as shown in the following example.

EXAMPLE 5   Identify each statement as *true* or *false*.

(a) For some real number x, $x < 5$ and $x > 2$.

Replacing x with 3 (as an example) gives $3 < 5$ and $3 > 2$. Since both $3 < 5$ and $3 > 2$ are true statements, the given statement is true by the *and* truth table. (Remember: *some* means "at least one.")

(b) For every real number b, $b > 0$ or $b < 1$.

No matter which real number might be tried as a replacement for b, at least one of the statements $b > 0$ and $b < 1$ will be true. Since an "or" statement is true if one or both component statements is true, the entire statement as given is true.

(c) For all real numbers x, $x^2 > 0$.

Since the quantifier is a universal quantifier, we need only find one case in which the inequality is false to make the entire statement false. Can we find a real number whose square is not positive (that is, not greater than 0)? Yes, we can—0 itself is a real number (and the *only* real number) whose square is not positive. Therefore, this statement is false. ●

Truth Tables

In the examples above, the truth value for a given statement was found by going back to the basic truth tables. In the long run, it is easier to first create a complete truth table for the given statement itself. Then final truth values can be read directly from this table. The procedure for making new truth tables is shown in the next few examples.

In this book we will use the following standard format for listing the possible truth values in compound statements involving two statements.

p	q	Compound Statement
T	T	
T	F	
F	T	
F	F	

EXAMPLE 6   **(a)** Construct a truth table for $(\sim p \wedge q) \vee \sim q$.

Begin by listing all possible combinations of truth values for p and q, as above. Then find the truth values of $\sim p \wedge q$. Start by listing the truth values of $\sim p$, which are the opposite of those of p.

p	q	$\sim p$
T	T	**F**
T	F	**F**
F	T	**T**
F	F	**T**

Use only the "$\sim p$" column and the "q" column, along with the *and* truth table, to find the truth values of $\sim p \wedge q$. List them in a separate column.

p	q	$\sim p$	$\sim p \wedge q$
T	T	F	**F**
T	F	F	**F**
F	T	T	**T**
F	F	T	**F**

Next include a column for $\sim q$.

p	q	$\sim p$	$\sim p \wedge q$	$\sim q$
T	T	F	F	**F**
T	F	F	F	**T**
F	T	T	T	**F**
F	F	T	F	**T**

Finally, make a column for the entire compound statement. To find the truth values, use *or* to combine $\sim p \wedge q$ with $\sim q$.

p	q	$\sim p$	$\sim p \wedge q$	$\sim q$	$(\sim p \wedge q) \vee \sim q$
T	**T**	F	F	F	**F**
T	**F**	F	F	T	**T**
F	**T**	T	T	F	**T**
F	**F**	T	F	T	**T**

(b) Suppose both p and q are true. Find the truth value of $(\sim p \wedge q) \vee \sim q$.

Look in the first row of the final truth table above, where both p and q have truth value T. Read across the row to find that the compound statement is false. ◆

EXAMPLE 7   Find the truth table for $p \wedge (\sim p \vee \sim q)$.

Proceed as shown.

p	q	$\sim p$	$\sim q$	$\sim p \vee \sim q$	$p \wedge (\sim p \vee \sim q)$
T	**T**	F	F	F	**F**
T	**F**	F	T	T	**T**
F	**T**	T	F	T	**F**
F	**F**	T	T	T	**F**

◆

In Need of Logic You might have to study this chapter several times to make logical sense out of this letter to a small business from the IRS (as quoted in *The Wall Street Journal*, February 20, 1985, p. 1).

The overpayment of $1,193.82 was moved to the June 30, 1983, 941 return after the refund of $1,376.16 was issued on July 23, 1984, and $125.55 refunded on July 23, 1984, from the Sep. 30, 1983, 941 return and a balance of $119.62 is due and $390.37 refunded July 23, 1984, from the June 30, 1083 (sic), 941 return and a balance of $371.93 is still due.

If a compound statement involves three component statements *p*, *q*, and *r*, we will use the following format in setting up the truth table.

p	*q*	*r*	Compound Statement
T	T	T	
T	T	F	
T	F	T	
T	F	F	
F	T	T	
F	T	F	
F	F	T	
F	F	F	

EXAMPLE 8   **(a)** Construct a truth table for $(\sim p \wedge r) \vee (\sim q \wedge \sim p)$.

This statement has three component statements, *p*, *q*, and *r*. The truth table thus requires eight rows to list all possible combinations of truth values of *p*, *q*, and *r*. The final truth table, however, can be found in much the same way as the ones above.

p	*q*	*r*	$\sim p$	$\sim p \wedge r$	$\sim q$	$\sim q \wedge \sim p$	$(\sim p \wedge r) \vee (\sim q \wedge \sim p)$
T	T	T	F	F	F	F	F
T	T	F	F	F	F	F	F
T	F	T	F	F	T	F	F
T	F	F	F	F	T	F	F
F	T	T	T	T	F	F	T
F	T	F	T	F	F	F	F
F	F	T	T	T	T	T	T
F	F	F	T	F	T	T	T

(b) Suppose *p* is true, *q* is false, and *r* is true. Find the truth value of $(\sim p \wedge r) \vee (\sim q \wedge \sim p)$.

By the third row of the truth table in part (a), the compound statement is false. (This is an alternate method for working part (c) of Example 4.) ●

PROBLEM SOLVING

Recall from the chapter on problem solving, one strategy for problem solving is noticing a pattern and using inductive reasoning. This strategy is used in the next example. ●

EXAMPLE 9   If *n* is a counting number, and a logical statement is composed of *n* component statements, how many rows will appear in the truth table for the compound statement?

To answer this question, let us examine some of the earlier truth tables in this section. The truth table for the negation has one statement and two rows. The truth tables for the conjunction and the disjunction have two component statements, and each has four rows. The truth table in Example 8(a) has three component statements and eight rows. Summarizing these in a table shows a pattern seen earlier.

Number of Statements	Number of Rows
1	$2 = 2^1$
2	$4 = 2^2$
3	$8 = 2^3$

Inductive reasoning leads us to the conjecture that, if a logical statement is composed of n component statements, it will have 2^n rows. This can be proved using more advanced concepts. ◆

Emilie, Marquise du Châtelet (1706–1749) participated in the scientific activity of the generation after Newton and Leibniz. She was educated in science, music, and literature, and she was studying mathematics at the time (1733) she began a long intellectual relationship with the philosopher François Voltaire (1694–1778). Her chateau was equipped with a physics laboratory. She and Voltaire competed independently in 1738 for a prize offered by the French Academy on the subject of fire. Although du Châtelet did not win, her dissertation was published by the academy in 1744. By that time she had published *Institutions of Physics* (expounding in part some ideas of Leibniz) and a work on Vital Forces. During the last four years of her life she translated Newton's *Principia* from Latin into French—the only French translation to date.

The result of Example 9 is reminiscent of the formula for the number of subsets of a set having n elements.

A logical statement having n component statements will have 2^n rows in its truth table.

Alternate Method for Finding Truth Tables

After making a reasonable number of truth tables, some people prefer the shortcut method shown in Example 10, which repeats Examples 6 and 8 above.

EXAMPLE 10   Find each truth table.

(a) $(\sim p \wedge q) \vee \sim q$

Start by inserting truth values for $\sim p$ and for q.

p	q	$(\sim p$	$\wedge$	$q)$	$\vee$	$\sim q$
T	T	F		T		
T	F	F		F		
F	T	T		T		
F	F	T		F		

Next, use the *and* truth table to obtain the truth values of $\sim p \wedge q$.

p	q	$(\sim p$	$\wedge$	$q)$	$\vee$	$\sim q$
T	T	F	**F**	T		
T	F	F	**F**	F		
F	T	T	**T**	T		
F	F	T	**F**	F		

Now disregard the two preliminary columns of truth values for $\sim p$ and for q, and insert truth values for $\sim q$.

p	q	$(\sim p$	$\wedge$	$q)$	$\vee$	$\sim q$
T	T		F			F
T	F		F			T
F	T		T			F
F	F		F			T

Finally, use the *or* truth table.

p	*q*	(~*p*	∧	*q*)	∨	~*q*
T	T		F		**F**	F
T	F		F		**T**	T
F	T		T		**T**	F
F	F		F		**T**	T

These steps can be summarized as follows.

p	*q*	(~*p*	∧	*q*)	∨	~*q*
T	**T**	F	F	T	**F**	F
T	**F**	F	F	F	**T**	T
F	**T**	T	T	T	**T**	F
F	**F**	T	F	F	**T**	T
		①	②	①	④	③

The circled numbers indicate the order in which the various columns of the truth table were found.

(b) (~*p* ∧ *r*) ∨ (~*q* ∧ ~*p*)

Work as follows.

p	*q*	*r*	(~*p*	∧	*r*)	∨	(~*q*	∧	~*p*)
T	**T**	**T**	F	F	T	**F**	F	F	F
T	**T**	**F**	F	F	F	**F**	F	F	F
T	**F**	**T**	F	F	T	**F**	T	F	F
T	**F**	**F**	F	F	F	**F**	T	F	F
F	**T**	**T**	T	T	T	**T**	F	F	T
F	**T**	**F**	T	F	F	**F**	F	F	T
F	**F**	**T**	T	T	T	**T**	T	T	T
F	**F**	**F**	T	F	F	**T**	T	T	T
			①	②	①	⑤	③	④	③

●

Equivalent Statements

One application of truth tables is illustrated by showing that two statements are equivalent; by definition, two statements are **equivalent** if they have the same truth value in *every* possible situation. The columns of each truth table that were the last to be completed will be exactly the same for equivalent statements.

EXAMPLE 11   Are the statements

$$\sim p \wedge \sim q \text{ and } \sim(p \vee q)$$

equivalent?

To find out, make a truth table for each statement, with the following results.

p	q	$\sim p \wedge \sim q$		p	q	$\sim(p \vee q)$
T	T	**F**		T	T	**F**
T	F	**F**		T	F	**F**
F	T	**F**		F	T	**F**
F	F	**T**		F	F	**T**

Since the truth values are the same in all cases, as shown in the columns in color, the statements $\sim p \wedge \sim q$ and $\sim(p \vee q)$ are equivalent. Equivalence is written with a three-bar symbol, $\equiv$. Using this symbol, $\sim p \wedge \sim q \equiv \sim(p \vee q)$. ◆

In the same way, the statements $\sim p \vee \sim q$ and $\sim(p \wedge q)$ are equivalent. We call these equivalences De Morgan's laws.

De Morgan's Laws

For any statements p and q,

$$\sim(p \vee q) \equiv \sim p \wedge \sim q$$
$$\sim(p \wedge q) \equiv \sim p \vee \sim q.$$

De Morgan's laws can be used to find the negations of certain compound statements.

EXAMPLE 12   Find a negation of each statement by applying De Morgan's laws.

(a) I got an A or I got a B.

If p represents "I got an A" and q represents "I got a B," then the compound statement is symbolized $p \vee q$. The negation of $p \vee q$ is $\sim(p \vee q)$; by one of De Morgan's laws, this is equivalent to

$$\sim p \wedge \sim q,$$

or, in words,

I didn't get an A and I didn't get a B.

This negation is reasonable—the original statement says that I got either an A or a B; the negation says that I didn't get *either* grade.

(b) She won't try and he will succeed.

From one of De Morgan's laws, $\sim(p \wedge q) \equiv \sim p \vee \sim q$, so the negation becomes

She will try or he won't succeed.

(c) $\sim p \vee (q \wedge \sim p)$

Negate both component statements and change $\vee$ to $\wedge$.

$$\sim[\sim p \vee (q \wedge \sim p)] \equiv p \wedge \sim(q \wedge \sim p)$$

Now apply De Morgan's law again.

$$p \wedge \sim(q \wedge \sim p) \equiv p \wedge (\sim q \vee \sim(\sim p))$$
$$\equiv p \wedge (\sim q \vee p)$$

A truth table will show that the statements

$$\sim p \vee (q \wedge \sim p) \qquad \text{and} \qquad p \wedge (\sim q \vee p)$$

are negations. ⬢

---

2 EXERCISES

Use the concepts introduced in this section to answer Exercises 1–6.

1. If we know that p is true, what do we know about the truth value of $p \vee q$ even if we are not given the truth value of q?

2. If we know that p is false, what do we know about the truth value of $p \wedge q$ even if we are not given the truth value of q?

3. If p is false, what is the truth value of $p \wedge (q \vee \sim r)$?

4. If p is true, what is the truth value of $p \vee (q \vee \sim r)$?

5. Explain in your own words the condition that must exist for a conjunction of two component statements to be true.

6. Explain in your own words the condition that must exist for a disjunction of two component statements to be false.

Let p represent a false statement and let q represent a true statement. Find the truth value of the given compound statement.

7. $\sim p$	8. $\sim q$	9. $p \vee q$	10. $p \wedge q$
11. $p \vee \sim q$	12. $\sim p \wedge q$	13. $\sim p \vee \sim q$	14. $p \wedge \sim q$
15. $\sim(p \wedge \sim q)$	16. $\sim(\sim p \vee \sim q)$	17. $\sim[\sim p \wedge (\sim q \vee p)]$	18. $\sim[(\sim p \wedge \sim q) \vee \sim q]$

19. Is the statement $5 \geq 2$ a conjunction or a disjunction?

20. Why is the statement $5 \geq 2$ true? Why is $5 \geq 5$ true?

Let p represent a true statement, and q and r represent false statements. Find the truth value of the given compound statement.

21. $(q \vee \sim r) \wedge p$	22. $(p \wedge r) \vee \sim q$
23. $(\sim p \wedge q) \vee \sim r$	24. $p \wedge (q \vee r)$
25. $(\sim r \wedge \sim q) \vee (\sim r \wedge q)$	26. $\sim(p \wedge q) \wedge (r \vee \sim q)$
27. $\sim[r \vee (\sim q \wedge \sim p)]$	28. $\sim[(\sim p \wedge q) \vee r]$

Let p represent the statement $2 > 3$, let q represent the statement $5 \not> 3$, and let r represent the statement $9 \geq 9$. Find the truth value of the given compound statement.

29. $p \wedge r$	30. $p \vee \sim q$	31. $\sim q \vee \sim r$	32. $\sim p \wedge \sim r$
33. $(p \wedge q) \vee r$	34. $\sim p \vee (\sim r \vee \sim q)$	35. $(\sim r \wedge q) \vee \sim p$	36. $\sim(p \vee \sim q) \vee \sim r$

Give the number of rows in the truth table for each of the following compound statements.

37. $p \vee \sim r$

38. $p \wedge (r \wedge \sim s)$

39. $(\sim p \wedge q) \vee (\sim r \vee \sim s) \wedge r$

40. $[(p \vee q) \wedge (r \wedge s)] \wedge (t \vee \sim p)$

41. $[(\sim p \wedge \sim q) \wedge (\sim r \wedge s \wedge \sim t)] \wedge (\sim u \vee \sim v)$

42. $[(\sim p \wedge \sim q) \vee (\sim r \vee \sim s)] \vee [(\sim m \wedge \sim n) \wedge (u \wedge \sim v)]$

43. If the truth table for a certain compound statement has 64 rows, how many distinct component statements does it have?

44. Is it possible for the truth table of a compound statement to have exactly 48 rows? Explain.

Construct a truth table for each compound statement.

45. $\sim p \wedge q$

46. $\sim p \vee \sim q$

47. $\sim (p \wedge q)$

48. $p \vee \sim q$

49. $(q \vee \sim p) \vee \sim q$

50. $(p \wedge \sim q) \wedge p$

51. $\sim q \wedge (\sim p \vee q)$

52. $\sim p \vee (\sim q \wedge \sim p)$

53. $(p \vee \sim q) \wedge (p \wedge q)$

54. $(\sim p \wedge \sim q) \vee (\sim p \vee q)$

55. $(\sim p \wedge q) \wedge r$

56. $r \vee (p \wedge \sim q)$

57. $(\sim p \wedge \sim q) \vee (\sim r \vee \sim p)$

58. $(\sim r \vee \sim p) \wedge (\sim p \vee \sim q)$

59. $\sim (\sim p \wedge \sim q) \vee (\sim r \vee \sim s)$

60. $(\sim r \vee s) \wedge (\sim p \wedge q)$

Use one of De Morgan's laws to write the negation of each statement.

61. You can pay me now or you can pay me later.

62. I am not going or she is going.

63. It is summer and there is no snow.

64. 1/2 is a positive number and -12 is less than zero.

65. I said yes but she said no.

66. Kelly Bell tried to sell the book, but she was unable to do so.

67. $5 - 1 = 4$ and $9 + 12 \neq 7$

68. $3 < 10$ or $7 \neq 2$

69. Dasher or Dancer will lead Santa's sleigh next Christmas.

70. The lawyer and the client appeared in court.

A conjunction of the form

$$a < x < b$$

is called a compound inequality, and translates as

$$a < x \quad \text{and} \quad x < b.$$

Therefore, in order for such a compound inequality to be true, both component statements must be true. Tell whether the compound inequality is true *or* false.

71. $3 < 4 < 7$

72. $-1 < 2 < 8$

73. $7 < 4 < 20$

74. $2 < 1 < 5$

75. $8 < 4 < 2$

76. $6 < 5 < 4$

77. There exists a real number x such that $5 < x < 6$.

78. There exists no integer x such that $5 < x < 6$.

79. For all real numbers x, $-10 < x < 10$.

80. For all whole numbers x, $-10 < x < 10$.

Identify each of the following statements as true *or* false.

81. For every real number y, $y < 12$ or $y > 4$.

82. For every real number t, $t > 3$ or $t < 3$.

83. For some integer p, $p \geq 5$ and $p \leq 5$.

84. There exists an integer n such that $n > 0$ and $n < 0$.

85. Lawyers sometimes use the phrase "and/or." This phrase corresponds to which usage of the word *or* as discussed in the text?

86. Complete the truth table for *exclusive disjunction*. The symbol $\veebar$ represents "one or the other is true, but not both."

p	q	$p \veebar q$
T	T	
T	F	
F	T	
F	F	

Exclusive disjunction

Decide whether the following compound statements are true *or* false. *Here,* or *is the exclusive disjunction; that is, assume "either p or q is true, but not both."*

87. $3 + 1 = 4$ or $2 + 5 = 7$

88. $3 + 1 = 4$ or $2 + 5 = 9$

89. $3 + 1 = 7$ or $2 + 5 = 7$

90. $3 + 1 = 7$ or $2 + 5 = 9$

91. The photograph shows the AND and OR game at the Ontario Science Center in Toronto. To win, you must release six of the twelve ping-pong balls at the top, with exactly one ping-pong ball making it to the bottom. A ball will pass through an AND gate only when both tubes entering the gate contain a ball. A ball passes through the OR gate if either or both tubes are filled.

(a) Pick six balls so that exactly one makes it to the bottom.

(b) Can you pick a different set of six balls so that exactly one gets through?

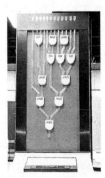

92. When Charlie Chan* neared the end of a case, he would gather all the suspects together in a room. As he recited the clues that he had unearthed, the circle of guilt would narrow until it contained only the suspect. Chan's method was derived from the greatest of all fictional detectives, Sherlock Holmes. Holmes' technique was summarized as follows: "To solve a mystery, I simply eliminate all that is impossible. Whatever remains, however improbable, is the solution." We can apply the Holmes method to solve whodunits by the use of truth tables. Consider the case in which we know

He did it or she did it, and he didn't do it.

(a) Let H represent "He did it," and let S represent "She did it." Use symbols to rewrite the statement displayed above.

There are two people involved, so that there are four possibilities: (1) Both he and she did it, (2) He did it and she didn't, (3) She did it and he didn't, (4) Neither did it. Each line in a truth table for the clue represents one of the possibilities. Holmes' method is to eliminate the impossible. The truth table shows what is impossible by having the row for those cases turn out to be false. (Another set of clues is given at the end of Section 4.)

(b) Form the truth table for $(H \vee S) \wedge {\sim}H$.

(c) Which row of the truth table leads to a true statement?

(d) Who did it?

*From "Solving Whodunits by Symbolic Logic," by Lawrence Sher, in *The Two-Year College Mathematics Journal*, December 1975, p. 36.

3

The Conditional

"If you build it, he will come."
The Voice in the 1990 movie *Field of Dreams*

Ray Kinsella, an Iowa farmer in the movie *Field of Dreams,* heard a voice from the sky. Ray interpreted it as a promise that if he would build a baseball field in his cornfield, then the ghost of Shoeless Joe Jackson (a baseball star in the early days of the twentieth century) would come to play on it. The promise came in the form of a conditional statement. A **conditional** statement is a compound statement that uses the connective *if . . . then*. For example, here are a few conditional statements.

If I read for too long, *then* I get a headache.
If looks could kill, *then* I would be dead.
If he doesn't get back soon, *then* you should go look for him.

In each of these conditional statements, the component coming after the word *if* gives a condition (but not necessarily the only condition) under which the statement coming after *then* will be true. For example, "If it is over 90°, then I'll go to the mountains" tells one possible condition under which I will go to the mountains—if the temperature is over 90°.

The conditional is written with an arrow, so that "if p, then q" is symbolized as

$$p \rightarrow q.$$

We read $p \rightarrow q$ as "p implies q" or "if p, then q." In the conditional $p \rightarrow q$, the statement p is the **antecedent,** while q is the **consequent.**

The conditional connective may not always be explicitly stated. That is, it may be "hidden" in an everyday expression. For example, the statement

Big girls don't cry

can be written in *if . . . then* form as

If you're a big girl, then you don't cry.

As another example, the statement

It is difficult to study when you are distracted

can be written

If you are distracted, then it is difficult to study.

As seen in the quote from the movie *Field of Dreams* earlier, the word "then" is sometimes not stated but understood there to be from the context of the statement. In that statement, "you build it" is the antecedent and "he will come" is the consequent.

The conditional truth table is a little harder to define than were the tables in the previous section. To see how to define the conditional truth table, let us analyze a statement made by a politician, Senator Julie Davis:

If I am elected, then taxes will go down.

As before, there are four possible combinations of truth values for the two simple statements. Let p represent "I am elected," and let q represent "Taxes will go down."

$x = 6 \quad n!$
$\{1, 2, 3, \ldots\} \quad \binom{n}{r}$
$5 > 3$
$15 + 2 \neq 1 \quad A \cup B$
$_nP_r$
$\int \quad \varnothing \quad \sqrt{x} \quad p \wedge q$
$\pi \quad \log_b x$

The importance of symbols was emphasized by the American philosopher-logician Charles Sanders Peirce (1839–1914), who asserted the nature of humans as symbol-using or sign-using organisms. Symbolic notation is half of mathematics, Bertrand Russell once said.

As we analyse the four possibilities, it is helpful to think in terms of the following: "Did Senator Davis lie?" If she lied, then the conditional statement is considered false; if she did not lie, then the conditional statement statement is considered true.

Possibility	Elected?	Taxes Go Down?	
1	Yes	Yes	p is T, q is T
2	Yes	No	p is T, q is F
3	No	Yes	p is F, q is T
4	No	No	p is F, q is F

The four possibilities are as follows:

1. In the first case assume that the senator was elected and taxes did go down (p is T, q is T). The senator told the truth, so place T in the first row of the truth table. (We do not claim that taxes went down *because* she was elected; it is possible that she had nothing to do with it at all.)
2. In the second case assume that the senator was elected and taxes did not go down (p is T, q is F). Then the senator did not tell the truth (that is, she lied). So we put F in the second row of the truth table.
3. In the third case assume that the senator was defeated, but taxes went down anyway (p is F, q is T). Senator Davis did not lie; she only promised a tax reduction if she were elected. She said nothing about what would happen if she were not elected. In fact, her campaign promise gives no information about what would happen if she lost. Since we cannot say that the senator lied, place T in the third row of the truth table.
4. In the last case assume that the senator was defeated but taxes did not go down (p is F, q is F). We cannot blame her, since she only promised to reduce taxes if elected. Thus, T goes in the last row of the truth table.

Truth Table for the Conditional If *p*, then *q*

If p, then q.

p	q	$p \rightarrow q$
T	T	T
T	F	F
F	T	T
F	F	T

The completed truth table for the conditional is defined as follows.

It must be emphasized that the use of the conditional connective in no way implies a cause-and-effect relationship. Any two statements may have an arrow placed between them to create a compound statement. For example,

If I pass mathematics, then the sun will rise the next day

is true, since the consequent is true. (See the box after Example 1.) There is, however, no cause-and-effect connection between my passing mathematics and the sun's rising. The sun will rise no matter what grade I get in a course.

EXAMPLE 1 Find the truth value of the statement $(p \rightarrow \sim q) \rightarrow (\sim r \rightarrow q)$ if p, q, and r are all false.

Using the short-cut method explained in Example 3 of Section 2, we can replace p, q, and r with F (since each is false) and proceed as before, using the negation and conditional truth tables as necessary.

$$(p \rightarrow \sim q) \rightarrow (\sim r \rightarrow q)$$
$$(F \rightarrow \sim F) \rightarrow (\sim F \rightarrow F)$$
$$(F \rightarrow T) \rightarrow (T \rightarrow F)$$

$T \rightarrow F$	Use the negation truth table.
F	Use the conditional truth table.

The statement $(p \rightarrow \sim q) \rightarrow (\sim r \rightarrow q)$ is false when p, q, and r are all false. ●

The following observations come from the truth table for $p \rightarrow q$.

Special Characteristics of Conditional Statements

1. $p \rightarrow q$ is false only when the antecedent is *true* and the consequent is *false*.
2. If the antecedent is *false*, then $p \rightarrow q$ is automatically *true*.
3. If the consequent is *true*, then $p \rightarrow q$ is automatically *true*.

EXAMPLE 2 Write *true* or *false* for each statement. Here T represents a true statement, and F represents a false statement.

(a) $T \rightarrow (6 = 3)$

Since the antecedent is true, while the consequent, $6 = 3$, is false, the given statement is false by the first point mentioned above.

(b) $(5 < 2) \rightarrow F$

The antecedent is false, so the given statement is true by the second observation.

(c) $(3 \neq 2 + 1) \rightarrow T$

The consequent is true, making the statement true by the third characteristic of conditional statements. ●

Truth tables for compound statements involving conditionals are found using the techniques described in the previous section. The next example shows how this is done.

EXAMPLE 3 Make a truth table for each statement.

(a) $(\sim p \rightarrow \sim q) \rightarrow (\sim p \wedge q)$

First insert the truth values of $\sim p$ and of $\sim q$. Then find the truth value of $\sim p \rightarrow \sim q$.

p	q	$\sim p$	$\sim q$	$\sim p \rightarrow \sim q$
T	T	F	F	**T**
T	F	F	T	**T**
F	T	T	F	**F**
F	F	T	T	**T**

Next use $\sim p$ and q to find the truth values of $\sim p \wedge q$.

p	q	$\sim p$	$\sim q$	$\sim p \rightarrow \sim q$	$\sim p \wedge q$
T	T	F	F	T	**F**
T	F	F	T	T	**F**
F	T	T	F	F	**T**
F	F	T	T	T	**F**

Now use the conditional truth table to find the truth values of $(\sim p \rightarrow \sim q) \rightarrow (\sim p \wedge q)$.

p	q	$\sim p$	$\sim q$	$\sim p \rightarrow \sim q$	$\sim p \wedge q$	$(\sim p \rightarrow \sim q) \rightarrow (\sim p \wedge q)$
T	**T**	F	F	T	F	**F**
T	**F**	F	T	T	F	**F**
F	**T**	T	F	F	T	**T**
F	**F**	T	T	T	F	**F**

(b) $(p \rightarrow q) \rightarrow (\sim p \vee q)$

Go through steps similar to the ones above.

p	q	$p \rightarrow q$	$\sim p$	$\sim p \vee q$	$(p \rightarrow q) \rightarrow (\sim p \vee q)$
T	**T**	T	F	T	**T**
T	**F**	F	F	F	**T**
F	**T**	T	T	T	**T**
F	**F**	T	T	T	**T**

As the truth table in Example 3(b) shows, the statement $(p \rightarrow q) \rightarrow (\sim p \vee q)$ is always true, no matter what the truth values of the components. Such a statement is called a **tautology.** Other examples of tautologies (as can be checked by forming truth tables) include $p \vee \sim p$, $p \rightarrow p$, $(\sim p \vee \sim q) \rightarrow \sim(q \wedge p)$, and so on. By the way, the truth tables in Example 3 also could have been found by the alternate method shown in the previous section.

Negation of $p \rightarrow q$

Suppose that someone makes the conditional statement

"If it rains, then I take my umbrella."

When will the person have lied to you? The only case in which you would have been misled is when it rains *and* the person does *not* take the umbrella. Letting p represent "it rains" and q represent "I take my umbrella," you might suspect that the symbolic statement

$$p \wedge \sim q$$

is a candidate for the negation of $p \rightarrow q$. That is,

$$\sim(p \rightarrow q) \equiv p \wedge \sim q.$$

It happens that this is indeed the case, as the next truth table indicates.

p	q	$p \rightarrow q$	$\sim(p \rightarrow q)$	$\sim q$	$p \wedge \sim q$
T	T	T	F	F	F
T	F	F	T	T	T
F	T	T	F	F	F
F	F	T	F	T	F

Negation of $p \rightarrow q$

The negation of $p \rightarrow q$ is $p \wedge \sim q$.

Since

$$\sim(p \rightarrow q) \equiv p \wedge \sim q,$$

by negating each expression we have

$$\sim[\sim(p \rightarrow q)] \equiv \sim(p \wedge \sim q).$$

The left side of the above equivalence is $p \rightarrow q$, and one of De Morgan's laws can be applied to the right side.

$$p \rightarrow q \equiv \sim p \vee \sim(\sim q)$$
$$p \rightarrow q \equiv \sim p \vee q$$

This final row indicates that a conditional may be written as a disjunction.

Writing a Conditional as an "or" Statement

$p \rightarrow q$ is equivalent to $\sim p \vee q$.

EXAMPLE 4   Write the negation of each statement.

(a) If you build it, he will come.

If b represents "you build it" and q represents "he will come," then the given statement can be symbolized $b \rightarrow q$. The negation of $b \rightarrow q$, as shown above, is $b \wedge \sim q$, so the negation of the statement is

You build it and he will not come.

(b) All dogs have fleas.

First, we must restate the given statement in *if. . . then* form:

If it is a dog, then it has fleas.

Based on our earlier discussion, the negation is

It is a dog and it does not have fleas.   ●

FOR FURTHER THOUGHT

Sets	Logic
A'	$\sim p$
$A \cap B$	$p \wedge q$
$A \cup B$	$p \vee q$
U	T
$\varnothing$	F

It may become evident that these two topics are closely related in concepts and symbols. The table above compares symbols in set theory and in logic.

Negations of statements are analogous to complements of sets. Intersection of sets plays the same role that the connective *and* plays in logic; similarly, union plays the same role as *or*. The universal and empty sets compare with the logical ideas of T and F, respectively.

If we are given two sets A and B, there are four possibilities for x being an element (member) of the sets:

$$x \in A \text{ and } x \in B$$
$$x \in A \text{ and } x \notin B$$
$$x \notin A \text{ and } x \in B$$
$$x \notin A \text{ and } x \notin B.$$

These possibilities can be listed in a table as follows.

A	**B**
$x \in A$	$x \in B$
$x \in A$	$x \notin B$
$x \notin A$	$x \in B$
$x \notin A$	$x \notin B$

For Group Discussion
1. How does the second table compare to a truth table format?
2. What significance does the expression 2^n have in both set theory and logic?
3. What are some other parallels between set theory and logic that you have noticed?

A common error occurs when students try to negate a conditional statement with another conditional statement. As seen in Example 4, the negation of a conditional statement is written as a conjunction.

EXAMPLE 5   Write each conditional as an equivalent statement without using *if . . . then.*

(a) If the Cubs win the pennant, then Gwen will be happy.

Since the conditional $p \rightarrow q$ is equivalent to $\sim p \vee q$, let p represent "The Cubs win the pennant" and q represent "Gwen will be happy." Restate the conditional as

The Cubs do not win the pennant or Gwen will be happy.

(b) If it's Borden's, it's got to be good.

If p represents "it's Borden's" and if q represents "it's got to be good," the conditional may be restated as

It's not Borden's or it's got to be good.   ●

Statements of the form $p \rightarrow q$ that contain a variable are normally handled as follows. First, *assume* the antecedent is true. Then if the consequent is necessarily true, the given statement is true. Otherwise the statement is false. For example,

$$\text{If } x = 2, \text{ then } x + 5 < 10$$

is true since the truth of the antecedent ($x = 2$) implies that $x + 5 = 7$ and $7 < 10$ are true, so the consequent is true. On the other hand, the statement

$$\text{If } x < 2, \text{ then } x < 0$$

is false since the antecedent can be true without the consequent being true (for example, if $x = 1$).

EXAMPLE 6   Decide whether the following statements are *true* or *false*.

(a) If $x + 3 \leq 5$, then $x \leq 2$.

We are given $x + 3 \leq 5$ as the antecedent. By subtracting 3 from both sides, we obtain $x \leq 2$, the consequent. Since the consequent *must* follow from the antecedent, the given statement is true.

(b) If $x + y = 6$, then $x = 3$ and $y = 3$.

We are given that the sum of two numbers, x and y, is 6. Must it follow that $x = 3$ and $y = 3$? No, since there are many other possible values of x and y that will satisfy the condition of the antecedent. The given statement is false.   ◆

---

3 EXERCISES

In Exercises 1–8, decide whether each statement is true *or* false.

1. If the antecedent of a conditional statement is false, the conditional statement is true.

2. If the consequent of a conditional statement is true, the conditional statement is true.

3. If q is true, then $(p \wedge q) \rightarrow q$ is true.

4. If p is true, then $\sim p \rightarrow (q \vee r)$ is true.

5. The negation of "If pigs fly, I'll believe it" is "If pigs don't fly, I won't believe it."

6. The statements "If it flies, then it's a bird" and "It does not fly or it's a bird" are logically equivalent.

7. "If $x = 3$, then $x^2 = 9$" is a true statement.

8. "If $x^2 = 9$, then $x = 3$" is a true statement.

9. In a few sentences, explain how we determine the truth value of a conditional statement.

10. Explain why the statement "If $3 = 5$, then $4 = 6$" is true.

Rewrite each statement using the if . . . then *connective. Rearrange the wording or add words as necessary.*

11. You can believe it if it's in *USA Today*.

12. It must be dead if it doesn't move.

13. Kathi Callahan's area code is 708.

14. Mark Badgett goes to Hawaii every summer.

15. All soldiers maintain their weapons.

16. Every dog has its day.

17. No koalas live in Mississippi.

18. No guinea pigs are scholars.

19. An alligator cannot live in these waters.

20. Romeo loves Juliet.

Tell whether each conditional is true *or* false. *Here* T *represents a true statement and* F *represents a false statement.*

21. $F \rightarrow (4 = 7)$

22. $T \rightarrow (4 < 2)$

23. $(6 = 6) \rightarrow F$

24. $F \rightarrow (3 = 3)$

25. $(4 = 11 - 7) \rightarrow (3 > 0)$

26. $(4^2 \neq 16) \rightarrow (4 + 4 = 8)$

Let s represent "I study in the library," *let p represent the statement* "I pass my psychology course," *and let m represent* "I major in mathematics." *Express each compound statement in words.*

27. $\sim m \rightarrow p$

28. $p \rightarrow \sim m$

29. $s \rightarrow (m \wedge p)$

30. $(s \wedge p) \rightarrow m$

31. $\sim p \rightarrow (\sim m \vee s)$

32. $(\sim s \vee \sim m) \rightarrow \sim p$

Let d represent "I drive my car," *let s represent* "it snows," *and let c represent* "classes are cancelled." *Write each compound statement in symbols.*

33. If it snows, then I drive my car.

34. If I drive my car, then classes are cancelled.

35. If I do not drive my car, then it does not snow.

36. If classes are cancelled, then it does not snow.

37. I drive my car, or if classes are cancelled then it snows.

38. Classes are cancelled, and if it snows then I do not drive my car.

39. I'll drive my car if it doesn't snow.

40. It snows if classes are cancelled.

Find the truth value of each statement. Assume that p and r are false, and q is true.

41. $\sim r \rightarrow q$

42. $\sim p \rightarrow \sim r$

43. $q \rightarrow p$

44. $\sim r \rightarrow p$

45. $p \rightarrow q$

46. $\sim q \rightarrow r$

47. $\sim p \rightarrow (q \wedge r)$

48. $(\sim r \vee p) \rightarrow p$

49. $\sim q \rightarrow (p \wedge r)$

50. $(\sim p \wedge \sim q) \rightarrow (p \wedge \sim r)$

51. $(p \rightarrow \sim q) \rightarrow (\sim p \wedge \sim r)$

52. $(p \rightarrow \sim q) \wedge (p \rightarrow r)$

53. Explain why, if we know that p is true, we also know that

$$[r \vee (p \vee s)] \rightarrow (p \vee q)$$

is true, even if we are not given the truth values of q, r, and s.

54. Construct a true statement involving a conditional, a conjunction, a disjunction, and a negation (not necessarily in that order), that consists of component statements p, q, and r, with all of these component statements false.

Construct a truth table for each statement. Identify any tautologies.

55. $\sim q \rightarrow p$

56. $p \rightarrow \sim q$

57. $(\sim p \rightarrow q) \rightarrow p$

58. $(\sim q \rightarrow \sim p) \rightarrow \sim q$

59. $(p \vee q) \rightarrow (q \vee p)$

60. $(p \wedge q) \rightarrow (p \vee q)$

61. $(\sim p \rightarrow \sim q) \rightarrow (p \wedge q)$

62. $r \rightarrow (p \wedge \sim q)$

63. $[(r \vee p) \wedge \sim q] \rightarrow p$

64. $(\sim r \rightarrow s) \vee (p \rightarrow \sim q)$

65. $(\sim p \wedge \sim q) \rightarrow (\sim r \rightarrow \sim s)$

66. What is the minimum number of Fs that need appear in the final column of a truth table for us to be assured that the statement is not a tautology?

Write the negation of each statement. Remember that the negation of $p \rightarrow q$ is $p \wedge \sim q$.

67. If you give your plants tender, loving care, they flourish.

68. If the check is in the mail, I'll be surprised.

69. If she doesn't, he will.

70. If I say yes, she says no.

71. All residents of Boise are residents of Idaho.

72. All men were once boys.

Write each statement as an equivalent statement that does not use the if . . . then *connective. Remember that $p \rightarrow q$ is equivalent to $\sim p \vee q$.*

73. If you give your plants tender, loving care, they flourish.

74. If the check is in the mail, I'll be surprised.

75. If she doesn't, he will.

76. If I say yes, she says no.

77. All residents of Boise are residents of Idaho.

78. All men were once boys.

Use truth tables to decide which of the pairs of statements are equivalent.

79. $p \rightarrow q$; $\sim p \vee q$

80. $\sim(p \rightarrow q)$; $p \wedge \sim q$

81. $p \rightarrow q$; $\sim q \rightarrow \sim p$

82. $q \rightarrow p$; $\sim p \rightarrow \sim q$

83. $\sim(\sim p)$; p

84. $p \rightarrow q$; $q \rightarrow p$

85. $p \wedge \sim q$; $\sim q \rightarrow \sim p$

86. $\sim p \wedge q$; $\sim p \rightarrow q$

87. From algebra, we know that the distributive law for multiplication with respect to addition holds; that is, for all real numbers *a, b,* and *c,*

$$a(b + c) = ab + ac.$$

From "For Further Thought" in the chapter on sets, we also know that the distributive law for intersection with respect to union holds; that is, for all sets *A, B,* and *C,*

$$A \cap (B \cup C) = (A \cap B) \cup (A \cap C).$$

Now show by truth tables that the distributive law for conjunction ($\wedge$) holds with respect to disjunction ($\vee$); that is, for all statements *p, q,* and *r,*

$$p \wedge (q \vee r) \equiv (p \wedge q) \vee (p \wedge r).$$

88. Show that the distributive law for disjunction holds with respect to conjunction; that is, for all statements *p, q,* and *r,*

$$p \vee (q \wedge r) \equiv (p \vee q) \wedge (p \vee r).$$

Decide whether each statement is true *or* false.

89. If $x = 6$, then $2x + 4 > 9$.

90. If $y > 4$, then $3y > 12$.

91. If $r = 5$, then $r^2 = 25$.

92. If $r = -5$, then $r^2 = 25$.

93. If $t^2 = 36$, then $t = 6$.

94. If $t^2 = 36$, then $t = 6$ or $t = -6$.

EXTENSION

Circuits

One of the first non-mathematical applications of symbolic logic was seen in the master's thesis of Claude Shannon, in 1937. Shannon showed how logic could be used as an aid in designing electrical circuits. His work was immediately taken up by the designers of computers. These computers, then in the developmental stage, could be simplified and built for less money using the ideas of Shannon.

To see how Shannon's ideas work, look at the electrical switch shown in Figure 1. We assume that current will flow through this switch when it is closed and not when it is open.

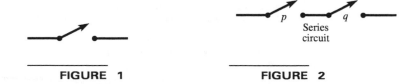

FIGURE 1   **FIGURE 2**

Claude E. Shannon was at Bell Telephone Laboratories in 1952 when he devised an experiment to show the capabilities of telephone relays. An electrical mouse (in his hand) can find its way through a maze without error, guided by information "remembered" in the kind of switching relays used in dial telephone systems.

Shannon had stated the ideas of information theory in 1948 in *The Mathematical Theory of Communication* (written with Warren Weaver). The theory is based on the concept of entropy, meaning disorder or randomness; thus it is closely related to probability.

Figure 2 shows two switches connected in *series;* in such a circuit, current will flow only when both switches are closed. Note how closely a series circuit corresponds to the conjunction $p \land q$. We know that $p \land q$ is true only when both p and q are true.

A circuit corresponding to the disjunction $p \lor q$ can be found by drawing a *parallel* circuit, as in Figure 3. Here, current flows if either p *or* q is closed or if both p *and* q are closed.

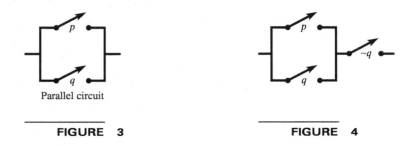

FIGURE 3   **FIGURE 4**

The circuit in Figure 4 corresponds to the statement $(p \lor q) \land {\sim}q$, which is a compound statement involving both a conjunction and a disjunction.

The way that logic is used to simplify an electrical circuit depends on the idea of equivalent statements, from Section 2. Recall that two statements are equivalent if they have exactly the same truth table. The symbol $\equiv$ is used to indicate that the two statements are equivalent. Some of the equivalent statements that we shall need are shown in the following box.

Equivalent Statements Used to Simplify Circuits

$$p \lor (q \land r) \equiv (p \lor q) \land (p \lor r) \qquad p \lor p \equiv p$$
$$p \land (q \lor r) \equiv (p \land q) \lor (p \land r) \qquad p \land p \equiv p$$
$$p \to q \equiv {\sim}q \to {\sim}p \qquad {\sim}(p \land q) \equiv {\sim}p \lor {\sim}q$$
$$p \to q \equiv {\sim}p \lor q \qquad {\sim}(p \lor q) \equiv {\sim}p \land {\sim}q$$

If T represents any true statement and F represents any false statement, then

$$p \lor \text{T} \equiv \text{T} \qquad p \lor {\sim}p \equiv \text{T}$$
$$p \land \text{F} \equiv \text{F} \qquad p \land {\sim}p \equiv \text{F}.$$

Circuits can be used as models of compound statements, with a closed switch corresponding to T, while an open switch corresponds to F. The method for simplifying circuits is explained in the following example.

EXAMPLE 1 Simplify the circuit of Figure 5.

FIGURE 5   **FIGURE 6**

At the top of Figure 5, *p* and *q* are connected in series, and at the bottom, *p* and *r* are connected in series. These are interpreted as the compound statements $p \wedge q$ and $p \wedge r$, respectively. These two conjunctions are connected in parallel, as indicated by the figure treated as a whole. Therefore, we write the disjunction of the two conjunctions:

$$(p \wedge q) \vee (p \wedge r).$$

(Think of the two switches labeled "*p*" as being controlled by the same handle.) By one of the pairs of equivalent statements above,

$$(p \wedge q) \vee (p \wedge r) \equiv p \wedge (q \vee r),$$

which has the circuit of Figure 6. This new circuit is logically equivalent to the one above, and yet contains only three switches instead of four—which might well lead to a large savings in manufacturing costs. ◆

EXAMPLE 2 Draw a circuit for $p \rightarrow (q \wedge {\sim}r)$.

From the list of equivalent statements in the box, $p \rightarrow q$ is equivalent to ${\sim}p \vee q$. This equivalence gives $p \rightarrow (q \wedge {\sim}r) \equiv {\sim}p \vee (q \wedge {\sim}r)$, which has the circuit diagram in Figure 7. ◆

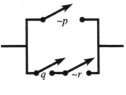

FIGURE 7

EXTENSION EXERCISES

Write a logical statement representing each of the following circuits. Simplify each circuit when possible.

1.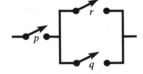

2.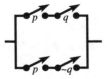

3.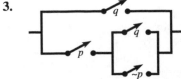

4. 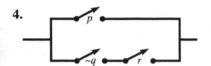   **5.** 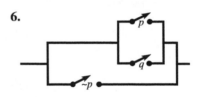   **6.**

Draw circuits representing the following statements as they are given. Simplify if possible.

7. $(\sim p \wedge \sim q) \wedge \sim r$

8. $p \wedge (q \vee \sim p)$

9. $(\sim q \wedge \sim p) \vee (\sim p \vee q)$

10. $(p \vee q) \wedge (\sim p \wedge \sim q)$

11. $[(\sim p \wedge \sim r) \vee \sim q] \wedge (\sim p \wedge r)$

12. $[(p \vee q) \wedge r] \wedge \sim p$

13. $\sim p \rightarrow (\sim p \vee \sim q)$

14. $\sim q \rightarrow (\sim p \rightarrow q)$

15. Refer to Figures 5 and 6 in Example 1. Suppose the cost of the use of one switch for an hour is 3¢. By using the circuit in Figure 6 rather than the circuit in Figure 5, what is the savings for a year of 365 days, assuming that the circuit is in continuous use?

16. Explain why the circuit

will always have exactly one open switch. What does this circuit simplify to?

4

More on the Conditional

The conditional statement, introduced in the previous section, is one of the most important of all compound statements. Many mathematical properties and theorems are stated in *if . . . then* form. Because of their usefulness, we need to study conditional statements that are related to a statement of the form $p \rightarrow q$.

Converse, Inverse, and Contrapositive

Any conditional statement is made up of an antecedent and a consequent. If they are interchanged, negated, or both, a new conditional statement is formed. Suppose that we begin with the direct statement

> If you stay, then I go,

and interchange the antecedent ("you stay") and the consequent ("I go"). We obtain the new conditional statement

> If I go, then you stay.

This new conditional is called the **converse** of the given statement.

By negating both the antecedent and the consequent, we obtain the **inverse** of the given statement:

> If you do not stay, then I do not go.

If the antecedent and the consequent are both interchanged *and* negated, the **contrapositive** of the given statement is formed:

If I do not go, then you do not stay.

These three related statements for the conditional $p \rightarrow q$ are summarized below. (Notice that the inverse is the contrapositive of the converse.)

Related Conditional Statements

Direct Statement	$p \rightarrow q$	(If p, then q.)
Converse	$q \rightarrow p$	(If q, then p.)
Inverse	$\sim p \rightarrow \sim q$	(If not p, then not q.)
Contrapositive	$\sim q \rightarrow \sim p$	(If not q, then not p.)

Alfred North Whitehead (1861–1947), above, and Bertrand Russell worked together on *Principia Mathematica*. During that time, Whitehead was teaching mathematics at Cambridge University and had written *Universal Algebra*. In 1910 he went to the University of London, exploring not only the philosophical basis of science but also the "aims of education" (as he called one of his books). It was as philosopher that he was invited to Harvard University in 1924. Whitehead died at the age of 86 in Cambridge, Massachusetts.

EXAMPLE 1 Given the direct statement

If I live in Tampa, then I live in Florida.

write each of the following.

(a) the converse
    Let p represent "I live in Tampa" and q represent "I live in Florida." Then the direct statement may be written $p \rightarrow q$. The converse, $q \rightarrow p$, is

If I live in Florida, then I live in Tampa.

Notice that for this statement, the converse is not necessarily true, even though the direct statement is.

(b) the inverse
    The inverse of $p \rightarrow q$ is $\sim p \rightarrow \sim q$. For the given statement, the inverse is

If I don't live in Tampa, then I don't live in Florida.

which is again not necessarily true.

(c) the contrapositive
    The contrapositive, $\sim q \rightarrow \sim p$, is

If I don't live in Florida, then I don't live in Tampa.

The contrapositive, like the direct statement, is true. ●

Example 1 shows that the converse and inverse of a true statement need not be true. They *can* be true, but they need not be. The relationship between the truth values of the direct statement, converse, inverse, and contrapositive is shown in the truth table that follows.

		Direct	Converse	Inverse	Contrapositive
		Equivalent			
			Equivalent		
p	q	$p \to q$	$q \to p$	$\sim p \to \sim q$	$\sim q \to \sim p$
T	T	T	T	T	T
T	F	F	T	T	F
F	T	T	F	F	T
F	F	T	T	T	T

As this truth table shows, the direct statement and the contrapositive always have the same truth values, making it possible to replace any statement with its contrapositive without affecting the logical meaning. Also, the converse and inverse always have the same truth values.

This discussion is summarized in the following sentence.

The direct statement and the contrapositive are equivalent, and the converse and the inverse are equivalent.

Bertrand Russell was a student of Whitehead's before they wrote the *Principia*. Like his teacher, Russell turned toward philosophy. His works include a critique of Leibniz, analyses of mind and of matter, and a history of Western thought.

Russell became a public figure because of his involvement in social issues. Deeply aware of human loneliness, he was "passionately desirous of finding ways of diminishing this tragic isolation." During World War I he was an anti-war crusader, and he was imprisoned briefly. Again in the 1960s he championed peace. He wrote many books on social issues, winning the Nobel Prize for Literature in 1950.

EXAMPLE 2   For the direct statement $\sim p \to q$, write each of the following.

(a) the converse

The converse of $\sim p \to q$ is $q \to \sim p$.

(b) the inverse

The inverse is $\sim(\sim p) \to \sim q$, which simplifies to $p \to \sim q$.

(c) the contrapositive

The contrapositive is $\sim q \to \sim (\sim p)$, which simplifies to $\sim q \to p$.   ●

Alternate Forms of "if p, then q"

The conditional statement "if p, then q" can be stated in several other ways in English. For example,

If you go to the shopping center, then you will find a place to park

can also be written

Going to the shopping center is *sufficient* for finding a place to park.

According to this statement, going to the shopping center is enough to guarantee finding a place to park. Going to other places, such as schools or office buildings, *might* also guarantee a place to park, but at least we *know* that going to the shopping center does. Thus, $p \rightarrow q$ can be written "*p* is sufficient for *q*." Knowing that *p* has occurred is sufficient to guarantee that *q* will also occur. On the other hand,

Turning on the set is necessary for watching television   [*]

has a different meaning. Here, we are saying that one condition that is necessary for watching television is that you turn on the set. This may not be enough; the set might be broken, for example. The statement labeled [*] could be written as

If you watch television, then you turned on the set.

As this example suggests, $p \rightarrow q$ is the same as "*q* is necessary for *p*." In other words, if *q* doesn't happen, then neither will *p*. Notice how this idea is closely related to the idea of equivalence between the direct statement and its contrapositive.

Some common translations of $p \rightarrow q$ are summarized in the following box.

Common Translations of $p \rightarrow q$

The conditional $p \rightarrow q$ can be translated in any of the following ways.

If *p*, then *q*.	*p* is sufficient for *q*.
If *p*, *q*.	*q* is necessary for *p*.
p implies *q*.	All *p*'s are *q*'s.
p only if *q*.	*q* if *p*.

The translation of $p \rightarrow q$ into these various word forms does not in any way depend on the truth or falsity of $p \rightarrow q$.

EXAMPLE 3   The statement

If you are 18, then you can vote

can be written in any of the following ways.

> You can vote if you are 18.
> You are 18 only if you can vote.
> Being able to vote is necessary for you to be 18.
> Being 18 is sufficient for being able to vote.
> All 18-year-olds can vote.
> Being 18 implies that you can vote.   ●

EXAMPLE 4   Write each statement in the form "if *p*, then *q*."

(a) $x < 2$ if $x + 1 < 3$
    If $x + 1 < 3$, then $x < 2$.

(b) $m = 3/4$ only if $m^2 = 9/16$
    If $m = 3/4$, then $m^2 = 9/16$.

(c) All nurses wear white shoes.
    If you are a nurse, then you wear white shoes.   ●

FOR FURTHER THOUGHT

How many times have you heard a wise saying like "A stitch in time saves nine," "A rolling stone gathers no moss," or "Birds of a feather flock together"? In many cases, such proverbial advice can be restated as a conditional in *if . . . then* form. For example, these three statements can be restated as follows.

> "If you make a stitch in time, then it will save you nine (stitches)."
> "If a stone rolls, then it gathers no moss."
> "If they are birds of a feather, then they flock together."

There is much wisdom in such sayings. How many times have you decided to have something repaired, even though it was working acceptably, and you could have lived with it as it was? Then it comes back from the repair shop in worse condition than before. And then, you thought of what someone once told you: "If it ain't broke, don't fix it."

For Group Discussion
1. Think of some wise sayings that have been around for a long time, and state them in *if . . . then* form.
2. You have probably heard the saying "All that glitters is not gold." Do you think that what is said here actually is what is meant? If not, restate it as you think it should be stated. (*Hint:* Write the original statement in *if . . . then* form.)

EXAMPLE 5   Let *p* represent "A triangle is equilateral," and let *q* represent "A triangle has three equal sides." Write each of the following in symbols.

(a) A triangle is equilateral if it has three equal sides.

$$q \rightarrow p$$

(b) A triangle is equilateral only if it has three equal sides.

$$p \rightarrow q \quad \bullet$$

Biconditionals

In elementary algebra we learn that both of these statements are true:

$$\text{If } x > 0, \text{ then } 5x > 0.$$
$$\text{If } 5x > 0, \text{ then } x > 0.$$

Notice that the second statement is the converse of the first. If we wish to make the statement that each condition ($x > 0$, $5x > 0$) implies the other, we use the following language:

$$x > 0 \text{ if and only if } 5x > 0.$$

This may also be stated as

$$5x > 0 \text{ if and only if } x > 0.$$

The compound statement *p if and only if q* (often abbreviated *p iff q*) is called a **biconditional.** It is symbolized $p \leftrightarrow q$, and is interpreted as the conjunction of the two conditionals $p \rightarrow q$ and $q \rightarrow p$. Using symbols, this conjunction is written

$$(q \rightarrow p) \wedge (p \rightarrow q)$$

so that, by definition,

$$p \leftrightarrow q \equiv (q \rightarrow p) \wedge (p \rightarrow q).$$

Using this definition, the truth table for the biconditional $p \leftrightarrow q$ can be determined.

Truth Table for the Biconditional *p* if and only if *q*

p if and only if q

p	q	$p \leftrightarrow q$
T	T	T
T	F	F
F	T	F
F	F	T

EXAMPLE 6   Tell whether each biconditional statement is *true* or *false*.

(a) $6 + 9 = 15$ if and only if $12 + 4 = 16$

Both $6 + 9 = 15$ and $12 + 4 = 16$ are true. By the truth table for the biconditional, this biconditional is true.

(b) $5 + 2 = 10$ if and only if $17 + 19 = 36$

Since the first component ($5 + 2 = 10$) is false, and the second is true, the entire biconditional statement is false.

(c) $6 = 5$ if and only if $12 \neq 12$

Both component statements are false, so by the last line of the truth table for the biconditional, the entire statement is true. (Understanding this might take some extra thought!) ◗

The final example shows how to determine truth values of conditional statements written in alternative ways, and of biconditionals, when a variable appears in the statement.

EXAMPLE 7   Determine whether each statement is *true* or *false*.

(a) $z^2 = \dfrac{81}{64}$ if $z = \dfrac{9}{8}$

Writing the statement as

$$\text{If } z = \frac{9}{8}, \text{ then } z^2 = \frac{81}{64}$$

shows that it is true, since the truth of the antecedent implies the truth of the consequent.

Principia Mathematica
The title chosen by
Whitehead and Russell was
a deliberate reference to
*Philosophiae naturalis
principia mathematica,* or
"mathematical principles of
the philosophy of nature,"
Issac Newton's epochal
work of 1687. Newton's
Principia pictured a kind of
"clockwork universe" that
ran via his Law of
Gravitation. Newton
independently invented the
calculus, unaware that
Leibniz had published his
own formulation of it earlier.
A controversy over their
priority continued into the
eighteenth century.

(b) $z^2 = \dfrac{81}{64}$ only if $z = \dfrac{9}{8}$

Rewrite this statement as

$$\text{If } z^2 = \frac{81}{64}, \text{ then } z = \frac{9}{8}.$$

Since the truth of the antecedent does not necessarily imply the truth of the consequent (z may equal $-9/8$), the statement is false.

(c) $z^2 = \dfrac{81}{64}$ if and only if $z = \dfrac{9}{8}$

Because of part (b), this statement is false. (It would become true if $z = 9/8$ were replaced with $z = \pm 9/8$.) ●

In this section and in the previous two sections, truth tables have been derived for several important types of compound statements. The summary that follows describes how these truth tables may be remembered.

Summary of Basic Truth Tables

1. $\sim p$, the **negation** of p, has truth value opposite that of p.
2. $p \wedge q$, the **conjunction**, is true only when both p and q are true.
3. $p \vee q$, the **disjunction**, is false only when both p and q are false.
4. $p \rightarrow q$, the **conditional**, is false only when p is true and q is false.
5. $p \leftrightarrow q$, the **biconditional**, is true only when p and q have the same truth value.

---

4 EXERCISES

For each given direct statement, write **(a)** *the converse,* **(b)** *the inverse, and* **(c)** *the contrapositive in* if . . . then *form. In Exercises 3–10, it may be helpful to restate the direct statement in* if . . . then *form.*

1. If you lead, then I will follow.

2. If beauty were a minute, then you would be an hour.

3. If I had a nickel for each time that happened, I would be rich.

4. If it ain't broke, don't fix it.

5. Milk contains calcium.

6. Walking in front of a moving car is dangerous to your health.

7. A rolling stone gathers no moss.

8. Birds of a feather flock together.

9. Where there's smoke, there's fire.

10. If you build it, he will come.

11. $p \rightarrow \sim q$

12. $\sim p \rightarrow q$

13. $\sim p \rightarrow \sim q$

14. $\sim q \rightarrow \sim p$

15. $p \rightarrow (q \vee r)$ (*Hint:* Use one of De Morgan's laws as necessary.)

16. $(r \vee \sim q) \rightarrow p$ (*Hint:* Use one of De Morgan's laws as necessary.)

17. Discuss the equivalences that exist among the direct conditional statement, the converse, the inverse, and the contrapositive.

18. State the contrapositive of "If the square of a natural number is even, then the natural number is even." The two statements must have the same truth value. Use several examples and inductive reasoning to decide whether both are true or both are false.

Write each of the following statements in the form "if p, then q."

19. If I finish studying, I'll go to the party.

20. If it is muddy, I'll wear my galoshes.

21. $x > 0$ implies that $x > -1$.

22. $x > 6$ implies that $2x > 12$.

23. All whole numbers are integers.

24. All integers are rational numbers.

25. Being in Fort Lauderdale is sufficient for being in Florida.

26. Doing crossword puzzles is sufficient for driving me crazy.

27. Being an environmentalist is necessary for being elected.

28. A day's growth of beard is necessary for Greg Odjakjian to shave.

29. The principal will hire more teachers only if the school board approves.

30. I can go from Park Place to Baltic Avenue only if I pass GO.

31. No integers are irrational numbers.

32. No whole numbers are not integers.

33. Rush will be a liberal when pigs fly.

34. The Phillies will win the pennant when their pitching improves.

35. A parallelogram is a four-sided figure with opposite sides parallel.

36. A rectangle is a parallelogram with a right angle.

37. A square is a rectangle with two adjacent sides equal.

38. A triangle with two sides of the same length is isosceles.

39. An integer whose units digit is 0 or 5 is divisible by 5.

40. The square of a two-digit number whose units digit is 5 will end in 25.

41. One of the following statements is not equivalent to all the others. Which one is it?
    (a) $x = 7$ only if $x^2 = 49$.
    (b) $x = 7$ implies $x^2 = 49$.
    (c) If $x = 7$, then $x^2 = 49$.
    (d) $x = 7$ is necessary for $x^2 = 49$.

42. Many students have difficulty interpreting *necessary* and *sufficient*. Use the statement "Being in Canada is sufficient for being in North America" to explain why "*p* is sufficient for *q*" translates as "if *p*, then *q*."

43. Use the statement "To be an integer, it is necessary that a number be rational" to explain why "*p* is necessary for *q*" translates as "if *q*, then *p*."

44. Explain why the statement "A week has eight days if and only if December has forty days" is true.

Identify each statement as true *or* false.

45. $5 = 9 - 4$ if and only if $8 + 2 = 10$.

46. $3 + 1 \neq 6$ if and only if $9 \neq 8$.

47. $8 + 7 \neq 15$ if and only if $3 \times 5 = 9$.

48. $6 \times 2 = 14$ if and only if $9 + 7 \neq 16$.

49. John F. Kennedy was president if and only if Ronald Reagan was not president.

50. Burger King sells Big Macs if and only if Guess sells jeans.

Identify each of the following as true *or* false.

51. If $z = -4$, then $z^2 = 16$.

52. If $x = 8$, then $x^2 = 64$.

53. If $z^2 = 16$, then $z = -4$.

54. If $x^2 = 64$, then $x = 8$.

55. $z = -4$ if and only if $z^2 = 16$.

56. $x = 8$ if and only if $x^2 = 64$.

57. $z = -4$ only if $z^2 = 16$.

58. $x = 8$ only if $x^2 = 64$.

Two statements that can both be true about the same object are **consistent**. *For example,* "It is green" *and*

"It is small" *are consistent statements. Statements that cannot both be true about the same object are called* **contrary**; *"It is a Ford" and* "It is a Chevrolet" *are contrary.*

Label the following pairs of statements as either contrary *or* consistent.

59. Elvis is alive. Elvis is dead.

60. Bill Clinton is a Democrat. Bill Clinton is a Republican.

61. That animal has four legs. That animal is a dog.

62. That book is nonfiction. That book costs over $40.

63. This number is an integer. This number is irrational.

64. This number is positive. This number is a natural number.

65. Make up two statements that are consistent.

66. Make up two statements that are contrary.

67. Let us take another example from the article by Lawrence Sher mentioned in Exercise 92 of Section 2. As we saw, when a row in the truth table for a group of clues is false, the case is impossible and we eliminate it. However, when a row ends in T, this does not mean that the case is the truth. It means that it is possible. The way to solve the mystery is to eliminate all but one possibility. The last remaining case is the truth.

Sometimes it takes more than one clue to eliminate all but one possibility. Consider the mystery for which we have the following clues.

1. If the butler did it, then the maid didn't.
2. The butler or the maid did it.
3. If the maid did it, then the butler did it.

(a) Write these clues in symbols. Use *b* for "The butler did it," and use *m* for "The maid did it."

(b) Make a truth table for the first clue.

(c) Which possibility can now be eliminated?

(d) We now know that the butler and the maid could not both have done it. Test the remaining three possibilities by completing a truth table for the second clue, $b \vee m$.

b	m	$b \vee m$
T	F	
F	T	
F	F	

(e) Which row is eliminated by this table? This now leaves only two possibilities to be tested by the last clue. Test these two cases, the butler did it alone and the maid did it alone, by completing a truth table for the last clue, $m \to b$.

b	m	$m \to b$
T	F	
F	T	

(f) Who did it?

68. There is a close connection between sets and logic, as this exercise shows. Start with a universal set

$$U = \{1, 2, 3, 4, 5, 6, 7, 8\}.$$

Let *p* be the statement "The integer is even." Statement *p* is satisfied by the elements of the set $P = \{2, 4, 6, 8\}$, the *truth set* for *p*. Statement ~*p* has truth set $\{1, 3, 5, 7\}$. Let *q* be "The integer is less than 6," with truth set $Q = \{1, 2, 3, 4, 5\}$. Both *p* and *q* are statements, so $p \vee q$ and $p \wedge q$ must also be statements.

(a) Find the truth sets for $p \vee q$ and $p \wedge q$.

(b) Find the truth sets for $\sim p \wedge \sim q$, $\sim p \vee q$, and $\sim(p \wedge \sim q)$.

(c) Complete this table.

Logic	p	q	$\sim p$	$\sim q$	$p \vee q$	$p \wedge q$	$p \to q$	T	F
Sets	P	Q							

Using Euler Diagrams to Analyze Arguments

In Section 1 we introduced two types of reasoning: inductive and deductive. So far we have concentrated on using inductive reasoning to observe patterns and solve problems. Now, in this section and the next, we will study how deductive reasoning may be used to determine whether logical arguments are valid or invalid. A logical argument is made up of **premises** (assumptions, laws, rules, widely held ideas, or observations) and a **conclusion.** Together, the premises and the conclusion make up the argument. Also recall that *deductive* reasoning involves drawing specific conclusions from given general premises. When reasoning from the premises of an argument to obtain a conclusion, we want the argument to be valid.

Valid and Invalid Arguments

An argument is **valid** if the fact that all the premises are true forces the conclusion to be true. An argument that is not valid is **invalid,** or a **fallacy.**

Leonhard Euler
(1707–1783) won the academy prize and edged out du Châtelet and Voltaire. That was a minor achievement, as was the invention of "Euler circles" (which antedated Venn diagrams). Euler was the most prolific mathematician of his generation despite blindness that forced him to dictate from memory.

It is very important to note that "valid" and "true" are not the same—an argument can be valid even though the conclusion is false. (See Example 4 below.)

Several techniques can be used to check whether an argument is valid. One of these is the visual technique based on **Euler diagrams,** illustrated by the following examples. (Another is the method of truth tables, shown in the next section.)

EXAMPLE 1   Is the following argument valid?

All cats are animals.
Tom is a cat.
_____
Tom is an animal.

Here we use the common method of placing one premise over another, with the conclusion below a line. To begin, draw a region to represent the first premise. This is the region for "animals." Since all cats are animals, the region for "cats" goes inside the region for "animals," as in Figure 8.

The second premise, "Tom is a cat," suggests that "Tom" would go inside the region representing "cats." Let *x* represent "Tom." Figure 9 shows that "Tom" is

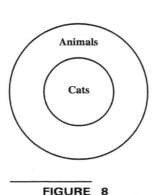

FIGURE 8

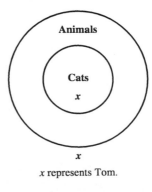

x represents Tom.

FIGURE 9

also inside the region for "animals." Therefore, if both premises are true, the conclusion that Tom is an animal must be true also. The argument is valid, as checked by Euler diagrams. ⬢

The method of Euler diagrams is especially useful for arguments involving the quantifiers *all, some,* or *none.*

EXAMPLE 2   Is the following argument valid?

All rainy days are cloudy.
Today is not cloudy.
―――――――――――――――
Today is not rainy.

In Figure 10 the region for "rainy days" is drawn entirely inside the region for "cloudy days." Since "Today is *not* cloudy," place an *x* for "today" *outside* the region for "cloudy days." (See Figure 11.) Placing the *x* outside the region for "cloudy days" forces it to be also outside the region for "rainy days." Thus, if the first two premises are true, then it is also true that today is not rainy. The argument is valid. ⬢

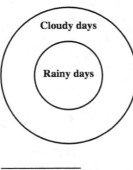

FIGURE 10

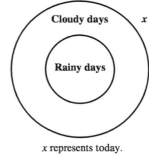

x represents today.

FIGURE 11

EXAMPLE 3   Is the following argument valid?

All banana trees have green leaves.
That plant has green leaves.
―――――――――――――――――――
That plant is a banana tree.

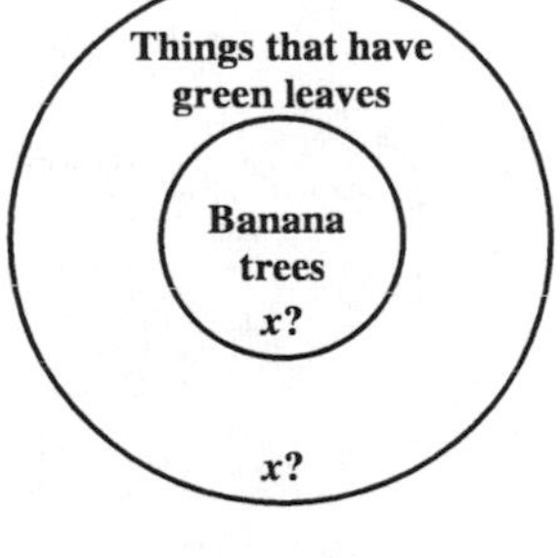

The region for "banana trees" goes entirely inside the region for "things that have green leaves." (See Figure 12.) There is a choice for locating the *x* that represents "that plant." The *x* must go inside the region for "things that have green leaves," but can go either inside or outside the region for "banana trees." Even if the premises are true, we are not forced to accept the conclusion as true. This argument is invalid; it is a fallacy. ⬢

FIGURE 12

As mentioned earlier, the validity of an argument is not the same as the truth of its conclusion. The argument in Example 3 was invalid, but the conclusion "That plant is a banana tree" may or may not be true. We cannot be sure.

EXAMPLE 4   Is the following argument valid?

All expensive things are desirable.
All desirable things make you feel good.
All things that make you feel good make you live longer.

All expensive things make you live longer.

A diagram for the argument is given in Figure 13. If each premise is true, then the conclusion must be true since the region for "expensive things" lies completely within the region for "things that make you live longer." Thus, the argument is valid. (This argument is an example of the fact that a *valid* argument need *not* have a true conclusion.) ◆

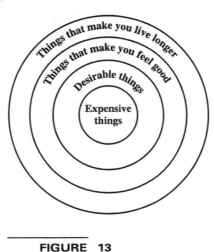

FIGURE 13

Arguments with the word "some" can be a little tricky. One is shown in the final example of this section.

EXAMPLE 5   Is the following argument valid?

Some students go to the beach.
I am a student.

I go to the beach.

The first premise is sketched in Figure 14. As the sketch shows, some (but not necessarily *all*) students go to the beach. There are two possibilities for *I*, as shown in Figure 15.

One possibility is that *I* go to the beach; the other is that *I* don't. Since the truth of the premises does not force the conclusion to be true, the argument is invalid.   ●

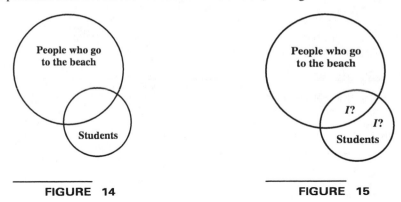

FIGURE 14   **FIGURE 15**

---

5 EXERCISES

Decide whether each argument is valid *or* invalid.

1. All psychology majors perform experiments with rats.
Chuck Miller is a psychology major.

Chuck Miller performs experiments with rats.

2. All architects love to draw.
Chris Batchelor is an architect.

Chris Batchelor loves to draw.

3. All homeowners have a plumber.
Vonalaine Crowe has a plumber.

Vonalaine Crowe is a homeowner.

4. All politicians have questionable ethics.
That man has questionable ethics.

That man is a politician.

5. All residents of St. Tammany parish live on farms.
Jay Beckenstein lives on a farm.

Jay Beckenstein is a resident of St. Tammany parish.

6. All dogs love to bury bones.
Nero is a dog.

Nero loves to bury bones.

7. All members of the credit union have savings accounts.
Michelle Beese does not have a savings account.

Michelle Beese is not a member of the credit union.

8. All engineers need mathematics.
Collene McHugh does not need mathematics.

Collene McHugh is not an engineer.

9. All residents of New Orleans have huge utility bills in July.
   Erin Kelly has a huge utility bill in July.
   _____
   Erin Kelly lives in New Orleans.

10. All people applying for a home loan must provide a down payment.
    Cynthia Herring provided a down payment.
    _____
    Cynthia Herring applied for a home loan.

11. Some mathematicians are absent-minded.
    Diane Gray is a mathematician.
    _____
    Diane Gray is absent-minded.

12. Some animals are nocturnal.
    Oliver Owl is an animal.
    _____
    Oliver Owl is nocturnal.

13. Some cars have automatic door locks.
    Some cars are red.
    _____
    Some red cars have automatic door locks.

14. Some doctors appreciate classical music.
    Kevin Howell is a doctor.
    _____
    Kevin Howell appreciates classical music.

15. Refer to Example 4 in this section. Give a different conclusion than the one given there so that the argument is still valid.

16. Construct a valid argument based on the Euler diagram shown here.

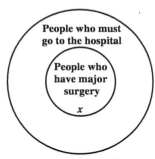

x represents Cynthia Biron.

As mentioned in the text, an argument can have a true conclusion yet be invalid. In these exercises, each argument has a true *conclusion. Identify each argument as* valid *or* invalid.

17. All birds fly.
    All planes fly.
    _____
    A bird is not a plane.

18. All cars have tires.
    All tires are rubber.
    _____
    All cars have rubber.

19. All chickens have a beak.
    All hens are chickens.
    _____
    All hens have a beak.

20. All chickens have a beak.
    All birds have a beak.
    _____
    All chickens are birds.

21. Quebec is northeast of Ottawa.
    Quebec is northeast of Toronto.
    _____
    Ottawa is northeast of Toronto.

22. Veracruz is south of Tampico.
    Tampico is south of Monterrey.
    _____
    Veracruz is south of Monterrey.

23. No whole numbers are negative.
−1 is negative.

−1 is not a whole number.

24. A scalene triangle has a longest side.
A scalene triangle has a largest angle.

The largest angle in a scalene triangle is opposite the longest side.

In Exercises 25–30, the premises marked A, B, and C are followed by several possible conclusions. Take each conclusion in turn, and check whether the resulting argument is valid *or* invalid.

A. *All people who drive contribute to air pollution.*

B. *All people who contribute to air pollution make life a little worse.*

C. *Some people who live in a surburb make life a little worse.*

25. Some people who live in a suburb drive.

26. Some people who live in a suburb contribute to air pollution.

27. Some people who contribute to air pollution live in a suburb.

28. Suburban residents never drive.

29. All people who drive make life a little worse.

30. Some people who make life a little worse live in a suburb.

31. Find examples of arguments in magazine ads. Check them for validity.

32. Find examples of arguments on television commercials. Check them for validity.

Logic puzzles of the type found in Exercises 33–34 can be solved by using a "grid" where information is entered in each box. If the situation is impossible, write No *in the grid. If it is possible write* Yes. *For example, consider the following puzzle.*

Norma, Harriet, Betty, and Geneva are married to Don, Bill, John, and Nathan, but not necessarily in the order given. One couple has first names that start with the same letter. Harriet is married to John. Don's wife is neither Geneva nor Norma. Pair up each husband and wife.

The grid that follows from the puzzle is shown below.

	Don	Bill	John	Nathan
Norma	No	No	No	Yes
Harriet	No	No	Yes	No
Betty	Yes	No	No	No
Geneva	No	Yes	No	No

From the grid, we deduce that Harriet is married to John, Norma is married to Nathan, Betty is married to Don, and Geneva is married to Bill.

Solve each of the following puzzles.

33. There are five boys in a room, two of whom are twins. Their names are Dan, Matt, Dave, and Barry and Billy (the twins). The four last names among the boys are Parker, Bennington, Petry, and Walsh. Dan's last name begins with P. The twins do not know the boy whose last name is Walsh. Matt has the longest last name. Find the first and last names of each boy.

34. Juanita, Evita, Li, Fred, and Butch arrived at a party at different times. Evita arrived after Juanita but before Butch. Butch was neither the first nor the last to arrive. Juanita and Evita arrived after Fred but all three of them were present when Li got there. In what order did the five arrive?

---

6 ## Using Truth Tables to Analyze Arguments

The previous section showed how to use Euler diagrams to test the validity of arguments. While Euler diagrams often work well for simple arguments, difficulties can develop with more complex ones. These difficulties occur because Euler diagrams require a sketch showing every possible case. In complex arguments it is hard to be sure that all cases have been considered.

In deciding whether to use Euler diagrams to test the validity of an argument, look for quantifiers such as "all," "some," or "no." These words often indicate arguments best tested by Euler diagrams. If these words are absent, it may be better to use truth tables to test the validity of an argument.

As an example of this method, consider the following argument:

> If the floor is dirty, then I must mop it.
> The floor is dirty.
> _____
> I must mop it.

In order to test the validity of this argument, we begin by identifying the *simple* statements found in the argument. They are "the floor is dirty" and "I must mop it." We shall assign the letters p and q to represent these statements:

> p represents "the floor is dirty."
>
> q represents "I must mop it."

Now we write the two premises and the conclusion in symbols:

> Premise 1: $p \rightarrow q$
> Premise 2: p
> _____
> Conclusion: q .

To decide if this argument is valid, we must determine whether the conjunction of both premises implies the conclusion for all possible cases of truth values for p and q. Therefore, write the conjunction of the premises as the antecedent of a conditional statement, and the conclusion as the consequent.

$$
\begin{array}{ccccc}
[(p \rightarrow q) & \wedge & p] & \longrightarrow & q \\
\uparrow & \uparrow & \uparrow & \uparrow & \uparrow \\
\text{premise} & \text{and} & \text{premise} & \text{implies} & \text{conclusion}
\end{array}
$$

Finally, construct the truth table for this conditional statement, as shown below.

p	q	$p \rightarrow q$	$(p \rightarrow q) \wedge p$	$[(p \rightarrow q) \wedge p] \rightarrow q$
T	T	T	T	T
T	F	F	F	T
F	T	T	F	T
F	F	T	F	T

Since the final column indicates that the conditional statement that represents the argument is true for all possible truth values of p and q, the statement is a tautology. Thus, the argument is valid.

The pattern of the argument in the floor-mopping example,

$$
\begin{array}{c}
p \rightarrow q \\
p \\
\hline
q
\end{array} \quad .
$$

is a common one, and is called **modus ponens,** or the *law of detachment*.

In summary, to test the validity of an argument using truth tables, follow the steps in the box that follows.

Testing the Validity of an Argument with a Truth Table

1. Assign a letter to represent each simple statement in the argument.
2. Express each premise and the conclusion symbolically.
3. Form the symbolic statement of the entire argument by writing the *conjunction* of *all* the premises as the antecedent of a conditional statement, and the conclusion of the argument as the consequent.
4. Complete the truth table for the conditional statement formed in part 3 above. If it is a tautology, then the argument is valid; otherwise, it is invalid.

EXAMPLE 1 Determine whether the argument is valid or invalid.

If my check arrives in time, I'll register for the Fall semester.
I've registered for the Fall semester.
_____
My check arrived in time.

Let p represent "my check arrives (arrived) in time" and let q represent "I'll register (I've registered) for the Fall semester." Using these symbols, the argument can be written in the form

$$p \to q$$
$$\underline{q \qquad}$$
$$p \qquad .$$

To test for validity, construct a truth table for the statement

$$[(p \to q) \wedge q] \to p.$$

p	q	$p \to q$	$(p \to q) \wedge q$	$[(p \to q) \wedge q] \to p$
T	T	T	T	T
T	F	F	F	T
F	T	T	T	F
F	F	T	F	T

The third row of the final column of the truth table shows F, and this is enough to conclude that the argument is invalid. ●

If a conditional and its converse were logically equivalent, then an argument of the type found in Example 1 would be valid. Since a conditional and its converse are *not* equivalent, the argument is an example of what is sometimes called the **fallacy of the converse**.

EXAMPLE 2 Determine whether the argument is valid or invalid.

If a man could be two places at one time, I'd be with you.
I am not with you.
_____
A man can't be two places at one time.

If *p* represents "a man could be two places at one time" and *q* represents "I'd be with you," the argument becomes

$$p \rightarrow q$$
$$\underline{\sim q}$$
$$\sim p \quad .$$

The symbolic statement of the entire argument is

$$[(p \rightarrow q) \wedge \sim q] \rightarrow \sim p.$$

The truth table for this argument, shown below, indicates a tautology, and the argument is valid.

p	*q*	*p* → *q*	~*q*	(*p* → *q*) ∧ ~*q*	~*p*	[(*p* → *q*) ∧ ~*q*] → ~*p*
T	T	T	F	F	F	T
T	F	F	T	F	F	T
F	T	T	F	F	T	T
F	F	T	T	T	T	T

The pattern of reasoning of this example is called **modus tollens,** or the *law of contraposition,* or *indirect reasoning.* ●

With reasoning similar to that used to name the fallacy of the converse, the fallacy

$$p \rightarrow q$$
$$\underline{\sim p}$$
$$\sim q$$

is often called the **fallacy of the inverse.** An example of such a fallacy is "If it rains, I get wet. It doesn't rain. Therefore, I don't get wet."

EXAMPLE 3   Determine whether the argument is valid or invalid.

I'll buy a car or I'll take a vacation.
I won't buy a car.
_____
I'll take a vacation.

If *p* represents "I'll buy a car" and *q* represents "I'll take a vacation," the argument becomes

$$p \vee q$$
$$\underline{\sim p}$$
$$q \quad .$$

We must set up a truth table for

$$[(p \vee q) \wedge \sim p] \rightarrow q.$$

p	*q*	*p* ∨ *q*	~*p*	(*p* ∨ *q*) ∧ ~*p*	[(*p* ∨ *q*) ∧ ~*p*] → *q*
T	T	T	F	F	T
T	F	T	F	F	T
F	T	T	T	T	T
F	F	F	T	F	T

The statement is a tautology and the argument is valid. Any argument of this form is valid by the law of **disjunctive syllogism.** ●

EXAMPLE 4 Determine whether the argument is valid or invalid.

If it squeaks, then I use WD-40.
If I use WD-40, then I must go to the hardware store.

If it squeaks, then I must go to the hardware store.

Let p represent "it squeaks," let q represent "I use WD-40," and let r represent "I must go to the hardware store." The argument takes on the general form

$$p \rightarrow q$$
$$q \rightarrow r$$
$$p \rightarrow r.$$

Make a truth table for the following statement:

$$[(p \rightarrow q) \wedge (q \rightarrow r)] \rightarrow (p \rightarrow r).$$

It will require eight rows.

p	q	r	$p \rightarrow q$	$q \rightarrow r$	$p \rightarrow r$	$(p \rightarrow q) \wedge (q \rightarrow r)$	$[(p \rightarrow q) \wedge (q \rightarrow r)] \rightarrow (p \rightarrow r)$
T	T	T	T	T	T	T	T
T	T	F	T	F	F	F	T
T	F	T	F	T	T	F	T
T	F	F	F	T	F	F	T
F	T	T	T	T	T	T	T
F	T	F	T	F	T	F	T
F	F	T	T	T	T	T	T
F	F	F	T	T	T	T	T

This argument is valid since the final statement is a tautology. The pattern of argument shown in this example is called **reasoning by transitivity,** or the *law of hypothetical syllogism.* ●

A summary of the valid and invalid forms of argument presented so far follows.

Valid Argument Forms

Modus Ponens	Modus Tollens	Disjunctive Syllogism	Reasoning by Transitivity
$p \rightarrow q$	$p \rightarrow q$	$p \vee q$	$p \rightarrow q$
p	$\sim q$	$\sim p$	$q \rightarrow r$
q	$\sim p$	q	$p \rightarrow r$

Invalid Argument Forms (*Fallacies*)

Fallacy of the Converse	Fallacy of the Inverse
$p \to q$	$p \to q$
q	$\sim p$
p	$\sim q$

When an argument contains three or more premises, it will be necessary to determine the truth value of the conjunction of all of them. Remember that if *at least one* premise in a conjunction of several premises is false, then the entire conjunction is false. This will be shown in the next example.

EXAMPLE 5   Determine whether the argument is valid or invalid.

If Eddie goes to town, then Mabel stays at home.
If Mabel does not stay at home, then Rita will cook.
Rita will not cook.
Therefore, Eddie does not go to town.

In an argument written in this manner, the premises are given first, and the conclusion is the statement which follows the word "Therefore." Let p represent "Eddie goes to town," let q represent "Mabel stays at home" and let r represent "Rita will cook." The symbolic form of the argument is

$$p \to q$$
$$\sim q \to r$$
$$\sim r$$
$$\overline{\sim p .}$$

To test validity, set up a truth table for the statement

$$[(p \to q) \land (\sim q \to r) \land \sim r] \to \sim p.$$

The table is shown below.

p	q	r	$p \to q$	$\sim q$	$\sim q \to r$	$\sim r$	$[(p \to q) \land (\sim q \to r) \land \sim r]$	$\sim p$	$[(p \to q) \land (\sim q \to r) \land \sim r] \to \sim p$
T	T	T	T	F	T	F	F	F	T
T	T	F	T	F	T	T	T	F	F
T	F	T	F	T	T	F	F	F	T
T	F	F	F	T	F	T	F	F	T
F	T	T	T	F	T	F	F	T	T
F	T	F	T	F	T	T	T	T	T
F	F	T	T	T	T	F	F	T	T
F	F	F	T	T	F	T	F	T	T

Because the final column does not contain all Ts, the statement is not a tautology.

The argument is invalid. ◗

Consider the following poem, which has been around for many years.

For want of a nail, the shoe was lost.
For want of a shoe, the horse was lost.
For want of a horse, the rider was lost.
For want of a rider, the battle was lost.
For want of a battle, the war was lost.
Therefore, for want of a nail, the war was lost.

Each line of the poem may be written as an *if . . . then* statement. For example, the first line may be restated as "if a nail is lost, then the shoe is lost." Other statements may be worded similarly. The conclusion, "for want of a nail, the war was lost," follows from the premises since repeated use of the law of transitivity applies. Arguments used by Lewis Carroll often take on a similar form. The next example comes from one of his works.

Tweedlogic "I know what you're thinking about," said Tweedledum, "but it isn't so, nohow." "Contrariwise," continued Tweedledee, "if it was so, it might be; and if it were so, it would be, but as it isn't, it ain't. That's logic."

EXAMPLE 6 Supply a valid conclusion for the following premises.

Babies are illogical.
Nobody is despised who can manage a crocodile.
Illogical persons are despised.

First, write each premise in the form *if . . . then.*

If you are a baby, then you are illogical.
If you can manage a crocodile, then you are not despised.
If you are illogical, then you are despised.

Let p be "you are a baby," let q be "you are logical," let r be "you can manage a crocodile," and let s be "you are despised." With these letters, the statements can be written symbolically as

$$p \rightarrow \sim q$$
$$r \rightarrow \sim s$$
$$\sim q \rightarrow s.$$

Now begin with any letter that appears only once. Here p appears only once. Using the contrapositive of $r \rightarrow \sim s$, which is $s \rightarrow \sim r$, rearrange the three statements as follows:

$$p \rightarrow \sim q$$
$$\sim q \rightarrow s$$
$$s \rightarrow \sim r.$$

From the three statements, repeated use of reasoning by transitivity gives the valid conclusion

$$p \rightarrow \sim r.$$

In words, "If you are a baby, then you cannot manage a crocodile," or, as Lewis Carroll would have written it, "Babies cannot manage crocodiles." ◗

FOR FURTHER THOUGHT

The field of advertising is notorious for logical errors. While the conclusion reached in an advertisement may be true, the logic used to reach that conclusion may be based on an invalid argument. One fallacy that is seen time and time again is the fallacy of experts. Here, an expert (or famous figure) is quoted in a field outside of that person's field of knowledge.

According to syndicated columnist Paul Harvey ("Celebrity Salesman," July 1, 1988, *Sacramento Union*), having well-known celebrities who "(seek) to transfer their own popularity to some product or service is a questionable practice." Some personalities and their endorsed products in recent years have been Jimmy Connors for a headache remedy, Ray Charles for a diet soft drink, and Kelsey Grammer for a lawnmower manufacturer.

The list goes on and on. Yet, according to Harvey, Video Storyboard, in a survey of effectiveness of television commercials, found that the most effective commercials are those that contain no "live people" at all. Some of the best ones were those that featured the California Raisins, Spuds MacKenzie, and Max Headroom.

In another illustration of the *fallacy of experts,* the following appeared as part of a question addressed to columnist Sue Rusche ("Education helps control alcoholism," July 9, 1988, *Sacramento Union*):

> The simple truth is that Congress and the press seldom listen to people who actually know something about a problem. They prefer to listen instead to those whose testimony or statements, though completely uninformed, will make a publicity splash. As a British friend of mine commented, "You Americans pick an actor who has played a drug addict in some film to testify before Congress as an expert on drugs. Lord Laurence Olivier has played Hamlet at least a thousand times, but Parliament has never called on him to testify on matters Danish."

Another common ploy in advertising is the fallacy of emotion, where an appeal is made to pity, passion, brute force, snobbishness, vanity, or some other emotion. Have you seen the tire advertisement that suggests that if you don't use a certain brand of tire, your infants will be unsafe? And have you ever seen an ad for beer that doesn't involve "beautiful people"?

For Group Discussion

1. What are some examples of the fallacy of experts that you have seen or heard?
2. What are some examples of the fallacy of emotion that you have seen or heard?

6 EXERCISES

Each of the following arguments is either valid by one of the forms of valid arguments discussed in this section, or a fallacy by one of the forms of invalid arguments discussed. (See the summary boxes.) Decide whether the argument is valid *or a* fallacy, *and give the form that applies.*

1. If you build it, he will come.
   If he comes, then you will see your father.
   _____
   If you build it, then you will see your father.

2. If Harry Connick, Jr. comes to town, then I will go to the concert.
   If I go to the concert, then I'll be broke until payday.
   _____
   If Harry Connick, Jr. comes to town, then I'll be broke until payday.

3. If Doug Gilbert sells his quota, he'll get a bonus.
   Doug Gilbert sold his quota.
   _____
   He got a bonus.

4. If Cyndi Keen works hard enough, she will get a raise.
   Cyndi Keen worked hard enough.
   _____
   She got a raise.

5. If she buys a dress, then she will buy shoes.
   She buys shoes.
   _____
   She buys a dress.

6. If I didn't have to write a term paper, I'd be ecstatic.
   I am ecstatic.
   _____
   I don't have to write a term paper.

7. If beggars were choosers, then I could ask for it.
   I cannot ask for it.
   _____
   Beggars aren't choosers.

8. If Nolan Ryan pitches, the Rangers will win.
   The Rangers will not win.
   _____
   Nolan Ryan will not pitch.

9. "If I have seen farther than others, it is because I have stood on the shoulders of giants." (Sir Isaac Newton)
   I have not seen farther than others.
   _____
   I have not stood on the shoulders of giants.

10. "If we evolved a race of Isaac Newtons, that would not be progress." (Aldous Huxley)
    We have not evolved a race of Isaac Newtons.
    _____
    That is progress.

11. Alice Lavin sings or Lida Lee dances.
    Lida Lee does not dance.
    _____
    Alice Lavin sings.

12. She charges it on Visa or she orders it C.O.D.
    She doesn't charge it on Visa.
    _____
    She orders it C.O.D.

Use a truth table to determine whether the argument is valid *or* invalid.

13. $p \wedge {\sim} q$
p
‾‾‾‾‾
${\sim} q$

14. $p \vee q$
p
‾‾‾‾‾
${\sim} q$

15. $p \vee {\sim} q$
p
‾‾‾‾‾
${\sim} q$

16. ${\sim} p \rightarrow {\sim} q$
q
‾‾‾‾‾
p

17. ${\sim} p \rightarrow q$
p
‾‾‾‾‾
${\sim} q$

18. $p \rightarrow q$
$q \rightarrow p$
‾‾‾‾‾
$p \wedge q$

19. $p \rightarrow {\sim} q$
${\sim} p$
‾‾‾‾‾
${\sim} q$

20. $p \rightarrow {\sim} q$
q
‾‾‾‾‾
${\sim} p$

21. $(p \rightarrow q) \wedge (q \rightarrow p)$
p
‾‾‾‾‾
$p \vee q$

22. $({\sim} p \vee q) \wedge ({\sim} p \rightarrow q)$
p
‾‾‾‾‾
${\sim} q$

23. $(r \wedge p) \rightarrow (r \vee q)$
$(q \wedge p)$
‾‾‾‾‾
$r \vee p$

24. $({\sim} p \wedge r) \rightarrow (p \vee q)$
$({\sim} r \rightarrow p)$
‾‾‾‾‾
$q \rightarrow r$

25. In Section 5, we showed how to analyze arguments using Euler diagrams. Refer to Example 4 in this section, restate each premise and the conclusion using a quantifier, and then draw an Euler diagram to illustrate the relationship.

26. Explain in a few sentences how to determine the statement for which a truth table will be constructed so that the arguments in Exercises 27–36 can be analyzed for validity.

Determine whether the following arguments are valid *or* invalid.

27. Wally's hobby is amateur radio. If Joanna likes to read, then Wally's hobby is not amateur radio. If Joanna does not like to read, then Nikolas likes cartoons. Therefore, Nikolas likes cartoons.

28. If you are infected with a virus, then it can be transmitted. The consequences are serious and it cannot be transmitted. Therefore, if the consequences are not serious, then you are not infected with a virus.

29. Paula Abdul sings or Tom Cruise is not a hunk. If Tom Cruise is not a hunk, then Garth Brooks does not win a Grammy. Garth Brooks wins a Grammy. Therefore, Paula Abdul does not sing.

30. If Bill so desires, then Al will be the vice president. Magic is a spokesman or Al will be the vice president. Magic is not a spokesman. Therefore, Bill does not so desire.

31. The Saints will be in the playoffs if and only if Morten is an all-pro. Janet loves the Saints or Morten is an all-pro. Janet does not love the Saints. Therefore, the Saints will not be in the playoffs.

32. If you're a big girl, then you don't cry. If you don't cry, then your momma does not say "Shame on you." You don't cry or your momma says "Shame on you." Therefore, if you're a big girl, then your momma says "Shame on you."

33. If I were your woman and you were my man, then I'd never stop loving you. I've stopped loving you. Therefore, I am not your woman or you are not my man.

34. If Charlie is a salesman, then he lives in Hattiesburg. Charlie lives in Hattiesburg and he loves to fish. Therefore, if Charlie does not love to fish, he is not a salesman.

35. All men are mortal. Socrates is a man. Therefore, Socrates is mortal.

36. All men are created equal. All people who are created equal are women. Therefore, all men are women.

37. Susan Katz made the following observation: "If I want to determine whether an argument leading to the statement

$$[(p \rightarrow q) \wedge {\sim} q] \rightarrow {\sim} p$$

is valid, I only need to consider the lines of the truth table which lead to T for the column headed $(p \rightarrow q) \wedge {\sim} q$." Susan was very perceptive. Can you explain why her observation was correct?

38. Refer to the margin note in this section titled *CB Static.* Is the argument valid? If so, what general form applies?

In the arguments used by Lewis Carroll, it is helpful to restate a premise in if . . . then *form in order to more easily lead to a valid conclusion. The following premises come from Lewis Carroll. Write each premise in* if . . . then *form.*

39. None of your sons can do logic.

40. All my poultry are ducks.

41. No teetotalers are pawnbrokers.

42. Guinea pigs are hopelessly ignorant of music.

43. Opium-eaters have no self-command.

44. No teachable kitten has green eyes.

45. All of them written on blue paper are filed.

46. I have not filed any of them that I can read.

The following exercises involve premises from Lewis Carroll. Write each premise in symbols, and then in the final part, give a valid conclusion.

47. Let p be "one is able to do logic," q be "one is fit to serve on a jury," r be "one is sane," and s be "he is your son."
  (a) Everyone who is sane can do logic.
  (b) No lunatics are fit to serve on a jury.
  (c) None of your sons can do logic.
  (d) Give a valid conclusion.

48. Let p be "it is a duck," q be "it is my poultry," r be "one is an officer," and s be "one is willing to waltz."
  (a) No ducks are willing to waltz.
  (b) No officers ever decline to waltz.
  (c) All my poultry are ducks.
  (d) Give a valid conclusion.

49. Let p be "it is a guinea pig," q be "it is hopelessly ignorant of music," r be "it keeps silent while the *Moonlight Sonata* is being played," and s be "it appreciates Beethoven."
  (a) Nobody who really appreciates Beethoven fails to keep silent while the *Moonlight Sonata* is being played.
  (b) Guinea pigs are hopelessly ignorant of music.
  (c) No one who is hopelessly ignorant of music ever keeps silent while the *Moonlight Sonata* is being played.
  (d) Give a valid conclusion.

50. Let p be "one is honest," q be "one is a pawnbroker," r be "one is a promise-breaker," s be "one is trustworthy," t be "one is very communicative," and u be "one is a wine-drinker."

(a) Promise-breakers are untrustworthy.
(b) Wine-drinkers are very communicative.
(c) A person who keeps a promise is honest.
(d) No teetotalers are pawnbrokers. (*Hint:* Assume "teetotaler" is the opposite of "wine-drinker.")
(e) One can always trust a very communicative person.
(f) Give a valid conclusion.

51. Let p be "he is going to a party," q be "he brushes his hair," r be "he has self-command," s be "he looks fascinating," t be "he is an opium-eater," u be "he is tidy," and v be "he wears white kid gloves."
  (a) No one who is going to a party ever fails to brush his hair.
  (b) No one looks fascinating if he is untidy.
  (c) Opium-eaters have no self-command.
  (d) Everyone who has brushed his hair looks fascinating.
  (e) No one wears white kid gloves unless he is going to a party. (*Hint:* "a unless b" ≡ $\sim b \rightarrow a$.)
  (f) A man is always untidy if he has no self-command.
  (g) Give a valid conclusion.

52. Let p be "it begins with 'Dear Sir'," q be "it is crossed," r be "it is dated," s be "it is filed," t be "it is in black ink," u be "it is in the third person," v be "I can read it," w be "it is on blue paper," x be "it is on one sheet," and y be "it is written by Brown."
  (a) All the dated letters in this room are written on blue paper.
  (b) None of them are in black ink, except those that are written in the third person.
  (c) I have not filed any of them that I can read.
  (d) None of them that are written on one sheet are undated.
  (e) All of them that are not crossed are in black ink.
  (f) All of them written by Brown begin with "Dear Sir."
  (g) All of them written on blue paper are filed.
  (h) None of them written on more than one sheet are crossed.
  (i) None of them that begin with "Dear Sir" are written in the third person.
  (j) Give a valid conclusion.

Symbols Used in This Chapter

Connectives	Symbols	Types of Statements
and	$\wedge$	Conjunction
or	$\vee$	Disjunction
not	$\sim$	Negation
if . . . then	$\rightarrow$	Conditional
if and only if	$\leftrightarrow$	Biconditional
is equivalent to	$\equiv$	Equivalent

1 Statements and Quantifiers

Universal Quantifiers all, each, every, no(ne)

Existential Quantifiers some, there exists, (for) at least one

Negations of Quantified Statements

Statement	Negation
All do.	Some do not. (Equivalently: Not all do.)
Some do.	None do. (Equivalently: All do not.)

2 Truth Tables

Truth Tables for Negation, Conjunction, and Disjunction

p	$\sim p$
T	F
F	T

p	q	$p \wedge q$	$p \vee q$
T	T	T	T
T	F	F	T
F	T	F	T
F	F	F	F

De Morgan's Laws
For any statements *p* and *q*,

$$\sim(p \vee q) \equiv \sim p \wedge \sim q$$
$$\sim(p \wedge q) \equiv \sim p \vee \sim q.$$

Two statements are equivalent if they have the same truth value in *every* possible situation.

A logical statement having *n* component statements will have 2^n lines in its truth table.

3 The Conditional

Truth Table for the Conditional *if p, then q*

p	q	$p \rightarrow q$
T	T	T
T	F	F
F	T	T
F	F	T

A statement that has all Ts in the final column completed in its truth table is a **tautology.**

Negation of $p \rightarrow q$ $p \wedge \sim q$

The disjunction $\sim p \vee q$ is equivalent to $p \rightarrow q$.

4   More on the Conditional

Statements Related to the Conditional

Direct statement	$p \rightarrow q$	(If p, then q.)
Converse	$q \rightarrow p$	(If q, then p.)
Inverse	$\sim p \rightarrow \sim q$	(If not p, then not q.)
Contrapositive	$\sim q \rightarrow \sim p$	(If not q, then not p.)

Various Translations of $p \rightarrow q$

The conditional $p \rightarrow q$ can be translated in any of the following ways.

If p, then q.	p is sufficient for q.
If p, q.	q is necessary for p.
p implies q.	All p's are q's.
p only if q.	q if p.

Truth Table for the Biconditional p *if and only if* q

p	q	$p \leftrightarrow q$
T	T	T
T	F	F
F	T	F
F	F	T

5   Using Euler Diagrams to Analyze Arguments

An argument is made up of premises (assumptions, laws, rules, widely held ideas, or observations) and a conclusion. An argument is valid if the fact that all the premises are true forces the conclusion to be true. An argument that is not valid is invalid, or a fallacy.

6   Using Truth Tables to Analyze Arguments

Testing the Validity of an Argument with a Truth Table

1. Assign a letter to represent each simple statement in the argument.
2. Express each premise and the conclusion symbolically.
3. Form the symbolic statement of the entire argument by writing the *conjunction* of *all* the premises as the antecedent of a conditional statement, and the conclusion of the argument as the consequent.
4. Complete the truth table for the conditional statement formed in part 3 above. If it is a tautology, then the agument is valid; otherwise, it is invalid.

Valid Argument Forms

Modus Ponens	Modus Tollens	Disjunctive Syllogism	Reasoning by Transitivity
$p \rightarrow q$	$p \rightarrow q$	$p \vee q$	$p \rightarrow q$
p	$\sim q$	$\sim p$	$q \rightarrow r$
q	$\sim p$	q	$p \rightarrow r$

Invalid Argument Forms

Fallacy of the Converse	Fallacy of the Inverse
$p \rightarrow q$	$p \rightarrow q$
q	$\sim p$
p	$\sim q$

CHAPTER TEST

Write a negation for each of the following statements.

1. $5 + 3 = 9$

2. Every good boy deserves favour.

3. Some people here can't play this game.

4. If it ever comes to that, I won't be here.

5. My mind is made up and you can't change it.

Let p represent "it is broken" *and let q represent* "you can fix it." *Write each of the following in symbols.*

6. If it isn't broken, then you can fix it.

7. It is broken or you can't fix it.

8. You can't fix anything that is broken.

Using the same directions as for Exercises 6–8, write each of the following in words.

9. $\sim p \wedge q$ 10. $p \leftrightarrow \sim q$

In each of the following, assume that p and q are true, with r false. Find the truth value of each statement.

11. $\sim p \wedge \sim r$ 12. $r \vee (p \wedge \sim q)$

13. $r \rightarrow (s \vee r)$ (The truth value of the statement *s* is unknown.)

14. $r \leftrightarrow (p \rightarrow \sim q)$

15. What are the necessary conditions for a conditional statement to be false? for a conjunction to be true?

16. Explain in your own words why, if *p* is a statement, the biconditional $p \leftrightarrow \sim p$ must be false.

Write a truth table for each of the following. Identify any tautologies.

17. $p \wedge (\sim p \vee q)$ 18. $\sim(p \wedge q) \rightarrow (\sim p \vee \sim q)$

Decide whether each statement is true *or* false.

19. All positive integers are whole numbers.   20. If $x + 4 = 6$, then $x > 1$.

Write each conditional statement in the form if . . . then.

21. All rational numbers are real numbers.

22. Being a rectangle is sufficient for a polygon to be a quadrilateral.

23. Being divisible by 2 is necessary for a number to be divisible by 6.

24. She cries only if she is hurt.

For each statement, write (**a**) *the converse,* (**b**) *the inverse, and* (**c**) *the contrapositive.*

25. If a picture paints a thousand words, the graph will help me understand it.

26. $\sim p \rightarrow (q \wedge r)$ (Use one of De Morgan's laws as necessary.)

27. Use an Euler diagram to determine whether the following argument is *valid* or *invalid*.

> All members of that music club save money.
> Dorothy Blanchard is a member of that music club.
> ───────────────────────────────
> Dorothy Blanchard saves money.

28. Match each argument in (a)–(d) with the law that justifies its validity, or the fallacy of which it is an example.
   A. Modus ponens
   B. Modus tollens
   C. Reasoning by transitivity
   D. Disjunctive syllogism
   E. Fallacy of the converse
   F. Fallacy of the inverse

(a) If you like ice cream, then you'll like Blue Bell.
   You don't like Blue Bell.
   ───────────────────────────
   You don't like ice cream.

(b) If I buckle up, I'll be safer.
   I don't buckle up.
   ─────────────────
   I'm not safer.

(c) If you love me, you will let me go.
   If you let me go, I'll try to forget.
   ──────────────────────────────
   If you love me, I'll try to forget.

(d) If it's a whole number, then it's an integer.
   It's not an integer.
   ─────────────────────────
   It's not a whole number.

Use a truth table to determine whether each argument is valid *or* invalid.

29. If I hear that song, it reminds me of my youth. If I get sentimental, then it does not remind me of my youth. I get sentimental. Therefore, I don't hear that song.

30. $\sim p \to \sim q$
   $\underline{q \to p}$
   $p \vee q$

CHAPTER 3

Numeration and Mathematical Systems

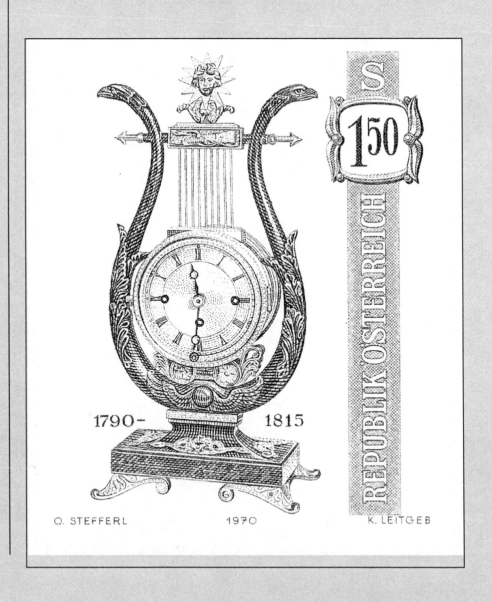

O. STEFFERL   1970   K. LEITGEB

A *set* is a collection of elements. A set, in itself, may have no particular structure. But when we introduce *ways of combining the elements* (called *operations*) and *ways of comparing the elements* (called *relations*), we obtain a **mathematical system.**

Mathematical System

A **mathematical system** is made up of three things:

1. a set of elements;
2. one or more operations for combining the elements;
3. one or more relations for comparing the elements.

Symbols designed to represent objects or ideas are among the oldest inventions of humans. These Indian symbols in Arizona are several hundred years old.

A familiar example of a mathematical system is the set of whole numbers {0, 1, 2, 3, . . .}, along with the operation of addition and the relation of equality.

Historically, the earliest mathematical system to be developed involved the set of counting numbers, or initially a limited subset of the "smaller" counting numbers. The development of this system was perhaps the most basic, as well as one of the most useful, of all mathematical ideas.

The various ways of symbolizing and working with the counting numbers are called **numeration systems.** The symbols of a numeration system are called **numerals.** In the first half of this chapter, we relate some historical numeration systems to our own modern system, observe how operations are carried out in our system, and see how certain technical applications call for basing numeration on numbers other than ten. The second half of the chapter involves some more abstract algebraic systems and their applications.

Historical Numeration Systems

Primitive societies have little need for large numbers. Even today, the languages of some cultures contain no numerical words beyond "one," "two," and maybe an indefinite word suggesting "many."

For example, according to UCLA physiologist Jared Diamond (*Discover,* Aug. 1987, p. 38), there are Gimi villages in New Guinea that use just two root words—*iya* for one and *rarido* for two. Slightly larger numbers are indicated using combinations of these two: for example, *rarido-rarido* is four and *rarido-rarido-iya* is five.

A practical method of keeping accounts by matching may have developed as humans established permanent settlements and began to grow crops and raise livestock. People might have kept track of the number of sheep in a flock by matching pebbles with the sheep, for example. The pebbles could then be kept as a record of the number of sheep.

A more efficient method is to keep a **tally stick.** With a tally stick, one notch or **tally** is made on a stick for each sheep. Tally sticks and tally marks have been found that appear to be many thousands of years old. Tally marks are still used today: for example, nine items are tallied by writing ⊬⊬⊬ ||||.

Tally sticks and groups of pebbles were an important advance. By these methods, the idea of *number* began to develop. Early people began to see that a group of three chickens and a group of three dogs had something in common: the idea of *three*. Gradually, people began to think of numbers separately from the things they represented. Words and symbols were developed for various numbers.

A numeration system, like an alphabet or any other symbolic system, is a medium of "information transfer." When information is transferred from one place to another (even if only to the person standing in front of you), we can think of it as *communication*. When the transfer is from one time to another, it involves *memory*. The numerical records of ancient people give us some idea of their daily lives and create a picture of them as producers and consumers. For example, Mary and Joseph went to Bethlehem to be counted in a census—a numerical record. Even earlier than that, as long as 5,000 years ago, the Egyptian and Sumerian peoples were using large numbers in their government and business records. Ancient documents reveal some of their numerical methods, as well as those of the Greeks, Romans, Chinese, and Hindus. Numeration systems became more sophisticated as the need arose.

Tally sticks like this one were used by the English in about 1400 to keep track of financial transactions. Each notch stands for one pound sterling.

Ancient Egyptian Numeration—Simple Grouping

Early matching and tallying led eventually to the basic essential ingredient of all more advanced numeration systems, that of **grouping.** We will see that grouping allows for less repetition of symbols and also makes numerals easier to interpret. Most historical systems, including our own, have used groups of ten, indicating that people commonly learn to count by using the fingers (of both hands). The size of the groupings (again, usually ten) is called the **base** of the number system. Bases of five, twenty and sixty have also been used.

The ancient Egyptian system is an example of a simple grouping system. It utilized ten as its base, and its various symbols are shown in Table 1. The symbol for 1 (I) is repeated, in a tally scheme, for 2, 3, and so on up to 9. A new symbol is introduced for 10 (∩), and that symbol is repeated for 20, 30, and so on, up to 90. This pattern enabled the Egyptians to express numbers up to 9,999,999 with just the seven symbols shown in the table.

The symbols used denote the various **powers** of the base (ten):

$$10^0 = 1, \ 10^1 = 10, \ 10^2 = 100, \ 10^3 = 1{,}000, \ 10^4 = 10{,}000,$$

$$10^5 = 100{,}000, \ \text{and} \ 10^6 = 1{,}000{,}000.$$

The smaller numerals at the right of the 10s, and slightly raised, are called **exponents.**

TABLE 1   Early Egyptian Symbols

Number	Symbol	Description
1	I	Stroke
10	∩	Heel bone
100	ๆ	Scroll
1,000	⚘	Lotus flower
10,000	⌒	Pointing finger
100,000	⌫	Burbot fish
1,000,000	𝕐	Astonished person

Applied Math An Egyptian tomb painting shows scribes tallying the count of a grain harvest. Egyptian mathematics was oriented more to practicality than was Greek or Babylonian mathematics, although the Egyptians did have a formula for finding the volume of a certain portion of a pyramid.

Number	Symbol
1	I
5	V
10	X
50	L
100	C
500	D
1,000	M

Roman numerals still appear today, mostly for decorative purposes: on clock faces, for chapter numbers in books, and so on. The system is essentially base ten, simple grouping, but with separate symbols for the intermediate values 5, 50, and 500, as shown above. If I is positioned left of V or X, it is subtracted rather than added. Likewise for X appearing left of L or C, and for C appearing left of D or M. Thus, for example, whereas CX denotes 110, XC denotes 90.

How deep is this ship in the water?

EXAMPLE 1   Write in our system the number below.

$$\text{⌒⌒} \, \mathcal{f}\mathcal{f}\mathcal{f}\mathcal{f}\mathcal{f} \, \text{9999} \, \overset{\cap\cap\cap\cap\cap\text{III}}{\cap\cap\cap\cap\text{IIII}}$$

Refer to Table 1 for the values of the Egyptian symbols. Each ⌒ represents 100,000. Therefore, two ⌒s represent $2 \times 100,000$, or 200,000. Proceed as follows:

two	⌒	$2 \times 100,000 =$	200,000
five	$\mathcal{f}$	$5 \times 1,000 =$	5,000
four	9	$4 \times 100 =$	400
nine	∩	$9 \times 10 =$	90
seven	I	$7 \times 1 =$	7
			205,497.

The number is 205,497. ●

EXAMPLE 2   Write 376,248 in Egyptian symbols.

Writing this number requires three ⌒s, seven ℓs, six $\mathcal{f}$s, two 9s, four ∩s, and eight Is, or

$$\text{⌒⌒} \, \ell\ell\ell \, \mathcal{f}\mathcal{f}\mathcal{f} \, \overset{}{99} \, \overset{\cap\cap\text{IIII}}{\cap\cap\text{IIII}}$$

Notice that the position or order of the symbols makes no difference in a simple grouping system. Each of the numbers 99∩∩IIII, IIII∩∩99, and II∩∩99∩II would be interpreted as 234. The most common order, however, is that shown in Examples 1 and 2, where like symbols are grouped together and groups of higher valued symbols are positioned to the left.

A simple grouping system is well suited to addition and subtraction. For example, to add $\mathcal{f}\mathcal{f}$99∩∩∩II and $\mathcal{f}$999∩IIIIII in the early Egyptian system, work as shown. Two Is plus six Is equal eight Is, and so on.

$$\begin{array}{r} \mathcal{f}\mathcal{f} \quad 99 \; \cap\cap\cap \; \text{II} \\ + \; \mathcal{f} \quad 999 \; \cap \; \text{IIIIII} \\ \hline \end{array}$$

Sum: $\mathcal{f}\mathcal{f}\mathcal{f}$999 ∩∩ IIII / 99 ∩∩ IIII

While we used a + sign for convenience and drew a line under the numbers, the Egyptians did not do this.

Sometimes regrouping, or "carrying," is needed, as in the example in which the answer contains more than nine heel bones. To regroup, get rid of ten heel bones from the tens group. Compensate for this by placing an extra scroll in the hundreds group.

Greek Numerals

1	α	60	ξ
2	β	70	o
3	γ	80	π
4	δ	90	φ
5	ϵ	100	ρ
6	ς	200	σ
7	ζ	300	τ
8	η	400	υ
9	θ	500	ϕ
10	ι	600	χ
20	κ	700	ψ
30	λ	800	ω
40	μ	900	χ
50	ν		

What About the Greeks?
Classical Greeks used letters of their alphabet as numerical symbols. The base of the system was 10, and numbers 1 through 9 were symbolized by the first nine letters of the alphabet. Rather than using repetition or multiplication, they assigned nine more letters to multiples of 10 (through 90), and more letters to multiples of 100 (through 900). This is called a ciphered system, and it sufficed for small numbers. For example, 57 would be $\nu\zeta$; 573 would be $\phi o\gamma$; and 803 would be $\omega\chi$. A small stroke was used with a units symbol for multiples of 1,000 (up to 9,000); thus 1,000 would be $\cdot\alpha$ or $'\alpha$. Often M would indicate tens of thousands (M for myriad = 10,000) with the multiples written above M.

Sum:

Regrouped answer:

Subtraction is done in much the same way, as shown in the next example.

EXAMPLE 3   Subtract in each of the following.

(a)

(b)

Difference:

In part (b), to subtract four Is from two Is, "borrow" one heel bone, which is equivalent to ten Is. Finish the problem after writing ten Is on the right.

Regrouped:

Difference:

A procedure such as those described above is called an **algorithm:** a rule or method for working a problem. The Egyptians used an interesting algorithm for multiplication which requires only an ability to add and to double numbers. Example 4 illustrates the way that the Egyptians multiplied. For convenience, this example uses our symbols rather than theirs.

EXAMPLE 4   A stone used in building a pyramid has a rectangular base measuring 5 by 18 cubits. Find the area of the base.

The area of a rectangle is found by multiplying the length and the width; in this problem, 5 times 18. To begin, build two columns of numbers, as shown below. Start the first column with 1, and the second column with 18. Each column is built downward by doubling the number above. Keep going until the first column contains numbers that can be added to make 5. Here $1 + 4 = 5$. To find 5×18, add only those numbers from the second column that correspond to 1 and 4. Here 18 and 72 are added to get the answer 90. The area of the base of the stone is 90 square cubits.

$$1 + 4 = 5 \begin{cases} \rightarrow 1 & \textbf{18} \leftarrow \text{Corresponds to 1} \\ 2 & 36 \\ \rightarrow 4 & \textbf{72} \leftarrow \text{Corresponds to 4} \end{cases} 18 + 72 = \textbf{90}$$

Finally, $5 \times 18 = 90$. ⬢

EXAMPLE 5   Use the Egyptian multiplication algorithm to find 19×70.

$\rightarrow 1$	$70 \leftarrow$
$\rightarrow 2$	$140 \leftarrow$
4	280
8	560
$\rightarrow 16$	$1{,}120 \leftarrow$

Census Records Knotted cords form a "quipu" used by Peruvian Indians for census. Larger knots are multiples of smaller; cord color indicates male or female.

Form two columns, headed by 1 and by 70. Keep doubling until there are numbers in the first column that add up to 19. (Here, $1 + 2 + 16 = 19$.) Then add corresponding numbers from the second column: $70 + 140 + 1,120 = 1,330$, so that $19 \times 70 = 1,330$. ●

Traditional Chinese Numeration—Multiplicative Grouping

Examples 1 through 3 above show that simple grouping, although an improvement over tallying, still requires considerable repetition of symbols. To denote 90, for example, the ancient Egyptian system must utilize nine ∩s: $\underset{\cap\cap\cap\cap}{\cap\cap\cap\cap\cap}$. If an additional symbol (a "multiplier") was introduced for nine, say "9," then 90 could be denoted 9 ∩. All possible numbers of repetitions of powers of the base could be handled by introducing a separate multiplier symbol for each counting number less than the base. Although the ancient Egyptian system apparently did not evolve in this direction, just such a system was developed many years ago in China. It was later adopted, for the most part, by the Japanese, with several versions occurring over the years. Here we show the predominant Chinese version, which used the symbols shown in Table 2. We call this type of system a **multiplicative grouping** system. In general, such a system would involve pairs of symbols, each pair containing a multiplier (with some counting number value less than the base) and then a power of the base. The Chinese numerals are read from top to bottom rather than from left to right.

Three features distinguish this system from a strictly pure multiplicative grouping system. First, the number of 1s is indicated using a single symbol rather than a pair. In effect, the multiplier (1, 2, 3, . . . , 9) is written but the power of the base (10^0) is not. Second, in the pair indicating 10s, if the multiplier is 1, then that multiplier is omitted. Just the symbol for 10 is written. Third, when a given power of the base is totally missing in a particular number, this omission is shown by the inclusion of the special zero symbol. (See Table 2.) If two or more consecutive powers are missing, just one zero symbol serves to note the total omission. The omission of 1s and 10s, and any other powers occurring at the extreme bottom of a numeral, need not be noted with a zero symbol. (Note that, for clarification in the examples that follow, we have emphasized the grouping into pairs by spacing and by using braces. These features are *not* part of the actual numeral.)

TABLE 2

Number	Symbol
1	一
2	二
3	三
4	∩
5	五
6	六
7	七
8	八
9	九
10	十
100	百
1,000	千
0	零

EXAMPLE 6 Interpret the Chinese numerals below.

(a) $\left.\begin{matrix}三\\千\end{matrix}\right\}$ $3 \times 1,000 = 3,000$

$\left.\begin{matrix}一\\百\end{matrix}\right\}$ $1 \times 100 \quad = \quad 100$

$\left.\begin{matrix}六\\十\end{matrix}\right\}$ $6 \times 10 \quad = \quad 60$

$\bigcirc$ $4(\times 1) \quad = \quad \underline{\quad 4}$

Total: 3,164

(b) $\left.\begin{matrix}七\\百\end{matrix}\right\}$ $7 \times 100 = 700$

零 $0(\times 10) = \quad 00$

三 $3(\times 1) = \quad \underline{\quad 3}$

Total: 703

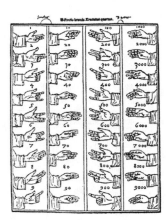

Finger Reckoning There is much evidence that early humans (in various cultures) used their fingers to represent numbers. As the various calculations of everyday life became more complicated, *finger reckoning,* as shown in this sketch, became popular. The Romans apparently became adept at this sort of calculating, carrying it to 10,000 or perhaps higher.

(c) 五千 } $5 \times 1{,}000 = 5{,}000$

零 { $0 (\times 100) = 000$
$\ \ 0 (\times 10) = 00$

九 $\qquad 9 (\times 1) = \underline{9}$
$\qquad\qquad$ Total: $\underline{5{,}009}$

(d) 四千 } $4 \times 1000 = 4{,}000$

二百 } $2 \times 100 = \underline{200}$
$\qquad\qquad$ Total: $\underline{4{,}200}$

EXAMPLE 7   Write Chinese numerals for these numbers.

(a) 614
   This number is made up of six 100s, one 10, and one 4, as depicted at the right.

6×100: { 六百

$(1 \times) 10$:   十

$4 (\times 1)$:   四

(b) 5,090
   This number consists of five 1,000s, no 100s, and nine 10s (no 1s).

$5 \times 1{,}000$: { 五千

$0 (\times 100)$: 零

9×10: { 九十

Hindu-Arabic Numeration—Positional System

A simple grouping system relies on repetition of symbols to denote the number of each power of the base. A multiplicative grouping system uses multipliers in place of repetition, which is more efficient. But the ultimate in efficiency is attained only when we proceed to the next step, a **positional** system, in which only the multipliers are used. The various powers of the base require no separate symbols, since the power associated with each multiplier can be understood by the position that the multiplier occupies in the numeral. If the Chinese system had evolved into a positional system, then the numeral for 7,482 could be written

七
四
八
二

rather than

七千
四百
八十
二

The lowest symbol is understood to represent two 1s (10^0), the next one up denotes eight 10s (10^1), then four 100s (10^2), and finally seven 1,000s (10^3). Each symbol in a numeral now has both a **face value,** associated with that particular symbol (the multiplier value) and a **place value** (a power of the base), associated with the place, or position, occupied by the symbol. Since these features are so important, we emphasize them as follows.

Number	Symbol
1	𒁹
10	𒌋

Babylonian numeration was positional, base sixty. But the face values within the positions were base ten simple grouping numerals, formed with the two symbols shown above. (These symbols resulted from the Babylonian method of writing on clay with a wedge-shaped stylus.) The numeral

𒌋𒌋𒁹𒁹𒁹 𒌋𒌋𒌋𒌋𒁹

denotes 1,421 ($23 \times 60 + 41 \times 1$).

Positional Numeration

In a positional numeral, each symbol (called a **digit**) conveys two things:
1. **face value**—the inherent value of the symbol
2. **place value**—the power of the base which is associated with the position that the digit occupies in the numeral.

The place values in a Hindu-Arabic numeral, from right to left, are 1, 10, 100, 1,000, and so on. The three 4s in the number 46,424 all have the same face value but different place values. The first 4, on the left, denotes four 10,000s, the next one denotes four 100s, and the one on the right denotes four 1s. Place values (in base ten) are named as shown here:

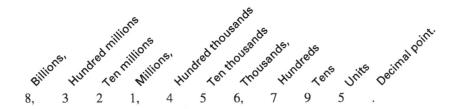

This numeral is read as eight billion, three hundred twenty-one million, four hundred fifty-six thousand, seven hundred ninety-five.

To work successfully, a positional system must have a symbol for zero, to serve as a **placeholder** in case one or more powers of the base are not needed. Because of this requirement, some early numeration systems took a long time to evolve to a positional form, or never did. Although the traditional Chinese system does utilize a zero symbol, it never did incorporate all the features of a positional system, but remained essentially a multiplicative grouping system.

The one numeration system that did achieve the maximum efficiency of positional form is our own system, the one commonly known, for historical reasons, as the **Hindu-Arabic** system. It developed over many centuries. Its symbols have been traced to the Hindus of 200 B.C. They were picked up by the Arabs and eventually transmitted to Spain, where a late tenth-century version appeared like this:

$$ \text{I Z Z Ƴ Ƴ Ƅ Ƅ 7 8 9.} $$

The earliest stages of the system evolved under the influence of navigational, trade, engineering and military requirements. And in early modern times, the advance of astronomy and other sciences led to a structure well suited to fast and accurate computation. The purely positional form that the system finally assumed was introduced to the West by Leonardo Fibonacci of Pisa (1170–1250) early in the thirteenth century. But widespread acceptance of standardized symbols and form was not achieved until the invention of printing during the fifteenth century. Since that time, no better system of numeration has been devised, and the positional base ten Hindu-Arabic system is commonly used around the world today. (In India, where it all began, standardization is still not totally achieved, as various local systems are still used today.)

Of course the Hindu-Arabic system that we know and use today also contains the placeholder 0 (zero). We are so accustomed to the positional structure of the system that most of us hardly give it a thought. For example, knowing that the system is based on ten, we readily interpret the numeral 5,407 as representing five 1,000s (10^3), four 100s (10^2), no 10s (10^1), and seven 1s (10^0).

In Section 2 we shall look in more detail at the structure of the Hindu-Arabic system and some early methods and devices for doing computation.

We have now considered the ancient Egyptian numeration system, which was simple grouping, the traditional Chinese system, which is (essentially) multiplicative grouping, and the Hindu-Arabic system, which is positional. Other well-documented numeration systems that have been used around the world at various times include the Babylonian, Greek, Roman, and Mayan systems. For our purposes here, the three systems already investigated are sufficient to illustrate the historical progression from the basic simple grouping approach to the more sophisticated and efficient positional structure.

1 EXERCISES

Convert each Egyptian numeral to Hindu-Arabic form.

1. ⌒⌒ 𝟿𝟿𝟿𝟿∩⎮⎮

2. 𝒞 ⌒⌒⌒ ∩∩∩⎮⎮⎮⎮⎮⎮

3. ⌶⌶⌶ ⌒⌒⌒⌒⌒ 𝟿𝟿∩∩∩⎮

4. ⌶⌶⌶⌶ ⌒⌒⌒ 𝓁𝓁𝓁 𝟿𝟿𝟿 ∩∩ ⎮⎮⎮⎮⎮ ⌶⌶⌶ ⌒⌒⌒ 𝟿𝟿𝟿𝟿 ⎮⎮⎮⎮

Convert each Hindu-Arabic numeral to Egyptian form.

5. 427 **6.** 23,145 **7.** 306,090 **8.** 8,657,000

Chapter 1 of the book of Numbers in the Bible describes a census of the draft-eligible men of Israel after Moses led them out of Egypt into the Desert of Sinai, about 1450 B.C. Write an Egyptian numeral for the number of available men from each tribe listed.

9. 46,500 from the tribe of Reuben **10.** 59,300 from the tribe of Simeon

11. 45,650 from the tribe of Gad **12.** 74,600 from the tribe of Judah

13. 54,400 from the tribe of Issachar **14.** 62,700 from the tribe of Dan

Convert each Chinese numeral to Hindu-Arabic form.

15. ⼆ 百 ⼞ ⼗ ⼋

16. 九 百 三 ⼗ 五

17. 〇 千 九 百 零 ⼆

18. 三 千 零 ⼁

Convert each Hindu-Arabic numeral to Chinese.

19. 63 **20.** 960 **21.** 2,416 **22.** 7,012

Though Chinese art forms began before written history, their highest development was achieved during four particular dynasties. Write traditional Chinese numerals for the beginning and ending dates of each dynasty listed.

23. Han (202 B.C. to A.D. 220)

24. T'ang (618 to 907)

25. Sung (960 to 1279)

26. Ming (1368 to 1644)

Work each of the following addition or subtraction problems, using regrouping as necessary. Convert each answer to Hindu-Arabic form.

27. 99∩∩∩ |||| / |||
　　+ 9∩∩∩ ||
　　　∩∩ |||

28. 9　∩∩ ||
　　　　∩∩
　　+ ∩∩∩∩ ||||
　　　∩∩∩

29. ℓℓℓ 99 ∩∩ ||
　　99 999∩∩
　　+ ℓℓ 999 ∩∩ |||
　　999 |||

30. ℓℓℓ ℓℓ 　∩ |||
　　+ ℓℓ ℓ 99 ∩∩∩∩||||
　　999∩∩∩∩ ||||

31. ∩∩∩ |||
　　∩∩ |||
　　− ∩∩∩ ||||

32. 99∩∩∩ ||||
　　− 9 ∩∩ |

33. ℓ 999 ∩∩∩ |||
　　99 |||
　　− 99 ∩∩∩ |||
　　∩∩∩∩

34. ℓ ℓ 99 ||||
　　− ℓℓℓ 999 |||
　　999 |||

Use the Egyptian algorithm to find each product.

35. 3×19 **36.** 5×26 **37.** 12×93 **38.** 21×44

Convert all numbers in the following problems to Egyptian numerals. Multiply using the Egyptian algorithm, and add using the Egyptian symbols. Give the final answer using a Hindu-Arabic numeral.

39. King Solomon told the King of Tyre (now Lebanon) that Solomon needed the best cedar for his temple, and that he would "pay you for your men whatever sum you fix." Find the total bill to Solomon if the King of Tyre used the following numbers of men: 5,500 tree cutters at two shekels per week each, for a total of seven weeks; 4,600 sawers of wood at three shekels per week each, for a total of 32 weeks; and 900 sailors at one shekel per week each, for a total of 16 weeks.

40. The book of Ezra in the Bible describes the return of the exiles to Jerusalem. When they rebuilt the temple, the King of Persia gave them the following items: thirty golden basins, a thousand silver basins, four hundred ten silver bowls, and thirty golden bowls. Find the total value of this treasure, if each gold basin is worth 3,000 shekels, each silver basin is worth 500 shekels, each silver bowl is worth 50 shekels, and each golden bowl is worth 400 shekels.

Explain why each of the following steps would be an improvement in the development of numeration systems.

41. progressing from carrying groups of pebbles to making tally marks on a stick

42. progressing from tallying to simple grouping

43. progressing from simple grouping to multiplicative grouping

44. progressing from multiplicative grouping to positional numeration

Recall that the ancient Egyptian system described in this section was simple grouping, used a base of ten, and contained seven distinct symbols. The largest number expressible in that system is 9,999,999. Identify the largest number expressible in each of the following simple grouping systems. (In Exercises 49–52, d can be any counting number.)

45. base ten, five distinct symbols

46. base ten, ten distinct symbols

47. base five, five distinct symbols

48. base five, ten distinct symbols

49. base ten, *d* distinct symbols

50. base five, *d* distinct symbols

51. base seven, *d* distinct symbols

52. base *b*, *d* distinct symbols (where *b* is any counting number 2 or greater)

The Hindu-Arabic system is positional and uses ten as the base. Describe any advantages or disadvantages that may have resulted in each of the following cases.

53. Suppose the base had been larger, say twelve or twenty for example.

54. Suppose the base had been smaller, maybe eight or five.

2

Arithmetic in the Hindu-Arabic System

The historical development of numeration culminated in positional systems, the most successful of which is the Hindu-Arabic system. This type of system gives us the easiest way of expressing numbers. But, just as importantly, it gives us the easiest way of computing with numbers. This section involves some of the structure and history of the basic arithmetic operations.

As stated in Section 1, Hindu-Arabic place values are powers of the base ten. For example, 10^4 denotes the fourth power of ten. Such expressions are often called **exponential expressions.** In this case, 10 is the **base** and 4 is the **exponent.** Exponents actually indicate repeated multiplication of the base:

$$10^4 = \underbrace{10 \times 10 \times 10 \times 10}_{\text{four factors of 10}} = 10,000.$$

In the same way, $10^2 = 10 \times 10 = 100$, $10^6 = 10 \times 10 \times 10 \times 10 \times 10 \times 10 = 1,000,000$, and so on. The base does not have to be 10; for example,

$$4^3 = 4 \times 4 \times 4 = 64, \qquad 2^2 = 2 \times 2 = 4,$$
$$3^5 = 3 \times 3 \times 3 \times 3 \times 3 = 243,$$

and so on. Expressions of this type are defined in general as follows.

Exponential Expressions

For any number *a* and any counting number *m*,

$$a^m = \underbrace{a \times a \times a \cdots \times a.}_{m \text{ factors of } a}$$

The number *a* is the **base,** *m* is the **exponent,** and a^m is read "*a* to the power *m*."

Digits This Iranian stamp should remind us that counting on fingers (and toes) is an age-old practice. In fact, our word *digit*, referring to the numerals 0–9, comes from a Latin word for "finger" (or "toe"). It seems reasonable to connect so natural a counting method with the fact that number bases of five, ten, or twenty are the most frequent in human cultures. Aristotle first noted the relationships between fingers and base ten in Greek numeration. Anthropologists go along with the notion. Some cultures, however, have used two, three, or four as number bases, for example, counting on the joints of the fingers or the spaces between them.

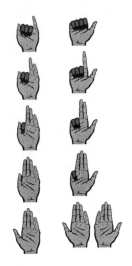

Finger Counting Many people of the world have learned to count without using the Hindu-Arabic digits 1, 2, 3, 4, 5, 6, 7, 8, 9, 0. The first digits people used were their fingers. In Africa the Zulu used the method shown here to count to ten. They started on the left hand with palm up and fist closed. The Zulu finger positions for 1–5 are shown above on the left. The Zulu finger positions for 6–10 are shown on the right.

EXAMPLE 1 Find each power.

(a) $10^3 = 10 \times 10 \times 10 = 1{,}000$
(10^3 is read "10 cubed," or "10 to the third power.")

(b) $7^2 = 7 \times 7 = 49$
(7^2 is read "7 squared," or "7 to the second power.")

(c) $5^4 = 5 \times 5 \times 5 \times 5 = 625$
(5^4 is read "5 to the fourth power.") ●

To simplify work with exponents, it is agreed that $a^0 = 1$ for any nonzero number a. By this agreement, $7^0 = 1$, $52^0 = 1$, and so on. At the same time, $a^1 = a$ for any number a. For example, $8^1 = 8$, and $25^1 = 25$. The exponent 1 is usually omitted.

With the use of exponents, numbers can be written in **expanded form** in which the value of the digit in each position is made clear. For example, write 924 in expanded form by thinking of 924 as nine 100s plus two 10s plus four 1s, or

$$924 = 900 + 20 + 4$$
$$924 = (9 \times 100) + (2 \times 10) + (4 \times 1).$$

By the definition of exponents, $100 = 10^2$, $10 = 10^1$, and $1 = 10^0$. Use these exponents to write 924 in expanded form as follows:

$$924 = (9 \times 10^2) + (2 \times 10^1) + (4 \times 10^0).$$

EXAMPLE 2 The following are written in expanded form.

(a) $1{,}906 = (1 \times 10^3) + (9 \times 10^2) + (0 \times 10^1) + (6 \times 10^0)$
Since $0 \times 10^1 = 0$, this term could be omitted, but the form is clearer with it included.

(b) $46{,}424 = (4 \times 10^4) + (6 \times 10^3) + (4 \times 10^2) + (2 \times 10^1) + (4 \times 10^0)$ ●

EXAMPLE 3 Each of the following expansions is simplified.

(a) $(3 \times 10^5) + (2 \times 10^4) + (6 \times 10^3) + (8 \times 10^2) + (7 \times 10^1) + (9 \times 10^0) = 326{,}879$

(b) $(2 \times 10^1) + (8 \times 10^0) = 28$ ●

Expanded notation can be used to see why standard algorithms for addition and subtraction really work. The key idea behind these algorithms is based on the **distributive property,** which will be discussed more fully in Section 5. It can be written in one form as follows.

Distributive Property

For all real numbers a, b, and c,

$$(b \times a) + (c \times a) = (b + c) \times a.$$

For example, $(3 \times 10^4) + (2 \times 10^4) = (3 + 2) \times 10^4$
$$= 5 \times 10^4.$$

EXAMPLE 4   Use expanded notation to add 23 and 64.

$$23 = (2 \times 10^1) + (3 \times 10^0)$$
$$+\ 64 = (6 \times 10^1) + (4 \times 10^0)$$
$$\overline{(8 \times 10^1) + (7 \times 10^0) = 87}$$ ⬡

Subtraction works in much the same way.

EXAMPLE 5   Find $695 - 254$.

$$695 = (6 \times 10^2) + (9 \times 10^1) + (5 \times 10^0)$$
$$-\ 254 = (2 \times 10^2) + (5 \times 10^1) + (4 \times 10^0)$$
$$\overline{(4 \times 10^2) + (4 \times 10^1) + (1 \times 10^0) = 441}$$ ⬡

Expanded notation and the distributive property can also be used to show how to solve addition problems where a power of 10 ends up with a multiplier of more than one digit.

EXAMPLE 6   Use expanded notation to add 75 and 48.

$$75 = (7 \times 10^1) + (5 \times 10^0)$$
$$+\ 48 = (4 \times 10^1) + (8 \times 10^0)$$
$$\overline{(11 \times 10^1) + (13 \times 10^0)}$$

Since the units position (10^0) has room for only one digit, 13×10^0 must be modified:

$$13 \times 10^0 = (10 \times 10^0) + (3 \times 10^0) \qquad \text{Distributive property}$$
$$= (1 \times 10^1) + (3 \times 10^0)$$

In effect, the 1 from 13 moved to the left from the units position to the tens position. This is called "carrying." Now our sum is

$$\underbrace{(\mathbf{11 \times 10^1}) + (\mathbf{1 \times 10^1})} + (3 \times 10^0)$$
$$= (\mathbf{12 \times 10^1}) + (3 \times 10^0) \qquad \text{Distributive property}$$
$$= (10 \times 10^1) + (2 \times 10^1) + (3 \times 10^0)$$
$$= (1 \ \times 10^2) + (2 \times 10^1) + (3 \times 10^0)$$
$$= 123.$$ ⬡

Subtraction problems often require "borrowing," which can also be clarified with expanded notation.

EXAMPLE 7   Use expanded notation to subtract 186 from 364.

$$364 = (3 \times 10^2) + (6 \times 10^1) + (4 \times 10^0)$$
$$-\ 186 = (1 \times 10^2) + (8 \times 10^1) + (6 \times 10^0)$$

The ***Carmen de Algorismo*** (opening verses shown here) by Alexander de Villa Dei, thirteenth century, popularized the new art of "algorismus":

. . . .from these twice five figures
0 9 8 7 6 5 4 3 2 1
of the Indians we benefit. . .

The *Carmen* related that Algor, an Indian king, invented the art. But actually, "algorism" (or "algorithm") comes in a roundabout way from the name Muhammad ibn Musa al-Khorârizmi, an Arabian mathematician of the ninth century, whose arithmetic book was translated into Latin. Furthermore, this Muhammad's book on equations, *Hisab al-jabr w'al-muqâbalah,* yielded the term "algebra" in a similar way.

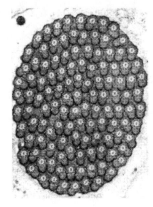

Exponents are used often in science, as when expressing the size of the region shown in this photomicrograph (photo taken through a microscope). The caddis fly sperm is shown 5,250 times as large as its actual size of about 6.5×10^{-3} mm wide and 8.8×10^{-3} mm long.

Combining New with Old
So you think an abacus is old-fashioned and a calculator is up to date? Then how about an instrument (not sold in North America) that combines a calculator and abacus? (Many Japanese use the calculator merely to check the results of the abacus.)

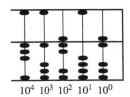

$10^4 \ 10^3 \ 10^2 \ 10^1 \ 10^0$

FIGURE 1

Since, in the units position, we cannot subtract 6 from 4, we modify the top expansion as follows (the units position borrows from the tens position):

$$(3 \times 10^2) + (\mathbf{6 \times 10^1}) + (4 \times 10^0)$$
$$= (3 \times 10^2) + \overbrace{(\mathbf{5 \times 10^1}) + (\mathbf{1 \times 10^1})} + (4 \times 10^0) \qquad \text{Distributive property}$$
$$= (3 \times 10^2) + (5 \times 10^1) + \underbrace{(\mathbf{10 \times 10^0}) + (\mathbf{4 \times 10^0})}$$
$$= (3 \times 10^2) + (5 \times 10^1) + (\mathbf{14 \times 10^0}). \qquad \text{Distributive property}$$

(We can now subtract 6 from 14 in the units position, but cannot take 8 from 5 in the tens position, so we continue the modification, borrowing from the hundreds to the tens position.)

$$\overbrace{(\mathbf{3 \times 10^2}) + (5 \times 10^1)} + (14 \times 10^0)$$
$$= \overbrace{(\mathbf{2 \times 10^2}) + (\mathbf{1 \times 10^2})} + (5 \times 10^1) + (14 \times 10^0) \qquad \text{Distributive property}$$
$$= (2 \times 10^2) + \underbrace{(\mathbf{10 \times 10^1}) + (\mathbf{5 \times 10^1})} + (14 \times 10^0)$$
$$= (2 \times 10^2) + (\mathbf{15 \times 10^1}) + (14 \times 10^0) \qquad \text{Distributive property}$$

Now we can complete the subtraction.

$$\begin{array}{r} (2 \times 10^2) + (15 \times 10^1) + (14 \times 10^0) \\ - (1 \times 10^2) + \ (8 \times 10^1) + \ (6 \times 10^0) \\ \hline (1 \times 10^2) + \ (7 \times 10^1) + \ (8 \times 10^0) = 178 \quad \blacklozenge \end{array}$$

Examples 4 through 7 used expanded notation and the distributive property to clarify our usual additional and subtraction methods. In practice, our actual work for these four problems would appear as follows:

$$\begin{array}{cccc} & & {}^{1} & {}^{2\ 15\ 1} \\ 23 & 695 & 75 & 3\,\cancel{6}\,4 \\ +64 & -254 & +48 & -1\,8\,6 \\ \hline 87 & 441 & 123 & 1\,7\,8. \end{array}$$

The procedures seen in this section also work for positional systems with bases other than ten.

Since our numeration system is based on powers of ten, it is often called the **decimal system,** from the Latin word *decem,* meaning ten.* Over the years, many methods have been devised for speeding calculations in the decimal system. One of the oldest is the **abacus,** a device made with a series of rods with sliding beads and a dividing bar. Reading from right to left, the rods have values of 1, 10, 100, 1,000, and so on. The bead above the bar has five times the value of those below. Beads moved *toward* the bar are in the "active" position, and those toward the frame are ignored.

In our illustrations of abaci (plural form of abacus), such as in Figure 1, the activated beads are shown in black for emphasis.

December was the tenth month in an old form of the calendar. It is interesting to note that *decem* became *dix* in the French language; a ten-dollar bill, called "dixie," was in use in New Orleans before the Civil War. And "Dixie Land" was a nickname for that city before Dixie came to refer to all the Southern states, as in Daniel D. Emmett's song, written in 1859.

EXAMPLE 8 The number on the abacus in Figure 1 is found as follows:

$$(3 \times 10{,}000) + (1 \times 1{,}000) + [(1 \times 500) + (2 \times 100)] + 0 + [(1 \times 5) + (1 \times 1)]$$
$$= 30{,}000 + 1{,}000 + 500 + 200 + 0 + 5 + 1$$
$$= 31{,}706. \quad \blacklozenge$$

As paper became more readily available, people gradually switched from devices like the abacus (though these are still commonly used in many areas) to paper-and-pencil methods of calculation. One early scheme, used both in India and Persia, was the **lattice method,** which arranged products of single digits into a diagonalized lattice, as shown in the following example.

Twice 2 are 4.
Pray hasten on before.

5 times 5 are 25.
I thank my stars I'm yet alive.

Merry Math These two rhymes illustrated with wood engravings (above) come from *Marmaduke Multiply's Merry Method of Making Minor Mathematicians*, a primer published in the late 1830s in Boston.

EXAMPLE 9 Find the product 38 × 794 by the lattice method. Work as follows.

Step 1 Write the problem, with one number at the side and one across the top.

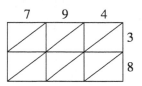

Step 2 Within the lattice, write the products of all pairs of digits from the top and side.

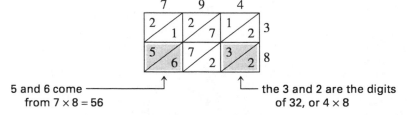

5 and 6 come from 7 × 8 = 56   the 3 and 2 are the digits of 32, or 4 × 8

Step 3 Starting at the right of the lattice add diagonally, carrying as necessary.

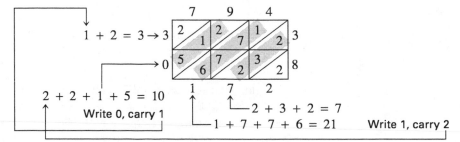

1 + 2 = 3 → 3

2 + 2 + 1 + 5 = 10   Write 0, carry 1

2 + 3 + 2 = 7
1 + 7 + 7 + 6 = 21   Write 1, carry 2

Step 4 Read the answer around the left side and bottom:

$$38 \times 794 = 30{,}172. \quad \blacklozenge$$

John Napier's most significant mathematical contribution, developed over a period of at least 20 years, was the concept of *logarithms*, which, among other things, allow multiplication and division to be accomplished with addition and subtraction, a great computational advantage given the state of mathematics at the time (1614).

Napier himself regarded his interest in mathematics as a recreation, his main involvements being political and religious. A supporter of John Knox and James I, he published a widely read anti-Catholic work which analyzed the Biblical book of Revelation and concluded that the Pope was the Antichrist and that the Creator would end the world between 1688 and 1700. Napier was one of many who, over the years, have miscalculated the end of the world. One of the most recent was a former NASA rocket engineer, Edgar C. Whisenant, who wrote the book *88 Reasons Why the Rapture Will Be in 1988.* Apparently we have not yet perfected our mathematics to the point of being able to calculate all the secrets of the Creator.

The Scottish mathematician John Napier (1550–1617) introduced a significant calculating tool called **Napier's rods,** or **Napier's bones.** Napier's invention, based on the lattice method of multiplication, is widely acknowledged as a very early forerunner of modern computers. It consisted of a set of strips, several for each digit 0 through 9, on which the multiples of each digit appeared in a sort of lattice column. See Figure 2.

FIGURE 2

FIGURE 3

An additional strip, called the index, could be laid beside any of the others to indicate the multiplier at each level. Napier's rods were used for mechanically multiplying, dividing, and taking square roots. Figure 3 shows how to multiply 2,806 by 7. Select the rods for 2, 8, 0, and 6; place them side by side. Then using the index, locate the level for a multiplier of 7. The resulting lattice, shown at the bottom of the figure, gives the product 19,642.

FOR FURTHER THOUGHT

The abacus has been used (and still is) to perform very rapid calculations. A simple example is adding 526 and 362. Start with 526 on the abacus:

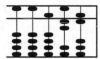

To add 362, start by "activating" an additional 2 on the 1s rod:

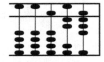

Next, activate an additional 6 on the 10s rod:

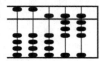

Finally, activate an additional 3 on the 100s rod:

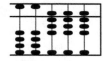

The sum, read from the abacus, is 888.

For problems where carrying or borrowing are required, it takes a little more thought and skill. Try to obtain an actual abacus (or, otherwise, make sketches) and practice some addition and subtraction problems until you can do them quickly.

For Group Discussion

1. Use an abacus to add: 13,728 + 61,455. Explain each step of your procedure.
2. Use an abacus to subtract: 6,512 − 4,816. Again, explain each step of your procedure.

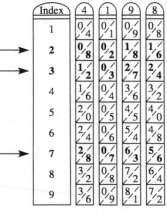

FIGURE 4

EXAMPLE 10 Use Napier's rods to find the product of 723 and 4,198.

We line up the rods for 4, 1, 9, and 8 next to the index as in Figure 4. The product 3 × 4,198 is found as described in Example 9 and written at the bottom of the figure. Then 2 × 4,198 is found similarly and written below, shifted one place to the left (why?). Finally, the product 7 × 4,198 is written shifted two places to the left. The final answer is found by addition to obtain

$$723 \times 4{,}198 = 3{,}035{,}154. \quad \bullet$$

One other paper-and-pencil method of multiplication is the **Russian peasant method,** which is similar to the Egyptian method of doubling explained in the previous section. (In fact both of these methods work, in effect, by expanding one of the numbers to be multiplied, but in base two rather than in base ten. Base two numerals are discussed in Section 3.) To multiply 37 and 42 by the Russian peasant method, make two columns headed by 37 and 42. Form the first column by dividing 37 by 2 again and again, ignoring any remainders. Stop when 1 is obtained. Form the second column by doubling each number down the column.

	37	42	
	18	84	
Divide by 2,	9	168	Double each
ignoring remainders.	4	336	number.
	2	672	
	1	1,344	

Now add up only the second column numbers that correspond to odd numbers in the first column. Omit those corresponding to even numbers in the first column.

→	**37**	**42**	←	
	18	84		
Odd numbers →	**9**	**168**	← Add these numbers.	
	4	336		
	2	672		
→	**1**	**1,344**	←	

Finally, $37 \times 42 = 42 + 168 + 1,344 = 1,554$.

---

2 EXERCISES

Write each number in expanded form. (See Example 2.)

1. 37 **2.** 814 **3.** 2,815 **4.** 15,504

5. three thousand, six hundred twenty-eight

6. fifty-three thousand, eight hundred twelve

7. thirteen million, six hundred six thousand, ninety

8. one hundred twelve million, fourteen thousand, one hundred twelve

Simplify each of the following expansions. (See Example 3.)

9. $(7 \times 10^1) + (3 \times 10^0)$

10. $(2 \times 10^2) + (6 \times 10^1) + (0 \times 10^0)$

11. $(5 \times 10^3) + (0 \times 10^2) + (7 \times 10^1) + (2 \times 10^0)$

12. $(4 \times 10^5) + (0 \times 10^4) + (7 \times 10^3) + (7 \times 10^2) + (5 \times 10^1) + (2 \times 10^0)$

13. $(5 \times 10^7) + (6 \times 10^5) + (2 \times 10^3) + (3 \times 10^0)$

14. $(6 \times 10^8) + (5 \times 10^7) + (1 \times 10^2) + (4 \times 10^0)$

In each of the following, add in expanded notation. (See Example 4.)

15. $63 + 26$ **16.** $693 + 305$

In each of the following, subtract in expanded notation. (See Example 5.)

17. $84 - 52$ **18.** $673 - 412$

Perform each addition using expanded notation. (See Example 6.)

19. $65 + 44$ **20.** $536 + 279$ **21.** $424 + 298$ **22.** $6,755 + 4,827$

Perform each subtraction using expanded notation. (See Example 7.)

23. $53 - 47$ **24.** $253 - 48$ **25.** $643 - 436$ **26.** $826 - 345$

Identify the number represented on each of these abaci.

27. **28.**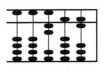

29. **30.**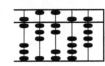

Sketch an abacus to show each number.

31. 38 **32.** 183 **33.** 2,547 **34.** 70,163

Use the lattice method to find each product.

35. 63×28 **36.** 29×635 **37.** 413×68 **38.** 845×396

Refer to Example 10, where Napier's rods were used to find the product of 723 and 4,198. Then complete Exercises 39 and 40.

39. Find the product of 723 and 4,198 by completing the lattice process shown here.

40. Explain how Napier's rods could have been used in Example 10 to set up one complete lattice product rather than adding three individual (shifted) lattice products.

Make use of Napier's rods (Figure 2) to find each product.

41. 8×62 **42.** 32×73 **43.** $26 \times 8,354$ **44.** $526 \times 4,863$

Use the Russian peasant method to find each product.

45. 5×82 **46.** 41×33 **47.** 62×429 **48.** 135×63

3

Converting Between Number Bases

Most of us can work with decimal numbers effectively, having used them all our lives. But that doesn't mean we necessarily have a deep understanding of the system we use so well. You may immediately recognize that the digit 4 in the numeral 1,473 denotes 4 "hundreds," but that may not be because you know the third digit

TABLE 3 Selected Powers of Some Alternate Number Bases

	Fourth Power	Third Power	Second Power	First Power	Zero Power
Base two	16	8	4	2	1
Base five	625	125	25	5	1
Base seven	2,401	343	49	7	1
Base eight	4,096	512	64	8	1
Base sixteen	65,536	4,096	256	16	1

from the right represents second powers of the base. By writing numbers in unfamiliar bases, and converting from one base to another, you can come to appreciate the nature of a positional system and realize that a base of ten is a choice, not a necessity.

Although the numeration systems discussed in Section 1 were all base ten, other bases have occurred historically. For example, the ancient Babylonians used 60 as their base. The Mayan Indians of Central America and Mexico used 20. In this section we consider bases other than ten, but we use the familiar Hindu-Arabic symbols. We will consistently indicate bases other than ten with a spelled-out subscript, as in the numeral 43_{five}. Whenever a number appears without a subscript, it is to be assumed that the intended base is ten. It will help to be careful how you read (or verbalize) numerals here. The numeral 43_{five} is read "four three base five." (Do *not* read it as "forty-three," as that terminology implies base ten and names a totally different number.)

For reference in doing number expansions and base conversions, Table 3 gives the first several powers of some numbers used as alternate bases in this section.

We begin our illustrations with the base five system, which requires just five distinct symbols, 0, 1, 2, 3, and 4. Table 4 compares the base five and decimal (base ten) numerals for the whole numbers 0 through 30. Notice that, while the base five system uses fewer distinct symbols, it normally requires more digits to denote the same number.

TABLE 4

Base Ten	Base Five
0	0
1	1
2	2
3	3
4	4
5	10
6	11
7	12
8	13
9	14
10	20
11	21
12	22
13	23
14	24
15	30
16	31
17	32
18	33
19	34
20	40
21	41
22	42
23	43
24	44
25	100
26	101
27	102
28	103
29	104
30	110

EXAMPLE 1 Convert $1{,}342_{\text{five}}$ to decimal form.

Referring to the powers of five in Table 3, we see that this number has one 125, three 25s, four 5s, and two 1s, so

$$1{,}342_{\text{five}} = (1 \times 125) + (3 \times 25) + (4 \times 5) + (2 \times 1)$$
$$= 125 + 75 + 20 + 2$$
$$= 222. \quad \blacklozenge$$

A shortcut for converting from base five to decimal form, which is *particularly useful when you use a calculator,* can be derived as follows. (We can illustrate this by repeating the conversion of Example 1.)

$$1{,}342_{\text{five}} = (1 \times 5^3) + (3 \times 5^2) + (4 \times 5) + 2$$

Now 5 can be factored out of the three quantities in parentheses, so

$$1{,}342_{\text{five}} = ((1 \times 5^2) + (3 \times 5) + 4) \times 5 + 2.$$

Now, factoring another five out of the two "inner" quantities, we get

$$1{,}342_{\text{five}} = (((1 \times 5) + 3) \times 5 + 4) \times 5 + 2.$$

The inner parentheses around 1×5 are not needed since the product would be automatically done before the 3 is added. Therefore, we can write

$$1{,}342_{\text{five}} = ((1 \times 5 + 3) \times 5 + 4) \times 5 + 2.$$

This series of products and sums is easily done as an uninterrupted sequence of operations on a calculator, with no intermediate results written down. The same thing works for converting to base ten from any other base. The procedure is summarized as follows.

Calculator Shortcut

To convert from another base to decimal form: Start with the first digit on the left and multiply by the base. Then add the next digit, multiply again by the base, and so on. The last step is to add the last digit on the right. Do *not* multiply it by the base.

Exactly how you accomplish these steps depends on the type of calculator you use. With some, only the digits, the multiplications, and the additions need to be entered, in order. With others, you may need to press the $\boxed{=}$ key following each addition of a digit. If you handle grouped expressions on your calculator by actually entering parentheses, then enter the expression just as illustrated above, and in the following example. (The number of left parentheses to start with will be two fewer than the number of digits in the original numeral.)

EXAMPLE 2   Use the calculator shortcut to convert $244{,}314_{\text{five}}$ to decimal form.

$$244{,}314_{\text{five}} = ((((2 \times 5 + 4) \times 5 + 4) \times 5 + 3) \times 5 + 1) \times 5 + 4$$
$$= 9{,}334. \quad \bullet$$

Knowledge of the base five place values (the powers of five, as in Table 3) enables us to convert from decimal form to base five as in the next example.

EXAMPLE 3   Convert 497 from decimal form to base five.

The base five place values, starting from the right, are 1, 5, 25, 125, 625, and so on. Since 497 is between 125 and 625, it will require no 625s, but some 125s, as well as possibly some 25s, 5s, and 1s. Dividing 497 by 125 determines the proper number of 125s. The quotient is 3, with remainder 122. So we need three 125s. Next, the remainder, 122, is divided by 25 (the next place value) to find the proper number of 25s. The quotient is 4, with remainder 22, so we need four 25s. Dividing 22 by 5 yields 4, with remainder 2. So we need four 5s. Dividing 2 by 1 yields 2 (with remainder 0), so we need two 1s. Finally, we see that 497 consists of three 125s, four 25s, four 5s, and two 1s, so $497 = 3{,}442_{\text{five}}$.

Trick or Tree? The octal number 31 is equal to the decimal number 25. This may be written as

   31 OCT = 25 DEC

Does this mean that Halloween and Christmas fall on the same day of the year?

Yin-yang The binary (base two) symbols of the *I Ching*, 2,000-year-old Chinese classic, permute into 8 elemental trigrams; 64 hexagrams are interpreted in casting oracles.

The basic symbol here is the ancient Chinese "yin-yang," in which the black and the white enfold each other, each containing a part of the other. A kind of duality is conveyed between destructive (yin) and beneficial (yang) aspects. Leibniz (1646–1716) studied Chinese ideograms in search of a universal symbolic language and promoted East-West cultural contact. He saw parallels between the trigrams and his binary arithmetic.

Niels Bohr (1885–1962), famous Danish Nobel laureate in physics (atomic theory), adopted the yin-yang symbol in his coat of arms to depict his principle of *complementarity*, which he believed was fundamental to reality at the deepest levels. Bohr also pushed for East-West cooperation.

(In its 1992 edition, The World Book Dictionary first judged "yin-yang" to have been used enough to become a permanent part of our ever-changing language, assigning it the definition, "made up of opposites.")

More concisely, this process can be written as follows.

$$497 \div 125 = 3 \qquad \text{Remainder } 122$$
$$122 \div 25 = 4 \qquad \text{Remainder } 22$$
$$22 \div 5 = 4 \qquad \text{Remainder } 2$$
$$2 \div 1 = 2 \qquad \text{Remainder } 0$$
$$497 = 3{,}442_{\text{five}}.$$

Check the answer:

$$3{,}442_{\text{five}} = (3 \times 125) + (4 \times 25) + (4 \times 5) + (2 \times 1)$$
$$= 375 + 100 + 20 + 2$$
$$= 497. \quad \blacklozenge$$

The calculator shortcut for converting from another base to decimal form involved repeated *multiplications* by the other base. (See Example 2.) A shortcut for converting from decimal form to another base makes use of repeated *divisions* by the other base. Just divide the original decimal numeral, and the resulting quotients in turn, by the desired base until the quotient 0 appears.

EXAMPLE 4 Repeat Example 3 using the shortcut just described.

Remainder

$$
\begin{array}{r|l}
5 & 497 \\
5 & 99 \leftarrow \qquad 2 \\
5 & 19 \leftarrow \qquad 4 \\
5 & 3 \leftarrow \qquad 4 \\
& 0 \leftarrow \qquad 3
\end{array}
$$

Read the answer from the remainder column, reading from the bottom up:

$$497 = 3{,}442_{\text{five}}. \quad \blacklozenge$$

To see why this shortcut works, notice the following:

The first division shows that four hundred ninety-seven 1s are equivalent to ninety-nine 5s and two 1s. (The two 1s are set aside and account for the last digit of the answer.)

The second division shows that ninety-nine 5s are equivalent to nineteen 25s and four 5s. (The four 5s account for the next digit of the answer.)

The third division shows that nineteen 25s are equivalent to three 125s and four 25s. (The four 25s account for the next digit of the answer.)

The fourth (and final) division shows that the three 125s are equivalent to no 625s and three 125s. The remainders, as they are obtained *from top to bottom*, give the number of 1s, then 5s, then 25s, then 125s.

The methods for converting between bases ten and five, including the shortcuts, can be adapted for conversions between base ten and any other base, as illustrated in the following examples.

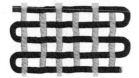

Woven fabric is a binary system of threads going lengthwise (warp threads—white in the diagram above) and threads going crosswise (weft, or woof). At any point in a fabric, either warp or weft is on top, and the variation creates the pattern.

Weaving is done on a loom, and there must be some way to lift the warp threads wherever the pattern dictates. Nineteenth-century looms operated using punched cards, "programmed" for pattern. The looms were set up with hooked needles, the hooks holding the warp. Where there were holes in cards, the needles moved, the warp lifted, the weft passed under. Where no holes were, the warp did not lift, and the weft was on top. The system parallels the on-off system in calculators and computers. In fact, the looms described here were models in the development of modern calculating machinery.

Joseph Marie Jacquard (1752–1823) is credited with improving the mechanical loom so that mass production of fabric was feasible.

EXAMPLE 5   Convert $6{,}343_{\text{seven}}$ to decimal form, by expanding in powers, and by using the calculator shortcut.

$$6{,}343_{\text{seven}} = (6 \times 7^3) + (3 \times 7^2) + (4 \times 7^1) + (3 \times 7^0)$$
$$= (6 \times 343) + (3 \times 49) + (4 \times 7) + (3 \times 1)$$
$$= 2{,}058 + 147 + 28 + 3$$
$$= 2{,}236$$

Calculator shortcut:

$$6{,}343_{\text{seven}} = ((6 \times 7 + 3) \times 7 + 4) \times 7 + 3 = 2{,}236. \quad \bullet$$

EXAMPLE 6   Convert 7,508 to base seven.

Divide 7,508 by 7, then divide the resulting quotient by 7, and so on, until a quotient of 0 results.

Remainder

$$
\begin{array}{r|r}
7 & 7{,}508 \\
7 & 1{,}072 \leftarrow \quad 4 \\
7 & 153 \leftarrow \quad 1 \\
7 & 21 \leftarrow \quad 6 \\
7 & 3 \leftarrow \quad 0 \\
& 0 \leftarrow \quad 3
\end{array}
$$

From the remainders, reading bottom to top, $7{,}508 = 30{,}614_{\text{seven}}$. $\bullet$

Because we are accustomed to doing arithmetic in base ten, most of us would handle conversions between arbitrary bases (where neither is ten) by going from the given base to base ten and then to the desired base. This method is illustrated in the next example.

EXAMPLE 7   Convert $3{,}164_{\text{seven}}$ to base five.

First convert to decimal form.

$$3{,}164_{\text{seven}} = (3 \times 7^3) + (1 \times 7^2) + (6 \times 7^1) + (4 \times 7^0)$$
$$= (3 \times 343) + (1 \times 49) + (6 \times 7) + (4 \times 1)$$
$$= 1{,}029 + 49 + 42 + 4$$
$$= 1{,}124.$$

Next convert this decimal result to base five.

Remainder

$$
\begin{array}{r|r}
5 & 1{,}124 \\
5 & 224 \leftarrow \quad 4 \\
5 & 44 \leftarrow \quad 4 \\
5 & 8 \leftarrow \quad 4 \\
5 & 1 \leftarrow \quad 3 \\
& 0 \leftarrow \quad 1
\end{array}
$$

From the remainders, $3{,}164_{\text{seven}} = 13{,}444_{\text{five}}$. $\bullet$

Computer Mathematics

There are three alternative base systems that are most useful in computer applications. These are the **binary** (base two), **octal** (base eight), and **hexadecimal** (base sixteen) systems. Computers and handheld calculators actually use the binary system for their internal calculations since that system consists of only two symbols, 0 and 1. All numbers can then be represented by electronic "switches," of one kind or another, where "on" indicates 1 and "off" indicates 0. The octal system is used extensively by programmers who work with internal computer codes. In a computer, the CPU (central processing unit) often uses the hexadecimal system to communicate with a printer or other output device.

The binary system is extreme in that it has only two available symbols (0 and 1); because of this, representing numbers in binary form requires more digits than in any other base. Table 5 shows the whole numbers up to 20 expressed in binary form.

Conversions between any of these three special base systems (binary, octal, and hexadecimal) and the decimal system can be done by the methods already discussed, including the shortcut methods.

TABLE 5

Base Ten (decimal)	Base Two (binary)
0	0
1	1
2	10
3	11
4	100
5	101
6	110
7	111
8	1,000
9	1,001
10	1,010
11	1,011
12	1,100
13	1,101
14	1,110
15	1,111
16	10,000
17	10,001
18	10,010
19	10,011
20	10,100

EXAMPLE 8 Convert $110,101_{two}$ to decimal form, by expanding in powers, and by using the calculator shortcut.

$$110,101_{two} = (1 \times 2^5) + (1 \times 2^4) + (0 \times 2^3) + (1 \times 2^2) + (0 \times 2^1) + (1 \times 2^0)$$
$$= (1 \times 32) + (1 \times 16) + (0 \times 8) + (1 \times 4) + (0 \times 2) + (1 \times 1)$$
$$= 32 + 16 + 0 + 4 + 0 + 1$$
$$= 53.$$

Calculator shortcut:

$$110,101_{two} = ((((1 \times 2 + 1) \times 2 + 0) \times 2 + 1) \times 2 + 0) \times 2 + 1$$
$$= 53. \quad \blacklozenge$$

EXAMPLE 9 Convert 9,583 to octal form.

Divide repeatedly by 8, writing the remainders at the side.

Remainder

```
8 | 9,583
 8 | 1,197  ←――――  7
  8 |  149  ←――――  5
   8 |  18  ←――――  5
    8 |  2  ←――――  2
       0  ←――――  2
```

From the remainders, $9,583 = 22,557_{eight}$. $\blacklozenge$

The hexadecimal system, having base 16, which is greater than 10, presents a new problem. Since distinct symbols are needed for every whole number from 0 up to one less than the base, base sixteen requires more symbols than are normally used in our decimal system. Computer programmers commonly use the letters A, B, C, D, E, and F as hexadecimal digits for the numbers ten through fifteen, respectively.

EXAMPLE 10 Convert FA5$_{\text{sixteen}}$ to decimal form.

Since the hexadecimal digits F and A represent 15 and 10, respectively,

$$\text{FA5}_{\text{sixteen}} = (15 \times 16^2) + (10 \times 16^1) + (5 \times 16^0)$$
$$= 3{,}840 + 160 + 5$$
$$= 4{,}005. \quad \bullet$$

EXAMPLE 11 Convert 748 from decimal form to hexadecimal form.

Use repeated division by 16.

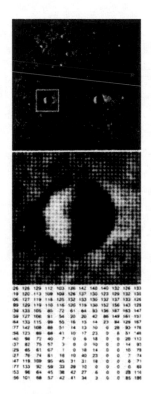

$$
\begin{array}{r}
16\,\lfloor\,748 \\
16\,\lfloor\,46 \\
16\,\lfloor\,2 \\
0
\end{array}
$$

Remainder / Hexadecimal notation

12 ← C
14 ← E
2 ← 2

From the remainders at the right, $748 = 2EC_{\text{sixteen}}$. ●

The decimal whole numbers 0 through 17 are shown in Table 6 along with their equivalents in the common computer-oriented bases (two, eight, and sixteen). Conversions among binary, octal, and hexadecimal systems can generally be accomplished by the shortcuts explained below, and are illustrated in the next several examples.

Photographs from Space
Spacecraft typically do not use ordinary photographic film. Instead, electronic sensors break an image into tiny spots, called *pixels*. Each pixel is assigned a number representing its brightness—0 for pure white and 63 for pure black, for example. These numbers are then sent back to Earth as binary digits, from 000000 to 111111. A computer then uses these binary digits to recreate the scene. (See Exercises 84 and 85 at the end of this section.)

TABLE 6 Some Decimal Equivalents in the Common Computer-Oriented Bases

Decimal (Base Ten)	Hexadecimal (Base Sixteen)	Octal (Base Eight)	Binary (Base Two)
0	0	0	0
1	1	1	1
2	2	2	10
3	3	3	11
4	4	4	100
5	5	5	101
6	6	6	110
7	7	7	111
8	8	10	1,000
9	9	11	1,001
10	A	12	1,010
11	B	13	1,011
12	C	14	1,100
13	D	15	1,101
14	E	16	1,110
15	F	17	1,111
16	10	20	10,000
17	11	21	10,001

Converting Calculators
A number of scientific calculators are available that will convert between decimal, binary, octal, and hexadecimal, and will also do calculations directly in all of these separate modes. Some examples are the Texas Instrument TI-35 PLUS, the Radio Shack EC-4014, the Casio FX-3600P, and the Hewlett-Packard 28S.

TABLE 7

Octal	Binary
0	000
1	001
2	010
3	011
4	100
5	101
6	110
7	111

TABLE 8

Hexadecimal	Binary
0	0000
1	0001
2	0010
3	0011
4	0100
5	0101
6	0110
7	0111
8	1000
9	1001
A	1010
B	1011
C	1100
D	1101
E	1110
F	1111

The binary system is the natural one for internal computer workings because of its compatibility with the two-state electronic switches. It is very cumbersome, however, for human use, because so many digits occur even in the numerals for relatively small numbers. The octal and hexadecimal systems are the choices of computer programmers mainly because of their close relationship with the binary system. *Both eight and sixteen are powers of two.* And when base conversions involve one base that is a power of the other, there is a quick conversion shortcut available. For example, since $8 = 2^3$, every octal digit (0 through 7) can be expressed as a 3-digit binary numeral. See Table 7.

EXAMPLE 12   Convert 473_{eight} to binary form.

Replace each octal digit with its 3-digit binary equivalent. (Leading zeros can be omitted only when they occur in the leftmost group.) Then combine all the binary equivalents into a single binary numeral.

$$
\begin{array}{ccc}
4 & 7 & 3_{eight} \\
\downarrow & \downarrow & \downarrow \\
100 & 111 & 011_{two}
\end{array}
$$

By this method, $473_{eight} = 100{,}111{,}011_{two}$. ◆

Convert from binary form to octal form in a similar way. Start at the right and break the binary numeral into groups of three digits. (Leading zeros in the leftmost group may be omitted.)

EXAMPLE 13   Convert $10{,}011{,}110_{two}$ to octal form.

Starting at the right, break the digits into groups of three. Then convert the groups to their octal equivalents.

$$
\begin{array}{ccc}
10 & 011 & 110_{two} \\
\downarrow & \downarrow & \downarrow \\
2 & 3 & 6_{eight}
\end{array}
$$

Finally, $10{,}011{,}110_{two} = 236_{eight}$. ◆

Since $16 = 2^4$, every hexadecimal digit can be equated to a 4-digit binary numeral (see Table 8), and conversions between binary and hexadecimal forms can be done in a manner similar to that used in Examples 12 and 13.

EXAMPLE 14   Convert $8{,}B4F_{sixteen}$ to binary form.

Each hexadecimal digit yields a 4-digit binary equivalent.

$$
\begin{array}{cccc}
8 & B & 4 & F_{sixteen} \\
\downarrow & \downarrow & \downarrow & \downarrow \\
1000 & 1011 & 0100 & 1111_{two}
\end{array}
$$

Combining these groups of digits, we see that

$$8{,}B4F_{sixteen} = 1{,}000{,}101{,}101{,}001{,}111_{two}. ◆$$

TABLE 9

A	B	C	D
1	2	4	8
3	3	5	9
5	6	6	10
7	7	7	11
9	10	12	12
11	11	13	13
13	14	14	14
15	15	15	15

Several games and tricks are based on the binary system. For example, Table 9 can be used to find the age of a person 15 years old or younger. The person need only tell you the columns that contain his or her age. For example, suppose Francisco says that his age appears in columns B and D only. To find his age, add the numbers from the top row of these columns:

Francisco is 2 + 8 = 10 years old.

Do you see how this trick works? If not, you can get help in Exercises 70–73.

FOR FURTHER THOUGHT

Julie Rislov, produce buyer for a supermarket, has received five large bins filled with bags of carrots. All bins should be filled with 10-pound bags of carrots, but Julie has learned that, through an error, some of the bins are filled with 9-pound bags. Julie's assistant, Dusty Rainbolt, claims that he can pile some bags from all five bins together on the scale and, from just a single weighing of them, tell exactly which bins have the 9-pound bags.

For Group Discussion
1. Remembering binary notation, verify the following: Every counting number can be broken down into ones, twos, fours, eights, sixteens, etc., with no more than one of each power of two needed.
2. Explain how Dusty can make good on his claim.

3 EXERCISES

List the first twenty counting numbers in each of the following bases.

1. seven (Only digits 0 through 6 are used in base seven.)

2. eight (Only digits 0 through 7 are used.)

3. nine (Only digits 0 through 8 are used.)

4. sixteen (The digits 0, 1, 2, . . . , 9, A, B, C, D, E, F are used in base sixteen.)

For each of the following, write (in the same base) the counting numbers just before and just after the given number. (Do not convert to base ten.)

5. 14_{five} 6. 555_{six} 7. $B6F_{\text{sixteen}}$ 8. $10,111_{\text{two}}$

Determine the number of distinct symbols needed in each of the following positional systems.

9. base three   10. base seven   11. base eleven   12. base sixteen

Determine, in each of the following bases, the smallest and largest four-digit numbers and their decimal equivalents.

13. three   14. sixteen

Convert each of the following to decimal form by expanding in powers and by using the calculator shortcut. (See Examples 1, 2, 5, 8, and 10.)

15. 24_{five} 16. 62_{seven} 17. $1,011_{\text{two}}$ 18. 35_{eight}

19. $3BC_{\text{sixteen}}$ 20. $34,432_{\text{five}}$ 21. $2,366_{\text{seven}}$ 22. $101,101,110_{\text{two}}$

23. $70,266_{\text{eight}}$ 24. A,BCD_{sixteen} 25. $2,023_{\text{four}}$ 26. $6,185_{\text{nine}}$

27. $41,533_{\text{six}}$ 28. $88,703_{\text{nine}}$

Convert each of the following from decimal form to the given base. (See Examples 3, 4, 6, 9, and 11.)

29. 86 to base five

30. 65 to base seven

31. 19 to base two

32. 935 to base eight

33. 147 to base sixteen

34. 2,730 to base sixteen

35. 36,401 to base five

36. 70,893 to base seven

37. 586 to base two

38. 12,888 to base eight

39. 8,407 to base three

40. 11,028 to base four

41. 9,346 to base six

42. 99,999 to base nine

Make the following conversions as indicated. (See Example 7.)

43. 43_{five} to base seven

44. 27_{eight} to base five

45. $C02_{\text{sixteen}}$ to base seven

46. $6,748_{\text{nine}}$ to base four

Convert each of the following from octal form to binary form. (See Example 12.)

47. 367_{eight}

48. $2,406_{\text{eight}}$

Convert each of the following from binary form to octal form. (See Example 13.)

49. $100,110,111_{\text{two}}$

50. $11,010,111,101_{\text{two}}$

Make the following conversions as indicated. (See Example 14.)

51. DC_{sixteen} to binary

52. $F,111_{\text{sixteen}}$ to binary

53. $101,101_{\text{two}}$ to hexadecimal

54. $101,111,011,101,000_{\text{two}}$ to hexadecimal

Identify the largest number from each list in Exercises 55 and 56.

55. $42_{\text{seven}}, 37_{\text{eight}}, 1D_{\text{sixteen}}$

56. $1,101,110_{\text{two}}, 407_{\text{five}}, 6F_{\text{sixteen}}$

Some people think that twelve would be a better base than ten. This is mainly because twelve has more divisors (1, 2, 3, 4, 6, 12) than ten (1, 2, 5, 10), which makes fractions easier in base twelve. The base twelve system is called the duodecimal *system. Just as in the decimal system we speak of a one, a ten, and a hundred (and so on), in the duodecimal system we say a* one, *a* dozen *(twelve), and a* gross *(twelve squared, or one hundred forty-four).*

57. Altogether, Otis Taylor's clients ordered 9 gross, 10 dozen, and 11 copies of *Math for Base Runners* during the last week of January. How many copies was that in base ten?

One very common method of converting symbols into binary digits for computer processing is called ASCII (American Standard Code of Information Interchange). The upper case letters A through Z are assigned the numbers 65 through 90, so A has binary code 1000001 and Z has code 1011010. Lowercase letters a through z have codes 97 through 122 (that is, 1100001 through 1111010). ASCII codes, as well as other numerical computer output, normally appear without commas.

Write the binary code for each of the following letters.

58. *C*

59. *X*

60. *k*

61. *r*

Break each of the following into groups of seven digits and write as letters.

62. 100100010001011001100101 0000

63. 1000011100100010101011000011 1001011

Translate each word into an ASCII string of binary digits. (Be sure to distinguish upper and lower case letters.)

64. New

65. Orleans

66. Explain why the octal and hexadecimal systems are convenient for people who code for computers.

67. There are thirty-seven counting numbers whose base eight numerals contain two digits but whose base three numerals contain four digits. Find the smallest and largest of these numbers.

68. What is the smallest counting number (expressed in base ten) that would require six digits in its base nine representation?

69. In a pure decimal (base ten) monetary system, the first three denominations needed are pennies, dimes, and dollars. Name the first three denominations of a base five monetary system.

Refer to Table 9 for Exercises 70–73.

70. After observing the binary forms of the numbers 1–15 (Table 5), identify a common property of all Table 9 numbers in each of the following columns.
   (a) Column A   **(b)** Column B   **(c)** Column C   **(d)** Column D

71. Explain how the "trick" of Table 9 works.

72. Extend Table 9 so that it will accommodate any age up to 31 years.

73. How many rows would be needed for Table 9 to include all ages up to 63?

In our decimal system, we distinguish odd and even numbers by looking at their ones (or units) digit. If the ones digit is even (0, 2, 4, 6, or 8) the number is even. If the ones digit is odd (1, 3, 5, 7, or 9) the number is odd. For Exercises 74–83, determine whether this same criterion works for numbers expressed in the given bases.

74. two   **75.** three   **76.** four   **77.** five

78. six   **79.** seven   **80.** eight   **81.** nine

82. all even bases. If it works for all, explain why. If not, find a criterion that does work for all even bases.

83. all odd bases. If it works for all, explain why. If not, find a criterion that does work for all odd bases.

Photographic Dots
A printed page works in much the same way that photographs are sent from space. At each point on a printed page, there is either ink or there is no ink. Similarly, black and white photographs are reproduced as a series of small dots, either black or white; the dots are so fine as to give the illusion of a continuous tone.

Photographs from space often are sent back to earth by being broken down into tiny spots called pixels, each represented by a binary number representing its brightness.

84. Suppose a photograph is divided into 1,000 pixels horizontally and 500 vertically. How many pixels is this altogether?

85. Each pixel requires six binary digits for transmission to earth. How many digits would be needed altogether?

86. What is the rule for telling when a base ten numeral represents a number that is divisible by ten?

Use the results of Exercise 86 to help you decide the answers to Exercises 87 and 88.

87. Which of the following base five numerals represent numbers that are divisible by five?

$$3,204, \quad 200, \quad 342, \quad 2,310, \quad 3,041$$

88. Which of the following base sixteen numerals represent numbers that are divisible by sixteen?

$$72, \quad 1B8, \quad F60, \quad 3A0, \quad E94, \quad B,0B0, \quad 1,994$$

4

Clock Arithmetic and Modular Systems

Recall from the introduction to this chapter that a "mathematical system" consists of (1) a set of elements, along with (2) one or more operations for combining those elements, and (3) one or more relations for comparing those elements. The chapter so far has dealt with the set of counting numbers (an infinite set), and with basic questions about them: how to denote them, and how to perform the arithmetic operations on them. In the remaining sections of the chapter, some of the more familiar properties of mathematical operations will be encountered in the context of some not-so-familiar systems, built mostly upon finite sets.

The first nontraditional system of this section, called the **12-hour clock system,** is based on an ordinary clock face, with the difference that 12 is replaced with 0 and the minute hand is left off. See Figure 5.

Plus 2 hours
$5 + 2 = 7$

FIGURE 5   **FIGURE 6**

The clock face yields the finite set {0, 1, 2, 3, 4, 5, 6, 7, 8, 9, 10, 11}. As an operation for this clock system, define addition as follows: add by moving the hour hand in a clockwise direction. For example, to add 5 and 2 on a clock, first move the hour hand to 5, as in Figure 6. Then, to add 2, move the hour hand 2 more hours in a clockwise direction. The hand stops at 7, so

$$5 + 2 = 7.$$

This result agrees with traditional addition. However, the sum of two numbers from the 12-hour clock system is not always what might be expected, as the following example shows.

EXAMPLE 1   Find each sum in clock arithmetic.

(a) $8 + 9$

Move the hour hand to 8, as in Figure 7. Then advance the hand clockwise through 9 more hours. It stops at 5, so that

$$8 + 9 = 5.$$

(b) $11 + 3$

Proceed as shown in Figure 8. Check that

$$11 + 3 = 2. \quad ⬡$$

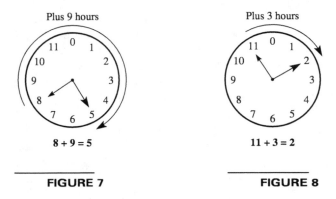

Plus 9 hours	Plus 3 hours
$8 + 9 = 5$	$11 + 3 = 2$
FIGURE 7	**FIGURE 8**

Since there are infinitely many whole numbers, it is not possible to write a complete table of addition facts for that set. Such a table, to show the sum of every possible pair of whole numbers, would have an infinite number of rows and columns, making it impossible to construct.

On the other hand, the 12-hour clock system uses only the whole numbers 0, 1, 2, 3, 4, 5, 6, 7, 8, 9, 10, and 11. A table of all possible sums for this system requires only 12 rows and 12 columns. The 12-hour clock **addition table** is shown in Table 10. (The significance of the colored diagonal line will be discussed later.) Since the 12-hour system is built upon a finite set, it is called a **finite mathematical system.**

TABLE 10   Table for 12-Hour Clock Addition

+	0	1	2	3	4	5	6	7	8	9	10	11
0	0	1	2	3	4	5	6	7	8	9	10	11
1	1	2	3	4	5	6	7	8	9	10	11	0
2	2	3	4	5	6	7	8	9	10	11	0	1
3	3	4	5	6	7	8	9	10	11	0	1	2
4	4	5	6	7	8	9	10	11	0	1	2	3
5	5	6	7	8	9	10	11	0	1	2	3	4
6	6	7	8	9	10	11	0	1	2	3	4	5
7	7	8	9	10	11	0	1	2	3	4	5	6
8	8	9	10	11	0	1	2	3	4	5	6	7
9	9	10	11	0	1	2	3	4	5	6	7	8
10	10	11	0	1	2	3	4	5	6	7	8	9
11	11	0	1	2	3	4	5	6	7	8	9	10

| EXAMPLE 2 | Use the 12-hour clock addition table to find each sum.

(a) $7 + 11$

Find 7 on the left of the addition table and 11 across the top. The intersection of the row headed 7 and the column headed 11 gives the number 6. Thus, $7 + 11 = 6$.

(b) Also from the table, $11 + 1 = 0$. ●

ASCENSION

Until the mid-1700s, sailors had no accurate way of telling their **longitude,** their east-west position on the earth (they had fairly accurate star charts which would tell them the latitude, or north-south position). The British government offered a prize for a method of finding longitude; the winner was Harrison's Chronometer, a very accurate clock. Not surprisingly, Harrison had a difficult time collecting the prize money from the government.

So far, our 12-hour clock system consists of the set {0, 1, 2, 3, 4, 5, 6, 7, 8, 9, 10, 11}, together with the operation of clock addition. Table 10 shows that the sum of two numbers on a clock face is always a number on the clock face. In other words: if a and b are any clock numbers in the set of the system, the $a + b$ is also in the set of the system. This is called the **closure property** for clock addition. (The set of the system is said to be *closed* under addition.)

Notice also that in this system, $6 + 8$ and $8 + 6$ both yield 2. Also $7 + 11$ and $11 + 7$ both yield 6. The order of the elements being added does not seem to matter. For any clock numbers a and b, $a + b = b + a$. This is called the **commutative property** of clock addition.

A quick way to test a finite system for commutativity is to draw a diagonal line through the table of the system, from upper left to lower right (as was done in Table 10). If the part of the table *above* the diagonal is a mirror image of the part *below* the diagonal, the system has the commutative property. Notice in Table 10 that wherever a given number occurs in the body of the chart, that same number also occurs straight through the diagonal, the same distance to the other side.

A third important property that holds in many mathematical systems is the **associative property,** which says that whenever three elements are combined in a given order, it does not matter whether the initial combination involves the first and second or the second and third; symbolically (for addition):

$$(a + b) + c = a + (b + c).$$

| EXAMPLE 3 | Is 12-hour clock addition associative?

It would take lots of work to prove that the required relationship *always* holds. But a few examples should either disprove it (by revealing a *counterexample*—a case where it fails to hold), or should make it at least plausible. Using the clock numbers 4, 5, and 9, we see that

$$(4 + 5) + 9 = 9 + 9 \qquad 4 + (5 + 9) = 4 + 2$$
$$= 6 \qquad\qquad\qquad = 6.$$

Thus, $(4 + 5) + 9 = 4 + (5 + 9)$. Try another example:

$$(7 + 6) + 3 = 1 + 3 \qquad 7 + (6 + 3) = 7 + 9$$
$$= 4 \qquad\qquad\qquad = 4.$$

So $(7 + 6) + 3 = 7 + (6 + 3)$. Any other examples tried would also work. Clock addition *does* satisfy the associative property. ●

The fourth property we consider here is the **identity property.** A system satisfying the identity property must include in its set an element which, when combined with any element (in either order), produces that same element. That is, the identity element e (for addition) must satisfy $a + e = a$ and $e + a = a$ for any element a of the system. Notice in the clock addition table (Table 10) that $4 + 0 = 0 + 4 = 4$, $6 + 0 = 0 + 6 = 6$, and so on. The number 0 is the identity element (just as for ordinary addition of whole numbers), so that clock addition *does* satisfy the identity property.

Generally, if a finite system has an identity element e, it can be located easily in the operation table. Check the body of Table 10 for a column that is identical to the column at the left side of the table. Since the column under 0 meets this requirement, $a + 0 = a$ holds for all elements a in the system. Thus 0 is *possibly* the identity. Now locate 0 at the left of the table. Since the corresponding row is identical to the row at the top of the table, $0 + a = a$ also holds for all elements a, which is the other requirement of an identity element. Hence 0 is *indeed* the identity.

Subtraction can be performed on a 12-hour clock. Subtraction may be interpreted on the clock face by a movement in the counterclockwise direction. For example, to perform the subtraction $2 - 5$, begin at 2 and move 5 hours counterclockwise, ending at 9, as shown in Figure 9. Therefore, in this system,

$$2 - 5 = 9.$$

In our usual system, subtraction may be checked by addition and this is also the case in clock arithmetic. To check that $2 - 5 = 9$, simply add $9 + 5$. The result on the clock face is 2, verifying the accuracy of this subtraction.

The *additive inverse*, $-a$, of an element a in clock arithmetic, is the element that satisfies the following statement: $a + (-a) = 0$ and $(-a) + a = 0$. The next example examines this idea.

Minus 5 hours

$2 - 5 = 9$

FIGURE 9

EXAMPLE 4 Determine the additive inverse of 5 in clock arithmetic.

The additive inverse for the clock number 5 is a number x such that

$$5 + x = 0.$$

Going from 5 to 0 on the clock face requires 7 more hours, so

$$5 + 7 = 0.$$

This means that 7 is the additive inverse of 5. ●

The method used in Example 4 may be used to verify that *every* element of the system has an additive inverse (also in the system). This is called the **inverse property** of clock addition.

Another simpler way to verify the inverse property, once you have the table, is to make sure the identity element appears exactly once in each row, and that the pair of elements that produces it also produces it in the opposite order. (This last condition is automatically true if the commutative property holds for the system.) For example, note in Table 10 that row 3 contains one 0, under the 9, so $3 + 9 = 0$, and that row 9 contains one 0, under the 3, so $9 + 3 = 0$ also. Therefore, 3 and 9 are inverses.

The following chart lists the elements and their additive inverses. Notice that one element, 6, is its own inverse for addition.

Clock value a	0	1	2	3	4	5	6	7	8	9	10	11
Additive inverse $-a$	0	11	10	9	8	7	6	5	4	3	2	1

Using the additive inverse symbol, we can say that in clock arithmetic,

$$-5 = 7, \qquad -11 = 1, \qquad -10 = 2,$$

and so on.

Subtraction on a Clock

If a and b are elements in clock arithmetic,

$$a - b = a + (-b).$$

Now that additive inverses have been discussed, a formal definition of subtraction in clock arithmetic may be given. Notice that it is the same definition that is used in our usual system. Use the definition of subtraction.

The additive inverse of 5 is 7, from the table of inverses.

EXAMPLE 5 Find each of the following differences.

(a) $8 - 5 = 8 + (-5)$
$\qquad = 8 + 7$
$8 - 5 = 3$

This result agrees with traditional arithmetic. Check by adding 5 and 3; the sum is 8.

(b) $6 - 11 = 6 + (-11)$
$\qquad = 6 + 1$
$6 - 11 = 7$ ●

Clock numbers can also be multiplied. For example, find the product 5×4 by adding 4 a total of 5 times:

$$5 \times 4 = 4 + 4 + 4 + 4 + 4 = 8.$$

EXAMPLE 6 Find each product, using clock arithmetic.

(a) $6 \times 9 = 9 + 9 + 9 + 9 + 9 + 9 = 6$

(b) $3 \times 4 = 4 + 4 + 4 = 0$

(c) $6 \times 0 = 0 + 0 + 0 + 0 + 0 + 0 = 0$

(d) $0 \times 8 = 0$ ⬢

Some properties of the system of 12-hour clock numbers with the operation of multiplication will be investigated in Exercises 6–8.

We now expand the ideas of clock arithmetic to **modular systems** in general. Recall that 12-hour clock arithmetic was set up so that answers were always whole numbers less than 12. For example, $8 + 6 = 2$. The traditional sum, $8 + 6 = 14$, reflects the fact that moving the clock hand forward 8 hours from 0,

and then forward another 6 hours, amounts to moving it forward 14 hours total. But since the final position of the clock hand is at 2, we see that 14 and 2 are, in a sense, equivalent. More formally we say that 14 and 2 are **congruent modulo** 12, which is written

$$14 \equiv 2 \ (\text{mod } 12) \qquad (\text{The sign} \equiv \text{indicates } congruence.)$$

By observing clock hand movements, you can also see that, for example,

---

Congruence Modulo m

The integers a and b are **congruent modulo** m (where m is a natural number greater than 1 called the **modulus**) if and only if the difference $a - b$ is divisible by m. Symbolically, this congruence is written

$$a \equiv b \ (\textbf{mod } m).$$

$$26 \equiv 2 \ (\text{mod } 12), \qquad 38 \equiv 2 \ (\text{mod } 12), \qquad \text{and so on.}$$

In each case, the congruence is true because the difference of two congruent numbers is a multiple of 12:

$$14 - 2 = 12 = 1 \times 12, \qquad 26 - 2 = 24 = 2 \times 12, \qquad 38 - 2 = 36 = 3 \times 12.$$

This suggests the following definition.

Since being divisible by m is the same as being a multiple of m, we can say that

$$a \equiv b \ (\text{mod } m) \text{ if and only if } a - b = km \text{ for some integer } k.$$

The basic ideas of congruence were introduced by Karl F. Gauss in 1801, when he was twenty-four years old.

Chess Clock The double clock shown here is used to time chess, backgammon, and scrabble games. Push one button, and that clock stops—the other begins simultaneously. When a player's allotted time for the game has expired, that player will lose if he or she has not made the required number of moves.

Mathematics and chess are often thought to be closely related. Actually that is not so. Both arts demand logical thinking. Chess requires psychological acumen and knowledge of the opponent. No mathematical knowledge is needed in chess.

Emanuel Lasker was able to achieve mastery in both fields. He is best known as a World Chess Champion for 27 years, until 1921. Lasker also was famous in mathematical circles for his work concerning the theory of primary ideals, algebraic analogies of prime numbers. An important result, the Lasker-Noether theorem, bears his name along with that of Emmy Noether. Noether extended Lasker's work. Her father had been Lasker's Ph.D. advisor.

EXAMPLE 7   Mark each statement as *true* or *false*.

(a) $16 \equiv 10 \ (\text{mod } 2)$
The difference $16 - 10 = 6$ is divisible by 2, so $16 \equiv 10 \ (\text{mod } 2)$ is true.

(b) $49 \equiv 32 \ (\text{mod } 5)$
False, since $49 - 32 = 17$, which is not divisible by 5.

Criterion for Congruence

$a \equiv b \pmod{m}$ if and only if the same remainder is obtained when a and b are divided by m.

G. H. Hardy (1877–1947) worked at Cambridge University in England on problems in number theory. He also wrote books, such as *A Mathematician's Apology*, explaining mathematics for the general public.

(c) $30 \equiv 345 \pmod 7$

True, since $30 - 345 = -315$ is divisible by 7. (It doesn't matter if we find $30 - 345$ or $345 - 30$.) ●

There is another method of determining if two numbers, a and b, are congruent modulo m.

For example, we know that $27 \equiv 9 \pmod 6$ because $27 - 9 = 18$, which is divisible by 6. Now, if 27 is divided by 6, the quotient is 4 and the remainder is 3. Also, if 9 is divided by 6, the quotient is 1 and the remainder is 3. According to the box above, $27 \equiv 9 \pmod 6$ since the remainder is the same in each case.

Addition, subtraction, and multiplication can be performed in any modulo system just as with clock numbers. Since final answers should be whole numbers less than the modulus, we can first find an answer using ordinary arithmetic. Then, as long as the answer is nonnegative, simply divide it by the modulus and keep the remainder. This produces the smallest nonnegative integer that is congruent (modulo m) to the ordinary answer.

EXAMPLE 8 Find each of the following sums and products.

(a) $(9 + 14) \pmod 3$

First add 9 and 14 to get 23. Then divide 23 by 3. The remainder is 2, so $23 \equiv 2 \pmod 3$ and

$$(9 + 14) \equiv 2 \pmod 3.$$

(b) $(27 - 5) \pmod 6$

$27 - 5 = 22$. Divide 22 by 6, obtaining 4 as a remainder:

$$(27 - 5) \equiv 4 \pmod 6.$$

(c) $(50 + 34) \pmod 7$

$50 + 34 = 84$. When 84 is divided by 7, a remainder of 0 is found:

$$(50 + 34) \equiv 0 \pmod 7.$$

(d) $(8 \times 9) \pmod{10}$

Since $8 \times 9 = 72$, and 72 leaves a remainder of 2 when divided by 10,

$$(8 \times 9) \equiv 2 \pmod{10}.$$

(e) $(12 \times 10) \pmod 5$

$$(12 \times 10) = 120 \equiv 0 \pmod 5 \quad ●$$

Public Codes One application of modulo systems comes from the recently discovered "trapdoor codes" involving a very simple method of encoding a message and an extremely complex method of decoding. In fact, the encoding method is so simple that it can be made public without helping the adversary discover how to decode the message.

PROBLEM SOLVING

Modulo systems can often be applied to questions involving cyclical changes. For example, our method of dividing time into weeks causes the days to repeatedly cycle through the same pattern of seven. Suppose today is Sunday and we want to know what day of the week it will be 45 days from now. Since we don't care how many weeks will pass between now and then, we can discard the largest whole number of weeks in 45 days and keep the remainder. (We are finding the smallest nonnegative integer that is congruent to 45 modulo 7.) Dividing 45 by 7 leaves remainder 3, so the desired day of the week is 3 days past Sunday, or *Wednesday*. ●

EXAMPLE 9   If today is Thursday, November 12, and *next* year is a leap year, what day of the week will it be one year from today?

A modulo 7 system applies here, but we need to know the number of days between today and one year from today. Today's date, November 12, is unimportant except that it shows we are later in the year than the end of February and therefore the next year (starting today) will contain 366 days. (This would not be so if today was, say, January 12.) Now dividing 366 by 7 produces 52 with remainder 2. Two days past Thursday is our answer. That is, one year from today will be a Saturday. ●

Just as in algebra, equations can be solved in modulo systems. A **modulo equation** (or just an *equation*) is a sentence such as $(3 + x) \equiv 5 \pmod 7$ that may or may not be true, depending upon the replacement value of the variable x. A method of solving these equations is given in the examples that follow.

EXAMPLE 10   Solve $(3 + x) \equiv 5 \pmod 7$.

In a modulo 7 system, any integer will be congruent to one of the integers 0, 1, 2, 3, 4, 5, or 6. So, the equation $(3 + x) \equiv 5 \pmod 7$ can be solved by trying, in turn, each of these integers as a replacement for x.

$x = 0$:   Is it true that $(3 + 0) \equiv 5 \pmod 7$?   No

$x = 1$:   Is it true that $(3 + 1) \equiv 5 \pmod 7$?   No

$x = 2$:   Is it true that $(3 + 2) \equiv 5 \pmod 7$?   Yes

Try $x = 3$, $x = 4$, $x = 5$, and $x = 6$ to see that none of them work. Of the integers from 0 through 6, only 2 is a solution of the equation $(3 + x) \equiv 5 \pmod 7$.

Since 2 is a solution, find other solutions to this mod 7 equation by repeatedly adding 7:

$$2$$
$$2 + 7 = 9$$
$$2 + 7 + 7 = 16$$
$$2 + 7 + 7 + 7 = 23,$$

and so on. The set of all positive solutions of $(3 + x) \equiv 5 \pmod 7$ is

$$\{2, 9, 16, 23, 30, 37, \ldots\}. \quad \bullet$$

EXAMPLE 11   Solve the equation $5x \equiv 4 \pmod 9$.

Because the modulus is 9, try 0, 1, 2, 3, 4, 5, 6, 7, and 8:

$$\text{Is it true that } 5 \times 0 \equiv 4 \pmod 9? \quad \text{No}$$
$$\text{Is it true that } 5 \times 1 \equiv 4 \pmod 9? \quad \text{No}$$

Continue trying numbers. You should find that none work except $x = 8$:

$$5 \times 8 = 40 \equiv 4 \pmod 9.$$

The set of all positive solutions to the equation $5x \equiv 4 \pmod 9$ is

$$\{8, 8 + 9, 8 + 9 + 9, 8 + 9 + 9 + 9, \ldots\} \quad \text{or}$$
$$\{8, 17, 26, 35, 44, 53, \ldots\}. \quad \bullet$$

EXAMPLE 12   Solve the equation $6x \equiv 3 \pmod 8$.

Try the numbers 0, 1, 2, 3, 4, 5, 6, and 7. You should find that none work. Therefore, the equation $6x \equiv 3 \pmod 8$ has no solutions at all. Write the set of all solutions as the empty set, $\varnothing$.

This result is reasonable since $6x$ will always be even, no matter which whole number is used for x. Since $6x$ is even and 3 is odd, the difference $6x - 3$ will be odd, and therefore not divisible by 8. $\bullet$

EXAMPLE 13   Solve $8x \equiv 8 \pmod 8$.

Trying the integers 0, 1, 2, 3, 4, 5, 6, and 7 shows that *any* integer can be used as a solution. $\bullet$

An equation like $8x \equiv 8 \pmod 8$ in Example 13 that is true for all values of the variable (x, y, and so on) is called an **identity.** Other examples of identities (in ordinary algebra) include $2x + 3x = 5x$ and $y^2 \cdot y^3 = y^5$.

Some problems can be solved by writing down two or more modulo equations and finding their common solutions. The next example illustrates the process.

EXAMPLE 14   Julio wants to arrange his CD collection in equal size stacks, but after trying stacks of 4, stacks of 5, and stacks of 6, he finds that there is always 1 disc left over. Assuming Julio owns more than one CD, what is the least possible number of discs in his collection?

The given information leads to three modulo equations,

$$x \equiv 1 \pmod 4, \quad x \equiv 1 \pmod 5, \quad x \equiv 1 \pmod 6,$$

FOR FURTHER THOUGHT

A Card Trick

Many card "tricks" that have been around for years are really not tricks at all, but are based on mathematical properties that allow anyone to do them with no special conjuring abilities. One of them is based on modulo 14 arithmetic.

In this trick, suits play no role. Each card has a numerical value: 1 for ace, 2 for two, . . . , 11 for jack, 12 for queen, and 13 for king. The deck is shuffled and given to a spectator who is instructed to place the deck of cards face up on a table, and is told to follow the procedure described: A card is laid down with its face up. (We shall call it the "starter" card.) The starter card will be at the bottom of a pile. In order to form a pile, note the value of the starter card, and then add cards on top of it while counting up to 13. For example, if the starter card is a six, pile up seven cards on top of it. If it is a jack, add two cards to it, and so on.

When the first pile is completed, it is picked up and placed face down. The next card becomes the starter card for the next pile, and the process is repeated. This continues until all cards are used or until there are not enough cards to complete the last pile. Any cards that are left over are put aside for later use. We shall refer to these as "leftovers."

The performer then requests that a spectator choose three piles at random. The remaining piles are added to the leftovers. The spectator is then instructed to turn over any two top cards from the piles. The performer is then able to determine the value of the third top card.

The secret to the trick is that the performer adds the values of the two top cards that were turned over, and then adds 10 to this sum. The performer then counts off this number of cards from the leftovers. The number of cards remaining in the leftovers is the value of the remaining top card!

For Group Discussion

1. Obtain a deck of playing cards and perform the "trick" as described above. (As with many activities, you'll find that doing it is simpler than describing it.) Does it work?
2. Explain why this procedure works. (If you want to see how someone else explained it, using modulo 14 arithmetic, see "An Old Card Trick Revisited," by Barry C. Felps, in the December 1976 issue of *The Mathematics Teacher*.)

4 EXERCISES

Find each of the following differences on the 12-hour clock.

1. $8 - 3$ **2.** $4 - 9$ **3.** $2 - 8$ **4.** $0 - 3$

5. Complete the 12-hour clock multiplication table at the right. You can use repeated addition and the addition table (for example, $3 \times 7 = 7 + 7 + 7 = 2 + 7 = 9$) or use modulo 12 multiplication techniques, as in Example 8, parts (d) and (e).

×	0	1	2	3	4	5	6	7	8	9	10	11
0	0	0	0	0	0	0	0	0	0	0	0	0
1	0	1	2	3	4	5	6	7	8	9	10	11
2	0	2	4	6	8	10		2	4		8	
3	0	3	6	9	0	3	6			3	6	
4	0	4	8			8		4			4	8
5	0	5	10	3	8		6	11	4			
6	0	6	0		0	6	0	6		6		6
7	0	7	2	9				1			10	
8	0	8	4	0				8	4		8	4
9	0	9			0		6		0			
10	0	10	8			2						2
11	0	11										1

By referring to your table in Exercise 5, determine which of the following properties hold for the system of 12-hour clock numbers with the operation of multiplication.

6. closure　　　　　　　　　**7.** commutative　　　　　　　　　**8.** identity

A 5-hour clock system utilizes the set {0, 1, 2, 3, 4}, and relates to the clock face shown here.

9. Complete this 5-hour clock addition table.

+	0	1	2	3	4
0	0	1	2	3	4
1	1	2	3	4	
2	2	3	4		1
3	3	4			
4	4				3

Which of the following properties are satisfied by the system of 5-hour clock numbers with the operation of addition?

10. closure　　　　　　　　　　　　　　　　**11.** commutative

12. identity (If so, what is the identity element?)

13. inverse (If so, name the inverse of each element.)

14. Complete this 5-hour clock multiplication table.

×	0	1	2	3	4
0	0	0	0	0	0
1	0	1	2	3	4
2	0	2	4		
3	0	3			
4	0	4			

Which of the following properties are satisfied by the system of 5-hour clock numbers with the operation of multiplication?

15. closure　　　　　　　　　　　　　　　　**16.** commutative

17. identity (If so, what is the identity element?)

In clock arithmetic, as in ordinary arithmetic, $a - b = d$ is true if and only if $b + d = a$. Similarly, $a \div b = q$ if and only if $b \times q = a$.

Use the idea above and your 5-hour clock multiplication table of Exercise 14 to find the following quotients on a 5-hour clock.

18. $1 \div 3$　　　　　**19.** $3 \div 1$　　　　　**20.** $2 \div 3$　　　　　**21.** $3 \div 2$

22. Is division commutative on a 5-hour clock? Explain.

23. Is there an answer for $4 \div 0$ on a 5-hour clock? Find it or explain why not.

The military uses a 24-hour clock to avoid the problems of "A.M." *and* "P.M." *For example,* 1100 *hours is* 11 A.M., *while* 2100 *hours is* 9 P.M. *(12 noon + 9 hours). In these designations, the last two digits represent minutes, and the digits before that represent hours. Find each of the following sums in the 24-hour clock system.*

24. 1400 + 500
25. 1300 + 1800
26. 0750 + 1630
27. 1545 + 0815

28. Explain how the following three statements can *all* be true. (*Hint:* Think of clocks.)

$$1145 + 1135 = 2280$$
$$1145 + 1135 = 1120$$
$$1145 + 1135 = 2320$$

Answer true *or* false *for each of the following.*

29. $5 \equiv 19 \pmod 3$

30. $35 \equiv 8 \pmod 9$

31. $5{,}445 \equiv 0 \pmod 3$

32. $7{,}021 \equiv 4{,}202 \pmod 6$

Do each of the following modular arithmetic problems.

33. $(12 + 7) \pmod 4$

34. $(62 + 95) \pmod 9$

35. $(35 - 22) \pmod 5$

36. $(82 - 45) \pmod 3$

37. $(5 \times 8) \pmod 3$

38. $(32 \times 21) \pmod 8$

39. $[4 \times (13 + 6)] \pmod{11}$

40. $[(10 + 7) \times (5 + 3)] \pmod{10}$

41. The text described how to do arithmetic modulo *m* when the ordinary answer comes out nonnegative. Explain what to do when the ordinary answer is negative.

Do each of the following modular arithmetic problems.

42. $(3 - 27) \pmod 5$
43. $(16 - 60) \pmod 7$
44. $[(-8) \times 11] \pmod 3$
45. $[2 \times (-23)] \pmod 5$

In each of Exercises 46 and 47:
(a) *Complete the given addition table.*
(b) *Decide whether the closure, commutative, identity, and inverse properties are satisfied.*
(c) *If the inverse property is satisfied, give the inverse of each number.*

46. modulo 4

+	0	1	2	3
0	0	1	2	3
1				
2				
3				

47. modulo 7

+	0	1	2	3	4	5	6
0	0	1	2	3	4	5	6
1	1	2	3	4	5	6	
2							
3							
4							
5							
6							

In each of Exercises 48–51:
(a) *Complete the given multiplication table.*
(b) *Decide whether the closure, commutative, identity, and inverse properties are satisfied.*
(c) *Give the inverse of each nonzero number that has an inverse.*

48. modulo 2

×	0	1
0	0	0
1	0	

49. modulo 3

×	0	1	2
0	0	0	0
1	0	1	2
2	0	2	

50. modulo 4

×	0	1	2	3
0	0	0	0	0
1	0	1	2	3
2	0	2		
3	0	3		

51. modulo 9

×	0	1	2	3	4	5	6	7	8
0	0	0	0	0	0	0	0	0	0
1	0	1	2	3	4	5	6	7	8
2	0	2	4	6	8		5		
3	0	3	6	0		6		3	6
4	0	4	8		7		6		5
5	0	5	1		2		3	8	
6	0	6	3	0	6	3	0	6	3
7	0	7	5			8			2
8	0	8	7			4	3		1

52. Complete this statement: a modulo system satisfies the inverse property for multiplication only if the modulo number is a(n) _____ number.

Find all positive solutions for each of the following equations. Note any identities.

53. $x \equiv 3 \pmod{7}$

54. $(2 + x) \equiv 7 \pmod{3}$

55. $6x \equiv 2 \pmod{2}$

56. $(5x - 3) \equiv 7 \pmod{4}$

57. Until recently, automobile odometers have generally shown five whole-number digits and a digit for tenths of a mile. (Some makers, such as Toyota and Honda, now account for larger mileage totals by showing six whole number digits.) For those odometers showing just five whole number digits, totals are recorded in modulo what number?

58. If a car's five-digit whole number odometer shows a reading of 29,306, *in theory* how many miles might the car have traveled?

59. Martin Rosen finds that whether he sorts his White Sox ticket stubs into piles of 10, piles of 15, or piles of 20, there are always 2 left over. What is the least number of stubs he could have (assuming he has more than 2)?

60. Barbara McLaurin has a collection of silver spoons from all over the world. She finds that she can arrange her spoons in sets of 7 with 6 left over, sets of 8 with 1 left over, or sets of 15 with 3 left over. If Barbara has fewer than 200 spoons, how many are there?

61. Refer to Example 9 in the text. (Recall that *next* year is a leap year.) Assuming today was Thursday, January 12, answer the following questions.

(a) How many days would the next year (starting today) contain?

(b) What day of the week would occur one year from today?

62. Assume again, as in Example 9, that *next* year is a leap year. If the next year (starting today) does *not* contain 366 days, what is the range of possible dates for today?

63. Jill Staut and Cynthia Wolfe, flight attendants for two different airlines, are close friends and like to get together as often as possible. Jill flies a 21-day schedule (including days off), which then repeats, while Cynthia has a repeating 30-day schedule. Both of their routines include stopovers in Chicago, New Orleans, and San Francisco. The table below shows which days of each of their individual schedules they are in these cities. (Assume the first day of a cycle is day number 1.)

	Days in Chicago	Days in New Orleans	Days in San Francisco
Jill	1, 2, 8	5, 12	6, 18, 19
Cynthia	23, 29, 30	5, 6, 17	8, 10, 15, 20, 25

If today is July 1 and Jill and Cynthia are both starting their schedules today (day 1), list the days during July and August that they will be able to see each other in each of the three cities.

The basis of the complex number system is the "imaginary" number i. The powers of i cycle through a repeating pattern of just 4 distinct values as shown here:

$$i^0 = 1, \quad i^1 = i, \quad i^2 = -1, \quad i^3 = -i, \quad i^4 = 1, \quad i^5 = i, \quad \text{and so on.}$$

Find the values of each of the following powers of i.

64. i^{16} **65.** i^{47} **66.** i^{98} **67.** i^{137}

The following formula can be used to find the day of the week on which a given year begins. * *Here y represents the year (after 1582, when our current calendar began). First calculate*

$$a = y + [\![(y-1)/4]\!] - [\![(y-1)/100]\!] + [\![(y-1)/400]\!],$$

where $[\![x]\!]$ represents the greatest integer less than or equal to x. (For example, $[\![9.2]\!] = 9$, and $[\![\pi]\!] = 3$.) After finding a, find the smallest nonnegative integer b such that

$$a \equiv b \pmod 7,$$

Then b gives the day of January 1, with b = 0 representing Sunday, b = 1 Monday, and so on.

Find the day of the week on which January 1 would occur in the following years.

68. 1812   **69.** 1865   **70.** 1994   **71.** 2001

Some people believe that Friday the thirteenth is unlucky. The table * below shows the months that will have a Friday the thirteenth if the first day of the year is known. A year is a leap year if it is divisible by 4. The only exception to this rule is that a century year (1900, for example) is a leap year only when it is divisible by 400.*

First Day of Year	Nonleap Year	Leap Year
Sunday	Jan., Oct.	Jan., April, July
Monday	April, July	Sept., Dec.
Tuesday	Sept., Dec.	June
Wednesday	June	March, Nov.
Thursday	Feb., March, Nov.	Feb., Aug.
Friday	August	May
Saturday	May	Oct.

Use the table to determine the months that have a Friday the thirteenth for the following years.

72. 1994   **73.** 1995   **74.** 1996   **75.** 2200

*An algorithm for determining the day of the week of any given date can be called a **perpetual calendar**. The one described here, based on modular arithmetic, will work for any date since the year 1700 and up through the year 2099. (See the text preceding Exercise 72 for the way to identify leap years.)*

Key numbers for the month, day, and century are determined by the following tables.

---

*Given in "An Aid to the Superstitious" by G. L. Ritter, S. R. Lowry, H. B. Woodruff and T. L. Isenhour. The Mathematics Teacher, May 1977, pages 456–57.

Month	Key		Day	Key		Century	Key
January	1 (0 if a leap year)		Saturday	0		1700s	4
February	4 (3 if a leap year)		Sunday	1		1800s	2
March	4		Monday	2		1900s	0
April	0		Tuesday	3		2000s	6
May	2		Wednesday	4			
June	5		Thursday	5			
July	0		Friday	6			
August	3						
September	6						
October	1						
November	4						
December	6						

The algorithm works as follows. (We use October 12, 1949 as an example.)

Step 1 Obtain the following five numbers. Example

  1. The number formed by the last two digits of the year 49

  2. The number in Step 1, divided by 4, with the remainder ignored 12

  3. The month key (1 for October in our example) 1

  4. The day of the month (12 for October 12) 12

  5. The century key (0 for the 1900s) 0

Step 2 Add these five numbers. 74

Step 3 Divide the sum by 7, and retain the remainder. (74/7 = 10, with remainder 4)

Step 4 Find this remainder in the day key table. (The number 4 implies that October 12, 1949 was a Wednesday.)

Find the day of the week on which each of the following dates fell, or will fall.

76. August 7, 1945

77. March 14, 2001

78. February 29, 1776

79. December 25, 2000

80. Modulo numbers can be used to create **modulo designs.** For example, to construct the design (11, 5) proceed as follows.

  (a) Draw a circle and divide the circumference into 10 equal parts. Label the division points as 1, 2, 3, . . . , 10.

  (b) Since $1 \times 5 \equiv 5$ (mod 11), connect 1 and 5. (We use 5 as a multiplier since we are making an (11, 5) design.)

  (c) $2 \times 5 \equiv 10$ (mod 11) Therefore, connect 2 and ____ .

  (d) $3 \times 5 \equiv$ ____ (mod 11) Connect 3 and ____ .

  (e) $4 \times 5 \equiv$ ____ (mod 11) Connect 4 and ____ .

  (f) $5 \times 5 \equiv$ ____ (mod 11) Connect 5 and ____ .

  (g) $6 \times 5 \equiv$ ____ (mod 11) Connect 6 and ____ .

  (h) $7 \times 5 \equiv$ ____ (mod 11) Connect 7 and ____ .

  (i) $8 \times 5 \equiv$ ____ (mod 11) Connect 8 and ____ .

  (j) $9 \times 5 \equiv$ ____ (mod 11) Connect 9 and ____ .

  (k) $10 \times 5 \equiv$ ____ (mod 11) Connect 10 and ____ .

  (l) You might want to shade some of the regions you have found to make an interesting pattern. Other modulo designs are shown at the side. For more information, see "Residue Designs," by Phil Locke in *The Mathematics Teacher,* March 1972, pages 260–263.

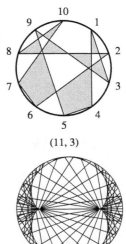

(11, 3)

(65, 3)

Identification numbers are used in various ways for all kinds of different products. *
*Books, for example, are assigned International Standard Book Numbers (ISBNs). Each
ISBN is a ten-digit number. It includes a check digit, which is determined on the basis of
modular arithmetic. The ISBN for this book is*

0-673-46738-4

*The first digit, 0, identifies the book as being published in an English-speaking country.
The next digits, 673, identify the publisher, while 46738 identifies this particular book.
The final digit, 4, is a check digit. To find this check digit, start at the left and multiply the
digits of the ISBN number by 10, 9, 8, 7, 6, 5, 4, 3, and 2, respectively. Then add these
products. For this book we get*

$$(10 \times 0) + (9 \times 6) + (8 \times 7) + (7 \times 3) + (6 \times 4) + (5 \times 6) + (4 \times 7) + (3 \times 3) + (2 \times 8) = 238.$$

*The check digit is the smallest number that must be added to this result to get a multiple
of 11. Since 238 + 4 = 242, a multiple of 11, the check digit is 4. (It is possible to have a
check "digit" of 10; the letter X is used instead of 10.)*

*When an order for this book is received, the ISBN is entered into a computer, and the
check digit evaluated. If this result does not match the check digit on the order, the order
will not be processed.*

Which of the following ISBNs have correct check digits?

81. 0-399-13615-4   **82.** 0-691-02356-5

Find the appropriate check digit for each of the following ISBNs.

83. *The Beauty of Fractals,* by H. O. Peitgen and P. H. Richter, 3-540-15851-

84. *Women in Science,* by Vivian Gornick, 0-671-41738-

85. *Beyond Numeracy,* by John Allen Paulos, 0-394-58640-

86. *Iron John,* by Robert Bly, 0-201-51720-

87. It is true that, for a common modulus, two numbers that are both congruent to a common third number must also be congruent to each other. That is, if $x \equiv a$ (mod m) and $y \equiv a$ (mod m), then $x \equiv y$ (mod m). Do you think that two numbers whose squares are congruent to the same number must be congruent to each other? That is, if $x^2 \equiv a$ (mod m) and $y^2 \equiv a$ (mod m), must it neccessarily be true that $x \equiv y$ (mod m)? Argue *yes* or *no* and support your argument with examples.

---

*For an interesting general discussion, see "The Mathematics of Identification Numbers," by Joseph
A. Gallian in *The College Mathematics Journal*, May 1991, page 194.*

5   ## Other Finite Mathematical Systems

We continue our study of finite mathematical systems. Some examples here will
consist of numbers, but others will be made up of elements denoted by letters. And
the operations are often represented by abstract symbols with no particular mathematical meaning. This is to make the point that a system is characterized by how its
elements behave under its operations, not by the choice of symbols used.

To begin, let us introduce a new finite mathematical system made up of the set
of elements {a, b, c, d}, and an operation we shall write with the symbol ☆. We
give meaning to operation ☆ by showing an **operation table,** which tells how operation ☆ is used to find the answer for any two elements from the set {a, b, c, d}. The

TABLE 11

☆	*a*	*b*	*c*	*d*
a	*a*	*b*	*c*	*d*
b	*b*	*d*	*a*	*c*
c	*c*	*a*	*d*	*b*
d	*d*	*c*	*b*	*a*

operation table for ☆ is shown in Table 11. To use the table to find, say, $c ☆ d$, first locate c on the left, and d across the top. This row and column give b, so that

$$c ☆ d = b.$$

As long as a system possesses a single operation, the properties we look for are the same as those mentioned in Section 4: closure, commutative, associative, identity, and inverse. The only difference now is that the operations are new and must be looked at with a fresh eye—it is hard to have preconceived ideas about operation ☆ and the table above. Let us now decide which properties are satisfied by the system made up of $\{a, b, c, d\}$ and operation ☆. (All of these properties are summarized later in this section.)

Closure Property

For this system to be closed under the operation ☆, the answer to any possible combination of elements from the system must be in the set $\{a, b, c, d\}$. A glance at Table 11 shows that the answers in the body of the table are all elements of this set. This means that the system is closed. If an element other than a, b, c, or d had appeared in the body of the table, the system would not have been closed.

Commutative Property

In order for the system to have the commutative property, it must be true that $\Gamma ☆ \Delta = \Delta ☆ \Gamma$, where Γ and Δ stand for any elements from the set $\{a, b, c, d\}$. For example,

$$c ☆ d = b \quad \text{and} \quad d ☆ c = b, \quad \text{so} \quad c ☆ d = d ☆ c.$$

To establish the commutative property for the system, apply the diagonal line test described in Section 4. Since Table 12 is symmetric about the line, ☆ is a commutative operation for this system.

TABLE 12

☆	*a*	*b*	*c*	*d*
a	*a*	*b*	*c*	*d*
b	*b*	*d*	*a*	*c*
c	*c*	*a*	*d*	*b*
d	*d*	*c*	*b*	*a*

Associative Property

The system is associative in the case $(\Gamma ☆ \Delta) ☆ Y = \Gamma ☆ (\Delta ☆ Y)$, where Γ, Δ, and Y represent any elements from the set $\{a, b, c, d\}$. There is no quick way to check a table for the associative property, as there was for the commutative property. All we can do is try some examples. Using the table that defines operation ☆,

$$(a ☆ d) ☆ b = d ☆ b = c, \quad \text{and} \quad a ☆ (d ☆ b) = a ☆ c = c,$$

so that

$$(a ☆ d) ☆ b = a ☆ (d ☆ b).$$

In the same way,

$$b ☆ (c ☆ d) = (b ☆ c) ☆ d.$$

In both these examples, changing the location of parentheses did not change the answers. Since the two examples worked, we suspect that the system is associative. We cannot be sure of this, however, unless every possible choice of three letters from the set is checked. (Although we have not completely verified it here, this system does, in fact, satisfy the associative property.)

Identity Property

For the identity property to hold, there must be an element Δ from the set of the system such that $\Delta ☆ X = X$ and $X ☆ \Delta = X$, where X represents any element from the set $\{a, b, c, d\}$. We can use the same criterion here as was used for clock addition in Section 4. Since the column below a (at the top) is identical to the column at the left, and the row across from a (at the left) is identical to the row at the top, a is in fact the identity element of the system. (It is shown in more advanced courses that if a system has an identity element, it has *only* one.)

Inverse Property

We found above that *a* is the identity element for the system using operation ☆. Is there any inverse in this system for, say, the element *b*? If Δ represents the inverse of *b* in this system, then

$$b ☆ Δ = a \quad \text{and} \quad Δ ☆ b = a \quad \text{(since } a \text{ is the identity element).}$$

Inspecting the table for operation ☆ shows that Δ should be replaced with *c*:

$$b ☆ c = a \quad \text{and} \quad c ☆ b = a.$$

Just as with clock addition in Section 4, we can inspect the table to see if every element of our system has an inverse in the system. We see (in Table 12) that the identity element *a* appears exactly once in each row, and that, in each case, the pair of elements that produces *a* also produces it in the opposite order. Therefore, we conclude that the system satisfies the inverse property.

In summary, the mathematical system made up of the set {*a*, *b*, *c*, *d*} and operation ☆ satisfies the closure, commutative, associative, identity, and inverse properties.

Let us now list the basic properties that may (or may not) be satisfied by a mathematical system involving a single operation.

Potential Properties of a Single-Operation System

Here *a*, *b*, and *c* represent elements from the set of the system, and ∘ represents the operation of the system.

Bernard Bolzano
(1781–1848) was an early exponent of rigor and precision in mathematics. Many early results in such areas as calculus were produced by the masters in the field; these masters knew what they were doing and produced accurate results. However, their sloppy arguments caused trouble in the hands of the less gifted. The work of Bolzano and others helped put mathematics on a strong footing.

Closure The system is closed if for all elements *a* and *b*,

$$a ∘ b$$

is in the set of the system.

Commutative The system has the commutative property if

$$a ∘ b = b ∘ a$$

for all elements *a* and *b* from the system.

Associative The system has the associative property if

$$(a ∘ b) ∘ c = a ∘ (b ∘ c)$$

for every choice of three elements *a*, *b*, and *c* of the system.

Identity The system has an identity element *e* (where *e* is in the set of the system) if

$$a ∘ e = a \quad \text{and} \quad e ∘ a = a,$$

for every element *a* in the system.

Inverse The system satisfies the inverse property if, for every element *a* of the system, there is an element *x* in the system such that

$$a ∘ x = e \quad \text{and} \quad x ∘ a = e,$$

where *e* is the identity element of the system.

×	0	1	2	3	4	5
0	0	0	0	0	0	0
1	0	1	2	3	4	5
2	0	2	4	0	2	4
3	0	3	0	3	0	3
4	0	4	2	0	4	2
5	0	5	4	3	2	1

EXAMPLE 1   The table in the margin is a multiplication table for the set {0, 1, 2, 3, 4, 5} under the operation of multiplication modulo 6. Which of the properties above are satisfied by this system?

All the numbers in the body of the table come from the set {0, 1, 2, 3, 4, 5}, so the system is closed. If we draw a line from upper left to lower right, we could fold the table along this line and have the corresponding elements match; the system has the commutative property.

To check for the associative property, try some examples:

$$2 \times (3 \times 5) = 2 \times 3 = 0 \quad \text{and} \quad (2 \times 3) \times 5 = 0 \times 5 = 0,$$

so that $\qquad\qquad\qquad\qquad 2 \times (3 \times 5) = (2 \times 3) \times 5.$

Also, $\qquad\qquad\qquad\qquad 5 \times (4 \times 2) = (5 \times 4) \times 2.$

Any other examples that we might try would also work. The system has the associative property.

Since the column at the left of the multiplication table is repeated under 1 in the body of the table, 1 is a candidate for the identity element in the system. To be sure that 1 is indeed the identity element here, check that the row corresponding to 1 at the left is identical with the row at the top of the table.

To find inverse elements, look for the identity element, 1, in the rows of the table. The identity element appears in the second row, $1 \times 1 = 1$; and in the bottom row, $5 \times 5 = 1$; so 1 and 5 are each their own inverses. There is no identity element in the rows opposite the numbers 0, 2, 3, and 4, so none of these elements have inverses.

In summary, the system made up of the set {0, 1, 2, 3, 4, 5} under multiplication modulo 6 satisfies the closure, associative, commutative, and identity properties, but not the inverse property. ●

×	1	2	3	4	5	6
1	1	2	3	4	5	6
2	2	4	6	1	3	5
3	3	6	2	5	1	4
4	4	1	5	2	6	3
5	5	3	1	6	4	2
6	6	5	4	3	2	1

EXAMPLE 2   The table in the margin is a multiplication table for the set of numbers {1, 2, 3, 4, 5, 6} under the operation of multiplication modulo 7. Which of the properties are satisfied by this system?

Notice here that 0 is not an element of this system. This is perfectly legitimate. Since we are defining the system, we can include (or exclude) whatever we wish. Check that the system satisfies the closure, commutative, associative, and identity properties, with identity element 1. Let us now check for inverses. The element 1 is its own inverse, since $1 \times 1 = 1$. In row 2, the identity element 1 appears under the number 4, so $2 \times 4 = 1$ (and $4 \times 2 = 1$), with 2 and 4 inverses of each other. Also, 3 and 5 are inverses of each other, and 6 is its own inverse. Since each number in the set of the system has an inverse, the system satisfies the inverse property. ●

When a mathematical system has two operations, rather than just one, we can look for an additional, very important property, namely the **distributive property.** For example, when we studied Hindu-Arabic arithmetic of counting numbers in Section 2, we saw that multiplication is distributive with respect to (or "over") addition.

$$3 \times (5 + 9) = 3 \times 5 + 3 \times 9 \quad \text{and} \quad (5 + 9) \times 3 = 5 \times 3 + 9 \times 3.$$

In each case, the factor 3 is "distributed" over the 5 and the 9.

Although the distributive property (as well as the other properties discussed here) can be applied to the real numbers in general, we state it here just for the system of integers.

Distributive *Property of* Multiplication *over* Addition

For integers a, b, and c, the **distributive property** holds for multiplication with respect to addition.

$$a \times (b + c) = a \times b + a \times c$$

and $$(b + c) \times a = b \times a + c \times a$$

EXAMPLE 3 Is addition distributive over multiplication?

To find out, exchange $\times$ and $+$ in the first equation above:

$$a + (b \times c) = (a + b) \times (a + c).$$

We need to find out whether this statement is true for *every* choice of three numbers that we might make. Try an example. If $a = 3$, $b = 4$, and $c = 5$,

$$a + (b \times c) = 3 + (4 \times 5) = 3 + 20 = 23,$$

while $$(a + b) \times (a + c) = (3 + 4) \times (3 + 5) = 7 \times 8 = 56.$$

Since $23 \neq 56$, we have $3 + (4 \times 5) \neq (3 + 4) \times (3 + 5)$. This false result is a *counterexample* (an example showing that a general statement is false). This counterexample shows that addition is *not* distributive over multiplication. ●

Because subtraction of real numbers is defined in terms of addition, the distributive property of multiplication also holds with respect to subtraction.

Distributive *Property of* Multiplication *over* Subtraction

For integers a, b, and c the **distributive property** holds for multiplication with respect to subtraction.

$$a \times (b - c) = a \times b - a \times c$$

and $$(b - c) \times a = b \times a - c \times a$$

The **general form of the distributive property** appears below.

General *Form of the* Distributive *Property*

Let $\star$ and $\circ$ be two operations defined for elements in the same set. Then $\star$ is distributive over $\circ$ if

$$a \star (b \circ c) = (a \star b) \circ (a \star c)$$

for every choice of elements a, b, and c from the set.

The final example illustrates how the distributive property may hold for a finite system.

EXAMPLE 4   Suppose that the set {*a, b, c, d, e*} has two operations ✩ and ∘ defined by the charts below.

✩	*a*	*b*	*c*	*d*	*e*
a	*a*	*a*	*a*	*a*	*a*
b	*a*	*b*	*c*	*d*	*e*
c	*a*	*c*	*e*	*b*	*d*
d	*a*	*d*	*b*	*e*	*c*
e	*a*	*e*	*d*	*c*	*b*

∘	*a*	*b*	*c*	*d*	*e*
a	*a*	*b*	*c*	*d*	*e*
b	*b*	*c*	*d*	*e*	*a*
c	*c*	*d*	*e*	*a*	*b*
d	*d*	*e*	*a*	*b*	*c*
e	*e*	*a*	*b*	*c*	*d*

The distributive property of ✩ with respect to ∘ holds in this system. Verify for the following case: $e ✩ (d ∘ b) = (e ✩ d) ∘ (e ✩ b)$.

First evaluate the left side of the equation by using the charts.

$$e ✩ (d ∘ b) = e ✩ e \qquad \text{Use the ∘ chart.}$$
$$= b \qquad \text{Use the ✩ chart.}$$

Now, evaluate the right side of the equation.

$$(e ✩ d) ∘ (e ✩ b) = c ∘ e \qquad \text{Use the ✩ chart twice.}$$
$$= b \qquad \text{Use the ∘ chart.}$$

In each case the final result is *b*, and the distributive property is verified for this case. ●

---

5 EXERCISES

For each system in Exercises 1–10, decide which of the properties of single operation systems are satisfied. If the identity property is satisfied, give the identity element. If the inverse property is satisfied, give the inverse of each element. If the identity property is satisfied but the inverse property is not, name the elements that have no inverses.

1. {1, 2, 3, 4};   multiplication modulo 5

×	1	2	3	4
1	1	2	3	4
2	2	4	1	3
3	3	1	4	2
4	4	3	2	1

2. {1, 2};   multiplication modulo 3

×	1	2
1	1	2
2	2	1

3. {1, 2, 3, 4, 5};   multiplication modulo 6

×	1	2	3	4	5
1	1	2	3	4	5
2	2	4	0	2	4
3	3	0	3	0	3
4	4	2	0	4	2
5	5	4	3	2	1

4. {1, 2, 3, 4, 5, 6, 7};   multiplication modulo 8

×	1	2	3	4	5	6	7
1	1	2	3	4	5	6	7
2	2	4	6	0	2	4	6
3	3	6	1	4	7	2	5
4	4	0	4	0	4	0	4
5	5	2	7	4	1	6	3
6	6	4	2	0	6	4	2
7	7	6	5	4	3	2	1

5. $\{1, 3, 5, 7\}$;   multiplication modulo 8

×	1	3	5	7
1	1	3	5	7
3	3	1	7	5
5	5	7	1	3
7	7	5	3	1

6. $\{1, 3, 5, 7, 9\}$;   multiplication modulo 10

×	1	3	5	7	9
1	1	3	5	7	9
3	3	9	5	1	7
5	5	5	5	5	5
7	7	1	5	9	3
9	9	7	5	3	1

7. $\{m, n, p\}$;   operation *J*

J	*m*	*n*	*p*
m	*n*	*p*	*n*
n	*p*	*m*	*n*
p	*n*	*n*	*m*

8. $\{A, B, F\}$;   operation ☆

☆	*A*	*B*	*F*
A	*B*	*F*	*A*
B	*F*	*A*	*B*
F	*A*	*B*	*F*

9. $\{A, J, T, U\}$;   operation #

#	*A*	*J*	*T*	*U*
A	*A*	*J*	*T*	*U*
J	*J*	*T*	*U*	*A*
T	*T*	*U*	*A*	*J*
U	*U*	*A*	*J*	*T*

10. $\{r, s, t, u\}$;   operation *Z*

Z	*r*	*s*	*t*	*u*
r	*u*	*t*	*r*	*s*
s	*t*	*u*	*s*	*r*
t	*r*	*s*	*t*	*u*
u	*s*	*r*	*u*	*t*

The tables in the finite mathematical systems that we developed in this section can be obtained in a variety of ways. For example, let us begin with a square, as shown in the figure. Let the symbols a, b, c, and d be defined as shown in the figure.

Let *a* represent zero rotation—leave the original square as is	Let *b* represent rotation of 90° clockwise from original position	Let *c* represent rotation of 180° clockwise from original position	Let *d* represent rotation of 270° clockwise from original position

Define an operation ☐ for these letters as follows. To evaluate b ☐ c, for example, first perform b by rotating the square 90°. (See the figure.) Then perform operation c by rotating the square an additional 180°. The net result is the same as if we had performed d only. Thus,

$$b \,\square\, c = d.$$

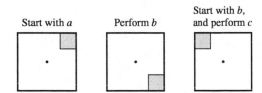

Start with *a*   Perform *b*   Start with *b*, and perform *c*

Use this method to find each of the following.

11. $b \,\square\, d$ **12.** $b \,\square\, b$ **13.** $d \,\square\, b$ **14.** $a \,\square\, b$

15. Complete the table at the right.

☐	*a*	*b*	*c*	*d*
a	*a*	*b*	*c*	*d*
b	*b*	*c*		*a*
c	*c*		*a*	
d	*d*	*a*		

16. Which of the properties from this section are satisfied by this system?

17. Define a universal set U as the set of counting numbers. Form a new set that contains all possible subsets of U. This new set of subsets together with the operation of set intersection forms a mathematical system. Which of the properties listed in this section are satisfied by this system?

18. Replace the word "intersection" with the word "union" in Exercise 17; then answer the same question.

19. Complete the table at the right so that the result is *not* the same as operation ☐ of the text, but so that the five properties listed in this section hold.

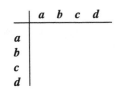

Try examples to help you decide whether or not the following operations, when applied to the integers, satisfy the distributive property.

20. subtraction over multiplication   21. addition over subtraction   22. subtraction over addition

Recall that Example 3 provided a counterexample for the general statement

$$a + (b \times c) = (a + b) \times (a + c).$$

Thus, addition is not *distributive over multiplication. Now do Exercises 23–26.*

23. Decide if the equation is true for each of the following sets of values.
    (a) $a = 2, b = -5, c = 4$ **(b)** $a = -7, b = 5, c = 3$
    (c) $a = -8, b = 14, c = -5$ **(d)** $a = 1, b = 6, c = -6$

24. Find another set of a, b, and c values that make the equation true.

25. Explain what general conditions will always cause the equation above to be true.

26. Explain why, regardless of the results in Exercises 23–25, addition is still *not* distributive over multiplication.

27. Give the conditions under which each of the following equations would be true.
    (a) $a + (b - c) = (a + b) - (a + c)$
    (b) $a - (b + c) = (a - b) + (a - c)$

28. **(a)** Find values of a, b, and c such that
    $$a - (b \times c) = (a - b) \times (a - c).$$
    (b) Does this mean that subtraction is distributive over multiplication? Explain.

Verify for the mathematical system of Example 4 that the distributive property holds for the following cases.

29. $c \star (d \circ e) = (c \star d) \circ (c \star e)$

30. $a \star (a \circ b) = (a \star a) \circ (a \star b)$

31. $d \star (e \circ c) = (d \star e) \circ (d \star c)$

32. $b \star (b \circ b) = (b \star b) \circ (b \star b)$

These exercises are for students who have studied the chapter on sets.

33. Use Venn diagrams to show that the distributive property for union with respect to intersection holds for sets A, B, and C. That is,
    $$A \cup (B \cap C) = (A \cup B) \cap (A \cup C).$$

34. Use Venn diagrams to show that *another* distributive property holds for sets A, B, and C. It is the distributive property of intersection with respect to union.
    $$A \cap (B \cup C) = (A \cap B) \cup (A \cap C)$$

These exercises are for students who have studied the chapter on logic.

35. Use truth tables to show that the following distributive property holds:
    $$p \vee (q \wedge r) \equiv (p \vee q) \wedge (p \vee r).$$

36. Use truth tables to show that *another* distributive property holds:
    $$p \wedge (q \vee r) \equiv (p \wedge q) \vee (p \wedge r).$$

6

Niels Henrik Abel

(1802–1829) of Norway was identified in childhood as a mathematical genius but never received in his lifetime the professional recognition his work deserved.

At 16, influenced by a perceptive teacher, he read the works of Newton, Euler, and Lagrange. In only a few years he began producing work of his own. One of Abel's achievements was the demonstration that a general formula for solving fifth-degree equations does not exist. The quadratic formula (for equations of degree 2) is well known, and formulas do exist for solving third- and fourth-degree equations. Abel's accomplishment ended a search that had lasted for years.

In the study of abstract algebra, groups which have the commutative property are referred to as **abelian** groups in honor of Abel.

When his father died, Abel assumed responsibility for his family and never escaped poverty. Even though a government grant enabled him to visit Germany and France, the leading mathematicians there failed to acknowledge his genius. He died of tuberculosis at age 27.

Groups

We have considered quite a few mathematical systems, most of which have satisfied some or all of the following properties: closure, associative, commutative, identity, inverse, and distributive. Systems are commonly classified according to which properties they satisfy. One of the most important categories ever studied is the mathematical **group,** which we define here.

Group

A mathematical system is called a **group** if, under its operation, it satisfies the closure, associative, identity, and inverse properties.

EXAMPLE 1   Does the set $\{-1, 1\}$ under the operation of multiplication form a group?

Check the necessary four properties.

Closure   The given system leads to the multiplication table below. All entries in the body of the table are either -1 or 1; the system is closed.

$\times$	-1	1
-1	1	-1
1	-1	1

Associative   Both -1 and 1 are integers, and multiplication of integers is associative.

Identity   The identity for multiplication is 1, an element of the set of the system, $\{-1, 1\}$.

Inverse   Both -1 and 1 are their own inverses for multiplication.

All four of the properties are satisfied, so the system is a group.   ●

EXAMPLE 2   Does the set $\{-1, 1\}$ under the operation of addition form a group?

The addition table below shows that closure is not satisfied, so there is no need to check further. The system is not a group.

$+$	-1	1
-1	-2	0
1	0	2	●

Amalie ("Emmy") Noether
(1882–1935) was an outstanding mathematician in the field of abstract algebra. She studied and worked in Germany at a time when it was very difficult for a woman to do so. At the University of Erlangen in 1900, Noether was one of only two women. Although she could sit in on classes, professors could and did deny her the right to take the exams for their courses. Not until 1904 was Noether allowed to register officially. She completed her doctorate four years later.

   In 1916 Emmy Noether went to Göttingen to work with David Hilbert on the general theory of relativity. But even with Hilbert's backing and prestige, it was three years before the faculty voted to make Noether a *Privatdozent*, the lowest rank in the faculty. In 1922 Noether was made an unofficial professor (or assistant). She received no pay for this post, although she was given a small stipend to lecture in algebra.

   Noether's area of interest was abstract algebra, particularly structures called rings and ideals. (Groups are structures, too, with different properties.) One special type of ring bears her name; she was the first to study its properties.

The system of Example 1 is a finite group. Let's look for an infinite group.

EXAMPLE 3   Does the set of integers {. . . , −3, −2, −1, 0, 1, 2, 3, . . .} under the operation of addition form a group?

Check the required properties.

Closure   The sum of any two integers is an integer; the system is closed.

Associative   Try some examples:

$$2 + (5 + 8) = 2 + 13 = 15$$

and
$$(2 + 5) + 8 = 7 + 8 = 15,$$

so
$$2 + (5 + 8) = (2 + 5) + 8.$$

$$-4 + (7 + 14) = -4 + 21 = 17$$

and
$$(-4 + 7) + 14 = 3 + 14 = 17,$$

so
$$-4 + (7 + 14) = (-4 + 7) + 14.$$

Apparently, addition of integers is associative.

Identity   We know that $a + 0 = a$ and $0 + a = a$ for any integer a. The identity element for addition of integers is 0.

Inverse   Given any integer a, its additive inverse, $-a$, is also an integer. For example 5 and −5 are inverses. The system satisfies the inverse property.

Since all four properties are satisfied, this (infinite) system *is* a group.   ●

Group structure applies not only to sets of numbers. One common group is the group of **symmetries of a square,** which we will develop. First, cut out a small square, and label it as shown in Figure 10.

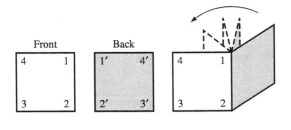

FIGURE 10

   Make sure that 1 is in front of 1′, 2 is in front of 2′, 3 is in front of 3′, and 4 is in front of 4′. Let the letter *M* represent a clockwise rotation of 90° *about the center of the square* (marked with a dot in Figure 11). Let *N* represent a rotation of 180°, and so on. A complete list of the symmetries of a square is given in Figure 11.

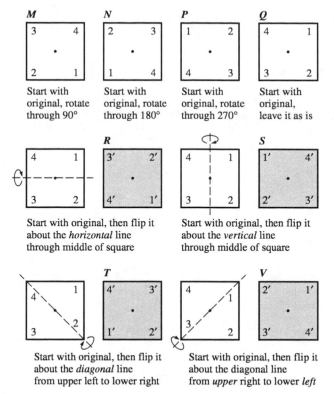

Symmetries of a square

FIGURE 11

Combine symmetries as follows: Let *NP* represent *N* followed by *P*. Performing *N* and then *P* is the same as performing just *M,* so that *NP* = *M.* See Figure 12.

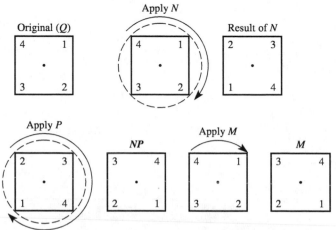

Think of *N* as advancing each corner two quarter turns clockwise. Thus 4 goes from upper left to lower right. To this result apply *P,* which advances each corner three quarter turns. Thus 2 goes from upper left to lower left. The result, *NP,* is the same as advancing each (original) corner one quarter turn, which *M* does. Thus, *NP* = *M.*

FIGURE 12

Évariste Galois

(1811–1832) About 160 years ago, as a young Frenchman, Galois agreed to fight a duel. He had been engaged in profound mathematical research for some time. Now, anticipating the possibility of his death, he summarized the essentials of his discoveries in a letter to a friend. His letter concluded: "You will publicly ask Jacobi or Gauss to give their opinion not on the truth, but on the importance of the theorems. After this there will be, I hope, some people who will find it to their advantage to decipher all this mess." The next day Galois was killed. He was not yet 21 years old when he died.

Galois's theories were never shown to Jacobi or Gauss. It was not until 1846 that they were published. Mathematicians began to appreciate the importance of Galois's work, which centered on solving equations by using groups. Galois found a way to derive a group which corresponds to each equation. This group, called "the group of the equation," contains the important properties of the equation. So-called Galois groups form an important part of modern abstract algebra.

EXAMPLE 4   Find *RT*.

First, perform *R* by flipping the square about a horizontal line through the middle. Then, perform *T* by flipping the result of *R* about a diagonal from upper left to lower right. The result of *RT* is the same as performing only *M*, so that *RT* = *M*.   ●

The method in Example 4 can be used to complete the following table for combining the symmetries of a square.

□	*M*	*N*	*P*	*Q*	*R*	*S*	*T*	*V*
M	*N*	*P*	*Q*	*M*	*V*	*T*	*R*	*S*
N	*P*	*Q*	*M*	*N*	*S*	*R*	*V*	*T*
P	*Q*	*M*	*N*	*P*	*T*	*V*	*S*	*R*
Q	*M*	*N*	*P*	*Q*	*R*	*S*	*T*	*V*
R	*T*	*S*	*V*	*R*	*Q*	*N*	*M*	*P*
S	*V*	*R*	*T*	*S*	*N*	*Q*	*P*	*M*
T	*S*	*V*	*R*	*T*	*P*	*M*	*Q*	*N*
V	*R*	*T*	*S*	*V*	*M*	*P*	*N*	*Q*

EXAMPLE 5   Show that the system made up of the symmetries of a square is a group.

For the system to be a group, it must satisfy the closure, associative, identity, and inverse properties.

Closure   All the entries in the body of the table come from the set {*M, N, P, Q, R, S, T, V* }. Thus, the system is closed.

Associative   Try examples:

$$P(MT) = P(R) = T.$$

Also, $$(PM)T = (Q)T = T,$$

so that $$P(MT) = (PM)T.$$

Other similar examples also work. (See Exercises 25–28.) Thus, the system has the associative property.

Identity   The column at the left in the table is repeated under *Q*. Check that *Q* is indeed the identity element.

Inverse   In the first row, *Q* appears under *P*. Check that *M* and *P* are inverses of each other. In fact, every element in the system has an inverse. (See Exercises 29–34.)

Since all four of the properties are satisfied, the system is a group.   ●

EXAMPLE 6   Form a mathematical system by using only the set {*M, N, P, Q*} from the group of symmetries of a square. Is this new system a group?

□	*M*	*N*	*P*	*Q*
M	*N*	*P*	*Q*	*M*
N	*P*	*Q*	*M*	*N*
P	*Q*	*M*	*N*	*P*
Q	*M*	*N*	*P*	*Q*

The table for the elements {*M, N, P, Q*} (shown on the left) is just one corner of the table for the entire system. Verify that the system represented by this table satisfies all four properties and thus is a group. This new group is a *subgroup* of the original group of the symmetries of a square. ⬡

Permutation Groups

A very useful example of a group comes from studying the arrangements, or permutations, of a list of numbers. Start with the symbols 1-2-3, in that order.

There are several ways in which the order could be changed—for example, 2-3-1. This rearrangement is written:

$$1\text{-}2\text{-}3$$
$$2\text{-}3\text{-}1.$$

Replace 1 with 2, replace 2 with 3, and 3 with 1. In the same way,

$$1\text{-}2\text{-}3$$
$$3\text{-}1\text{-}2$$

means replace 1 with 3, 2 with 1, and 3 with 2, while

$$1\text{-}2\text{-}3$$
$$3\text{-}2\text{-}1$$

says to replace 1 with 3, leave the 2 unchanged, and replace 3 with 1. All possible rearrangements of the symbols 1-2-3 are listed below where, for convenience, a name has been given to each rearrangement.

A^*: 1-2-3	B^*: 1-2-3	C^*: 1-2-3	D^*: 1-2-3
2-3-1	2-1-3	1-2-3	1-3-2

	E^*: 1-2-3	F^*: 1-2-3	
	3-1-2	3-2-1	

Two rearrangements can be combined as with the symmetries of a square; for example, the symbol B^*F^* means to first apply B^* to 1-2-3 and then apply F^* to the result. Rearrangement B^* changes 1-2-3 into 2-1-3. Then apply F^* to this result: 1 becomes 3, 2 is unchanged, and 3 becomes 1. In summary:

1-2-3

2-1-3 Rearrange according to B^*.

⬇

3 By F^*, 1 is replaced by 3.

2-3 Next, 2 remains unchanged.

2-3-1 As a last step, 3 changes into 1.

The net result of B^*F^* is to change 1-2-3 into 2-3-1, which is exactly what A^* does to 1-2-3. Therefore

$$B^*F^* = A^*.$$

Monster Groups Much research in group theory now is devoted to "simple" groups (which are not at all simple). These groups are fundamental—other groups are built up from them. One of the largest of these simple groups has

$$2^{46} \cdot 3^{20} \cdot 5^9 \cdot 7^6 \cdot 11^2 \cdot 13^3 \cdot 17 \cdot 19 \cdot 23 \cdot 29 \cdot 31 \cdot 41 \cdot 47 \cdot 59 \cdot 71$$

different elements. This huge number of elements is why the group is called the "monster group." If this "monster group" contains too many elements, how about the "baby monster" simple group, with only

$$2^{41} \cdot 3^{13} \cdot 5^6 \cdot 7^2 \cdot 11 \cdot 13 \cdot 17 \cdot 19 \cdot 23 \cdot 31 \cdot 47$$

different elements? (For more information, see "The Classification of the Finite Simple Groups," by Michael Aschbacher in *The Mathematical Intelligencer*, Issue 2, 1981.)

Group theory is essential to a detailed study of optical illusions such as the ones shown on these stamps.

| EXAMPLE 7 | Find $D*E*$. |

Use the procedure described above.

$$1\text{-}2\text{-}3$$
$$1\text{-}3\text{-}2$$
$$3$$
$$3 \quad 1$$
$$3\text{-}2\text{-}1$$

Apply $D*$. To apply $E*$, first replace 1 with 3. Next, replace 2 with 1. The last step is to replace 3 with 2. The result: $D*E*$ converts 1-2-3 into 3-2-1, as does $F*$, so

$$D*E* = F*. \quad \blacklozenge$$

As further examples, $A*B* = D*$ and $F*E* = B*$.

Once again, we see that we have encountered a mathematical system: the set $\{A*, B*, C*, D*, E*, F*\}$ and the operation of the combination of two rearrangements. To see whether or not this system is a group, check the requirements.

Closure Combine any two rearrangements and the result is another rearrangement, so the system is closed.

Associative Try an example:

First, $\qquad\qquad (B*D*)A* = E*A* = C*,$

while $\qquad\qquad B*(D*A*) = B*B* = C*,$

so that $\qquad\qquad (B*D*)A* = B*(D*A*).$

Since other examples will work out similarly, the system is associative.

Identity The identity element is $C*$. If x is any rearrangement, then $xC* = C*x = x$.

Inverse Does each rearrangement have an inverse rearrangement? Begin with the basic order 1-2-3 and then apply, say, $B*$, resulting in 2-1-3. The inverse of $B*$ must convert this 2-1-3 back into 1-2-3, by changing 2 into 1 and 1 into 2. But $B*$ itself will do this. Hence $B*B* = C*$ and $B*$ is its own inverse. By the same process, $E*$ and $A*$ are inverses of each other. Also, each of $C*$, $D*$, and $F*$ is its own inverse.

Since all four requirements are satisfied, the system is a group. Rearrangements are also referred to as *permutations*, so this group is sometimes called the **permutation group on three symbols.**

Sophus Lie (1842–1899), a Norwegian mathematician, built the Galois work into a full branch of mathematics, cataloging a huge collection of groups which now bear his name. Originally seen as pure and totally impractical, Lie group theory, with its very extensive symmetry, is now so essential in the grand unified theories of modern physics that the physicist Dr. Michio Kaku has called it the "foundation for all of the physical universe!" Yet even Lie himself, thinking he had catalogued all possible types of groups, completely missed the ones most crucial in modern physics, probably for the same reason that nearly all physicists rejected their use for many years, namely that they are based on numbers that violate the commutative property of multiplication. Noncommutative multiplication, which is counter to our intuition, is encountered in a number of important mathematical systems.

FOR FURTHER THOUGHT

Marja Strutz, Robert Spence, and Sonya Neal are all members (elements?) of a small (finite?) support group that meets on campus each Wednesday. All three also happen to be in the same math class, and after studying mathematical systems they became curious as to whether their Wednesday group was actually a *group* in the mathematical sense. Marja said:

> Everyone in the group is learning to be supportive and trusting. The more the members get together the closer we become. No one has left the group all year. So I believe it must satisfy the **closure** property.

Robert responded:

> Yes, and I've noticed a couple of the members who used to be so hidden within themselves they could never talk to anyone. Now they have opened up and seem to feel comfortable associating freely with the other members. That's what makes me sure that we satisfy the **associative** property.

And Sonya added:

> I just know that before I found our group, I felt like a real nobody. But with the support of these friends, I've begun to realize that I'm somebody. I *do* have an identity of my own. And so does each of the other members. So I would say the **identity** property is surely satisfied.

For Group Discussion

1. Comment on the interpretations offered by Marja, Robert, and Sonya.
2. Do you suppose the support group satisfies the **inverse** property? Explain.

6 EXERCISES

In Exercises 1 and 2, explain how you would respond to each of the following questions.

1. Do the integers form a group?

2. Does multiplication satisfy all of the group properties?

Decide whether or not each system is a group. If not a group, identify all properties that are not satisfied. (Recall that any system failing to satisfy the identity property automatically fails to satisfy the inverse property also.) For the finite systems, it may help to construct tables. For infinite systems, try some examples to help you decide.

3. {0}; addition

4. {0}; multiplication

5. {0}; subtraction

6. {0, 1}; addition

7. {0, 1}; multiplication

8. {−1, 1}; division

9. {−1, 0, 1}; addition

10. {−1, 0, 1}; multiplication

11. Integers; multiplication

12. Integers; subtraction

13. Counting numbers; addition

14. Odd integers; multiplication

15. Even integers; addition

16. Rational numbers; addition

17. Non-zero rational numbers; multiplication

18. Prime numbers; addition

19. Explain why a *finite* group based on the operation of addition of numbers cannot contain the element 1.

20. Explain why a group based on the operation of addition of numbers *must* contain the element 0.

Exercises 21–34 apply to the system of symmetries of a square presented in the text.

Find each of the following.

21. *RN*   **22.** *PR*   **23.** *TV*   **24.** *VP*

Verify each of the following statements.

25. $N(TR) = (NT)R$ **26.** $V(PS) = (VP)S$

27. $S(MR) = (SM)R$ **28.** $T(VN) = (TV)N$

Find the inverse of each element.

29. *N*   **30.** *Q*   **31.** *R*   **32.** *S*   **33.** *T*   **34.** *V*

Determine whether or not each of the following systems is a group.

35. $\{0, 1, 2\}$;   addition modulo 3   **36.** $\{0, 1, 2, 3\}$;   addition modulo 4

37. $\{0, 1, 2, 3, 4\}$;   addition modulo 5   **38.** $\{0, 1, 2, 3, 4, 5\}$;   addition modulo 6

39. Complete this statement: _____ modular addition systems are groups.

Determine whether or not each of the following systems is a group.

40. $\{1, 2, 3\}$;   multiplication modulo 4   **41.** $\{1, 2, 3, 4\}$;   multiplication modulo 5

42. $\{1, 2, 3, 4, 5\}$;   multiplication modulo 6   **43.** $\{1, 2, 3, 4, 5, 6\}$;   multiplication modulo 7

44. $\{1, 2, 3, 4, 5, 6, 7\}$;   multiplication modulo 8   **45.** $\{1, 2, 3, 4, 5, 6, 7, 8\}$;   multiplication modulo 9

46. Notice that in constructing modular multiplication systems, we excluded the element 0. Complete this statement: a modular multiplication system is a group only when the modulus is _____.

Consider the set $\{1, 2, 3, 4\}$ under the operation of multiplication modulo 5. Find each of the following in this system.

47. 2^1 **48.** 2^2 **49.** 2^3 **50.** 2^4 **51.** 2^5

The answers for Exercises 47–51 should have been the elements in the set $\{1, 2, 3, 4\}$, although not in that order. Thus, the various powers of 2 lead to all the elements in the set of the system. For this reason, 2 is called a **generator** *of the group, and the group itself is called a* **cyclic group.**

Check whether the following elements are generators of this same group.

52. 3   **53.** 4   **54.** 1

55. Is the mathematical system made up of the set $\{1, 2, 3, 4, 5, 6\}$ under multiplication modulo 7 a cyclic group? If so, identify all possible generators.

56. Is the group of symmetries of the square a cyclic group? If so, identify all possible generators.

57. Is the subgroup of symmetries of Example 6 a cyclic group? If so, identify all possible generators.

58. Make a chart for the group of rearrangements of three symbols.

Use the chart of Exercise 58 to decide whether each of the following sets of rearrangements is a group under the operation of combinations. If it is a group, decide whether it is cyclic. If it is cyclic, identify all possible generators.

59. $\{C^*\}$ **60.** $\{C^*, D^*\}$ **61.** $\{A^*, B^*, C^*\}$ **62.** $\{C^*, D^*, E^*, F^*\}$

A group that also satisfies the commutative property is called a commutative *group (or an* abelian *group, after Niels Henrik Abel).*

Determine whether each of the following groups is commutative.

63. $\{0, 1, 2, 3\}$ under addition modulo 4

64. $\{1, 2\}$ under multiplication modulo 3

65. the group of symmetries of a square

66. the subgroup of Example 6

67. the integers under addition

68. the permutation group on three symbols

Give illustrations to back up your answers for Exercises 69–72.

69. Produce a mathematical system with two operations which is a group under one operation but not a group under the other operation.

70. Explain what property is gained when the system of counting numbers is extended to the system of whole numbers.

71. Explain what property is gained when the system of whole numbers is extended to the system of integers.

72. Explain what property is gained when the system of integers is extended to the system of rational numbers.

CHAPTER SUMMARY

1 Historical Numeration Systems

Ancient Egyptian (Simple Grouping, Base Ten)

1   10   100   1,000   10,000   100,000   1,000,000

Traditional Chinese (Multiplicative Grouping, Base Ten)

1	2	3	4	5	6	7	8	9	10	100	1,000	0

Hindu-Arabic (Positional, Base Ten)

0   1   2   3   4   5   6   7   8   9

Basics of a Positional Numeral

Each digit conveys

1. face value: the inherent value of the digit symbol
2. place value: the power of the base associated with the digit's position

2 Arithmetic in the Hindu-Arabic System

Modern Algorithms Based on Expanded Notation with the Distributive Property

Early Calculating Schemes

    Mechanical devices: Abacus—still used in some areas today

                 Napier's rods—early forerunner of the modern computer

   "Paper and pencil" algorithms: Lattice method—used in India and Persia

                 Russian peasant method—related to base two

3 Converting Between Number Bases

Converting from Another Base to Decimal

Expanded form　　*Example:* $342_{\text{five}} = (3 \times 5^2) + (4 \times 5^1) + (2 \times 5^0)$
$$= (3 \times 25) + (4 \times 5) + (2 \times 1)$$
$$= 75 + 20 + 2$$
$$= 97$$

Calculator shortcut　　*Example:* $5{,}624_{\text{seven}} = ((5 \times 7 + 6) \times 7 + 2) \times 7 + 4$
$$= 2{,}027$$

Converting from Decimal to Another Base

Repeated division by the new base　　*Example:* Convert 548 to base five.

Remainder

$$5 \,|\, 548$$
$$5 \,\overline{|\, 109} \qquad 3$$
$$5 \,\overline{|\, 21} \qquad\; 4$$
$$5 \,\overline{\underline{|\, 4}} \qquad\quad 1$$
$$0 \qquad\qquad 4 \qquad 548 = 4{,}143_{\text{five}}$$

Some Decimal Equivalents in the Common Computer-Oriented Bases

Decimal (base ten)	Hexadecimal (base sixteen)	Octal (base eight)	Binary (base two)
0	0	0	0
1	1	1	1
2	2	2	10
3	3	3	11
4	4	4	100
5	5	5	101
6	6	6	110
7	7	7	111
8	8	10	1,000
9	9	11	1,001
10	A	12	1,010
11	B	13	1,011
12	C	14	1,100
13	D	15	1,101
14	E	16	1,110
15	F	17	1,111
16	10	20	10,000
17	11	21	10,001

4 Clock Arithmetic and Modular Systems

Example: a 4-hour clock

Addition table

+	0	1	2	3
0	0	1	2	3
1	1	2	3	0
2	2	3	0	1
3	3	0	1	2

Multiplication table

×	0	1	2	3
0	0	0	0	0
1	0	1	2	3
2	0	2	0	2
3	0	3	2	1

Congruence Modulo *m*

$a \equiv b \pmod{m}$ if and only if $a - b$ is divisible by m.

5 Other Finite Mathematical Systems

Potential Properties of a Single-Operation System

Here a, b, and c represent elements from the set of the system, and $\circ$ represents the operation of the system.

Closure   The system is closed if for all elements a and b,

$$a \circ b$$

is in the set of the system.

Commutative   The system has the commutative property if

$$a \circ b = b \circ a$$

for all elements a and b from the system.

Associative   The system has the associative property if

$$(a \circ b) \circ c = a \circ (b \circ c)$$

for every choice of three elements a, b, and c of the system.

Identity   The system has an identity element e (where e is in the set of the system) if

$$a \circ e = a \qquad \text{and} \qquad e \circ a = a,$$

for every element a in the system.

Inverse   The system satisfies the inverse property if, for every element a of the system, there is an element x in the system such that

$$a \circ x = e \qquad \text{and} \qquad x \circ a = e,$$

where e is the identity element of the system.

General Form of the Distributive Property

Let $\star$ and $\circ$ be two operations defined for elements in the same set. Then $\star$ is distributive over $\circ$ if

$$a \star (b \circ c) = (a \star b) \circ (a \star c)$$

for every choice of elements a, b, and c from the set.

6 Groups

Group

A mathematical system is called a **group** if, under its operation, it satisfies the closure, associative, identity, and inverse properties.

Examples of a Group

The symmetries of a square
The permutations (rearrangements) of three symbols

Subgroup

A (proper) subset of a group that is also a group under the same operation

Abelian group

A group that also satisfies the commutative property

CHAPTER TEST

1. For the numeral 𝟃𝟃 𝟡𝟡𝟡∩∩∩|||, identify the numeration system, and give the Hindu-Arabic equivalent.

2. Simplify: $(8 \times 10^3) + (3 \times 10^2) + (6 \times 10^1) + (4 \times 10^0)$.

3. Write in expanded notation: 60,923.

Convert each of the following to base ten.

4. 424_{five}

5. $100,110_{two}$

6. $A,80C_{sixteen}$

Convert as indicated.

7. 58 to base two

8. 1,846 to base five

9. $10,101,110_{two}$ to base eight

10. $B52_{sixteen}$ to base two

Briefly explain each of the following.

11. the advantage of multiplicative grouping over simple grouping

12. the advantage, in a positional numeration system, of a smaller base over a larger base

13. the advantage, in a positional numeration system, of a larger base over a smaller base

Do the following arithmetic problems on a 12-hour clock.

14. $11 + 9$

15. $6 - 9$

16. 8×9

Do the following modular arithmetic problems.

17. $(7 \times 18) \pmod 8$

18. $(52 + 39) \pmod 6$

19. $(23 \times 56) \pmod 2$

20. Construct an addition table for a modulo 6 system.

21. Construct a multiplication table for a modulo 6 system.

Find all positive solutions for the following.

22. $x \equiv 5 \pmod{12}$

23. $5x \equiv 3 \pmod 8$

24. Find the smallest positive integer that satisfies both $x \equiv 3 \pmod{12}$ and $x \equiv 5 \pmod 7$.

25. Describe in general what constitutes a mathematical *group*.

A mathematical system is defined by the table here.

V	a	e	i	o	u
a	o	e	u	a	i
e	u	o	a	e	i
i	e	u	o	i	a
o	a	e	i	o	u
u	i	a	e	u	o

26. (a) Is there an identity element in this system?   (b) If so, what is it?

27. (a) Is closure satisfied by this system?   (b) Explain.

28. (a) Is this system commutative?   (b) Explain.

29. (a) Is the distributive property satisfied in this system?   (b) Explain.

30. (a) Is the system a group?   (b) Explain.

The Real Number System

CHAPTER 4

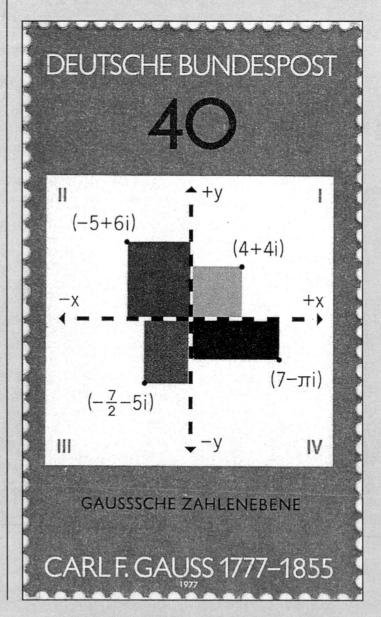

As mathematics developed, it was discovered that the numbers *1, 2, 3, 4*, and so on (the *counting* or *natural* numbers), did not satisfy all of the requirements of mathematicians. Consequently, new, expanded number systems were created. The mathematician Leopold Kronecker (1823–1891) once made the statement "God made the integers, all the rest is the work of man." In this chapter we look at those sets that, according to Kronecker, are the work of mankind.

The *whole numbers* consist of the counting numbers with the important number 0 included. By taking the negatives of the counting numbers along with the whole numbers, the set of *integers* is formed. The concept of fractional quantities is introduced when quotients of integers are formed. Counting numbers, whole numbers, integers, and quotients of integers all are examples of *rational numbers*. There are other useful numbers, such as $\sqrt{2}$ and π, that are not rational numbers. They cannot be represented exactly as quotients of integers, although they may be approximated that way. The very large set containing all of these numbers is called the set of *irrational numbers*. The union of the set of rational numbers and the set of irrational numbers is called the set of *real numbers*.

1

Introduction to Sets of Real Numbers

By including 0 in the set of natural numbers, we obtain the set of whole numbers.

The Origins of Zero The Mayan Indians of Mexico and Central America had one of the earliest numeration systems that included a symbol for 0. The very early Babylonians had a positional system, but they placed only a space between "digits" to indicate a missing power. When the Greeks absorbed Babylonian astronomy, they quickly saw the need for a symbol to represent "no powers." As early as 150 A.D. they used o or ō to represent "no power," or "zero." By the year 500, the Greeks were using the letter omicron, o, of their alphabet for "zero." The Greek numeration system gradually lost out to the Roman numeration system throughout Western Europe.

The Roman system was the one most commonly used in Europe from the time of Christ until perhaps 1400, when the Hindu-Arabic system began to take over. Zero was fundamental

---

Natural Numbers

$\{1, 2, 3, 4, \ldots\}$ is the set of **natural numbers.**

Whole Numbers

$\{0, 1, 2, 3, \ldots\}$ is the set of **whole numbers.**

These numbers, along with many others, can be represented on **number lines** like the one pictured in Figure 1. We draw a number line by locating any point on the line and calling it 0. Choose any point to the right of 0 and call it 1. The distance between 0 and 1 gives a unit of measure used to locate other points, as shown in Figure 1. The points labeled in Figure 1 and those continuing in the same way to the right correspond to the set of whole numbers.

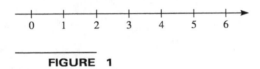

FIGURE 1

All the whole numbers starting with 1 are located to the right of 0 on the number line. But numbers may also be placed to the left of 0. These numbers, written $-1, -2, -3$, and so on, are shown in Figure 2. (The minus sign is used to show that the numbers are located to the *left* of 0.)

to the Hindu-Arabic system. The original Hindu word for zero was *sunya*, meaning "void." The Arabs adopted this word as *sifr*, or "vacant." There was a considerable battle over the new system in Europe, with most people sticking with the Roman system. Gradually, however, the advantages of the new Hindu-Arabic system became clear, and it replaced the cumbersome Roman system. The word *sifr* passed into Latin as *zephirum*, which over the years became *zevero*, *zepiro*, and finally, *zero*.

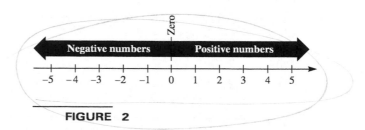

FIGURE 2

The numbers to the *left* of 0 are **negative numbers.** The numbers to the *right* of 0 are **positive numbers.** The number 0 itself is neither positive nor negative. Positive numbers and negative numbers are called **signed numbers.**

There are many practical applications of negative numbers. For example, temperatures sometimes fall below zero. The lowest temperature ever recorded in meteorological records was −128.6°F at Vostok, Antarctica, on July 22, 1983. A business that spends more than it takes in has a negative "profit." Altitudes below sea level can be represented by negative numbers. The shore surrounding the Dead Sea is 1,312 feet below sea level; this can be represented as −1,312 feet.

The set of numbers marked on the number line in Figure 2, including positive and negative numbers and zero, is part of the set of *integers*.

Integers

$\{. . . , -3, -2, -1, 0, 1, 2, 3, . . .\}$ is the set of **integers.**

Not all numbers are integers. For example, 1/2 is not; it is a number halfway between the integers 0 and 1. Also, 3 1/4 is not an integer. Several numbers that are not integers are *graphed* in Figure 3. The **graph** of a number is a point on the number line. Think of the graph of a set of numbers as a picture of the set. All the numbers in Figure 3 can be written as quotients of integers. These numbers are examples of *rational numbers*.

The Origins of Negative Numbers Negative numbers can be traced back to the Chinese between 200 B.C. and 220 A.D. Mathematicians at first found negative numbers ugly and unpleasant, even though they kept cropping up in the solutions of problems. For example, an Indian text of about 1150 A.D. gives the solution of an equation as −5 and then makes fun of anything so useless.

Leonardo of Pisa (Fibonacci), while working on a financial problem, was forced to conclude that the solution must be a negative number, that is, a financial loss. In 1545, the rules governing operations with negative numbers were published by Girolamo Cardano in his *Ars Magna* (Great Art).

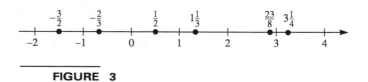

FIGURE 3

Rational Numbers

$\{x \mid x$ is a quotient of two integers, with denominator not equal to 0$\}$ is the set of **rational numbers.**

(Read the part in the braces as "the set of all numbers x such that x is a quotient of two integers, with denominator not equal to 0.")

The set symbolism used in the definition of rational numbers,

$$\{x \mid x \text{ has a certain property}\},$$

is called **set-builder notation.** This notation is convenient to use when it is not possible to list all the elements of the set.

Since any integer can be written as the quotient of itself and 1, all integers also are rational numbers.

All numbers that can be represented by points on the number line are called *real numbers.*

Real Numbers

$\{x \mid x \text{ is a number that can be represented by a point on the number line}\}$ is the set of **real numbers.**

Although a great many numbers are rational, not all are. For example, a floor tile one foot on a side has a diagonal whose length is the square root of 2 (written $\sqrt{2}$). It will be shown in Section 4 that $\sqrt{2}$ cannot be written as a quotient of integers. Because of this, $\sqrt{2}$ is not rational; it is *irrational.*

Irrational Numbers

$\{x \mid x \text{ is a real number that is not rational}\}$ is the set of **irrational numbers.**

Examples of irrational numbers include $\sqrt{3}$, $\sqrt{7}$, $-\sqrt{10}$, and π, which is the ratio of the distance around a circle to the distance across it.

Real numbers can be written as decimal numbers. Any rational number will have a decimal that will come to an end (terminate), or repeat in a fixed "block" of digits. For example, $2/5 = .4$ and $27/100 = .27$ are rational numbers with terminating decimals; $1/3 = .3333\ldots$ and $3/11 = .27272727\ldots$ are repeating decimals. The decimal representation of an irrational number will neither terminate nor repeat. More will be discussed about decimal representation of rational and irrational numbers later in this chapter.

Figure 4 illustrates two ways to represent the relationships among the various sets of real numbers.

EXAMPLE 1   List the numbers in the set

$$\left\{-5, \quad -\frac{2}{3}, \quad 0, \quad \sqrt{2}, \quad \frac{13}{4}, \quad 5, \quad 5.8\right\}$$

that belong to each of the following sets of numbers.

(a) natural numbers
The only natural number in the set is 5.

(b) whole numbers
The whole numbers consist of the natural numbers and 0. So the elements of the set that are whole numbers are 0 and 5.

(c) integers

The integers in the set are −5, 0, and 5.

(d) rational numbers

The rational numbers are −5, −2/3, 0, 13/4, 5, and 5.8, since each of these numbers *can* be written as the quotient of two integers. For example, 5.8 = 58/10.

(e) irrational numbers

The only irrational number in the set is $\sqrt{2}$.

(f) real numbers

All the numbers in the set are real numbers. ●

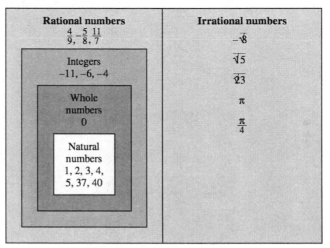

All numbers shown are real numbers.

(a)

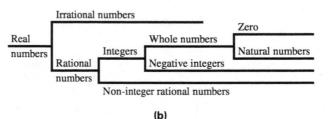

(b)

FIGURE 4

Two real numbers may be compared using the ideas of equality and inequality. Suppose that a and b represent two real numbers. If their graphs on the number line are the same point, they are **equal.** If the graph of a lies to the left of b, a **is less than** b, and if the graph of a lies to the right of b, a **is greater than** b. We use symbols to represent these ideas.

When read from left to right, the symbol < represents "is less than," so that "7 is less than 8" is written

$$7 < 8.$$

Also, we write "6 is less than 9" as 6 < 9.

The symbol > means "is greater than." Write "8 is greater than 2" as

$$8 > 2.$$

The statement "17 is greater than 11" becomes 17 > 11.

We can keep the meanings of the symbols < and > clear by remembering that the symbol always points to the smaller number. For example, write "8 is less than 15" by pointing the symbol toward the 8:

$$8 < 15$$

Two other symbols, ≤ and ≥, also represent the idea of inequality. The symbol ≤ means "is less than or equal to," so that

$$5 \leq 9$$

means "5 is less than or equal to 9." This statement is true, since 5 < 9 is true. If either the < part or the = part is true, then the inequality ≤ is true.

The symbol ≥ means "is greater than or equal to." Again,

$$9 \geq 5$$

is true because 9 > 5 is true. Also, 8 ≤ 8 is true since 8 = 8 is true. But it is not true that 13 ≤ 9 because neither 13 < 9 nor 13 = 9 is true.

The symbol for equality, =, was first introduced by the Englishman Robert Recorde in his 1557 algebra text *The Whetstone of Witte*. He used two parallel line segments because, he claimed, no two things can be more equal.

The symbols for order relationships, < and >, were first used by Thomas Harriot (1560–1621), another Englishman. These symbols were not immediately adopted by other mathematicians.

EXAMPLE 2   Determine whether each statement is *true* or *false*.

(a) 6 ≠ 6

The statement is false because 6 *is equal to* 6.

(b) 5 < 19

Since 5 represents a number that is indeed less than 19, this statement is true.

(c) 15 ≤ 20

The statement 15 ≤ 20 is true, since 15 < 20.

(d) 25 ≥ 30

Both 25 > 30 and 25 = 30 are false. Because of this, 25 ≥ 30 is false.

(e) 12 ≥ 12

Since 12 = 12, this statement is true.   ●

By a property of the real numbers, for any real number *x* (except 0), there is exactly one number on the number line the same distance from 0 as *x* but on the opposite side of 0. For example, Figure 5 shows that the numbers 3 and −3 are both the same distance from 0 but are on opposite sides of 0. The numbers 3 and −3 are called **additive inverses,** or **opposites,** of each other.

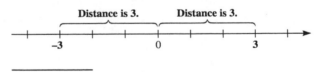

FIGURE 5

The additive inverse of the number 0 is 0 itself. This makes 0 the only real number that is its own additive inverse. Other additive inverses occur in pairs. For example, 4 and −4, and 5 and −5, are additive inverses of each other. Several pairs of additive inverses are shown in Figure 6.

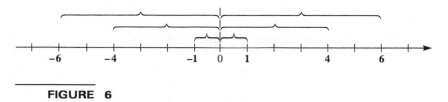

FIGURE   6

EXAMPLE 3   The following chart shows several numbers and their additive inverses.

Number	Additive Inverse
−4	−(−4), or 4
0	0
−2	2
19	−19
3	−3

An important property of additive inverses will be studied in more detail in a later section of this chapter: $a + (−a) = (−a) + a = 0$ for all real numbers a.

As mentioned above, additive inverses are numbers that are the same distance from 0 on the number line. This idea can also be expressed by saying that a number and its additive inverse have the same absolute value. The **absolute value** of a real number can be defined as the distance between 0 and the number on the number line. The symbol for the absolute value of the number x is $|x|$, read "the absolute value of x." For example, the distance between 2 and 0 on the number line is 2 units, so that

$$|2| = 2.$$

Because the distance between −2 and 0 on the number line is also 2 units,

$$|−2| = 2.$$

Since distance is a physical measurement, which is never negative, the absolute value of a number is never negative. For example, $|12| = 12$ and $|−12| = 12$, since both 12 and −12 lie at a distance of 12 units from 0 on the number line. Also, since 0 is a distance 0 units from 0, $|0| = 0$.

In symbols, the absolute value of x is defined as follows.

Formal Definition of Absolute Value

$$|x| = \begin{cases} x \text{ if } x \geq 0 \\ -x \text{ if } x < 0 \end{cases}$$

By this definition, if x is a positive number or 0, then its absolute value is x itself. For example, since 8 is a positive number, $|8| = 8$. However, if x is a negative number, then its absolute value is the additive inverse of x. For example, since -9 is a negative number, $|-9| = -(-9) = 9$, since the additive inverse of -9 is 9.

EXAMPLE 4   Simplify by removing absolute value symbols.

(a) $|5| = 5$

(b) $|-5| = -(-5) = 5$

(c) $-|5| = -(5) = -5$

(d) $-|-14| = -(14) = -14$

(e) $|8 - 2| = |6| = 6$ ●

---

1 EXERCISES

Graph each set on a number line.

1. $\{2, 3, 4, 5\}$

2. $\{0, 2, 4, 6, 8\}$

3. $\{-4, -3, -2, -1, 0, 1\}$

4. $\{-6, -5, -4, -3, -2\}$

5. $\left\{ -\dfrac{1}{2}, \dfrac{3}{4}, \dfrac{5}{3}, \dfrac{7}{2} \right\}$

6. $\left\{ -\dfrac{3}{5}, -\dfrac{1}{10}, \dfrac{9}{8}, \dfrac{12}{5}, \dfrac{13}{4} \right\}$

List the numbers in the given set that belong to (a) the natural numbers, (b) the whole numbers, (c) the integers, (d) the rational numbers, (e) the irrational numbers, and (f) the real numbers.

7. $\left\{ -9, -\sqrt{7}, -\dfrac{5}{4}, -\dfrac{3}{5}, 0, \sqrt{5}, 3, 5.9, 7 \right\}$

8. $\left\{ -5.3, -5, -\sqrt{3}, -1, -\dfrac{1}{9}, 0, 1.2, 1.8, 3, \sqrt{11} \right\}$

Decide whether each of the following statements is true *or* false.

9. $-2 < -1$

10. $-8 < -4$

11. $-3 \geq -7$

12. $-9 \geq -12$

13. $-15 \leq -20$

14. $-21 \leq -27$

15. $-8 \leq -(-4)$

16. $-9 \leq -(-6)$

17. $0 \leq -(-4)$

18. $0 \geq -(-6)$

19. $6 > -(-2)$

20. $-8 > -(-2)$

Give (a) the additive inverse and (b) the absolute value of each of the following.

21. 5

22. 9

23. -6

24. -8

25. A statement commonly heard is "Absolute value is always positive." Is this true? If not, explain.

26. If a is a negative number, then is $-|a|$ positive or negative?

27. Fill in the blanks with the correct values: The opposite of -3 is ———, while the absolute value of -3 is ———. The additive inverse of -3 is ———, while the additive inverse of the absolute value of -3 is ———.

28. True or false: For all real numbers a and b, $|a - b| = |b - a|$.

Specify each set by listing its elements. If there are no elements, write $\varnothing$.

29. $\{x \mid x \text{ is a natural number less than } 7\}$

30. $\{m \mid m \text{ is a whole number less than } 9\}$

31. $\{a \mid a \text{ is an even integer greater than } 10\}$

32. $\{k \mid k \text{ is a natural number less than } 1\}$

33. $\{x \mid x$ is an irrational number that is also rational$\}$
34. $\{r \mid r$ is a negative integer greater than $-1\}$
35. $\{p \mid p$ is a number whose absolute value is 3$\}$
36. $\{w \mid w$ is a number whose absolute value is 12$\}$
37. $\{z \mid z$ is a whole number multiple of 5$\}$
38. $\{n \mid n$ is a natural number multiple of 3$\}$

Give three examples of numbers that satisfy the given condition.

39. positive real numbers but not integers
40. real numbers but not positive numbers
41. real numbers but not whole numbers
42. rational numbers but not integers
43. real numbers but not rational numbers
44. rational numbers but not negative numbers

Tell whether each statement is true *or* false.

45. Every rational number is an integer. *False*

46. Every natural number is an integer. *True*
47. Every integer is a rational number. *True*
48. Every whole number is a real number. *True*
49. Some rational numbers are irrational. *False*
50. Some natural numbers are whole numbers. *True*
51. Some rational numbers are integers. *True*
52. Some real numbers are integers. *True*
53. Every rational number is a real number. *True*
54. Some integers are not real numbers. *False*
55. Every integer is positive. *False*
56. Every whole number is positive. *false*
57. Some irrational numbers are negative. *True*
58. Some real numbers are not rational. *True*
59. Not every rational number is positive. *True*
60. Some whole numbers are not integers. *whole #s are integers*

Simplify each expression by removing absolute value symbols.

61. $|3|$ 62. $|-8|$ 63. $-|7|$ 64. $-|-9|$
65. $|7 - 4|$ 66. $-|12 - 3|$ 67. $-|-(5 - 1)|$ 68. $|-(3 - 1)|$

Complete the following table, writing yes *if the number belongs to the specified set or* no *if it does not.*

	Number	Whole	Integer	Rational	Irrational	Real
69.	8	yes			no	yes
70.	-3		yes		no	
71.	$\dfrac{1}{4}$					
72.	$\dfrac{3}{17}$	no	no			
73.	6.15	no			no	yes
74.	-9.92	no				yes
75.	0					
76.	.666. . .				no	
77.	$\sqrt{2}$			no		
78.	$\sqrt{-1}$					no

2

Operations, Properties, and Applications of Real Numbers

The answer to an addition problem is called the **sum.** The rules for addition of real numbers are given below.

Adding Real Numbers

Like Signs Add two numbers with the *same* sign by adding their absolute values. The sign of the sum (either + or −) is the same as the sign of the two numbers.

Unlike Signs Add two numbers with *different* signs by subtracting the smaller absolute value from the larger. The sum is positive if the positive number has the larger absolute value. The sum is negative if the negative number has the larger absolute value.

For example, to add −12 and −8, first find their absolute values:

$$|-12| = \mathbf{12} \quad \text{and} \quad |-8| = \mathbf{8}.$$

Since these numbers have the *same* sign, add their absolute values: $12 + 8 = 20$. Give the sum the sign of the two numbers. Since both numbers are negative, the sign is negative and

$$-12 + (-8) = -20.$$

Find $-17 + 11$ by subtracting the absolute values, since these numbers have different signs.

$$|-17| = \mathbf{17} \quad \text{and} \quad |11| = \mathbf{11}$$
$$17 - 11 = 6$$

Give the result the sign of the number with the larger absolute value.

$$-17 + 11 = -6$$

⌐ Negative since $|-17| > |11|$

Practical Arithmetic From the time of Egyptian and Babylonian merchants, practical aspects of arithmetic complemented mystical (or "Pythagorean") tendencies. This was certainly true in the time of Adam Riese (1489–1559), a "reckon master" influential when commerce was growing in Northern Europe. Riese's likeness on the stamp above comes from the title page of one of his popular books on *Rechnung* (or "reckoning"). He championed new methods of reckoning using Hindu-Arabic numerals and quill pens. (The Roman methods in use moved counters on a ruled board.) Riese thus fulfilled Fibonacci's efforts three hundred years earlier to supplant Roman numerals and methods.

EXAMPLE 1 Find each of the following sums.

(a) $(-6) + (-3) = -(6 + 3) = -9$ **(b)** $(-12) + (-4) = -(12 + 4) = -16$

(c) $4 + (-1) = 3$ **(d)** $-9 + 16 = 7$

(e) $-16 + 12 = -4$ ●

We now turn our attention to subtraction of real numbers. The result of subtraction is called the **difference.** Thus, the difference between 7 and 5 is 2. To see how subtraction should be defined, compare the two statements below.

$$7 - 5 = 2$$
$$7 + (-5) = 2$$

In a similar way,

$$9 - 3 = 9 + (-3).$$

That is, to subtract 3 from 9, add the additive inverse of 3 to 9. These examples suggest the following rule for subtraction.

Definition of Subtraction

For all real numbers a and b,

$$a - b = a + (-b).$$

(Change the sign of the second number and add.)

EXAMPLE 2   Perform the indicated operations.

┌─ Change to addition.
│ ┌─ Change sign of second number.
↓ ↓

(a) $6 - 8 = 6 + (-8) = -2$

┌─ Change to addition.
│ ┌─ Change sign of secon⟨
↓ ↓

(b) $6 - 8 = 6 + (-8) = -2$

(c) $-10 - (-7) = -10 + [-(-7)]$ This step can be omitted.
$$= -10 + 7$$
$$= -3$$

(d) $15 - (-3) - 5 - 12$

When a problem with both addition and subtraction is being worked, perform the additions and subtractions in order from left to right.

$$15 - (-3) - 5 - 12 = (\mathbf{15 + 3}) - 5 - 12$$
$$= \mathbf{18} - 5 - 12$$
$$= 13 - 12$$
$$= 1 \quad \bullet$$

We now turn our attention to the operations of multiplication and division of real numbers. Any rules for multiplication with negative real numbers should be consistent with the usual rules for multiplication of positive real numbers and zero. To inductively obtain a rule for multiplying a positive real number and a negative real number, observe the pattern of products below. (The **product** is the result of a multiplication problem.)

$$\mathbf{4 \cdot 5 = 20}$$
$$\mathbf{4 \cdot 4 = 16}$$
$$\mathbf{4 \cdot 3 = 12}$$
$$\mathbf{4 \cdot 2 = 8}$$
$$\mathbf{4 \cdot 1 = 4}$$
$$\mathbf{4 \cdot 0 = 0}$$
$$\mathbf{4 \cdot (-1) = ?}$$

Early ways of writing the four basic operation symbols were quite different from those used today. The addition symbol shown below was derived from the Italian word *piú* (plus) in the sixteenth century. The + sign used today is shorthand for the Latin *et* (and).

The subtraction symbol shown below was used by Diophantus in Greece sometime during the second or third century A.D. Our subtraction bar may be derived from a bar used by medieval traders to mark differences in weights of products.

In the seventeenth century, Leibniz used the symbol below for multiplication to avoid × as too similar to the "unknown" x. The multiplication symbol × is based on St. Andrew's Cross.

The division symbol shown below was used by Gallimard in the eighteenth century. The familiar ÷ symbol may come from the fraction bar, embellished with the dots above and below.

What number must be assigned as the product $4 \cdot (-1)$ so that the pattern is maintained? The numbers just to the left of the equals signs decrease by 1 each time, and the products to the right decrease by 4 each time. To maintain the pattern, the number to the right in the bottom equation must be 4 less than 0, which is -4, or

$$4 \cdot (-1) = -4.$$

The pattern continues with

$$4 \cdot (-2) = -8$$
$$4 \cdot (-3) = -12$$
$$4 \cdot (-4) = -16,$$

and so on. In the same way,

$$-4 \cdot 2 = -8$$
$$-4 \cdot 3 = -12$$
$$-4 \cdot 4 = -16,$$

and so on.

A similar observation can be made about the product of two negative real numbers. Look at the pattern that follows.

$$-5 \cdot 4 = -20$$
$$-5 \cdot 3 = -15$$
$$-5 \cdot 2 = -10$$
$$-5 \cdot 1 = -5$$
$$-5 \cdot 0 = 0$$
$$-5 \cdot (-1) = ?$$

The numbers just to the left of the equals signs decrease by 1 each time. The products on the right increase by 5 each time. To maintain the pattern, the product $-5 \cdot (-1)$ must be 5 more than 0, or

$$-5 \cdot (-1) = 5.$$

Continuing this pattern gives

$$-5 \cdot (-2) = 10$$
$$-5 \cdot (-3) = 15$$
$$-5 \cdot (-4) = 20,$$

and so on.

These observations lead to the following rules for multiplication.

Multiplying Real Numbers

Like Signs Multiply two numbers with the *same* sign by multiplying their absolute values. The product is positive.

Unlike Signs Multiply two numbers with *different* signs by multiplying their absolute values. The product is negative.

EXAMPLE 3   Find each of the following products.

(a) $-9 \cdot -7 = -63$

(b) $-14 \cdot (-5) = 70$

(c) $-8 \cdot (-4) = 32$ ⬢

Let us now consider the operation of division. The result obtained by dividing real numbers is called the **quotient.** For real numbers a, b, and c, where $b \neq 0$, $\dfrac{a}{b} = c$ means that $a = b \cdot c$. To illustrate this, consider the division problem

$$\frac{10}{-2}.$$

The value of this quotient is obtained by asking "What number multiplied by -2 gives 10?" From our discussion of multiplication, the answer to this question must be "-5." Therefore,

$$\frac{10}{-2} = -5,$$

because $(-2) \cdot (-5) = 10$. Similar reasoning leads to the following results.

$$\frac{-10}{2} = -5 \qquad \frac{-10}{-2} = 5$$

These facts, along with the fact that the quotient of two positive numbers is positive, lead to the following rules for division.

Dividing Real Numbers

Like Signs   Divide two numbers with the *same* sign by dividing their absolute values. The quotient is positive.

Unlike Signs   Divide two numbers with *different* signs by dividing their absolute values. The quotient is negative.

EXAMPLE 4   Find each of the following quotients.

(a) $\dfrac{15}{-5} = -3$ This is true because $-5 \cdot (-3) = 15$.

(b) $\dfrac{-100}{-25} = 4$

(c) $\dfrac{-60}{-3} = 20$ ⬢

If 0 is divided by a nonzero number, the quotient is 0. That is,

$$\frac{0}{a} = 0 \quad \text{for } a \neq 0.$$

This is true because $a \cdot 0 = 0$. However, we cannot divide *by* 0. There is a good reason for this. Whenever a division is performed, we want to obtain one and only one quotient. Now consider the division problem

$$\frac{7}{0}.$$

We must ask ourselves "What number multiplied by 0 gives 7?" There is no such number, since the product of 0 and any number is zero. On the other hand, if we consider the quotient

$$\frac{0}{0},$$

there are infinitely many answers to the question "What number multiplied by 0 gives 0?" Since division by 0 does not yield a *unique* quotient, it is not permitted. To summarize these two situations, we make the following statement.

Division by 0 is undefined.

Order of Operations

Given a problem such as $5 + 2 \cdot 3$, should 5 and 2 be added first or should 2 and 3 be multiplied first? When a problem involves more than one operation, we use the following **order of operations.** (This is the order used by computers and many calculators.)

Order of Operations

If parentheses or square brackets are present:

Step 1 Work separately above and below any fraction bar.

Step 2 Use the rules below within each set of parentheses or square brackets. Start with the innermost set and work outward.

If no parentheses or brackets are present:

Step 1 Apply all exponents.

Step 2 Do any multiplications or divisions in the order in which they occur, working from left to right.

Step 3 Do any additions or subtractions in the order in which they occur, working from left to right.

The sentence "Please excuse my dear Aunt Sally" is often used to help remember the rule for order of operations. The letters P, E, M, D, A, S are the first letters of the words of the sentence, and they stand for *parentheses, exponents, multiply, divide, add, subtract.*

It is important to be careful when evaluating an exponential expression that involves a negative sign. In particular, we should be aware that $(-a)^n$ and $-a^n$ do not necessarily represent the same quantity. For example, if $a = 2$ and $n = 6$,

$$(-2)^6 = (-2)(-2)(-2)(-2)(-2)(-2) = 64$$

while

$$-2^6 = -(2 \cdot 2 \cdot 2 \cdot 2 \cdot 2 \cdot 2) = -64.$$

Notice that for $(-2)^6$, the $-$ sign is used in each factor of the expanded form, while for -2^6, the $-$ sign is treated as a factor of -1, and the base of the exponential expression is 2 (not -2).

EXAMPLE 5   Use the order of operations to simplify each of the following.

(a) $5 + 2 \cdot 3$

First multiply, and then add.

$$5 + \mathbf{2 \cdot 3} = 5 + \mathbf{6} \qquad \text{Multiply.}$$
$$= 11 \qquad \text{Add.}$$

(b) $4 \cdot 3^2 + 7 - (2 + 8)$

Work inside the parentheses.

$$4 \cdot 3^2 + 7 - \mathbf{(2 + 8)} = 4 \cdot 3^2 + 7 - \mathbf{10}$$

Apply all exponents. Since $3^2 = 3 \cdot 3 = 9$,

$$4 \cdot \mathbf{3^2} + 7 - 10 = 4 \cdot \mathbf{9} + 7 - 10.$$

Do all multiplications or divisions, working from left to right.

$$\mathbf{4 \cdot 9} + 7 - 10 = \mathbf{36} + 7 - 10$$

Finally, do all additions or subtractions, working from left to right.

$$\mathbf{36 + 7} - 10 = \mathbf{43} - 10$$
$$= \mathbf{33}$$

(c) $\dfrac{2(8 - 12) - 11(4)}{5(-2) - 3} = \dfrac{2(-4) - 11(4)}{5(-2) - 3} = \dfrac{-8 - 44}{-10 - 3} = \dfrac{-52}{-13} = 4$

(d) $-4^4 = -(4 \cdot 4 \cdot 4 \cdot 4) = -256$

(e) $(-4)^4 = (-4)(-4)(-4)(-4) = 256$

(f) $(-8)(-3) - [4 - (3 - 6)] = (-8)(-3) - [4 - (-3)]$
$$= (-8)(-3) - [4 + 3]$$
$$= (-8)(-3) - 7$$
$$= 24 - 7$$
$$= 17 \quad \blacksquare$$

Properties of Addition and Multiplication of Real Numbers

Several properties of addition and multiplication of real numbers that are essential to our study in this chapter are summarized in the following box.

Properties of Addition and Multiplication

For real numbers a, b, and c, the following properties hold.

Closure Properties If a and b are real numbers, then $a + b$ and ab are real numbers.

Commutative Properties
$$a + b = b + a \qquad ab = ba$$

Associative Properties
$$(a + b) + c = a + (b + c)$$
$$(ab)c = a(bc)$$

Identity Properties There is a real number 0 such that
$$a + 0 = a \qquad \text{and} \qquad 0 + a = a.$$

There is a real number 1 such that
$$a \cdot 1 = a \qquad \text{and} \qquad 1 \cdot a = a.$$

Inverse Properties For each real number a, there is a single real number $-a$ such that
$$a + (-a) = 0 \qquad \text{and} \qquad (-a) + a = 0.$$

For each nonzero real number a, there is a single real number $\dfrac{1}{a}$ such that
$$a \cdot \frac{1}{a} = 1 \qquad \text{and} \qquad \frac{1}{a} \cdot a = 1.$$

Distributive Property of Multiplication with Respect to Addition
$$a(b + c) = ab + ac$$
$$(b + c)a = ba + ca$$

The set of real numbers is said to be closed with respect to the operations of addition and multiplication. This means that the sum of two real numbers and the product of two real numbers are real numbers themselves. The commutative properties state that two real numbers may be added or multiplied in any order without affecting the result. The associative properties allow us to group terms or factors in any manner we wish without affecting the result. The number 0 is called the **identity element for addition**, and it may be added to any real number to obtain that real number as a sum. Similarly, 1 is called the **identity element for multiplication**, and multiplying a real number by 1 will always yield that real number. Each real number a has an **additive inverse**, $-a$, such that the sum is the additive identity element 0. Each nonzero real number a has a **multiplicative inverse**, or **reciprocal**, $1/a$, such that their product is the multiplicative identity element 1. The distributive property allows us to change a product to a sum or a sum to a product.

EXAMPLE 6   Some specific examples of the properties of addition and multiplication of real numbers are given here.

(a) $5 + 7$ is a real number.   Closure property for addition

(b) $5 + (6 + 8) = (5 + 6) + 8$ Associative property of addition

(c) $8 + 0 = 8$ Identity property of addition

(d) $-4(-1/4) = 1$ Inverse property of multiplication

(e) $4 + (3 + 9) = 4 + (9 + 3)$ Commutative property of addition

(f) $5(x + y) = 5x + 5y$ Distributive property ●

Applications of Real Numbers

The usefulness of negative numbers can be seen by considering situations that arise in everyday life. For example, we need negative numbers to express the temperatures on January days in Anchorage, Alaska, where they often drop below zero. If a company loses money, its "profits" are negative. Such money-losing companies are said to be "in the red" (an expression from the Renaissance, when losses were written in red ink and profits in black ink). And, of course, haven't we all experienced a checking account balance below zero, with hopes that our deposit will make it to the bank on time before our outstanding checks "bounce"?

PROBLEM SOLVING

When problems deal with gains and losses, the gains may be interpreted as positive numbers and the losses as negative numbers. Temperatures below 0° are negative, and those above 0° are positive. Altitudes above sea level are considered positive and those below sea level are considered negative. The next examples show applications of these ideas. ●

EXAMPLE 7   Paul Van Erden gained 3 yards on the first play from scrimmage, lost 12 yards on the second play, and then gained 13 yards on the third play. How many yards did Paul gain or lose altogether?

The gains are represented by positive numbers and the loss by a negative number.

$$3 + (-12) + 13$$

Add from left to right.

$$3 + (-12) + 13 = [3 + (-12)] + 13 = (-9) + 13 = 4$$

Paul gained 4 yards altogether. ●

EXAMPLE 8   The record high temperature of 134°F in the United States was recorded in Death Valley, California, in 1913. The record low was -80°F at Prospect Creek, Alaska, in 1971. What is the difference between the highest and the lowest temperatures?

We must find the value of the highest temperature minus the lowest temperature.

$$134 - (-80) = 134 + 80 \qquad \text{Use the definition of subtraction.}$$
$$= 214 \qquad\qquad \text{Add.}$$

The difference between the highest and the lowest temperatures is 214° F.   ●

---

2 EXERCISES

Decide whether each statement is true *or* false.

1. The sum of two negative numbers must be negative.

2. The difference between two negative numbers must be negative.

3. The product of two negative numbers must be negative.

4. The quotient of two negative numbers must be negative.

5. If $a > 0$ and $b < 0$, then $\dfrac{a}{b} < 0$.

6. The product of 648 and −927 is a real number.

Perform the indicated operations, using the order of operations as necessary.

7. $-12 + (-8)$
8. $-5 + (-2)$
9. $12 + (-16)$

10. $-6 + 17$
11. $-12 - (-1)$
12. $-3 - (-8)$

13. $-5 + 11 + 3$
14. $-9 + 16 + 5$
15. $12 - (-3) - (-5)$

16. $15 - (-6) - (-8)$
17. $-9 - (-11) - (4 - 6)$
18. $-4 - (-13) + (-5 + 10)$

19. $(-12)(-2)$
20. $(-3)(-5)$
21. $9(-12)(-4)(-1)3$

22. $-5(-17)(2)(-2)4$
23. $\dfrac{-18}{-3}$
24. $\dfrac{-100}{\rule{1.5em}{0.4pt}}$

25. $\dfrac{36}{-6}$
26. $\dfrac{52}{-13}$
27. $\dfrac{0}{12}$

28. $\dfrac{0}{\rule{1.5em}{0.4pt}}$
29. $-6 + [5 - (3 + 2)]$
30. $-8[4 + (7 - 8)]$

31. $-8(-2) - [(4^2) + (7 - 3)]$
32. $-7(-3) - [(2^3) - (3 - 4)]$
33. $-4 - 3(-2) + 5^2$

34. $-6 - 5(-8) + 3^2$
35. $(-6 - 3)(-2 - 3)$
36. $(-8 - 5)(-2 - 1)$

37. $\dfrac{(-10 + 4) \cdot (-3)}{-7 - 2}$
38. $\dfrac{(-6 + 3) \cdot (-4)}{-5 - 1}$

39. Which of the following expressions are undefined?

   (a) $\dfrac{8}{0}$ (b) $\dfrac{9}{6 - 6}$ (c) $\dfrac{4 - 4}{5 - 5}$ (d) $\dfrac{0}{-1}$

40. If you have no money in your pocket and you divide it equally among your three siblings, how much does each get? Use this situation to explain division of zero by a nonzero number.

Identify the property illustrated by each of the following statements.

41. $6 + 9 = 9 + 6$

42. $8 \cdot 4 = 4 \cdot 8$

43. $7 + (2 + 5) = (7 + 2) + 5$

44. $(3 \cdot 5) \cdot 4 = 4 \cdot (3 \cdot 5)$

45. $9 + (-9) = 0$

46. $12 + 0 = 12$

47. $9 \cdot 1 = 9$

48. $(-1/3) \cdot (-3) = 1$

49. $0 + 283 = 283$

50. $6 \cdot (4 \cdot 2) = (6 \cdot 4) \cdot 2$

51. $2 \cdot (4 + 3) = 2 \cdot 4 + 2 \cdot 3$

52. $9 \cdot 6 + 9 \cdot 8 = 9 \cdot (6 + 8)$

53. $19 + 12$ is a real number.

54. $19 \cdot 12$ is a real number.

55. **(a)** Evaluate $6 - 8$ and $8 - 6$.
   (b) By the results of part (a), we may conclude that subtraction is not a(n) ——— operation.
   (c) Are there *any* real numbers a and b for which $a - b = b - a$? If so, give an example.

56. **(a)** Evaluate $4 \div 8$ and $8 \div 4$.
   (b) By the results of part (a), we may conclude that division is not a(n) ——— operation.
   (c) Are there *any* real numbers a and b for which $a \div b = b \div a$? If so, give an example.

57. Many everyday occurrences can be thought of as operations that have opposites or inverses. For example, the inverse operation for "going to sleep" is "waking up." For each of the given activities, specify its inverse activity.
   (a) cleaning up your room
   (b) earning money
   (c) increasing the volume on your portable radio

58. Many everyday activities are commutative; that is, the order in which they occur does not affect the outcome. For example, "putting on your shirt" and "putting on your pants" are commutative operations. Decide whether the given activities are commutative.
   (a) putting on your shoes; putting on your socks
   (b) getting dressed;   taking a shower
   (c) combing your hair;   brushing your teeth

59. The following conversation actually took place between one of the authors of this text and his son, Jack, when Jack was four years old.

Daddy: "Jack, what is $3 + 0$?"
Jack: "3"
Daddy: "Jack, what is $4 + 0$?"
Jack: "4 . . . and Daddy, *string* plus zero equals *string*!"

What property of addition of real numbers did Jack recognize?

60. The phrase *defective merchandise counter* is an example of a phrase that can have different meanings depending upon how the words are grouped (think of the associative properties). For example, *(defective merchandise) counter* is a location at which we would return an item that does not work, while *defective (merchandise counter)* is a broken place where items are bought and sold. For each of the following phrases, explain why the associative property does not hold.
   (a) difficult test question
   (b) woman fearing husband
   (c) man biting dog

61. The distributive property holds for multiplication with respect to addition. Does the distributive property hold for addition with respect to multiplication? That is, is $a + (b \cdot c) = (a + b) \cdot (a + c)$ true for all values of a, b, and c? (*Hint:* Let $a = 2$, $b = 3$, and $c = 4$.)

62. Suppose someone makes the following claim: The distributive property for addition with respect to multiplication (from Exercise 61) is valid, and here's why: Let $a = 2$, $b = -4$, and $c = 3$. Then $a + (b \cdot c) = 2 + (-4 \cdot 3) = 2 + (-12) = -10$, and $(a + b) \cdot (a + c) = [2 + (-4)] \cdot [2 + 3] = -2 \cdot 5 = -10$. Since both expressions are equal, the property must be valid. How would you respond to this reasoning?

63. Suppose that a student shows you the following work.
$$-3(4 - 6) = -3(4) - 3(6) = -12 - 18 = -30$$
The student has made a very common error in applying the distributive property. Write a short paragraph explaining the student's mistake, and work the problem correctly.

64. Work the following problem in two ways, first using the order of operations, and then using the distributive property: Evaluate $9(11 + 15)$.

Recall from the text that an expression such as -2^4 *is evaluated as follows:*

$$-2^4 = -(2 \cdot 2 \cdot 2 \cdot 2) = -16.$$

The expression $(-2)^4$ *is evaluated as follows:*

$$(-2)^4 = (-2)(-2)(-2)(-2) = 16.$$

Each of the expressions in Exercises 65–72 is equal to either 81 *or* −81. *Decide which of these is the correct value.*

65. -3^4 **66.** $-(3^4)$ **67.** $(-3)^4$ **68.** $-(-3^4)$

69. $-(-3)^4$ **70.** $[-(-3)]^4$ **71.** $-[-(-3)]^4$ **72.** $-[-(-3^4)]$

73. Find a real number value of x such that $-x^3 = (-x)^3$.

74. Find a real number value of x such that $-x^2 = (-x)^2$.

Solve each of the following problems.

75. On January 23, 1943, the temperature in Spearfish, South Dakota, rose 49°F in two minutes. If the starting temperature was −4°F, what was the temperature two minutes later?

76. Marc Garza's checking account balance is $54. After writing a check for $68 he hopes to make a deposit before the check clears. What is his new balance before he makes a deposit? (Write the balance as a signed number.)

77. The lowest temperature ever recorded in Spokane, Washington, was −25°F. The highest recorded temperature there was 108°F. Find the difference between the highest and lowest temperatures.

78. On a series of three consecutive running plays, Dalton Hilliard of the New Orleans Saints gained 7 yd, lost 9 yd, and gained 1 yd. What positive or negative number represents his total net yardage for this series of plays?

79. Fontaine Evaldo, a pilot for a major airline, announced to her passengers that their plane, currently at 34,000 ft, would descend 2,500 ft to avoid turbulence, and then ascend 3,000 ft once they were out of danger from the turbulence. What would their final altitude be?

80. The top of Mount Whitney, visible from Death Valley, has an altitude of 14,494 ft above sea level. The bottom of Death Valley is 282 ft below sea level. Letting zero represent sea level, find the difference between these two elevations.

81. The highest point in Louisiana is Driskill Mountain, at an altitude of 535 ft. The lowest point is at Spanish Fort, 8 ft below sea level. Letting zero represent sea level, find the difference between these two elevations.

82. The highest temperature ever recorded in Albany, New York, was 99°F. The lowest temperature ever recorded there was 112 degrees less than the highest. What was the lowest temperature?

83. Ellen Endres, a chemist, was conducting an experiment at a constant temperature of −50°C. For three consecutive hours, she lowered the temperature 20 degrees per hour. What was the temperature at the end of the three hours?

84. A certain Greek mathematician was born in 426 B.C. His father was born 43 years earlier. In what year was his father born?

85. A piece of luggage falls from a plane flying 2,500 ft above a lake, and plunges to a point 140 ft below the water level of the lake. How many feet did the piece of luggage fall? (Write this solution as a subtraction problem.)

86. Kevin Carlson enjoys playing Triominoes every Thursday night. Last Thursday, on four successive turns, his scores were −19, 28, −5, and 13. What was his total score for the four turns?

87. David Fleming enjoys scuba diving. He dives to 34 ft below the surface of a lake. His partner, Jeremy Gowing, dives to 40 ft below the surface, but then ascends 20 ft. What is the vertical distance between Jeremy and David?

88. Write a problem similar to the ones found in Exercises 75–87, and solve it.

It is possible to actually prove that the product of two even integers is even, the sum of an odd integer and an even integer is odd, and so on. To do these, we use the following definitions:

> An integer is **even** if and only if it can be written in the form $2k$, where k is an integer.
> An integer is **odd** if and only if it can be written in the form $2m + 1$, where m is an integer.

We also must use the fact that the integers are closed for the operations of addition and multiplication.

EXAMPLE   Prove that the product of two even integers is even.

Proof Let $2k$ and $2m$ represent the two even integers. Then their product is $(2k)(2m)$. But $(2k)(2m) = 2(k \cdot 2m)$ by the associative property. Since $k \cdot 2m$ is an integer by closure, $2(k \cdot 2m)$ represents an even integer. Therefore, the product of two even integers is even.   ●

Use a similar method to prove each of the following.

89. The sum of two even integers is even.

90. The sum of two odd integers is even.

91. The product of an odd integer and an even integer is even.

92. The product of two odd integers is odd.

EXTENSION

Defining Whole Number Operations Using Sets

We can use the concepts of set theory to define addition and multiplication of whole numbers. We assume that all sets discussed here are finite sets. Recall that $n(A)$ represents the cardinal number of set A.

The set of **whole numbers** may be defined as the set of all cardinal numbers of finite sets. For example, $0 = n(\emptyset)$, $1 = n(\{a\})$, $2 = n(\{a, b\})$, and so on. The operation of addition of whole numbers is defined as follows.

Addition of Whole Numbers

If $n(A) = a$ and $n(B) = b$,   and if $A \cap B = \emptyset$,   then

$$a + b = n(A \cup B).$$

This definition can be illustrated as follows: Let $A = \{a, b\}$ and $B = \{c, d, e\}$. As required by the definition, $A \cap B = \emptyset$. Now $n(A) = 2$ and $n(B) = 3$. $A \cup B = \{a, b, c, d, e\}$, and so $n(A \cup B) = 5$. Therefore,

$$2 + 3 = n(A \cup B) = 5.$$

EXAMPLE 1 Show that addition of whole numbers is commutative by using the commutative property of union of sets: $A \cup B = B \cup A$.

Let A and B be sets such that $n(A) = a$ and $n(B) = b$, where $A \cap B = \varnothing$.

$$a + b = n(A) + n(B) \qquad \text{Given}$$
$$= n(A \cup B) \qquad \text{Definition of addition of whole numbers}$$
$$= n(B \cup A) \qquad \text{Commutative property of the union operation of sets}$$
$$= n(B) + n(A) \qquad \text{Definition of addition of whole numbers}$$
$$= b + a \quad \blacklozenge$$

Multiplication of whole numbers can also be defined in terms of set operations. Recall that $A \times B$ represents the Cartesian product of A and B.

Multiplication of Whole Numbers

If $n(A) = a$ and $n(B) = b$, then

$$a \cdot b = n(A \times B).$$

For example, let $A = \{1, 5, 9\}$ and $B = \{6, 7\}$. Pair each element of A with each element of B to find the product of the sets: $A \times B = \{(1, 6), (1, 7), (5, 6), (5, 7), (9, 6), (9, 7)\}$. Note that $n(A) = 3$, $n(B) = 2$, and $n(A \times B) = 6$.

Once we have defined addition and multiplication in terms of set operations, definitions of subtraction and division may also be given.

Subtraction and Division of Whole Numbers

For whole numbers a, b, and c,

$$a - b = c \qquad \text{if and only if} \qquad a = b + c.$$

For whole numbers a, b, and c, where $b \neq 0$,

$$a \div b = c \qquad \text{if and only if} \qquad a = b \cdot c.$$

EXAMPLE 2 Use the definitions of whole number subtraction and whole number division to find the following:

(a) $8 - 2$
$8 - 2 = \mathbf{6}$ because $8 = 2 + \mathbf{6}$.

(b) $8 \div 2$
$8 \div 2 = \mathbf{4}$ because $8 = 2 \cdot \mathbf{4}$. $\blacklozenge$

EXTENSION EXERCISES

1. Use the set theory definition of addition of whole numbers to find the sum $3 + 4$.

2. Use the set theory definition of multiplication of whole numbers to find the product $3 \cdot 4$.

In Exercises 3–6, let $A = \{m, n, o, p\}$ and let $B = \{p, q\}$.

3. Find $n(A)$.   4. Find $n(B)$.   5. Find $A \cup B$.   6. Find $n(A \cup B)$.

7. Is it true that in all cases, $n(A) + n(B) = n(A \cup B)$?

8. Why is it necessary to have the condition $A \cap B = \varnothing$ in the definition of addition of whole numbers?

9. Fill in the blank with $\geq$ or $\leq$ to make the statement true: For any sets A and B,
   $n(A) + n(B) \text{——} n(A \cup B)$.

Use the definitions of subtraction and division to justify each statement.

10. $7 - 3 = 4$ 11. $5 - 5 = 0$ 12. $16 \div 2 = 8$ 13. $26 \div 26 = 1$

14. The zero property of multiplication may be justified by using the ideas of set theory. Give the definition or property which justifies each statement below. Assume that $n(A) = a$.

$$0 = n(\varnothing) \qquad \text{————}$$
$$a \cdot 0 = n(A) \cdot n(\varnothing) \qquad \text{————}$$
$$= n(A \times \varnothing) \qquad \text{————}$$
$$= n(\varnothing) \qquad \text{————}$$
$$= 0 \qquad \text{————}$$

15. A definition of "less than" in terms of sets is given below.

If $n(A) = a$ and $n(B) = b$,

$a < b$ if and only if A is equivalent to a proper subset of B.

Give an example using this definition to illustrate that 3 is less than 5.

16. How would you change the definition in Exercise 15 to define "less than or equal to?"

3

Rational Numbers and Decimals

The set of real numbers is composed of two important mutually exclusive subsets: the rational numbers and the irrational numbers. (Two sets are *mutually exclusive* if they contain no elements in common.) In this section and the next, we will look at these two sets in some detail. Let us begin by examining the set of rational numbers.

Quotients of integers are called **rational numbers.** Think of the rational numbers as being made up of all the fractions (quotients of integers with denominator not equal to 0) and all the integers. Any integer can be written as the quotient of two integers. For example, the integer 9 can be written as the quotient 9/1, or 18/2, or 27/3, and so on. Also, −5 can be expressed as a quotient of integers as −5/1 or −10/2, and so on. (How can the integer 0 be written as a quotient of integers?) Since both fractions and integers can be written as quotients of integers, the set of rational numbers is defined as follows.

Rational Numbers

Rational numbers = $\{x \mid x \text{ is a quotient of two integers, with denominator not } 0\}$

Benjamin Banneker
(1731–1806) spent the first half of his life tending a farm in Maryland. He gained a reputation locally for his mechanical skills and abilities in mathematical problem-solving. In 1772 he acquired astronomy books from a neighbor and devoted himself to learning astronomy, observing the skies, and making calculations. In 1789 Banneker joined the team that surveyed what is now the District of Columbia.

Banneker published almanacs yearly from 1792 to 1802. His almanacs contained the usual astronomical data and information about the weather and seasonal planting. He also wrote social commentary and made proposals for the establishment of a peace office in the president's Cabinet, for a department of the interior, and for a league of nations. He sent a copy of his first almanac to Thomas Jefferson along with an impassioned letter against slavery. Jefferson subsequently championed the cause of this early African-American mathematician.

A rational number is said to be in **lowest terms** if the greatest common factor of the numerator (top number) and the denominator (bottom number) is 1. Rational numbers are written in lowest terms by using the *fundamental property of rational numbers.*

Fundamental Property of Rational Numbers

If a, b, and k are integers with $b \neq 0$ and $k \neq 0$, then

$$\frac{a \cdot k}{b \cdot k} = \frac{a}{b}.$$

The following example illustrates the fundamental property of rational numbers. We find the greatest common factor of the numerator and denominator and use it for k in the statement of the property.

EXAMPLE 1   Reduce 36/54 to lowest terms.

Since the greatest common factor of 36 and 54 is 18,

$$\frac{36}{54} = \frac{2 \cdot 18}{3 \cdot 18} = \frac{2}{3}. \quad \blacklozenge$$

In the above example it was shown that 36/54 = 2/3. If we multiply the numerator of the fraction on the left by the denominator of the fraction on the right, we obtain $36 \cdot 3 = 108$. Now if we multiply the denominator of the fraction on the left by the numerator of the fraction on the right, we obtain $54 \cdot 2 = 108$. It is not just coincidence that the result is the same in both cases. In fact, one way of determining whether two fractions are equal is to perform this test. If the product of the "extremes" (36 and 3 in this case) equals the product of the "means" (54 and 2), the fractions are equal. This method of checking for equality of rational numbers is called the **cross-product method.** It is given in the following box.

Cross-Product Test for Equality of Rational Numbers

For rational numbers a/b and c/d, $b \neq 0, d \neq 0$,

$$\frac{a}{b} = \frac{c}{d} \qquad \text{if and only if} \qquad a \cdot d = b \cdot c.$$

FIGURE 7

The operation of addition of rational numbers can be illustrated by the sketches in Figure 7. The rectangle on the left is divided into three equal portions, with one of the portions shaded. The rectangle on the right is divided into five equal parts, with two of them shaded.

The total of the shaded areas shaded is represented by the sum

$$\frac{1}{3} + \frac{2}{5}.$$

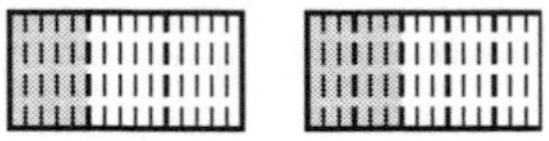

$\frac{5}{15}$
of the
rectangle
is shaded.

$\frac{6}{15}$
of the
rectangle
is shaded.

FIGURE 8

To evaluate this sum, the shaded areas must be redrawn in terms of a common unit. Since the least common multiple of 3 and 5 is 15, redraw both rectangles with 15 parts. See Figure 8. In the figure, 11 of the small rectangles are shaded, so

$$\frac{1}{3} + \frac{2}{5} = \frac{5}{15} + \frac{6}{15} = \frac{11}{15}.$$

In general, the sum

$$\frac{a}{b} + \frac{c}{d}$$

may be found by writing a/b and c/d with the common denominator bd, retaining this denominator in the sum, and adding the numerators:

$$\frac{a}{b} + \frac{c}{d} = \frac{ad}{bd} + \frac{bc}{bd} = \frac{ad + bc}{bd}.$$

A similar case can be made for the difference between rational numbers. A formal definition of addition and subtraction of rational numbers follows.

Adding and Subtracting Rational Numbers

If a/b and c/d are rational numbers, then

$$\frac{a}{b} + \frac{c}{d} = \frac{ad + bc}{bd} \qquad \text{and} \qquad \frac{a}{b} - \frac{c}{d} = \frac{ad - bc}{bd}.$$

This formal definition is seldom used in practice. In practical problems involving addition and subtraction of rational numbers, we usually rewrite the fractions with the least common multiple of their denominators. This is called the **least common denominator,** and finding the least common denominator may be done by inspection, or by the method of prime factorization. Rewrite the fractions so that the least common multiple of their denominators becomes the denominator of each one.

EXAMPLE 2   (a) Add: $\dfrac{2}{15} + \dfrac{1}{10}$

The least common multiple of 15 and 10 is 30. Now write 2/15 and 1/10 with denominators of 30, and then add the numerators. Proceed as follows:

Since $30 \div 15 = 2$, $\dfrac{2}{15} = \dfrac{2 \cdot 2}{15 \cdot 2} = \dfrac{4}{30}$,

and since $30 \div 10 = 3$, $\dfrac{1}{10} = \dfrac{1 \cdot 3}{10 \cdot 3} = \dfrac{3}{30}$.

Thus, $\dfrac{2}{15} + \dfrac{1}{10} = \dfrac{4}{30} + \dfrac{3}{30} = \dfrac{7}{30}$.

(b) Subtract: $\dfrac{173}{180} - \dfrac{69}{1{,}200}$

The least common multiple of 180 and 1,200 is 3,600.

$$\frac{173}{180} - \frac{69}{1{,}200} = \frac{3{,}460}{3{,}600} - \frac{207}{3{,}600} = \frac{3{,}460 - 207}{3{,}600} = \frac{3{,}253}{3{,}600}$$ ⬢

The product of two rational numbers is defined as follows.

Multiplying Rational Numbers

If a/b and c/d are rational numbers, then

$$\frac{a}{b} \cdot \frac{c}{d} = \frac{ac}{bd}.$$

Exercises 39 and 40 in this section illustrate a justification for this definition.

EXAMPLE 3   Find each of the following products.

(a) $\dfrac{3}{4} \cdot \dfrac{7}{10} = \dfrac{3 \cdot 7}{4 \cdot 10} = \dfrac{21}{40}$

(b) $\dfrac{5}{18} \cdot \dfrac{3}{10} = \dfrac{5 \cdot 3}{18 \cdot 10} = \dfrac{15}{180} = \dfrac{1 \cdot 15}{12 \cdot 15} = \dfrac{1}{12}$

In practice, a multiplication problem such as this is often solved by using slash marks to indicate that common factors have been divided out of the numerator and denominator.

$$\overset{1}{\underset{6}{\cancel{18}}} \cdot \overset{1}{\underset{2}{\cancel{10}}}$$

  3 is divided out of the terms 3 and 18;
  5 is divided out of 5 and 10.

$$= \frac{1}{6} \cdot \frac{1}{2}$$

$$= \frac{1}{12}$$ ⬢

In a fraction, the fraction bar indicates the operation of division. Recall that, in the previous section, we defined the multiplicative inverse, or reciprocal, of the nonzero number b. The multiplicative inverse of b is $1/b$. We can now define division using multiplicative inverses.

Definition of Division

If a and b are real numbers, $b \neq 0$, then

$$\frac{a}{b} = a \cdot \frac{1}{b}.$$

You have probably heard the rule "To divide fractions, invert the divisor and multiply." But have you ever wondered why this rule works? To illustrate it, suppose that you have 7/8 of a gallon of milk and you wish to find how many quarts you have. Since a quart is 1/4 of a gallon, you must ask yourself, "How many 1/4s are there in 7/8?" This would be interpreted as

$$\frac{7}{8} \div \frac{1}{4} \qquad \text{or} \qquad \frac{\frac{7}{8}}{\frac{1}{4}}.$$

The fundamental property of rational numbers discussed earlier can be extended to rational number values of a, b, and k. With $a = 7/8$, $b = 1/4$, and $k = 4$,

$$\frac{a}{b} = \frac{a \cdot k}{b \cdot k} = \frac{\frac{7}{8} \cdot 4}{\frac{1}{4} \cdot 4} = \frac{\frac{7}{8} \cdot 4}{1} = \frac{7}{8} \cdot \frac{4}{1}.$$

Now notice that we began with the division problem 7/8 ÷ 1/4 which, through a series of equivalent expressions, led to the multiplication problem 7/8 · 4/1. So dividing by 1/4 is equivalent to multiplying by its reciprocal, 4/1. By the definition of multiplication of fractions,

$$\frac{7}{8} \cdot \frac{4}{1} = \frac{28}{8} = \frac{7}{2},$$

and thus there are 7/2 or 3 1/2 quarts in 7/8 gallon.*

We now state the rule for dividing a/b by c/d.

Dividing Rational Numbers

If a/b and c/d are rational numbers, where $c/d \neq 0$, then

$$\frac{a}{b} \div \frac{c}{d} = \frac{a}{b} \cdot \frac{d}{c} = \frac{ad}{bc}.$$

---

*3 1/2 is a **mixed number.** Mixed numbers are covered in the exercises for this section.

EXAMPLE 4   Find each of the following quotients.

(a) $\dfrac{3}{5} \div \dfrac{7}{15} = \dfrac{3}{5} \cdot \dfrac{15}{7} = \dfrac{45}{35} = \dfrac{9 \cdot 5}{7 \cdot 5} = \dfrac{9}{7}$

(b) $\dfrac{-4}{7} \div \dfrac{3}{14} = \dfrac{-4}{7} \cdot \dfrac{14}{3} = \dfrac{-56}{21} = \dfrac{-8 \cdot 7}{3 \cdot 7} = \dfrac{-8}{3} = -\dfrac{8}{3}$

(c) $\dfrac{2}{9} \div 4 = \dfrac{2}{9} \div \dfrac{4}{1} = \dfrac{2}{9} \cdot \dfrac{1}{4} = \dfrac{\overset{1}{2}}{9} \cdot \dfrac{1}{\underset{2}{4}} = \dfrac{1}{18}$ ◆

There is no integer between two consecutive integers, such as 3 and 4. However, a rational number can always be found between any two distinct rational numbers. For this reason, the set of rational numbers is said to be *dense*.

Density Property of the Rational Numbers

If r and t are distinct rational numbers, with $r < t$, then there exists a rational number s such that

$$r < s < t.$$

Simon Stevin (1548–1620) worked as a bookkeeper in Belgium and became an engineer in the Netherlands army. He is usually given credit for the development of decimals. His work was an attempt to place whole numbers and fractions on common ground, but he did it in such a confusing way that nothing came of it for many years. Stevin's notation was clumsy; he did not use a decimal point. In fact, historians do not agree on who invented it. There is, however, agreement that the decimal point (or comma) did not come into common use until the seventeenth century. A comma is used instead of a decimal point in many European countries. The British use a point, but in an elevated position, as $23 \cdot 298$.

Example 5 shows how to find the rational number that is halfway between two given rational numbers—the average of the numbers.

EXAMPLE 5   Find the rational number halfway between 2/3 and 5/6.
Add the numbers:

$$\dfrac{2}{3} + \dfrac{5}{6} = \dfrac{4}{6} + \dfrac{5}{6} = \dfrac{9}{6} = \dfrac{3}{2}.$$

Take half this sum:

$$\dfrac{1}{2} \cdot \dfrac{3}{2} = \dfrac{3}{4}.$$

The number 3/4 is halfway between 2/3 and 5/6.   ◆

Repeated application of the density property implies that between two given rational numbers are *infinitely many* rational numbers. It is also true that between any two *real* numbers there are infinitely many *real* numbers. Thus, we may say that the set of real numbers is dense.

Decimal Form of Rational Numbers

Up to now in this section, we have discussed rational numbers in the form of quotients of integers. Rational numbers can also be expressed as decimals. Decimal numerals have place values that are powers of 10. For example, the decimal numeral

483.039475 is read "four hundred eighty three and thirty nine thousand, four hundred seventy five millionths." The place values are as shown here.

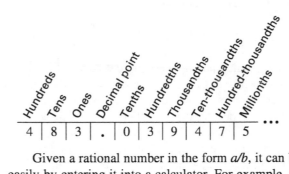

Given a rational number in the form *a/b*, it can be expressed as a decimal most easily by entering it into a calculator. For example, to write 3/8 as a decimal, enter 3, then enter the operation of division, then enter 8. Press the equals key to find the following equivalence.

$$\frac{3}{8} = .375$$

Of course, this same result may be obtained by long division, as shown in the margin. By this result, the rational number 3/8 is the same as the decimal .375. A decimal such as .375, which stops, is called a **terminating decimal.** Other examples of terminating decimals are

$$\frac{1}{4} = .25 \qquad \frac{7}{10} = .7, \qquad \text{and} \qquad \frac{89}{1,000} = .089.$$

Not all rational numbers can be represented by terminating decimals. For example, convert 4/11 into a decimal by dividing 11 into 4 using a calculator. The display shows

.36363636363,   or perhaps   .363636364.

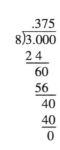

However, we see that the long division process, shown in the margin, indicates that we will actually get .3636 . . . , with the digits 36 repeating over and over indefinitely. To indicate this, we write a bar (called a *vinculum*) over the "block" of digits that repeats. Therefore, we can write

$$\frac{4}{11} = .\overline{36}.$$

Because of the limitations of the display of a calculator, and because some rational numbers have repeating decimals, it is important to be able to interpret calculator results accordingly when obtaining repeating decimals.

While we shall distinguish between *terminating* and *repeating* decimals in this book, some mathematicians prefer to consider all rational numbers as repeating decimals. This can be justified by thinking this way: if the division process leads to a remainder of 0, then zeros repeat indefinitely in the decimal form. For example, we can consider the decimal form of 3/4 as follows.

$$\frac{3}{4} = .75\overline{0}$$

EXAMPLE 6   A calculator or long division shows the following decimals for the given quotients of integers.

(a) $\dfrac{5}{11} = .\overline{45}$ (b) $\dfrac{1}{3} = .\overline{3}$ (c) $\dfrac{5}{6} = .8\overline{3}$ ●

By considering the possible remainders that may be obtained when converting a quotient of integers to a decimal, we can draw an important conclusion about the decimal form of rational numbers. If the remainder is never zero, the division will produce a repeating decimal. This happens because each step of the division process must produce a remainder that is less than the divisor. Since the number of different possible remainders is less than the divisor, the remainders must eventually begin to repeat. This makes the digits of the quotient repeat, producing a repeating decimal.

Any rational number can be expressed as either a terminating decimal or a repeating decimal.

Table 1 shows the reciprocals of the first twenty counting numbers. Recall that the reciprocal of a number n is $1/n$. Reciprocals of counting numbers are rational numbers.

In order to find a baseball player's batting average, we divide the number of hits by the number of at-bats. A surprising paradox exists concerning averages; it is possible for Player *A* to have a higher batting average than Player *B* in each of two successive years, yet for the two-year period, Player *B* can have a higher total batting average. Look at the chart.

Year	Player *A*	Player *B*
1991	$\dfrac{20}{40} = .500$	$\dfrac{90}{200} = .450$
1992	$\dfrac{60}{200} = .300$	$\dfrac{10}{40} = .250$
Two-year total	$\dfrac{80}{240} = .333$	$\dfrac{100}{240} = .417$

TABLE 1

Number	Reciprocal	Number	Reciprocal
1	1.0	11	$.\overline{09}$
2	.5	12	$.08\overline{3}$
3	$.\overline{3}$	13	$.\overline{076923}$
4	.25	14	$.0\overline{714285}$
5	.2	15	$.0\overline{6}$
6	$.1\overline{6}$	16	.0625
7	$.\overline{142857}$	17	$.\overline{58823594117647}$
8	.125	18	$.0\overline{5}$
9	$.\overline{1}$	19	$.\overline{052631578947368421}$
10	.1	20	.05

To determine whether the decimal form of a quotient of integers will terminate or repeat, use the following rule.

Criteria for Terminating and Repeating Decimals

A rational number a/b in lowest terms results in a **terminating decimal** if the only prime factors of the denominator are 2 or 5 (or both).

A rational number a/b in lowest terms results in a **repeating decimal** if a prime other than 2 or 5 appears in the prime factorization of the denominator.

The justification of this is based on the fact that the prime factors of 10 are 2 and 5, and the decimal system uses ten as its base.

EXAMPLE 7   Without actually dividing, determine whether the decimal form of the given rational number terminates or repeats.

(a) $\dfrac{7}{8}$

Since 8 factors as 2^3, the decimal form will terminate. No primes other than 2 or 5 divide the denominator.

(b) $\dfrac{13}{150}$

$150 = 2 \cdot 3 \cdot 5^2$. Since 3 appears as a prime factor of the denominator, the decimal form will repeat.

(c) $\dfrac{6}{\rule{1cm}{0.4pt}}$

Before performing the test it is necessary to reduce the rational number to lowest terms.

$$\frac{6}{75} = \frac{2}{25}$$

Since $25 = 5^2$, the decimal form will terminate.   ●

We have seen that a rational number will be represented by either a terminating or a repeating decimal. What about the reverse process? That is, must a terminating decimal or a repeating decimal represent a rational number? The answer is *yes*. For example, the terminating decimal .6 represents a rational number:

$$.6 = \frac{6}{10} = \frac{3}{5}.$$

EXAMPLE 8   Write each terminating decimal as a quotient of integers.

(a) .437

Think of .437 in words as "four hundred thirty-seven thousandths," or

$$.437 = \frac{437}{1,000}.$$

(b) $8.2 = 8 + \dfrac{2}{10} = \dfrac{82}{10} = \dfrac{41}{5}$ ⬢

Repeating decimals cannot be converted into quotients of integers quite so quickly. The steps for making this conversion are given in the next example. (This example uses basic algebra.)

$$1 = .99999999999999\cdots$$

Terminating or Repeating?
One of the most baffling truths of elementary mathematics is the following:

$$1 = .9999\ldots$$

Most people believe that $.\overline{9}$ has to be less than 1, but this is not the case. The following argument shows otherwise. Let $x = .9999\ldots$. Then

$$\begin{aligned} 10x &= 9.9999\ldots \\ x &= .9999\ldots \\ \hline 9x &= 9 \quad \text{Subtract.} \\ x &= 1. \end{aligned}$$

Therefore, $1 = .9999\ldots$. Similarly, it can be shown that any terminating decimal can be represented as a repeating decimal with an endless string of 9s. For example, $.5 = .49999\ldots$ and $2.6 = 2.59999\ldots$. This is another way of justifying what was stated in the text: any rational number may be represented as a repeating decimal.

For more on the fact that $1 = .\overline{9}$, see the article "Persuasive Arguments: $.9999\ldots = 1$" by Lucien T. Hall, Jr., in the December 1971 issue of *The Mathematics Teacher*. See also Exercises 117 and 118 at the end of this section.

EXAMPLE 9   Find a quotient of two integers equal to $.\overline{85}$.

Step 1   Let $x = .\overline{85}$, so that $x = .858585\ldots$.

Step 2   Multiply both sides of the equation $x = .858585\ldots$ by 100. (Use 100 since there are two digits in the part that repeats.)

$$\begin{aligned} x &= .858585\ldots \\ 100x &= 100(.858585\ldots) \\ 100x &= 85.858585\ldots \end{aligned}$$

Step 3   Subtract the expressions in Step 1 from the final expression in Step 2.

$$\begin{aligned} 100x &= 85.858585\ldots \\ x &= .858585\ldots \\ \hline 99x &= 85 \end{aligned}$$
(Recall that $x = 1x$ and $100x - x = 99x$.)

Step 4   Solve the equation $99x = 85$ by dividing both sides by 99:

$$99x = 85$$
$$\frac{99x}{99} = \frac{85}{99}$$
$$x = \frac{85}{99}.$$

Since x equals $.\overline{85}$,

$$.\overline{85} = \frac{85}{99}.$$

This result may be checked with a calculator. Remember, however, that the calculator will only show a finite number of decimal places, and may round off in the final decimal place shown. ●

EXAMPLE 10   Express $.3\overline{2}$ as the quotient of two integers.

Follow the steps given in the previous example.

Step 1 $x = .3\overline{2} = .322222\ldots$

Step 2 $10x = 3.2222\ldots$

Step 3
$$\begin{aligned} 10x &= 3.22222\ldots \\ x &= .32222\ldots \\ \hline 9x &= 2.9 \end{aligned}$$

Step 4   Since $9x = 2.9$, we have $x = \dfrac{2.9}{9}$.

Since 2.9 is not an integer as required, multiply numerator and denominator by 10:

$$x = \frac{2.9}{9} = \frac{2.9 \cdot 10}{9 \cdot 10} = \frac{29}{90}.$$

Finally, $.3\overline{2} = 29/90$. ●

3 EXERCISES

Decide whether each statement is true *or* false.

1. If *p* and *q* are different prime numbers, the rational number *p/q* is reduced to lowest terms.

2. The same number may be added to both the numerator and the denominator of a fraction without changing the value of the fraction.

3. A nonzero fraction and its reciprocal will always have the same sign.

4. The set of integers has the property of density.

Use the fundamental property of rational numbers to write each of the following in lowest terms.

5. $\dfrac{16}{48}$

6. $\dfrac{21}{28}$

7. $-\dfrac{15}{35}$

8. $-\dfrac{8}{48}$

Use the fundamental property to write each of the following in three other ways.

9. $\dfrac{3}{8}$

10. $\dfrac{9}{10}$

11. $-\dfrac{5}{7}$

12. $-\dfrac{7}{12}$

13. For each of the following, write a fraction in lowest terms that represents the portion of the figure that is shaded.

(a)   (b)   (c)   (d)

14. For each of the following, write a fraction in lowest terms that represents the region described.

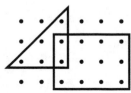

   (a) the dots in the rectangle as a part of the dots in the entire figure
   (b) the dots in the triangle as a part of the dots in the entire figure
   (c) the dots in the rectangle as a part of the dots in the union of the triangle and the rectangle
   (d) the dots in the intersection of the triangle and the rectangle as a part of the dots in the union of the triangle and the rectangle

15. Refer to the figure for Exercise 14 and write a description of the region that is represented by the fraction 1/12.

16. In the local softball league, the first five games produced the following results: David Glenn got 8 hits in 20 at-bats, and Chalon Bridges got 12 hits in 30 at-bats. David claims that he and Chalon did equally well. Is he correct? Why or why not?

17. After ten games in the local softball league, the following batting statistics were obtained.

Player	At-bats	Hits	Home Runs
Bishop, Kelly	40	9	2
Carlton, Robert	36	12	3
De Palo, Theresa	11	5	1
Crowe, Vonalaine	16	8	0
Marshall, James	20	10	2

Answer each of the following, using estimation skills as necessary.
(a) Which player got a hit in exactly 1/3 of his or her at-bats?
(b) Which player got a hit in just less than 1/2 of his or her at-bats?
(c) Which player got a home run in just less than 1/10 of his or her at-bats?
(d) Which player got a hit in just less than 1/4 of his or her at-bats?
(e) Which two players got hits in exactly the same fractional parts of their at-bats? What was the fractional part, reduced to lowest terms?

18. Use estimation skills to determine the best approximation for the following sum:

$$\frac{14}{26} + \frac{98}{99} + \frac{100}{51} + \frac{90}{31} + \frac{13}{27}.$$

(a) 6   **(b)** 7   **(c)** 5   **(d)** 8

Perform the indicated operations and express answers in lowest terms. Use the order of operations as necessary.

19. $\dfrac{3}{8} + \dfrac{1}{8}$ **20.** $\dfrac{7}{9} + \dfrac{1}{9}$ **21.** $\dfrac{5}{16} + \dfrac{7}{12}$ **22.** $\dfrac{1}{15} + \dfrac{7}{18}$

23. $\dfrac{2}{3} - \dfrac{7}{8}$ **24.** $\dfrac{13}{20} - \dfrac{5}{12}$ **25.** $\dfrac{5}{8} - \dfrac{3}{14}$ **26.** $\dfrac{19}{15} - \dfrac{7}{12}$

27. $\dfrac{3}{4} \cdot \dfrac{9}{5}$ **28.** $\dfrac{3}{8} \cdot \dfrac{2}{7}$ **29.** $-\dfrac{2}{3} \cdot -\dfrac{5}{8}$ **30.** $-\dfrac{2}{4} \cdot \dfrac{3}{9}$

31. $\dfrac{5}{12} \div \dfrac{15}{4}$ **32.** $\dfrac{15}{16} \div \dfrac{30}{8}$ **33.** $-\dfrac{9}{16} \div -\dfrac{3}{8}$ **34.** $-\dfrac{3}{8} \div \dfrac{5}{4}$

35. $\left(\dfrac{1}{3} \div \dfrac{1}{2}\right) + \dfrac{5}{6}$

36. $\dfrac{2}{5} \div \left(-\dfrac{4}{5} \div \dfrac{3}{10}\right)$

37. $\left(\dfrac{6}{11} + \dfrac{2}{3}\right) - \left(-\dfrac{1}{4} + \dfrac{5}{12}\right)$

38. $-\dfrac{1}{5}\left(\dfrac{1}{3} + \dfrac{1}{15}\right) - \dfrac{2}{3}\left(\dfrac{2}{5} - \dfrac{1}{2}\right)$

Explain how the following diagrams illustrate the given multiplication problems.

39. $\dfrac{1}{2} \cdot \dfrac{5}{6} = \dfrac{5}{12}$

40. $\dfrac{5}{8} \cdot \dfrac{1}{3} = \dfrac{5}{24}$

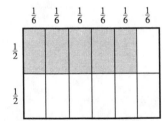

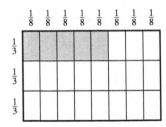

The **mixed number** 2 5/8 represents the sum 2 + 5/8. We can convert 2 5/8 to a fraction as follows:

$$2\frac{5}{8} = 2 + \frac{5}{8} = \frac{2}{1} + \frac{5}{8} = \frac{16}{8} + \frac{5}{8} = \frac{21}{8}.$$

The fraction 21/8 can be converted back to a mixed number by dividing 8 into 21. The quotient is 2 and the remainder is 5.

Convert each mixed number in the following exercises to a fraction, and convert each fraction to a mixed number.

41. $4\dfrac{1}{3}$ **42.** $3\dfrac{7}{8}$ **43.** $2\dfrac{9}{10}$ **44.** $\dfrac{18}{5}$ **45.** $\dfrac{27}{4}$ **46.** $\dfrac{19}{3}$

It is possible to add mixed numbers by first converting them to fractions, adding, and then converting the sum back to a mixed number. For example,

$$2\frac{1}{3} + 3\frac{1}{2} = \frac{7}{3} + \frac{7}{2} = \frac{14}{6} + \frac{21}{6} = \frac{35}{6} = 5\frac{5}{6}.$$

The other operations with mixed numbers may be performed in a similar manner.

Perform each operation and express your answer as a mixed number.

47. $3\dfrac{1}{4} + 2\dfrac{7}{8}$ **48.** $6\dfrac{1}{5} - 2\dfrac{7}{15}$ **49.** $-4\dfrac{7}{8} \cdot 3\dfrac{2}{3}$ **50.** $-4\dfrac{1}{6} \div 1\dfrac{2}{3}$

*A quotient of fractions (with denominator not zero) is called a **complex fraction.** There are two methods that are used to simplify a complex fraction.*

Method 1: *Simplify the numerator and denominator separately. Then rewrite as a division problem, and proceed as you would when dividing fractions.*

Method 2: *Multiply both the numerator and denominator by the least common denominator of all the fractions found within the complex fraction. (This is, in effect, multiplying the fraction by 1, which does not change its value.) Apply the distributive property, if necessary, and simplify.*

EXAMPLE   Simplify the complex fraction $\dfrac{\dfrac{1}{2} + \dfrac{2}{3}}{\dfrac{5}{6} + \dfrac{1}{12}}$.

Using Method 1, we have

$$\frac{\dfrac{1}{2} + \dfrac{2}{3}}{\dfrac{5}{6} + \dfrac{1}{12}} = \frac{\dfrac{3}{6} + \dfrac{4}{6}}{\dfrac{10}{12} + \dfrac{1}{12}} = \frac{\dfrac{7}{6}}{\dfrac{11}{12}} = \frac{7}{6} \div \frac{11}{12} = \frac{7}{6} \cdot \frac{12}{11} = \frac{84}{66} = \frac{14}{11}.$$

Using Method 2, we have

$$\frac{\dfrac{1}{2} + \dfrac{2}{3}}{\dfrac{5}{6} + \dfrac{1}{12}} = \frac{\mathbf{12}\left(\dfrac{1}{2} + \dfrac{2}{3}\right)}{\mathbf{12}\left(\dfrac{5}{6} + \dfrac{1}{12}\right)} = \frac{12\left(\dfrac{1}{2}\right) + 12\left(\dfrac{2}{3}\right)}{12\left(\dfrac{5}{6}\right) + 12\left(\dfrac{1}{12}\right)} = \frac{6 + 8}{10 + 1} = \frac{14}{11}. \quad \blacklozenge$$

Use one of the methods above to simplify each of the following complex fractions.

51. $\dfrac{\dfrac{1}{2}+\dfrac{1}{4}}{\dfrac{1}{2}-\dfrac{1}{4}}$

52. $\dfrac{\dfrac{2}{3}+\dfrac{1}{6}}{\dfrac{2}{3}-\dfrac{1}{6}}$

53. $\dfrac{\dfrac{5}{8}-\dfrac{1}{4}}{\dfrac{1}{8}+\dfrac{3}{4}}$

54. $\dfrac{\dfrac{3}{16}+\dfrac{1}{2}}{\dfrac{5}{16}-\dfrac{1}{8}}$

55. $\dfrac{\dfrac{7}{11}+\dfrac{3}{10}}{\dfrac{1}{11}-\dfrac{9}{10}}$

56. $\dfrac{\dfrac{11}{15}+\dfrac{1}{9}}{\dfrac{13}{15}-\dfrac{2}{3}}$

The **continued fraction** *corresponding to the rational number p/q is an expression of the form*

$$a_1+\cfrac{1}{a_2+\cfrac{1}{a_3+\cfrac{1}{a_4+.\quad.\quad.}}}$$

where each of the a's is an integer. For example, the continued fraction for 29/8 may be found using the following procedure.

$$\frac{29}{8}=3+\frac{5}{8}=3+\frac{1}{\dfrac{8}{5}}=3+\cfrac{1}{1+\dfrac{3}{5}}=3+\cfrac{1}{1+\cfrac{1}{\dfrac{5}{3}}}$$

$$=3+\cfrac{1}{1+\cfrac{1}{1+\dfrac{2}{3}}}=3+\cfrac{1}{1+\cfrac{1}{1+\cfrac{1}{\dfrac{3}{2}}}}=3+\cfrac{1}{1+\cfrac{1}{1+\cfrac{1}{1+\dfrac{1}{2}}}}$$

Use this procedure to find the continued fraction representation for each of the following rational numbers.

57. $\dfrac{28}{13}$

58. $\dfrac{73}{31}$

59. $\dfrac{52}{11}$

60. $\dfrac{29}{13}$

Write each of the following continued fractions in the form p/q, reduced to lowest terms. (Hint: Start at the bottom, and work upward.)

61. $2+\cfrac{1}{1+\cfrac{1}{3+\dfrac{1}{2}}}$

62. $4+\cfrac{1}{2+\cfrac{1}{1+\dfrac{1}{3}}}$

63. $2+\cfrac{1}{2+\cfrac{1}{2+\cfrac{1}{2+\dfrac{1}{2}}}}$

64. $3+\cfrac{1}{3+\cfrac{1}{3+\cfrac{1}{3+\dfrac{1}{3}}}}$

Solve the following problems.

65. The diagram shown appears in the book *Woodworker's 39 Sure-Fire Projects*. It is the front view of a corner bookcase/desk. Add the fractions shown in the diagram to find the height of the bookcase/desk.

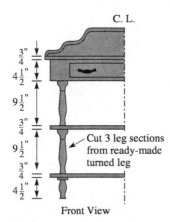

Front View

66. Adam Bryer, a motel owner, has decided to expand his business by buying a piece of property next to the motel. The property has an irregular

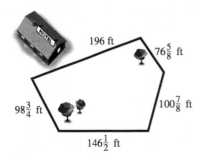

shape, with five sides as shown in the figure. Find the total distance around the piece of property.

67. Karen LaBonte's favorite recipe for barbecue sauce calls for 2 1/3 cups of tomato sauce. The recipe makes enough barbecue sauce to serve 7 people. How much tomato sauce is needed for 1 serving?

68. If an upholsterer needs 2 1/4 yd of fabric to re-cover a reclining chair, how many chairs can be re-covered with 27 yd of fabric?

69. Last month, the Salvage Recycling Center received 3 1/4 tons of newspaper, 2 3/8 tons of aluminum cans, 7 1/2 tons of glass, and 1 5/16 tons of used writing paper. Find the total number of tons of material received by the center during the month.

70. A hardware store sells a 40-piece socket wrench set. The measure of the largest socket is 3/4 in, while the measure of the smallest socket is 3/16 in. What is the difference between these measures?

71. A cent is equal to 1/100 of one dollar. Two dimes added to three dimes gives an amount equal to that of one half-dollar. Give an arithmetic problem using fractions that describes this equality, using 100 as a denominator throughout.

72. Three nickels added to twelve nickels gives an amount equal to that of three quarters. Give an arithmetic problem using fractions that describes this equality, using 100 as a denominator throughout.

Each of the following recipes serves four people. On Monday night Byron Hopkins is cooking just for his wife and himself, while on Thursday, he is cooking for a group of eight. Take half of each ingredient in each recipe for Monday, and double each recipe for Thursday.

73. Crabmeat Dip
1 lb lump crabmeat
1 1/2 bunches green onions
1 green pepper
5 stalks celery
2 1/2 teaspoons Worcestershire sauce
3 teaspoons parsley
1/2 cup Parmesan cheese
3 cans mushroom soup
1/2 stick butter

74. Cajun Cake
2 cups flour
1 1/2 teaspoons soda
2 eggs
1 1/2 cup sugar
1 can pineapple

Find the rational number halfway between the two given rational numbers.

75. $\frac{1}{2}$, $\frac{3}{4}$

76. $\frac{1}{3}$, $\frac{5}{12}$

77. $\frac{3}{5}$, $\frac{2}{3}$

78. $\frac{7}{12}$, $\frac{5}{8}$

79. $-\frac{2}{3}$, $-\frac{5}{6}$

80. -3, $-\frac{5}{2}$

In the March 1973 issue of The Mathematics Teacher *there appeared an article by Laurence Sherzer, an eighth-grade mathematics teacher, that immortalized one of his students, Robert McKay. The class was studying the density property and Sherzer was explaining how to find a rational number between two given positive rational numbers by finding the average. McKay pointed out that there was no need to go to all that trouble. To find a number (not necessarily their average) between two positive rational numbers a/b and c/d, he claimed, simply "add the tops and add the bottoms." Much to Sherzer's surprise, this method really does work. For example, to find a rational number between 1/3 and 1/4, add $1 + 1 = 2$ to get the numerator and $3 + 4 = 7$ to get the denominator. Therefore, by* **McKay's theorem,** *2/7 is between 1/3 and 1/4. Sherzer provided a proof of this method in the article.*

Use McKay's theorem *to find a rational number between the two given rational numbers.*

81. $\frac{5}{6}$ and $\frac{9}{13}$

82. $\frac{10}{11}$ and $\frac{13}{19}$

83. $\frac{4}{13}$ and $\frac{9}{16}$

84. $\frac{6}{11}$ and $\frac{8}{9}$

85. 2 and 3

86. 3 and 4

87. Apply McKay's theorem to any pair of consecutive integers, and make a conjecture about what happens in this case.

88. Explain in your own words how to find the rational number that is one-fourth of the way between two different rational numbers.

Convert each rational number into either a repeating or a terminating decimal. Use a calculator if your instructor so allows.

89. $\frac{3}{4}$

90. $\frac{7}{8}$

91. $\frac{3}{16}$

92. $\frac{9}{32}$

93. $\frac{3}{11}$

94. $\frac{9}{11}$

95. $\frac{2}{7}$

96. $\frac{11}{15}$

Convert each terminating decimal into a quotient of integers. Write each in lowest terms.

97. .4　　**98.** .9　　**99.** .85　　**100.** .105　　**101.** .934　　**102.** .7984

Convert each repeating decimal into a quotient of integers. Write each in lowest terms.

103. $.\overline{8}$　　**104.** $.\overline{1}$　　**105.** $.\overline{54}$　　**106.** $.\overline{36}$

107. $.4\overline{3}$　　**108.** $.2\overline{6}$　　**109.** $1.\overline{9}$　　**110.** $3.0\overline{9}$

Use the method of Example 7 to decide whether each of the following rational numbers would yield a repeating or a terminating decimal. (Hint: Write in lowest terms before trying to decide.)

111. $\frac{8}{15}$

112. $\frac{8}{35}$

113. $\frac{13}{125}$

114. $\frac{3}{24}$

115. $\frac{22}{55}$

116. $\frac{24}{75}$

117. Follow through on each part of this exercise in order.
  (a) Find the decimal for 1/3.
  (b) Find the decimal for 2/3.
  (c) By adding the decimal expressions obtained in parts (a) and (b), obtain a decimal expression for $1/3 + 2/3 = 3/3 = 1$.
  (d) Does your result seem bothersome? Read the margin note on terminating and repeating decimals in this section, which refers to this idea.

118. It is a fact that $1/3 = .333. \ . \ . \ .$. Multiply both sides of this equation by 3. Does your answer bother you? See the margin note on terminating and repeating decimals in this section.

4

Irrational Numbers and Decimals

In the previous section we saw that any rational number has a decimal form that terminates or repeats. Also, every repeating or terminating decimal represents a rational number. Some decimals, however, neither repeat nor terminate. For example, the decimal

.102001000200001000002. . .

does not terminate and does not repeat. (It is true that there is a pattern in this decimal, but no single block of digits repeats indefinitely.)*

A number represented by a nonrepeating, nonterminating decimal is called an **irrational** number. As the name implies, it cannot be represented as a quotient of integers. The decimal number above is an irrational number. Other irrational numbers include $\sqrt{2}$, $\sqrt{7}$, and π. The number π represents the ratio of the circumference of a circle to its diameter, and is one of the most important irrational numbers. (See "For Further Thought" in this section.)

There are infinitely many irrational numbers. In fact, the magnitude of the infinity of the irrational numbers has been shown to be greater than that of the rational numbers. The cardinal number of the set of rational numbers is $\aleph_0$, while that of the irrational numbers is c.

The first number determined to be irrational was $\sqrt{2}$, discovered by the Pythagoreans in about 500 B.C. This discovery was a great setback to their philosophy that everything is based upon the whole numbers. The Pythagoreans kept their findings secret, and legend has it that members of the group who divulged this discovery were sent out to sea, and, according to Proclus (410–485), "perished in a shipwreck, to a man."

It is not difficult to construct a line segment whose length is $\sqrt{2}$. We begin with a square, one unit on a side (Figure 9). A diagonal of this square cuts the square into two right triangles. By the Pythagorean theorem, the length of the diagonal (the *hypotenuse* of each of the right triangles) is given by

$$c^2 = 1^2 + 1^2$$
$$= 1 + 1$$
$$c^2 = 2, \quad \text{or} \quad c = \sqrt{2}.$$

Tsu Ch'ung-chih (about 500 A.D.), the Chinese mathematician honored in the above stamp, calculated π as 3.1415929. . ., which is quite accurate.
Aryabhata, his Indian contemporary, gave 3.1416 as the value.

---

*In this section we will assume that the digits of a number such as this continues indefinitely in the pattern established. The next few digits would be 000000100000002, and so on.

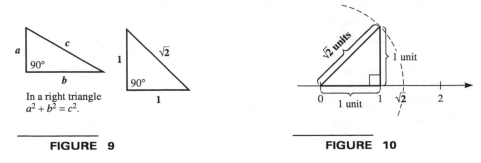

FIGURE 9   FIGURE 10

By this result, the diagonal of a square one unit on a side is given by an irrational number. The point representing $\sqrt{2}$ can be located on a number line as shown in Figure 10.

To find $\sqrt{2}$ on the number line, first construct a right triangle with each short side 1 unit in length. The hypotenuse must then be $\sqrt{2}$ units. Draw a circle with the point 0 as center and the hypotenuse of the triangle as radius. The dashed line in the figure indicates an arc of the circle. The arc intersects the number line at the point $\sqrt{2}$.

We will now prove that $\sqrt{2}$ is irrational. This proof is a classic example of a **proof by contradiction.** We begin by assuming that it is rational, and lead to a contradiction, or absurdity. The method is also called ***reductio ad absurdum*** (Latin for "reduce to the absurd").

In order to understand the proof, we consider three preliminary facts:

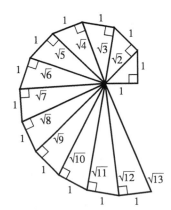

An interesting way to represent the lengths corresponding to $\sqrt{2}$, $\sqrt{3}$, $\sqrt{4}$, $\sqrt{5}$, and so on, is shown in the figure. Use the Pythagorean theorem to verify the lengths in the figure.

1. When a rational number is reduced to lowest terms, the greatest common factor of the numerator and denominator is 1.
2. If an integer is even, then it has 2 as a factor and may be written in the form $2k$, where k is an integer.
3. If a perfect square is even, then its square root is even.

THEOREM $\sqrt{2}$ is an irrational number.

Proof: Assume that $\sqrt{2}$ is a rational number. Then by definition,

$$\sqrt{2} = \frac{p}{q}, \quad \text{for some integers } p \text{ and } q.$$

Furthermore, assume that p/q is the form of $\sqrt{2}$ which is reduced to lowest terms, so that the greatest common factor of p and q is 1. Squaring both sides of the equation gives

$$2 = \frac{p^2}{q^2}$$

and multiplying through by q^2 gives

$$2q^2 = p^2.$$

This last equation indicates that 2 is a factor of p^2. So p^2 is even, and thus p is even. Since p is even, it may be written in the form $2k$, where k is an integer.

Now, substitute $2k$ for p in the last equation and simplify:

$$2q^2 = (2k)^2$$
$$2q^2 = 4k^2$$
$$q^2 = 2k^2.$$

Since 2 is a factor of q^2, q^2 must be even, and thus, q must be even. However, this leads to a contradiction: p and q cannot both be even because they would then have a common factor of 2, although it was assumed that their greatest common factor is 1.

Therefore, since the original assumption that $\sqrt{2}$ is rational has led to a contradiction, it must follow that $\sqrt{2}$ is irrational. ⬡

A calculator with a square root key can give approximations of square roots of numbers that are not perfect squares. To show that they are approximations, we use the $\approx$ symbol to indicate "is approximately equal to." Some such calculator approximations are as follows:

$$\sqrt{2} \approx 1.414213562$$
$$\sqrt{7} \approx 2.645751311$$
$$\sqrt{1,949} \approx 44.14748011.$$

Not all square roots are irrational. For example, $\sqrt{4} = 2$, $\sqrt{36} = 6$, and $\sqrt{100} = 10$ are all rational numbers. However, if n is a positive integer that is not the square of an integer, then $\sqrt{n}$ is an irrational number.

EXAMPLE 1   The chart below shows some examples of rational numbers and irrational numbers.

Rational Numbers	Irrational Numbers	
$\dfrac{3}{4}$	$\sqrt{2}$	
.64	.23233233323333. . .	
$.\overline{74}$	$\sqrt{5}$	
$\sqrt{16}$	π	
1.618	$\dfrac{1+\sqrt{5}}{2}$	The exact value of the golden ratio
2.718	e	An important number in higher mathematics— see the margin note. ⬡

One of the most useful irrational numbers is π, the ratio of the circumference to the diameter of a circle. Many formulas from geometry involve π, such as the formulas for area of a circle ($A = \pi r^2$) and volume of a sphere ($V = \dfrac{4}{3}\pi r^3$). For some four thousand years mathematicians have been finding better and better approximations for π. The ancient Egyptians used a method for finding the area of a circle that is equivalent to a value of 3.1605 for π. The Babylonians used numbers that give

The symbol for π in use today is a Greek letter. It was first used in England in the 1700s. In 1859 the symbol for π shown above was proposed by Professor Benjamin Peirce of Harvard.

3 1/8 for π. In the Bible (I Kings 7:23), a verse describes a circular pool at King Solomon's temple, about 1000 B.C. The pool is said to be ten cubits across, "and a line of 30 cubits did compass it round about." This implies a value of 3 for π.

FOR FURTHER THOUGHT

The March 22, 1992, issue of *The New Yorker* contains the article "The Mountains of Pi," profiling Gregory and David Chudnovsky. With their own computer, housed in their Manhattan apartment, the Chudnovskys have become two

$$\pi$$

The computation of pi

of today's foremost researchers on the investigation of the decimal digits of π. Their research deals with observing the digits for possible patterns in the digits. For example, one conjecture about π deals with what mathematicians term "normalcy." The normality conjecture says that all digits appear with the same average frequency. According to Gregory "There is absolutely no doubt that π is a 'normal' number. Yet we can't prove it. We don't even know how to *try* to prove it."

In mid-1991, the Chudnovskys stopped their calculation of the decimal digits of π at 2,260,321,336 digits. If printed in ordinary type, they would stretch from New York to Southern California.

The computation of π has fascinated mathematicians and laymen for centuries. In the nineteenth century the British mathematician William Shanks spent many years of his life calculating π to 707 decimal places. It turned out that only the first 527 were correct. The advent of the computer greatly revolutionized the quest in calculating π. In fact, the accuracy of computers and computer programs is sometimes tested by performing the computation of π.

Despite the fact that, in 1767, J. H. Lambert proved that π is irrational (and thus its decimal will never terminate and never repeat), the 1897 Indiana state legislature considered a bill that would have *legislated* the value of π. In one part of the bill, the value was stated to be 4, and in another part, 3.2. Amazingly, the bill passed the House, but the Senate postponed action on the bill indefinitely!

The following expressions are some which may be used to compute π to more and more decimal places.

$$\frac{\pi}{2} = \frac{2 \cdot 2 \cdot 4 \cdot 4 \cdot 6 \cdot 6 \cdot 8 \ldots}{1 \cdot 3 \cdot 3 \cdot 5 \cdot 5 \cdot 7 \cdot 7 \ldots}$$

$$\frac{\pi}{4} = 1 - \frac{1}{3} + \frac{1}{5} - \frac{1}{7} + \cdots$$

$$\frac{2}{\pi} = \frac{\sqrt{2}}{2} \cdot \frac{\sqrt{2+\sqrt{2}}}{2} \cdot \frac{\sqrt{2+\sqrt{2+\sqrt{2}}}}{2} \cdots$$

This poem, dedicated to Archimedes ("the immortal Syracusan"), allows us to learn the first thirty digits of the decimal representation of π. By replacing each word with the number of letters it contains, with a decimal point following the initial 3, the decimal is found. The poem was written by one A. C. Orr, and appeared in the *Literary Digest* in 1906.

Now I, even I, would
    celebrate
In rhymes unapt, the great
Immortal Syracusan, rivaled
    nevermore,
Who in his wondrous lore
Passed on before,
Left men his guidance
How to circles mensurate.

From this poem, we can determine these digits of π:
3.14159265358979323846264
3383279.

Archimedes was able to use circles inscribed and

The fascinating history of π has been chronicled by Petr Beckman in the book *A History of Pi.*

For Group Discussion
1. Have each class member ask someone outside of class "What is π?" Then as a class, discuss the various responses obtained.
2. As with Mount Everest, some people enjoy climbing the mountain of π simply because it is there. Have you ever tackled a project for no reason other than to simply say "I did it"? Share any such experiences with the class.
3. Divide the class into three groups, and, armed with calculators, spend a few minutes calculating the expressions above to approximate π. Compare your results to see which one of the expressions converges toward π the fastest.

circumscribed by polygons to find that the value of π is somewhere between 223/71 and 22/7. Because it is not difficult to find the perimeter of the polygons inscribed and circumscribed around the circle, he concluded that the circumference of the circle must be between these two perimeters. By choosing polygons of larger and larger numbers of sides, he was able to approximate the circumference of the circle (and thus the value of π) with greater and greater accuracy.

Through the centuries mathematicians have calculated π in various ways. For example, in 1579 François Viète used polygons having 393,216 sides to find π to nine decimal places. A computer was programmed by Shanks and Wrench in 1961 to compute 100,265 decimal places of π. In recent years, the Japanese mathematician Yasumasa Kanada and the brothers Gregory and David Chudnovsky, associated with Columbia University, have been at the forefront of the research being done in the evaluation of decimal digits of π. (See "For Further Thought" in this section.) As of the summer of 1991, the Chudnovskys had evaluated the first 2,260,321,336 digits of π.

Mathematicians have done research in observing patterns in the decimal for π. For example, six 9s in a row appear relatively early in the decimal, within the first 800 decimal places. And past the half-billion mark appears the sequence 123456789.

Square Roots

In everyday mathematical work, nearly all of our calculations deal with rational numbers, usually in decimal form. In our *study* of the various branches of mathematics, however, we are sometimes required to perform operations with irrational numbers, and in many instances the irrational numbers are square roots. Recall that $\sqrt{a}$, for $a \geq 0$, is the nonnegative number whose square is a; that is, $(\sqrt{a})^2 = a$. We will now look at some simple operations with square roots.

Notice that

$$\sqrt{4} \cdot \sqrt{9} = 2 \cdot 3 = 6$$

and
$$\sqrt{4 \cdot 9} = \sqrt{36} = 6.$$

It is no coincidence that $\sqrt{4} \cdot \sqrt{9}$ is equal to $\sqrt{4 \cdot 9}$. This is a particular case of the following product rule.

Product Rule for Square Roots

For nonnegative real numbers a and b,

$$\sqrt{a} \cdot \sqrt{b} = \sqrt{a \cdot b}.$$

The symbol above comes from the Latin word for root, *radix*. It was first used by Leonardo da Pisa (Fibonacci) in 1220. The sixteenth-century German symbol we use today probably is also derived from the letter r.

Just as every rational number a/b can be written in simplest (lowest) terms (by using the fundamental property of rational numbers), every square root radical has a simplest form. A square root radical is in **simplified form** if the three following conditions are met.

Simplified Form of a Square Root Radical

1. The number under the radical (**radicand**) has no factor (except 1) that is a perfect square.
2. The radicand has no fractions.
3. No denominator contains a radical.

EXAMPLE 2 Simplify $\sqrt{27}$.

Since 9 is a factor of 27 and 9 is a perfect square, $\sqrt{27}$ is not in simplified form, as the first condition in the box above is not met. We use the product rule to simplify as follows.

$$\sqrt{27} = \sqrt{9 \cdot 3}$$
$$= \sqrt{9} \cdot \sqrt{3} \qquad \text{Use the product rule.}$$
$$= 3\sqrt{3} \qquad \sqrt{9} = 3, \text{ since } 3^2 = 9.$$

The simplified form of $\sqrt{27}$ is $3\sqrt{3}$. ◓

Expressions like $\sqrt{27}$ and $3\sqrt{3}$ are called *exact values* of the square root of 27. We can use a calculator to strengthen our understanding that $\sqrt{27}$ and $3\sqrt{3}$ are equal. If we use the square root key of a calculator, we find

$$\sqrt{27} \approx 5.196152423.$$

If we find $\sqrt{3}$ and then multiply the result by 3, we get

$$3\sqrt{3} \approx 3(1.732050808) \approx 5.196152423.$$

Notice that these approximations are the same, as we would expect. (Due to various methods of calculating, there may be a discrepancy in the final digit of the calculation.) Understand, however, that the calculator approximations do not actually *prove* that the two numbers are equal, but only strongly suggest the equality. The work done in Example 2 actually provides the mathematical justification that they are indeed equal.

A rule similar to the product rule exists for quotients.

Quotient Rule for Square Roots

For nonnegative numbers a and positive numbers b,

$$\frac{\sqrt{a}}{\sqrt{b}} = \sqrt{\frac{a}{b}}.$$

EXAMPLE 3 Simplify each radical.

(a) $\sqrt{\dfrac{25}{9}}$

Because the radicand contains a fraction, the radical expression is not simplified. (See condition 2 in the box preceding Example 2.) Use the quotient rule as follows.

$$\sqrt{\frac{25}{9}} = \frac{\sqrt{25}}{\sqrt{9}} = \frac{5}{3}$$

(b) $\sqrt{\dfrac{3}{4}} = \dfrac{\sqrt{3}}{\sqrt{4}} = \dfrac{\sqrt{3}}{2}$

(c) $\sqrt{\dfrac{1}{2}}$

$$\sqrt{\frac{1}{2}} = \frac{\sqrt{1}}{\sqrt{2}}$$

$$= \frac{1}{\sqrt{2}}$$

This expression is not in simplified form, since condition 3 is not met. In order to give an equivalent expression with no radical in the denominator, we use a procedure called **rationalizing the denominator.** Multiply $1/\sqrt{2}$ by $\sqrt{2}/\sqrt{2}$, which is a form of 1, the identity element for multiplication.

$$\frac{1}{\sqrt{2}} = \frac{1}{\sqrt{2}} \cdot \frac{\sqrt{2}}{\sqrt{2}}$$

$$= \frac{\sqrt{2}}{2} \qquad\qquad \sqrt{2} \cdot \sqrt{2} = 2$$

The simplified form of $\sqrt{1/2}$ is $\sqrt{2}/2$.

(The results in each part of this example may be illustrated by calculator approximations. Verify in (a) that each expression is equal to $1.\overline{6}$, in (b) that each is approximately equal to .866025404, and in (c) that each is approximately equal to .707106781.) ◖

Is it true that $\sqrt{4} + \sqrt{9}$ is equal to $\sqrt{4 + 9}$? Simple computation here shows that the answer is "no," since $\sqrt{4} + \sqrt{9} = 2 + 3 = 5$, while $\sqrt{4 + 9} = \sqrt{13}$, and $5 \neq \sqrt{13}$. Square root radicals may be added, however, if they have the same radicand. Such radicals are **like** or **similar radicals.** We add (and subtract) similar radicals with the distributive property, as shown in the next example.

> **The ancient Greeks** found approximate values of π expressing the ratio of the circumference of a circle to its diameter d as a sum of fractions. One sum of this sort gave
>
> $$\pi \approx 3 + \frac{8}{60} + \frac{30}{(60)^2}$$
>
> $$= 3.141\overline{6}$$
>
> which is correct to four decimal places. A later mathematician, Nehemiah, approximated the value of π by writing the area of a circle as
>
> $$A = d^2 - \frac{d^2}{7} - \frac{d^2}{14}$$
>
> $$\frac{1}{7} - \frac{1}{14}\left(\frac{1}{}\right)d^2$$
>
> $$= \frac{11}{14}d^2.$$
>
> The actual area of a circle is
>
> $$A = \pi r^2 = \pi\left(\frac{1}{2}d\right)^2 = \frac{\pi}{4}d^2.$$
>
> Thus, Nehemiah found
>
> $$\frac{\pi}{4} \approx \frac{11}{14}$$
>
> $$\pi \approx \frac{44}{14} \approx 3.1429.$$

EXAMPLE 4   **(a)** Add: $3\sqrt{6} + 4\sqrt{6}$.

Since both terms contain $\sqrt{6}$, they are like radicals, and may be combined.

$$3\sqrt{6} + 4\sqrt{6} = (\mathbf{3 + 4})\sqrt{6} \qquad \text{Distributive property}$$
$$= 7\sqrt{6} \qquad\qquad \mathbf{3 + 4 = 7}$$

(b) Subtract: $\sqrt{18} - \sqrt{32}$.

At first glance it seems that we cannot combine these terms. However, if we first simplify $\sqrt{18}$ and $\sqrt{32}$, then it can be done.

$$\sqrt{18} - \sqrt{32} = \sqrt{9 \cdot 2} - \sqrt{16 \cdot 2}$$
$$= \sqrt{9} \cdot \sqrt{2} - \sqrt{16} \cdot \sqrt{2} \qquad \text{Product rule}$$
$$= 3\sqrt{2} - 4\sqrt{2} \qquad\qquad \text{Take square roots.}$$
$$= (3 - 4)\sqrt{2} \qquad\qquad \text{Distributive property}$$
$$= -1\sqrt{2} \qquad\qquad\quad 3 - 4 = -1$$
$$= -\sqrt{2} \qquad\qquad\quad -1 \cdot a = -a$$

Use a calculator to verify that in part (a), both expressions are approximately equal to 17.1464282, and in part (b) both are approximately equal to −1.414213562. ◖

From Example 4, we see that like radicals may be added or subtracted by adding or subtracting their coefficients (the numbers by which they are multiplied), and keeping the same radical. For example,

$$9\sqrt{7} + 8\sqrt{7} = 17\sqrt{7} \quad (\text{since } 9 + 8 = 17)$$
$$4\sqrt{3} - 12\sqrt{3} = -8\sqrt{3} \quad (\text{since } 4 - 12 = -8)$$

and so on.

In the statements of the product and quotient rules for square roots, the radicands could not be negative. While $-\sqrt{2}$ is a real number, for example, $\sqrt{-2}$ is not: there is no real number whose square is -2. The same may be said for any negative radicand. In order to handle this situation, mathematicians have extended our number system to include *complex numbers,* discussed in the Extension at the end of this chapter.

4 EXERCISES

Identify each of the following as rational *or* irrational.

1. $\frac{4}{7}$ **2.** $\frac{5}{8}$ **3.** $\sqrt{6}$ **4.** $\sqrt{13}$

5. .89 **6.** .76 **7.** $.\overline{89}$ **8.** $.\overline{76}$

9. .878778777877778. . . **10.** .434334333433334. . . **11.** 3.14159

12. $\frac{22}{7}$ **13.** π **14.** 0

15. (a) Find the following sum:

$$.272772777277772. . .$$
$$+ .616116111611116. . .$$

(b) Based on the result of part (a), we can conclude that the sum of two ——— numbers may be a(n) ——— number.

16. (a) Find the following sum:

$$.010110111011110. . .$$
$$+ .252552555255552. . .$$

(b) Based on the result of part (a), we can conclude that the sum of two ——— numbers may be a(n) ——— number.

Use a calculator to find a rational decimal approximation for each of the following irrational numbers. Give as many places as your calculator shows.

17. $\sqrt{39}$ **18.** $\sqrt{44}$ **19.** $\sqrt{15.1}$ **20.** $\sqrt{33.6}$

21. $\sqrt{884}$ **22.** $\sqrt{643}$ **23.** $\sqrt{\frac{9}{8}}$ **24.** $\sqrt{\frac{6}{5}}$

Complete the following table.

Number	Whole	Integer	Rational	Irrational	Real
25. 10	yes			no	yes
26. −2		yes		no	
27. $\dfrac{1}{3}$					
28. $\dfrac{13}{19}$	no	no			
29. 4.25	no			no	yes
30. −8.46	no				yes
31. $-\sqrt{11}$			no		
32. $-\sqrt{32}$			no		

33. Find the first eight digits in the decimal for 355/113. Compare the result to the decimal for π given in the margin note. What do you find?

34. Using a calculator with a square root key, divide 2,143 by 22, and then press the square root key twice. Compare your result to the decimal for π given in the margin note.

35. A **mnemonic** device is a scheme whereby one is able to recall facts by memorizing something completely unrelated to the facts. One way of learning the first few digits of the decimal for π is to memorize a sentence (or several sentences) and count the letters in each word of the sentence. For example, "See, I know a digit," will give the first 5 digits of π: "See" has 3 letters, "I" has 1 letter, "know" has 4 letters, "a" has 1 letter, and "digit" has 5 letters. So the first five digits are 3.1415.

Verify that the following mnemonic devices work. Use the decimal for π given in the margin note.

(a) "May I have a large container of coffee?"

(b) "See, I have a rhyme assisting my feeble brain, its tasks ofttimes resisting."

(c) "How I want a drink, alcoholic of course, after the heavy lectures involving quantum mechanics."

36. Make up your own mnemonic device to obtain the first eight digits of π.

37. You may have seen the statements "use 22/7 for π" and "use 3.14 for π." Since 22/7 is the quotient of two integers, and 3.14 is a terminating decimal, do these statements suggest that π is rational?

38. Use a calculator with an exponential key to find values for the following: $(1.1)^{10}$, $(1.01)^{100}$, $(1.001)^{1000}$, $(1.0001)^{10,000}$, and $(1.00001)^{100,000}$. Compare your results to the approximation given for the irrational number e in the margin note in this section. What do you find?

Use the methods of Examples 2 and 3 to simplify each of the following expressions. Then, use a calculator to approximate both the given expression and the simplified expression. (Both should be the same.)

39. $\sqrt{50}$ **40.** $\sqrt{32}$ **41.** $\sqrt{75}$ **42.** $\sqrt{150}$ **43.** $\sqrt{288}$ **44.** $\sqrt{200}$ **45.** $\dfrac{5}{\sqrt{6}}$ **46.** $\dfrac{3}{\sqrt{2}}$

47. $\sqrt{\dfrac{7}{4}}$ **48.** $\sqrt{\dfrac{8}{9}}$ **49.** $\sqrt{\dfrac{7}{3}}$ **50.** $\sqrt{\dfrac{14}{5}}$

51. Read over the directions for Exercises 39–50, and refer to them as you write a short paragraph explaining the distinction between exact and approximate values of square roots.

52. Use a calculator to show that, in general, $\sqrt{a+b} \neq \sqrt{a} + \sqrt{b}$, by letting $a = 25$ and $b = 144$.

Use the method of Example 4 to perform the indicated operations.

53. $\sqrt{6} + \sqrt{6}$ **54.** $\sqrt{11} + \sqrt{11}$ **55.** $\sqrt{17} + 2\sqrt{17}$ **56.** $3\sqrt{19} + \sqrt{19}$

57. $5\sqrt{7} - \sqrt{7}$ **58.** $3\sqrt{27} - \sqrt{27}$ **59.** $3\sqrt{18} + \sqrt{2}$ **60.** $2\sqrt{48} - \sqrt{3}$

61. $-\sqrt{12} + \sqrt{75}$ **62.** $2\sqrt{27} - \sqrt{300}$ **63.** $5\sqrt{72} - 2\sqrt{50}$ **64.** $6\sqrt{18} - 4\sqrt{32}$

65. In algebra the expression $a^{1/2}$ is defined to be $\sqrt{a}$ for nonnegative values of a. Use a calculator with an exponential key to evaluate each of the following, and compare to the value obtained with the square root key. (Both should be the same.)

(a) $2^{1/2}$ (b) $7^{1/2}$ (c) $13.2^{1/2}$ (d) $25^{1/2}$

66. The method for simplifying square root radicals, as explained in Examples 2 and 3, can be generalized to cube roots, using the perfect cubes $8 = 2^3$, $27 = 3^3$, $64 = 4^3$, $125 = 5^3$, $216 = 6^3$, and so on. Simplify each of the following cube roots.

(a) $\sqrt[3]{16}$ (b) $\sqrt[3]{54}$

(c) $\sqrt[3]{24}$ (d) $\sqrt[3]{250}$

67. Based on Exercises 65 and 66, answer the following.

(a) How do you think that the expression $a^{1/3}$ is defined as a radical?

(b) Use a calculator with a cube root key to approximate $\sqrt[3]{16}$.

(c) Use a calculator with an exponential key to approximate $16^{1/3}$.

(d) Compare your results in parts (b) and (c). What do you find?

(e) Compare the calculator approximation for the answer in Exercise 66(a) to the results in parts (b) and (c). What do you find?

68. Historians have determined that the Babylonians used the following formula to approximate square roots: If $n = a^2 + b$, then

$$\sqrt{n} \approx a + \frac{b}{2a} \quad \text{if } 0 < |b| < a^2.$$

(a) Use $2 = (4/3)^2 + 2/9$ (that is, $a = 4/3$ and $b = 2/9$) to find a rational approximation for $\sqrt{2}$.

(b) Use a calculator to compare your result in part (a) with the calculator approximation of $\sqrt{2}$ using the square root key.

(c) Use $10 = 3^2 + 1$ to find a rational approximation of $\sqrt{10}$.

(d) Use a calculator to compare your result in part (c) with the calculator approximation of $\sqrt{10}$ using the square root key.

(e) The ancient Hindus sometimes used $\sqrt{10}$ as an approximation for π. To how many digits do these two numbers agree?

Applications of Decimals and Percents

Perhaps the most frequent use of mathematics in everyday life concerns operations with decimal numbers and the concept of percent. When we use dollars and cents, we are dealing with decimal numbers. Sales tax on purchases made at the grocery store is computed using percent. The educated consumer must have a working knowledge of decimals and percent in financial matters. Look at any newspaper and you will see countless references to percent and percentages. In this section we will study the basic ideas of operations with decimals, the concept of percent, and applications of decimals and percents.

Because calculators have, for the most part, replaced paper-and-pencil methods for operations with decimals and percent, we will only briefly mention these latter methods. *We strongly suggest that the work in this section be done with a calculator at hand.*

Addition and Subtraction of Decimals

To add or subtract decimal numbers, line up the decimal points in a column and perform the operation.

EXAMPLE 1   **(a)** To compute the sum .46 + 3.9 + 12.58, use the following method:

$$
\begin{array}{r}
.46 \\
3.9 \\
12.58 \\
\hline
16.94. \leftarrow \text{Sum}
\end{array}
$$

(b) To compute the difference 12.1 − 8.723, use this method:

$$
\begin{array}{rl}
12.100 & \text{Attach zeros.} \\
-8.723 & \\
\hline
3.377. & \leftarrow \text{Difference} \quad \bullet
\end{array}
$$

Recall that when two numbers are multiplied, the numbers are called *factors* and the answer is called their *product*. When two numbers are divided, the number being divided is called the *dividend,* the number doing the dividing is called the *divisor,* and the answer is called the *quotient.* The rules for paper-and-pencil multiplication and division of decimals follow.

Multiplication and Division of Decimals

1. To multiply decimals, perform the multiplication in the same manner as integers are multiplied. The number of decimal places to the right of the decimal point in the product is the *sum* of the numbers of places to the right of the decimal points in the factors.
2. To divide decimals, move the decimal point to the right the same number of places in the divisor and the dividend so as to obtain a whole number in the divisor. Perform the division in the same manner as integers are divided. The number of decimal places to the right of the decimal point in the quotient is the same as the number of places to the right in the dividend.

EXAMPLE 2   **(a)** To find the product 4.613 × 2.52, use the following method:

$$
\begin{array}{r}
4.613 \leftarrow 3 \text{ decimal places} \\
\times\ 2.52 \leftarrow 2 \text{ decimal places} \\
\hline
9\,226 \\
2\,30\,65 \\
9\,22\,6 \\
\hline
11.62\,476. \leftarrow 3 + 2 = 5 \text{ decimal places}
\end{array}
$$

(b) To find the quotient 65.175 ÷ 8.25, follow these steps:

$$
8.25\overline{)65.175} \longrightarrow
\begin{array}{r}
7.9 \\
825\overline{)6517.5} \\
\underline{5775} \\
742\,5 \\
\underline{742\,5} \\
0. \quad \bullet
\end{array}
$$

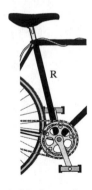

Bicycle Mathematics
Experiments done in England, using racing cyclists on stationary bicycles, show that the most efficient saddle height is 109% of a cyclist's inside-leg measurement. You can get the most mileage (or kilometrage) out of your leg work by following these directions:

1. Stand up straight, without shoes. Have someone measure your leg on the inside (from floor to crotch bone).
2. Multiply this length by 109% (that is, by 1.09) to get a measure *R*.
3. Adjust your saddle so that the measure *R* equals the distance between the top of the saddle and the lower pedal spindle when the pedals are positioned as in the diagram above.

Students often ask "Why do these rules for operations with decimals work the way they do?" See Exercises 91 and 92, which deal with the justification for these rules.

Decimal calculations with calculators are performed quite easily. While you should read your instruction manual carefully to see how this is done, Example 3 gives the typical keystrokes for performing the calculations done on paper in Examples 1 and 2.

EXAMPLE 3 (a) $.46 + 3.9 + 12.58$

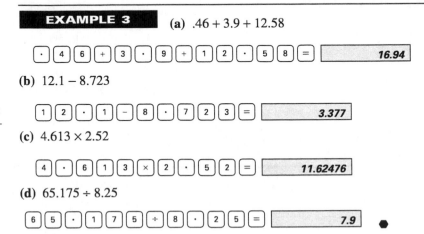

(b) $12.1 - 8.723$

(c) 4.613×2.52

(d) $65.175 \div 8.25$

Rounding Decimals

Operations with decimals often result in long strings of digits in the decimal places. Since all these digits may not be needed in a practical problem, it is common to *round* a decimal to the necessary number of decimal places. For example, in preparing federal income tax, money amounts are rounded to the nearest dollar. Round as shown in the next example.

EXAMPLE 4 Round 3.917 to the nearest hundredth.

The hundredths place in 3.917 contains the digit 1.

$$3.917$$

↑ Hundredths place

To round this decimal, think of a number line. Locate 3.91 and 3.92 on the number line as in Figure 11.

FIGURE 11

The distance from 3.91 to 3.92 is divided into ten equal parts. The seventh of these ten parts locates the number 3.917. As the number line shows, 3.917 is closer to 3.92 than it is to 3.91, so

3.917 rounded to the nearest hundredth is 3.92. ●

FOR FURTHER THOUGHT

Do you have the "knack"? We are all born with different abilities. That's what makes us all unique individuals. Some people have musical talents, while others can't carry a tune. Some people can repair automobiles, sew, or build things while others can't do any of these. And some people have a knack for percents, while others are completely befuddled by them. Do you have the knack?

For example, suppose that you need to compute 20% of 50. You have the knack if you use one of these methods:

1. You think "Well, 20% means 1/5, and to find 1/5 of something I divide by 5, so 50 divided by 5 is 10. The answer is 10."

2. You think "20% is twice 10%, and to find 10% of something I move the decimal point one place to the left. So, 10% of 50 is 5, and 20% is twice 5, or 10. The answer is 10."

If you don't have the knack, you probably search for a calculator whenever you need to compute a percent, and hope like crazy that you'll work it correctly. Keep in mind one thing, however: there's nothing to be ashamed of if you don't have the knack. The methods explained in this section allow you to learn how to compute percents using tried-and-true mathematical methods. And just because you don't have the knack, it doesn't mean that you can't succeed in mathematics or can't learn other concepts. One ability does not necessarily assure success in another seemingly similar area. Case in point: The nineteenth century German Zacharias Dase was a lightning-swift calculator, and could do things like multiply 79,532,853 by 93,758,479 in his head in less than one minute, but had no concept of theoretical mathematics!

HERMAN®

"I got 6 percent in math.
is that good or bad?"

For Group Discussion Have class members share their experiences on how they compute percents.

If the number line method of Example 4 were used to round 3.915 to the nearest hundredth, a problem would develop—the number 3.915 is exactly halfway between 3.91 and 3.92. An arbitrary decision is then made to round *up:* 3.915 rounded to the nearest hundredth is 3.92.

The number line method in Example 4 suggests the following rules for rounding decimals.

Rules for Rounding Decimals

Step 1   Locate the **place** to which the number is being rounded.

Step 2   Look at the next **digit to the right** of the place to which the number is being rounded.

Step 3A If this digit is **less than 5,** drop all digits to the right of the place to which the number is being rounded. Do *not change* the digit in the place to which the number is being rounded.	*Step 3B* If this digit is **5 or greater,** drop all digits to the right of the place to which the number is being rounded. *Add 1* to the digit in the place to which the number is being rounded.

 EXAMPLE 5   Round 14.39656 to the nearest thousandth.

Step 1   Use an arrow to locate the place to which the number is being rounded.

$$14.39656$$
$$\uparrow \text{ Thousandths place}$$

Step 2   Check to see if the first digit to the right of the arrow is 5 or greater.

$$14.396 \;\; \textcircled{5} \;\; 6 \qquad \text{Digit to the right of the arrow is 5.}$$
$$\uparrow$$

Step 3   If the digit to the right of the arrow is 5 or greater, increase by 1 the digit to which the arrow is pointing. Drop all digits to the right of the arrow.

$$14.39656 \qquad \text{Drop.}$$
$$\uparrow$$
$$14.397 \qquad \text{Increase by 1.}$$

Finally, 14.39656 rounded to the nearest thousandth is 14.397.   ●

Some calculators have a key that allows the user to round answers to a specific decimal place. This key is usually labeled $\boxed{\text{fix}}$ (as in "to fix the number of decimal places"). It is often a second function as well.

Percent

One of the main applications of decimals comes from problems involving **percents.** Percents are widely used. In consumer mathematics, interest rates and discounts are often given as percents.

Do you think that this call *really* costs less than a penny?

According to information in the Thirty-first yearbook of the National Council of Teachers of Mathematics, the percent sign, %, probably evolved from a symbol introduced in an Italian manuscript of 1425. Instead of "per 100," "P 100" or "P cento," which were common at that time, the author used "P $\hat{}$." By about 1650 the $\hat{}$ had become $\frac{0}{0}$, so "per $\frac{0}{0}$" was often used. Finally the "per" was dropped, leaving $\frac{0}{0}$ or %.

The word *percent* means "per hundred." This idea is used in the basic definition of percents: if the symbol % represents "percent," then

$$1\% = \frac{1}{100} = .01.$$

For example, $45\% = 45(1\%) = 45(.01) = .45$.

EXAMPLE 6   Convert each percent to a decimal.

(a) $98\% = 98(1\%) = 98(.01) = .98$

(b) $3.4\% = .034$

(c) $.2\% = .002$ ●

A decimal can be converted to a percent in much the same way.

EXAMPLE 7   Convert each decimal to a percent.

(a) $.13 = 13(.01) = 13(1\%) = 13\%$

(b) $.532 = 53.2(.01) = 53.2(1\%) = 53.2\%$

(c) $2.3 = 230\%$ ●

From Examples 6 and 7, it can be seen that the following procedures can be used when converting between percents and decimals.

Converting Between Decimals and Percents

1. *To convert a percent to a decimal,* drop the % sign and move the decimal point two places to the left, inserting zeros as placeholders if necessary.
2. *To convert a decimal to a percent,* move the decimal point two places to the right, inserting zeros as placeholders if necessary, and attach a % sign.

EXAMPLE 8   Convert each fraction to a percent.

(a) $\dfrac{3}{5}$

First write 3/5 as a decimal. Dividing 5 into 3 gives $3/5 = .6 = 60\%$.

(b) $\dfrac{14}{25} = .56 = 56\%$ ●

The procedure of Example 8 is summarized as follows.

Converting a Fraction to a Percent

To convert a fraction to a percent, convert the fraction to a decimal, and then convert the decimal to a percent.

The following examples show how to work the various types of problems involving percents. In each example, three methods are shown. The second method in each case involves the cross-product method from Section 3, and some basic algebra. The third method involves the percent key of a calculator.

EXAMPLE 9   Find 18% of 250.

Method 1:   The key word here is "of." The word "of" translates as "times," with 18% of 250 given by

$$(18\%)(250) = (.18)(250) = 45.$$

Method 2:   Think "18 is to 100 as what (x) is to 250?" This translates into the equation

$$\frac{18}{100} = \frac{x}{250}$$

$$100x = 18 \cdot 250 \qquad a/b = c/d \text{ if and only if } ad = bc.$$

$$x = \frac{18 \cdot 250}{100} = 45. \qquad \text{Divide by 100 and simplify.}$$

Method 3:   Use the percent key on a calculator with the following keystrokes:

$$\boxed{2}\;\boxed{5}\;\boxed{0}\;\boxed{\times}\;\boxed{1}\;\boxed{8}\;\boxed{\%}\;\boxed{\mathbf{45}}\;.$$

With any of these methods, we find that 18% of 250 is 45. ●

EXAMPLE 10   What percent of 500 is 75?

Method 1:   Let the phrase "what percent" be represented by $x \cdot 1\%$ or $.01x$. Again the word "of" translates as "times," while "is" translates as "equals." Thus,

$$.01x \cdot (500) = 75$$

$$5x = 75 \qquad \text{Multiply on the left side.}$$

$$x = 15. \qquad \text{Divide by 5 on both sides.}$$

Method 2: Think "What (x) is to 100 as 75 is to 500?" This translates as

$$\frac{x}{100} = \frac{75}{500}$$

$$500x = 7{,}500$$

$$x = 15.$$

Method 3: ⎡7⎤⎡5⎤⎡÷⎤⎡5⎤⎡0⎤⎡0⎤⎡%⎤ ▢ **15**

In each case, 15 is the percent, so we may conclude that 75 is 15% of 500. ●

EXAMPLE 11   38 is 5% of what number?

Method 1: $38 = .05x$

$$x = \frac{38}{.05}$$

$$x = 760.$$

Method 2:   Think "38 is to what number (x) as 5 is to 100?"

$$\frac{38}{x} = \frac{5}{100}$$

$$5x = 3{,}800$$

$$x = 760.$$

Method 3: ⎡3⎤⎡8⎤⎡÷⎤⎡5⎤⎡%⎤ ▢ **760**

Each method shows us that 38 is 5% of 760. ●

PROBLEM SOLVING

The methods of working with percents described in Examples 9, 10 and 11 can be extended to include more meaningful work. When applying percent, it is a good idea to restate the given problem as a question similar to those found in the preceding examples, and then proceed to answer that question. One method of problem solving deals with solving a simpler, similar problem. This is an excellent chance for us to utilize this problem-solving method. And because approximations are often sufficient for everyday use, we also can apply estimation techniques. ●

EXAMPLE 12   Las Vegas, Nevada, has the fastest growth rate of any city in the United States. In 1980, its population was approximately 463,000, and by 1990 it had grown to approximately 741,500.

(a) Use estimation skills to approximate the percent increase over these ten years.

If we round the figures to 460,000 and 740,000, respectively, we can easily determine that the increase in population is approximately 740,000 − 460,000 = 280,000. Then we must answer the question "What percent of 450,000 (the *original* population) is 280,000?". Since 280 is a little less than 2/3 of 450 (thinking in terms of thousands), and 2/3 ≈ 67%, the percent increase is a bit less than 67%.

(b) Use mathematics to find the percent increase over these ten years.

We must find the difference between the two populations, and then determine what percent of 463,000 comprises this difference.

$$\underbrace{741,500}_{\substack{\text{Population} \\ \text{in 1990}}} - \underbrace{463,000}_{\substack{\text{Population} \\ \text{in 1980}}} = \underbrace{278,500}_{\substack{\text{Increase in} \\ \text{population}}}$$

Now solve the problem "What percent of 463,000 is 278,500?" This is similar to the problem in Example 10. Any of the methods explained there will show that the answer is approximately 60%. ●

PROBLEM SOLVING

Much information can be depicted by using a graph, and in many instances, information in the graph is given with percents. We should be able to use this information and our general knowledge of percent to be able to answer questions like those found in the next example. Again, the simple problems found in Examples 9, 10, and 11 provide techniques to solve more realistic ones as in the next example. ●

EXAMPLE 13   The graphs shown in Figure 12 accompanied a newspaper article. According to the article, 17,252 tornadoes were reported sighted in the past twenty years. Use the graphs to answer the following questions.

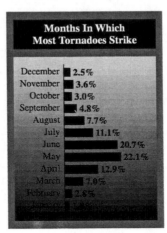

Months In Which Most Tornadoes Strike

December	2.5%
November	3.6%
October	3.0%
September	4.8%
August	7.7%
July	11.1%
June	20.7%
May	22.1%
April	12.9%
March	7.0%
February	2.8%
January	

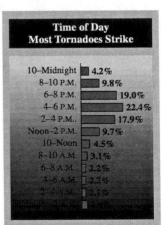

Time of Day Most Tornadoes Strike

10–Midnight	4.2%
8–10 P.M.	9.8%
6–8 P.M.	19.0%
4–6 P.M.	22.4%
2–4 P.M.	17.9%
Noon–2 P.M.	9.7%
10–Noon	4.5%
8–10 A.M.	3.1%
6–8 A.M.	2.2%
4–6 A.M.	2.2%
2–4 A.M.	2.1%

FIGURE 12

(a) How many of the reported tornadoes occurred during the hours of 6–8 P.M.?

According to the graph on the left, 19% of the tornadoes occurred during this time, so we must ask the question "What is 19% of 17,252?" This is similar to the problem posed in Example 9. Using any of the methods described there, we find that the answer is approximately 3,278. (**Note:** If we only need a "ballpark figure" we can use the fact that 19% is about 20%, and 20% is twice 10%. Ten percent of about 17,000 is 17,000/10 = 1,700, and twice 1,700 is 3,400. Compare this result to the answer found above.)

(b) How many more tornadoes occurred during March than October?

Method 1: Seven percent occurred in March and 3% occurred in October, so 7% − 3% = 4% of the total occurrences will give us the answer. Again, as in Example 9, we must find a percent of a number: "Find 4% of 17,252." Any of the described methods gives approximately 690.

Method 2: We can find 7% of 17,252 and then 3% of 17,252, and subtract the results.

Number of tornadoes in March: 7% of 17,252 is .07(17,252) ≈ 1,208

Number of tornadoes in October: 3% of 17,252 is .03(17,252) ≈ 518

Therefore, there were approximately 1,208 − 518 = 690 more tornadoes in March than October.   ◗

PROBLEM SOLVING

In many applications we are asked to find the percent increase or percent decrease from one quantity to another. The following guidelines summarize how to do this.

Finding Percent Increase or Decrease

1. To find the percent increase from *a* to *b*, where *b* > *a*, subtract *a* from *b*, and divide this result by *a*. Convert to a percent.

Example: The percent increase from 4 to 7 is $\dfrac{7-4}{4} = \dfrac{3}{4} = 75\%$.

2. To find the percent decrease from *a* to *b*, where *b* < *a*, subtract *b* from *a*, and divide this result by *a*. Convert to a percent.

Example: The percent decrease from 8 to 6 is $\dfrac{8-6}{8} = \dfrac{2}{8} = \dfrac{1}{4} = 25\%$.

These ideas will be used in some of the applications in the exercises for this section.   ◗

5 EXERCISES

Decide whether each of the following is true *or* false.

1. 50% of a quantity is the same as 1/2 of the quantity.

2. 200% of 8 is 16.

3. When 435.67 is rounded to the nearest ten, the answer is 435.7.

4. When 668.342 is rounded to the nearest hundredth, the answer is 668.34.

5. A football team that wins 10 games and loses 6 games has a winning percentage of 60%.

6. To find 25% of a quantity, we may simply divide the quantity by 4.

7. If 60% is a passing grade and a test has 40 items, then answering more than 22 items correctly will assure you of a passing grade.

8. To find 40% of a quantity, we may find 10% of that quantity and multiply our answer by 4.

9. 15 is less than 30% of 45.

10. If an item usually costs $50.00 and it is discounted 10%, the sale price is $5.00.

Work each of the following using either a calculator or paper-and-pencil methods, as directed by your instructor.

11. $8.53 + 2.785$

12. $9.358 + 7.2137$

13. $8.74 - 12.955$

14. $2.41 - 3.997$

15. $25.7 \times .032$

16. 45.1×8.344

17. $1,019.825 \div 21.47$

18. $-262.563 \div 125.03$

19. $\dfrac{118.5}{1.45 + 2.3}$

20. $2.45(1.2 + 3.4 - 5.6)$

Solve each of the following problems. Use a calculator if allowed by your instructor.

21. To prepare for her daughter's birthday party, Sharon Hollobow bought a cake for $19.95, ice cream for $5.75, and spent $35.78 on party favors. What was the total price of these items?

22. Last month Marjorie Seachrist, a video dealer, collected $2,345.97 in video rentals, $754.28 in video sales, and $321.45 in late penalty fees. What was her total income from these sources?

23. Brian Hayes manages the payroll accounts for a computer company. In February, he determined that the employees' salaries totaled $6,238.23. From these salaries he deducted $935.75 for federal tax, $235.23 for state tax, and $754.11 for other miscellaneous expenses. What was the net salary for these employees?

24. The bank balance of Tammy's Hobby Shop was $1,856.12 on March 1. During March, Tammy deposited $1,742.18 received from the sale of goods, $9,271.94 paid by customers on their accounts, and a $28.37 tax refund. She paid out $7,195.14 for merchandise, $511.09 for salaries, and $1,291.03 for other expenses.

(a) How much did Tammy deposit during March?

(b) How much did she pay out?

(c) What was her bank balance at the end of March?

25. On a recent trip to Wal-Mart, David Horwitz bought three curtain rods at $4.57 apiece, five picture frames at $2.99 each, and twelve packs of gum at $.39 per pack. If 6% sales tax was added to his purchase, what was his total bill?

26. Ray Kelley drove 411.4 mi on 12.1 gallons of gasoline. How many miles per gallon did he get?

Exercises 27–30 are based on formulas found in Auto Math Handbook: Mathematical Calculations, Theory, and Formulas for Automotive Enthusiasts, *by John Lawlor (1991, HP Books).*

27. The Blood Alcohol Concentration (BAC) of a person who has been drinking is given by the formula

$$\text{BAC} = \frac{(\text{ounces} \times \text{percent alcohol} \times .075)}{\text{body weight in lb}}$$

$$- (\text{hours of drinking} \times .015).$$

Suppose a policeman stops a 190-pound man who, in two hours, has ingested four 12-ounce beers with each beer having a 3.2 percent alcohol content. The formula would then read

$$\text{BAC} = \frac{[(4 \times 12) \times 3.2 \times .075]}{190} - (2 \times .015).$$

(a) Find this BAC.

(b) Find the BAC for a 135-pound woman who, in three hours, has drunk three 12-ounce beers with each beer having a 4.0 percent alcohol content.

28. The approximate rate of an automobile in miles per hour (MPH) can be found in terms of the engine's revolutions per minute (rpm), the tire diameter in inches, and the overall gear ratio by the formula

$$\text{MPH} = \frac{\text{rpm} \times \text{tire diameter}}{\text{gear ratio} \times 336}.$$

If a certain automobile has an rpm of 5,600, a tire diameter of 26 inches, and a gear ratio of 3.12, what is its approximate rate (MPH)?

29. Horsepower can be found from indicated mean effective pressure (mep) in pounds per square inch, engine displacement in cubic inches, and revolutions per minute (rpm) using the formula

$$\text{Horsepower} = \frac{\text{mep} \times \text{displacement} \times \text{rpm}}{792,000}.$$

Suppose that an engine has displacement of 302 cubic inches, and indicated mep of 195 pounds per square inch at 4,000 rpm. What is its approximate horsepower?

30. To determine the torque at a given value of rpm, the formula below applies:

$$\text{Torque} = \frac{5,252 \times \text{horsepower}}{\text{rpm}}.$$

If the horsepower of a certain vehicle is 400 at 4,500 rpm, what is the approximate torque?

Round each of the following numbers to the nearest (**a**) *tenth;* (**b**) *hundredth. Always round from the original number.*

31. 78.414   **32.** 3,689.537   **33.** .0837

34. .0658   **35.** 12.68925   **36.** 43.99613

Convert each decimal to a percent.

37. .42   **38.** .87   **39.** .365   **40.** .792

41. .008   **42.** .0093   **43.** 2.1   **44.** 8.9

Convert each fraction to a percent.

45. $\dfrac{1}{5}$ **46.** $\dfrac{2}{5}$ **47.** $\dfrac{1}{100}$ **48.** $\dfrac{1}{50}$

49. $\dfrac{3}{8}$ **50.** $\dfrac{5}{6}$ **51.** $\dfrac{3}{2}$ **52.** $\dfrac{7}{4}$

53. Explain the difference between 1/2 of a quantity and 1/2% of the quantity.

54. In the left column of the chart below there are some common percents, found in many everyday situations. In the right column are fractional equivalents of these percents. Match the fractions in the right column with their equivalent percents in the left column.

    (**a**) 25%   **A.** $\dfrac{1}{3}$

    (**b**) 10%   **B.** $\dfrac{1}{50}$

    (**c**) 2%   **C.** $\dfrac{3}{4}$

    (**d**) 20%   **D.** $\dfrac{1}{10}$

    (**e**) 75%   **E.** $\dfrac{1}{4}$

    (**f**) $33\dfrac{1}{3}\%$ **F.** $\dfrac{1}{5}$

55. Fill in each blank with the appropriate numerical response.

    (**a**) 5% means _____ in every 100.
    (**b**) 25% means 6 in every _____.
    (**c**) 200% means _____ for every 4.
    (**d**) .5% means _____ in every 100.
    (**e**) _____% means 12 for every 2.

56. The following Venn diagram shows the number of elements in the four regions formed.

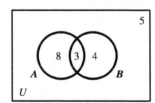

    (**a**) What percent of the elements in the universe are in $A \cap B$?
    (**b**) What percent of the elements in the universe are in A but not in B?
    (**c**) What percent of the elements in $A \cup B$ are in $A \cap B$?
    (**d**) What percent of the elements in the universe are in neither A nor B?

57. Suppose that an item regularly costs $50.00 and it is discounted 10%. If it is then marked up 10%, is the resulting price $50.00? If not, what is it?

58. At the start of play on August 16, 1992, the standings of the Eastern division of the National League were as follows:

	Won	Lost
Pittsburgh	65	51
Montreal	64	53
Chicago	56	60
St. Louis	54	61
New York	52	63
Philadelphia	49	67

"Winning percentage" is commonly expressed as a decimal rounded to the nearest thousandth. To find the winning percentage of a team, divide the number of wins by the total number of games played. Find the winning percentage of each of the teams in the division.

59. Refer to the figures in Exercise 13 of Section 3, and express each of the fractional parts represented by the shaded areas as percents.

60. If there is a 40% chance of rain tomorrow, what *fraction* in lowest terms represents the chance that it will not rain?

Work each of the following problems involving percent.

61. What is 26% of 480?

62. Find 38% of 12.

63. Find 10.5% of 28.

64. What is 48.6% of 19?

65. What percent of 30 is 45?

66. What percent of 48 is 20?

67. 25% of what number is 150?

68. 12% of what number is 3,600?

69. .392 is what percent of 28?

70. 78.84 is what percent of 292?

Use mental techniques to answer each of the following. Try to avoid using paper and pencil or a calculator.

71. Johnny Cross had his allowance raised from $4.00 per week to $5.00 per week. What was the percent of the increase?
    (a) 25%   (b) 20%
    (c) 50%   (d) 30%

72. Jane Gunton bought a boat five years ago for $5,000 and sold it this year for $2,000. What percent of her original purchase did she lose on the sale?
    (a) 40%   (b) 50%   (c) 20%
    (d) 60%

73. The 1990 United States census showed that the population of Alabama was 4,040,587, with 25.3% representing African-Americans. What is the best estimate of the African-American population of Alabama?
    (a) 500,000   (b) 750,000   (c) 1,000,000
    (d) 1,500,000

74. The 1990 United States census showed that the population of New Mexico was 1,515,069, with 38.2% being Hispanic. What is the best estimate of the Hispanic population of New Mexico?
    (a) 600,000   (b) 60,000   (c) 750,000
    (d) 38,000

Work each of the following problems. Round all money amounts to the nearest dollar.

75. According to a Knight-Ridder Newspapers report, as of May 31, 1992, the nation's "consumer-debt burden" was 16.4%. This means that the average American had consumer debts, such as credit card bills, auto loans, and so on, totaling 16.4% of his or her take-home pay. Suppose that George Duda has a take-home pay of $3,250 per month. What is 16.4% of his monthly take-home pay?

76. In 1992 General Motors announced that it would raise prices on its 1993 vehicles by an average of 1.6%. If a certain vehicle had a 1992 price of $10,526 and this price was raised 1.6%, what would the 1993 price be?

77. An advertisement for a dot matrix printer gives the sale price of $149.99. The regular price is $169.99. What is the percent discount on this printer?

78. Devorah Harris earns $3,200 per month. If she wants to save 18% of this amount, how much should she set aside monthly?

79. The 1916 dime minted in Denver is quite rare. The 1979 edition of *A Guide Book of United States Coins* listed its value in extremely fine condition as $625.00. The 1991 value had increased to $1,750. What was the percent increase in the value of this coin?

80. In 1963, the value of a 1903 Morgan dollar minted in New Orleans in uncirculated condition was $1,500. Due to a discovery of a large hoard of these dollars late that year, the value plummeted. Its value as listed in the 1991 edition of *A Guide Book of United States Coins* was $200. What percent of its 1963 value was its 1991 value?

81. The manufacturer's suggested retail price of a 1992 Mazda MX 3 was $14,295. A dealer advertised a $2,300 discount. What percent discount was this?

82. According to a report by Freeport-McMoRan Copper Co., Inc., its Grasberg prospect in Indonesia has a large copper find. It has at least 50 million metric tons of ore at an average grade of 1.4% copper and 1.3 grams of gold per ton. Assuming that there actually are 50 million metric tons of ore,
   (a) find the number of metric tons of pure copper;
   (b) find the number of grams of gold.

Refer to Example 13 and Figure 6.12 to solve the problems in Exercises 83 and 84.

83. How many fewer tornadoes occurred during August than June?

84. How many tornadoes occurred from midnight to noon during the twenty year period?

85. By law, a cord of wood is 128 cubic feet of wood, or a stack 4 ft by 4 ft by 8 ft. The wood must be well stoved (tightly stacked) as shown in the top photograph.
   (a) The middle photograph shows the wood from the first photograph stacked in a looser way. The pile of wood in front represents the wood not received by the customer. This wood occupies 20 cu ft when properly stacked. What percent of a proper cord does the customer not receive?
   (b) Finally, stacking the original cord of wood "log cabin" style, as in the bottom photograph, leaves 64 cu ft of wood that the customer does not get. What percent of a proper cord does the customer not get?

A tightly packed face cord has split side of wood down, all voids filled.

The same 4-by-8 face cord loosely stacked, bark side down, gives 20 cu ft less wood—shown in the front pile.

The same size face cord stacked "log cabin" style means you lose 64 cu ft of the wood.

86. What percent of a cord of wood is 320 cubic feet of wood? (See Exercise 85.)

It is customary in our society to "tip" waiters and waitresses when eating in restaurants. The usual rate of tipping is 15%. A quick way of figuring a tip that will give a close approximation of 15% is as follows:

1. Round off the bill to the nearest dollar.
2. Find 10% of this amount by moving the decimal point one place to the left.
3. Take half of the amount obtained in Step 2 and add it to the result of Step 2.

This will give you approximately 15% of the bill. The amount obtained in Step 3 is 5%, and 10% + 5% = 15%.

Use the method above to find an approximation of 15% of each of the following restaurant bills.

87. $29.57

88. $38.32

89. $5.15

90. $7.89

91. Example 2(a) shows a paper-and-pencil method of multiplying 4.613 × 2.52. The following discussion gives a mathematical justification of this method. Fill in the blanks with the appropriate responses.

$$4.613 = 4\frac{613}{1,000} = \frac{4,613}{1,000} = \frac{4,613}{10^3}$$

$$2.52 = 2\frac{52}{100} = \frac{252}{100} = \frac{252}{10^2}$$

$$4.613 \times 2.52 = \frac{4,613}{10^3} \cdot \frac{252}{10^2} \qquad [*]$$

(a) In algebra, we learn that multiplying powers of the same number is accomplished by *adding* the exponents. Thus,

$$10^3 \cdot 10^2 = 10^{\underline{} + \underline{}} = 10^{\underline{}}.$$

(b) The product in the line indicated by [*] is obtained by multiplying the fractions.

$$\frac{4,613 \cdot 252}{10^5} = \frac{1,162,476}{10^5} = 11.62476$$

The _____ places to the right of the decimal point in the product are the result of division by $10^{\underline{}}$.

92. Develop an argument justifying the paper-and-pencil method of dividing decimal numbers, as shown in Example 2(b).

93. A television reporter once asked a professional wrist-wrestler what percent of his sport was physical and what percent was mental. The athlete responded "I would say it's 50% physical and 90% mental." Comment on this response.

94. We often hear the claim "(S)he gave 110%." Comment on this claim. Do you think that this is actually possible?

EXTENSION

Complex Numbers

Early mathematicians would often come up with a solution to a problem such as $-2 + \sqrt{-16}$. If negative numbers and square roots were bad enough, what sense could be made from the square root of a negative number? These numbers were called *imaginary* by the early mathematicians, who would not permit these numbers to be used as solutions to problems.

Gradually, however, applications were found that required the use of these numbers, making it necessary to enlarge the set of real numbers to form the set of **complex numbers.** By doing this, an end is reached: the set of complex numbers provides a solution for just about any equation that can be written.

To develop the basic ideas of the complex number system, consider the equation $x^2 + 1 = 0$. It has no real number solution, since any solution must be a number whose square is -1. In the set of real numbers all squares are nonnegative numbers, because the product of either two positive numbers or two negative numbers is positive. To provide a solution for the equation $x^2 + 1 = 0$, a new number i is defined so that

$$i^2 = -1.$$

That is, i is a number whose square is -1. This definition of i makes it possible to define the square root of any negative number as follows.

For any positive real number b, $\qquad \sqrt{-b} = i\sqrt{b}.$

Gauss and the Complex Numbers The above stamp honors the many contributions made by Gauss to our understanding of complex numbers. In about 1831 he was able to show that numbers of the form $a + bi$ can be represented as points on the plane (as the stamp on page 265 diagrams) just as real numbers are. He shares this contribution with Robert Argand, a bookkeeper in Paris, who wrote an essay on the geometry of the complex numbers in 1806. This went unnoticed at the time.

EXAMPLE 1   Write each number as a product of a real number and i.

(a) $\sqrt{-100} = i\sqrt{100} = 10i$

(b) $\sqrt{-2} = \sqrt{2}i = i\sqrt{2}$

It is easy to mistake $\sqrt{2}i$ for $\sqrt{2i}$, with the i under the radical. For this reason, it is common to write $\sqrt{2}i$ as $i\sqrt{2}$. ●

When finding a product such as $\sqrt{-4} \cdot \sqrt{-9}$, the product rule for radicals cannot be used, since that rule applies only when both radicals represent real numbers. For this reason, always change $\sqrt{-b}$ ($b > 0$) to the form $i\sqrt{b}$ before performing any multiplications or divisions. For example,

$$\sqrt{-4} \cdot \sqrt{-9} = i\sqrt{4} \cdot i\sqrt{9} = i \cdot 2 \cdot i \cdot 3 = 6i^2.$$

Since $i^2 = -1$,

$$6i^2 = 6(-1) = -6.$$

An *incorrect* use of the product rule for radicals would give a wrong answer.

$$\sqrt{-4} \cdot \sqrt{-9} = \sqrt{(-4)(-9)} = \sqrt{36} = 6 \qquad \text{Incorrect}$$

EXAMPLE 2   Multiply.

(a) $\sqrt{-3} \cdot \sqrt{-7} = i\sqrt{3} \cdot i\sqrt{7} = i^2\sqrt{3 \cdot 7} = (-1)\sqrt{21} = -\sqrt{21}$

(b) $\sqrt{-2} \cdot \sqrt{-8} = i\sqrt{2} \cdot i\sqrt{8} = i^2)\sqrt{2 \cdot 8} = (-1)\sqrt{16} = (-1)4 = -4$

(c) $\sqrt{-5} \cdot \sqrt{6} = i\sqrt{5} \cdot \sqrt{6} = i\sqrt{30}$ ⬢

The methods used to find products also apply to quotients, as the next example shows.

EXAMPLE 3   Divide.

(a) $\dfrac{\sqrt{-75}}{\sqrt{-3}} = \dfrac{i\sqrt{75}}{i\sqrt{3}} = \sqrt{\dfrac{75}{3}} = \sqrt{25} = 5$

(b) $\dfrac{\sqrt{-32}}{\sqrt{8}} = \dfrac{i\sqrt{32}}{\sqrt{8}} = i\sqrt{\dfrac{32}{8}} = i\sqrt{4} = 2i$ ●

With the new number i and the real numbers, a new set of numbers can be formed that includes the real numbers as a subset. The *complex numbers* are defined as follows.

Complex Numbers

If a and b are real numbers, then any number of the form $a + bi$ is called a **complex number.**

In the complex number $a + bi$, the number a is called the **real part** and b is called the **imaginary part.** When $b = 0$, $a + bi$ is a real number, so the real numbers are a subset of the complex numbers. Complex numbers with $b \neq 0$ are called **imaginary numbers**. In spite of their name, imaginary numbers are very useful in applications, particularly in work with electricity.

The relationships among the various sets of numbers discussed in this chapter are shown in Figure 13.

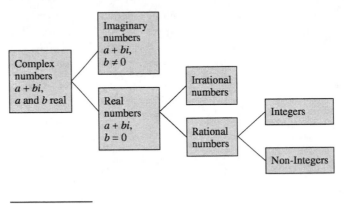

FIGURE 13

An interesting pattern emerges when we consider various powers of i. By definition, $i^0 = 1$, and $i^1 = i$. We have seen that $i^2 = -1$, and higher powers of i can be found as shown in the following list.

$$i^3 = i \cdot i^2 = i(-1) = -i \qquad i^6 = i^2 \cdot i^4 = (-1) \cdot 1 = -1$$
$$i^4 = i^2 \cdot i^2 = (-1)(-1) = 1 \qquad i^7 = i^3 \cdot i^4 = (-i) \cdot 1 = -i$$
$$i^5 = i \cdot i^4 = i \cdot 1 = i \qquad i^8 = i^4 \cdot i^4 = 1 \cdot 1 = 1$$

A few powers of i are listed here.

Powers of i

$i^1 = i$	$i^5 = i$	$i^9 = i$	$i^{13} = i$
$i^2 = -1$	$i^6 = -1$	$i^{10} = -1$	$i^{14} = -1$
$i^3 = -i$	$i^7 = -i$	$i^{11} = -i$	$i^{15} = -i$
$i^4 = 1$	$i^8 = 1$	$i^{12} = 1$	$i^{16} = 1$

As these examples suggest, the powers of i rotate through the four numbers i, -1, $-i$, and 1. Larger powers of i can be simplified by using the fact that $i^4 = 1$. For example, $i^{75} = (i^4)^{18} \cdot i^3 = 1^{18} \cdot i^3 = 1 \cdot i^3 = -i$. This example suggests a quick method for simplifying large powers of i.

Extension **Simplifying Large Powers of *i***

Step 1 Divide the exponent by 4.

Step 2 Observe the remainder obtained in Step 1. The large power of *i* is the same as *i* raised to the power determined by this remainder. Refer to the chart above to complete the simplification. (If the remainder is 0, the power simplifies to $i^0 = 1$.)

EXAMPLE 4   Find each power of *i*.

(a) $i^{12} = (i^4)^3 = 1^3 = 1$

(b) i^{39}

We can use the guidelines shown above. Start by dividing 39 by 4 (Step 1).

$$\begin{array}{r} 9 \\ 4\overline{)39} \\ 36 \\ \hline 3 \leftarrow \text{Remainder} \end{array}$$

The remainder is 3. So $i^{39} = i^3 = -i$ (Step 2).

Another way of simplifying i^{39} is as follows.

$$i^{39} = i^{36} \cdot i^3 = (i^4)^9 \cdot i^3 = 1^9 \cdot (-i) = -i \quad \blacklozenge$$

EXTENSION EXERCISES

Use the method of Examples 1–3 to write each as a real number or a product of a real number and i.

1. $\sqrt{-144}$ **2.** $\sqrt{-196}$ **3.** $-\sqrt{-225}$ **4.** $-\sqrt{-400}$

5. $\sqrt{-3}$ **6.** $\sqrt{-19}$ **7.** $\sqrt{-75}$ **8.** $\sqrt{-125}$

9. $\sqrt{-5} \cdot \sqrt{-5}$ **10.** $\sqrt{-3} \cdot \sqrt{-3}$ **11.** $\sqrt{-9} \cdot \sqrt{-36}$ **12.** $\sqrt{-4} \cdot \sqrt{-81}$

13. $\sqrt{-16} \cdot \sqrt{-100}$ **14.** $\sqrt{-81} \cdot \sqrt{-121}$ **15.** $\dfrac{\sqrt{-200}}{\sqrt{-100}}$ **16.** $\dfrac{\sqrt{-50}}{\sqrt{-2}}$

17. $\dfrac{\sqrt{-54}}{\sqrt{6}}$ **18.** $\dfrac{\sqrt{-90}}{\sqrt{10}}$ **19.** $\dfrac{\sqrt{-288}}{\sqrt{-8}}$ **20.** $\dfrac{\sqrt{-48} \cdot \sqrt{-3}}{\sqrt{-2}}$

21. Why is it incorrect to use the product rule for radicals to multiply $\sqrt{-3} \cdot \sqrt{-12}$?

22. In your own words describe the relationship between complex numbers and real numbers.

Use the method of Example 4 to find each power of i.

23. i^8 **24.** i^{16} **25.** i^{42} **26.** i^{86}

27. i^{47} **28.** i^{63} **29.** i^{101} **30.** i^{141}

31. Explain the difference between $\sqrt{-1}$ and $-\sqrt{1}$. Which one of these is defined as *i*?

32. Is it possible to give an example of a real number that is not a complex number? Why or why not?

1 Introduction to Sets of Real Numbers

Sets of Numbers

Natural Numbers	$\{1, 2, 3, 4, \ldots\}$
Whole Numbers	$\{0, 1, 2, 3, \ldots\}$
Integers	$\{\ldots, -3, -2, -1, 0, 1, 2, 3, \ldots\}$
Rational Numbers	$\{x \mid x$ is a quotient of two integers, with denominator not equal to $0\}$
Real Numbers	$\{x \mid x$ is a number that can be represented by a point on the number line$\}$
Irrational Numbers	$\{x \mid x$ is a real number that is not rational$\}$

Absolute Value

$$|x| = \begin{cases} x & \text{if } x \geq 0 \\ -x & \text{if } x < 0 \end{cases}$$

2 Operations, Properties, and Applications of Real Numbers

Adding Real Numbers

Like Signs   Add two numbers with the *same* sign by adding their absolute values. The sign of the sum is the same as the sign of the two numbers.

Unlike Signs   Add two numbers with *different* signs by subtracting the smaller absolute value from the larger. The sum is positive if the positive number has the larger absolute value. The sum is negative if the negative number has the larger absolute value.

Definition of Subtraction

For all real numbers a and b,

$$a - b = a + (-b).$$

Multiplying and Dividing Real Numbers

Like Signs   Multiply or divide two numbers with the *same* sign by multiplying or dividing their absolute values. The product or quotient is positive.

Unlike Signs   Multiply or divide two numbers with *different* signs by multiplying or dividing their absolute values. The product or quotient is negative.

Order of Operations

If parentheses or square brackets are present:

Step 1   Work separately above and below any fraction bar.

Step 2   Use the rules below within each set of parentheses or square brackets. Start with the innermost set and work outward.

If no parentheses or brackets are present:

Step 1   Apply all exponents.

Step 2   Do any multiplications or divisions in the order in which they occur, working from left to right.

Step 3   Do any additions or subtractions in the order in which they occur, working from left to right.

Properties of Addition and Multiplication of Real Numbers
For any real numbers a, b, and c, the following properties hold.

Closure Properties If a and b are real numbers, then $a + b$ and ab are real numbers.

Commutative Properties $$a + b = b + a \qquad ab = ba$$

Associative Properties $$(a + b) + c = a + (b + c)$$
$$(ab)c = a(bc)$$

Identity Properties There is a real number 0 such that
$$a + 0 = a \quad \text{and} \quad 0 + a = a.$$
There is a real number 1 such that
$$a \cdot 1 = a \quad \text{and} \quad 1 \cdot a = a.$$

Inverse Properties For each real number a, there is a single real number $-a$ such that
$$a + (-a) = 0 \quad \text{and} \quad (-a) + a = 0.$$
For each nonzero real number a, there is a single real number $\dfrac{1}{a}$ such that
$$a \cdot \frac{1}{a} = 1 \quad \text{and} \quad \frac{1}{a} \cdot a = 1.$$

Distributive Property
of Multiplication $$a(b + c) = ab + ac$$
with Respect to Addition $$(b + c)a = ba + ca$$

3   Rational Numbers and Decimals

Fundamental Property of Rational Numbers
If a, b, and k are integers with $b \neq 0$ and $k \neq 0$, then
$$\frac{a \cdot k}{b \cdot k} = \frac{a}{b}.$$

Cross-Product Test for Equality of Rational Numbers
For rational numbers a/b and c/d, $b \neq 0$, $d \neq 0$,
$$\frac{a}{b} = \frac{c}{d} \quad \text{if and only if} \quad a \cdot d = b \cdot c.$$

Adding and Subtracting Rational Numbers
If a/b and c/d are rational numbers, then
$$\frac{a}{b} + \frac{c}{d} = \frac{ad + bc}{bd}$$
$$\text{and} \quad \frac{a}{b} - \frac{c}{d} = \frac{ad - bc}{bd}.$$

Multiplying Rational Numbers

If a/b and c/d are rational numbers, then

$$\frac{a}{b} \cdot \frac{c}{d} = \frac{ac}{bd}.$$

Definition of Division

If a and b are real numbers, $b \neq 0$, then

$$\frac{a}{b} = a \cdot \frac{1}{b}.$$

Dividing Rational Numbers

If a/b and c/d are rational numbers, where $c/d \neq 0$, then

$$\frac{a}{b} \div \frac{c}{d} = \frac{a}{b} \cdot \frac{d}{c} = \frac{ad}{bc}.$$

Any rational number can be expressed as either a terminating decimal or a repeating decimal. A rational number a/b in lowest terms results in a terminating decimal if the only prime factors of the denominator are 2 or 5 (or both). It results in a repeating decimal if a prime other than 2 or 5 appears in the prime factorization of the denominator.

Density Property of the Rational Numbers

If r and t are distinct rational numbers, with $r < t$, then there exists a rational number s such that

$$r < s < t.$$

4   Irrational Numbers and Decimals

The chart shows some examples of rational numbers and irrational numbers.

Rational Numbers	Irrational Numbers
$\dfrac{2}{3}$	$\sqrt{3}$
$.43$	$.45455455545555\ldots$
$.\overline{83}$	$\sqrt{10}$
$\dfrac{355}{113}$	π
1.618	$\dfrac{1+\sqrt{5}}{2}$ The golden ratio
2.718	e An important number in higher mathematics

$\sqrt{a}$

For $a \geq 0$, $\sqrt{a}$ is the nonnegative real number whose square is a; that is, $(\sqrt{a})^2 = a$.

Product Rule for Square Roots

For nonnegative real numbers a and b,

$$\sqrt{a} \cdot \sqrt{b} = \sqrt{a \cdot b}.$$

Simplified Form of a Square Root Radical
1. The number under the radical (radicand) has no factor (except 1) that is a perfect square.
2. The radicand has no fractions.
3. No denominator contains a radical.

Quotient Rule for Square Roots
For nonnegative real numbers a and positive numbers b,

$$\frac{\sqrt{a}}{\sqrt{b}} = \sqrt{\frac{a}{b}}.$$

5 Applications of Decimals and Percents

Rules for Rounding Decimals
Step 1   Locate the **place** to which the number is being rounded.
Step 2   Look at the next **digit to the right** of the place to which the number is being rounded.

Step 3A If this digit is **less than 5,** drop all digits to the right of the place to which the number is being rounded. Do *not change* the digit in the place to which the number is being rounded.	*Step 3B* If this digit is **5 or greater,** drop all digits to the right of the place to which the number is being rounded. *Add one* to the digit in the place to which the number is being rounded.

Conversion Rules
1. To convert a percent to a decimal, drop the % sign and move the decimal point two places to the left, inserting zeros as place holders, if necessary.
2. To convert a decimal to a percent, move the decimal point two places to the right, inserting zeros as place holders, if necessary, and attach a % sign.
3. To convert a fraction to a decimal, divide the numerator by the denominator.
4. To convert a fraction to a percent, follow Rule 3 and then follow Rule 2.

CHAPTER TEST

1. List the numbers in the set $\{-8, -\sqrt{6}, -4/3, -.6, 0, \sqrt{2}, 3.9, 10\}$ that are **(a)** natural numbers, **(b)** whole numbers, **(c)** integers, **(d)** rational numbers, **(e)** irrational numbers, **(f)** real numbers.

2. Explain what is wrong with the following statement: "The absolute value of a number is always positive."

3. Specify the set $\{x \mid x$ is a positive integer less than $4\}$ by listing its elements.

4. Give three examples of a number that is a positive rational number, but not an integer.

5. True or false: The absolute value of -5 is $-(-5)$.

6. Perform the indicated operations, using the order of operations as necessary.

   (a) $5^2 - 3(2 + 6)$ **(b)** $(-3)(-2) - [5 + (8 - 10)]$ **(c)** $\dfrac{(-8 + 3) - (5 + 10)}{7 - 9}$

7. Which one of the following is undefined: $\dfrac{7-7}{7+7}$ or $\dfrac{7+7}{7-7}$?

8. Match each of the statements on the left with the property that justifies it.
   (a) $7 \cdot (8 \cdot 5) = (7 \cdot 8) \cdot 5$ **A.** Distributive property
   (b) $3x + 3y = 3(x + y)$ **B.** Identity property
   (c) $8 \cdot 1 = 1 \cdot 8 = 8$ **C.** Closure property
   (d) $7 + (6 + 9) = (6 + 9) + 7$ **D.** Commutative property
   (e) $9 + (-9) = -9 + 9 = 0$ **E.** Associative property
   (f) $5 \cdot 8$ is a real number.   **F.** Inverse property

9. The temperature at 4 A.M. was $-19°$. It then increased $39°$ by noon. Find the temperature at noon.

10. Which one of the following is not written in lowest terms?
    (a) $\dfrac{21}{29}$ (b) $\dfrac{2}{3}$ (c) $\dfrac{9}{4}$ (d) $\dfrac{17}{51}$

11. The five starters on the local high school basketball team had the following shooting statistics after the first three games.

Player	Field Goal Attempts	Field Goals Made
Camp, Jim	40	13
Cooper, Daniel	10	4
Cornett, Bill	20	8
Hickman, Chuck	6	4
Levinson, Harold	7	2

Answer each of the following, using estimation skills as necessary.
   (a) Which player made more than half of his attempts?
   (b) Which players made just less than 1/3 of their attempts?
   (c) Which player made exactly 2/3 of his attempts?
   (d) Which two players made the same fractional parts of their attempts? What was the fractional part, reduced to lowest terms?

Perform each operation. Reduce your answer to lowest terms.

12. $\dfrac{3}{16} + \dfrac{1}{2}$ 13. $\dfrac{9}{20} - \dfrac{3}{32}$ 14. $\dfrac{3}{8} \cdot \left(-\dfrac{16}{15}\right)$ 15. $\dfrac{7}{9} \div \dfrac{14}{27}$

16. Dottie Fogell works 40 hours per week in a stationery store. She worked 8 1/4 hours on Monday, 6 3/8 hours on Tuesday, 7 2/3 hours on Wednesday, and 8 3/4 hours on Thursday. How many hours did Dottie work on Friday?

Convert each rational number into a repeating or terminating decimal. Use a calculator if your instructor so allows.

17. $\dfrac{9}{20}$ 18. $\dfrac{5}{12}$

Convert each decimal into a quotient of integers, reduced to lowest terms.

19. $.72$ 20. $.\overline{58}$

21. Identify each number as rational or irrational.
    (a) $\sqrt{10}$ (b) $\sqrt{16}$ (c) $.01$ (d) $.\overline{01}$ (e) $.0101101110\ldots$

For each of the following (**a**) *use a calculator to find a decimal approximation and* (**b**) *simplify the radical according to the guidelines in Section 4.*

22. $\sqrt{150}$

23. $\dfrac{13}{\sqrt{7}}$

24. $2\sqrt{32} - 5\sqrt{128}$

25. A student using his powerful new calculator states that the *exact* value of $\sqrt{65}$ is 8.062257748. Is he correct? If not, explain.

Work each of the following using either a calculator or paper-and-pencil methods, as directed by your instructor.

26. $4.6 + 9.21$

27. $12 - 3.725 - 8.59$

28. $86(.45)$

29. $236.439 \div (-9.73)$

30. Round 9.0449 to the following place values: (**a**) hundredths (**b**) thousandths.

31. Find 18.5% of 90.

32. What number is 145% of 70?

33. 28 is what percent of 7?

34. Use mental techniques to answer the following: In 1990, James Ertl sold $150,000 worth of books. In 1991, he sold $450,000 worth of books. His 1991 sales were _____ of his 1990 sales.
(**a**) 200%   (**b**) 33 1/3%   (**c**) 300%   (**d**) 30%

35. The population of Manistee, Michigan, declined from 7,665 to 6,734 between the 1980 and 1990 censuses. What percent decrease in population does this represent?

Refer to the figure to answer the questions in Exercises 36–37.

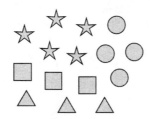

36. What percent of the total number of shapes are circles?

37. What percent of the total number of shapes are not stars?

Answer true *or* false *to each of the following.*

38. 1/2%, .5%, and 1/200 all represent the same fractional part of a quantity.

39. "1 in every 4" represents 1/4%.

40. "4 for every 1" represents 400%.

Counting Methods

MAGYAR POSTA

RUBIK KOCKA
VILÁGBAJNOKSÁG
BUDAPEST 1982

2Ft

1982   VARGA F.

Counting methods can be used to find the number of moves required to solve a Rubik's Cube (see the illustration on the facing page). The scrambled cube must be modified so that each face is a solid color. Rubik's royalties from sales of the cube in Western countries made him Hungary's richest man.

There are many situations where a *task* is to be performed and where it is useful to know how many different *results* are possible. Depending on the nature of the task, there are various ways to find the answer to the question, "How many possible results are there?" We shall refer to any procedure for answering the question "How many?" as a **counting method.** Counting methods are especially important in the study of probability. Just as with other kinds of mathematical problems, we can attack counting problems by applying Polya's four-step process for problem solving. After understanding the problem (step 1), we devise a plan (step 2). In the case of counting problems, the plan will be the selection of a strategy, namely an appropriate counting method. Commonly used strategies are the use of tables, charts and diagrams, observing patterns, drawing a sketch, and utilizing an appropriate equation or formula. And perhaps most importantly, remember that your own common sense can be the most helpful strategy of all. This chapter will present some approaches that have proved helpful over the years, but you should also feel free to apply your own reasoning skills to design your own methods. Counting problems will provide you the opportunity to utilize a great many of your mathematical skills.

1 Counting by Systematic Listing

The methods of counting presented in this section all involve coming up with an actual list of the possible results for a given task. This approach is only practical for fairly short lists. Other methods, developed in the remainder of the chapter, will enable us to often find "how many" without actually listing all the possibilities.

When listing possible results, it is extremely important to use a *systematic* approach. If we just start listing the possibilities as they happen to occur to us, we are very likely to miss some of them.

One-Part Tasks

The results for simple tasks consisting of one part can often be listed easily. For the task of tossing a single fair coin, for example, the list looks like this: *heads, tails.* There are two possible results. If the task is to roll a single fair die (a cube with faces numbered 1 through 6), the different results are 1, 2, 3, 4, 5, 6, a total of six possibilities.

EXAMPLE 1 Consider a club *N* with five members:

$$N = \{\text{Andy, Bill, Cathy, David, Evelyn}\},$$

or, as a shortcut,

$$N = \{A, B, C, D, E\}.$$

In how many ways can this group select a president (assuming all members are eligible)?

The task in this case is to select one of the five members as president. There are five possible results: *A, B, C, D,* and *E.* ●

Two-Part Tasks; Using Product Tables

EXAMPLE 2 Determine the number of two-digit numbers that can be written using digits from the set {1, 2, 3}.

This task consists of two parts: choose a first digit and choose a second digit. The results for a two-part task can be pictured in a **product table** such as Table 1. From the table we obtain our list of possible results: 11, 12, 13, 21, 22, 23, 31, 32, 33. There are nine possibilities. ◗

TABLE 1

	Second Digit		
	1	**2**	**3**
First Digit 1	11	12	13
2	21	22	23
3	31	32	33

EXAMPLE 3 Determine the number of different possible results when two ordinary dice are rolled.

For clarity, assume the dice are easily distinguishable. Perhaps one is red and the other green. Then the task consists of two parts: roll the red die and roll the green die. Table 2 is a product table showing the thirty-six possible results. ◗

TABLE 2

	Green Die					
	1	**2**	**3**	**4**	**5**	**6**
Red Die 1	(1, 1)	(1, 2)	(1, 3)	(1, 4)	(1, 5)	(1, 6)
2	(2, 1)	(2, 2)	(2, 3)	(2, 4)	(2, 5)	(2, 6)
3	(3, 1)	(3, 2)	(3, 3)	(3, 4)	(3, 5)	(3, 6)
4	(4, 1)	(4, 2)	(4, 3)	(4, 4)	(4, 5)	(4, 6)
5	(5, 1)	(5, 2)	(5, 3)	(5, 4)	(5, 5)	(5, 6)
6	(6, 1)	(6, 2)	(6, 3)	(6, 4)	(6, 5)	(6, 6)

You will want to refer back to Table 2 when various dice-rolling problems occur in the remainder of this chapter and the next.

Bone dice were unearthed in the remains of a Roman garrison, Vindolanda, near the border between England and Scotland. Life on the Roman frontier was occupied with gaming as well as fighting. Some of the Roman dice were loaded in favor of 6 and 1.

Life on the American frontier was reflected in cattle brands that were devised to keep alive the memories of hardships, feuds, and romances. A rancher named Ellis from Paradise Valley in Arizona liked a pun now and then. He even designed his cattle brand in the shape of a pair of dice. You can guess that the pips were 6 and 1.

EXAMPLE 4 Find the number of ways that club *N* of Example 1 can elect both a president and a secretary. Assume that all members are eligible, but that no one can hold both offices.

Again, the required task has two parts: determine the president and determine the secretary. Constructing Table 3 gives us the following list (where, for example, *AB* denotes president *A* and secretary *B*, while *BA* denotes president *B* and secretary *A*):

AB, AC, AD, AE, BA, BC, BD, BE, CA, CB,
CD, CE, DA, DB, DC, DE, EA, EB, EC, ED.

Notice that certain entries (down the main diagonal, from upper left to lower right) are omitted from the table, since the cases *AA, BB,* and so on would imply one person holding both offices. We see that there are twenty possibilities. ●

TABLE 3

		Secretary				
		A	*B*	*C*	*D*	*E*
President	*A*		*AB*	*AC*	*AD*	*AE*
	B	*BA*		*BC*	*BD*	*BE*
	C	*CA*	*CB*		*CD*	*CE*
	D	*DA*	*DB*	*DC*		*DE*
	E	*EA*	*EB*	*EC*	*ED*	

EXAMPLE 5   Find the number of ways that club *N* can appoint a committee of two members to represent them at an association conference.

The required task again has two parts. In fact, we can refer to Table 3 again, but this time, the order of the two letters (people) in a given pair really makes no difference. For example, *BD* and *DB* are the same committee. (In Example 4, *BD* and *DB* were different results since the two people would be holding different offices.) In the case of committees, we eliminate not only the main diagonal entries, but also all entries below the main diagonal. Our resulting list contains ten possibilities:

AB,   AC,   AD,   AE,   BC,   BD,   BE,   CD,   CE,   DE. ●

Tasks with Three or More Parts; Using Tree Diagrams

When a task has more than two parts, it is not so easy to analyze it with a product table, since it would require a table of more than two dimensions, which is hard to construct on paper. Another helpful device is the **tree diagram,** which we use in the following examples.

EXAMPLE 6   Find the number of three-digit numbers that can be written using digits from the set {1, 2, 3}, assuming that (a) repeated digits are allowed, (b) repeated digits are not allowed.

(a) The task of constructing such a number has three parts: select the first digit, select the second digit, and select the third digit. As we move from left to right through the tree diagram in Figure 1, the tree branches at the first stage to all possibilities for the first digit. Then each first stage branch again branches, or splits, to the second stage, to all possibilities for the second digit. Finally, the third stage branching shows the third-digit possibilities. The list of possible results (27 of them) is shown at the right.

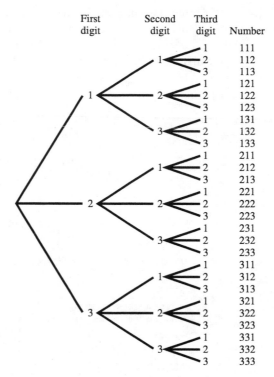

Tree diagram for three-digit numbers
with digits from the set {1, 2, 3}

FIGURE 1

(b) For the case of non-repeating digits, we could construct a whole new tree diagram, as in Figure 2, or we could simply go down the list of numbers from the first tree diagram and strike out any that contain repeated digits. In either case we obtain only six possibilities. ●

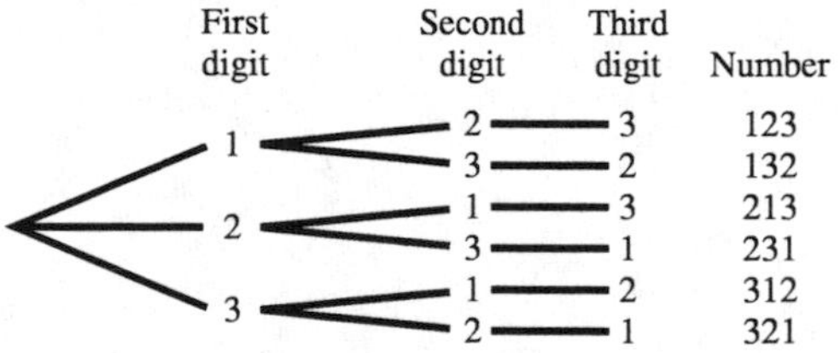

First digit	Second digit	Third digit	Number
1	2	3	123
1	3	2	132
2	1	3	213
2	3	1	231
3	1	2	312
3	2	1	321

Tree diagram for non-repeating three-digit
numbers with digits from the set {1, 2, 3}

FIGURE 2

EXAMPLE 7   Mollie Schlue's computer allows for optional settings with a panel of four on-off switches in a row. How many different settings can Mollie select if no two adjacent switches can both be off?

This situation is typical of user-selectable options on various devices, including computer equipment, garage door openers, and other appliances. In Figure 3 we denote "on" and "off" with 1 and 0, respectively (a common practice). The number of possible settings is seen to be eight. Notice that each time on the tree diagram that a switch is indicated as off (0), the next switch can only be on (1). This is to satisfy the restriction that no two adjacent switches can both be off. ●

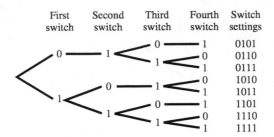

Tree diagram for printer settings

FIGURE 3

▉ **EXAMPLE 8** ▉   Andy, Betty, Clyde, and Dawn have tickets for four reserved seats in a row at a concert. In how many different ways can they seat themselves so that Andy and Betty will sit next to each other?

Here we have a four-part task: assign people to the first, second, third, and fourth seats. The tree diagram in Figure 4 again avoids repetitions, since no person can occupy more than one seat. Also, once *A* or *B* appears at any stage of the tree, the other one must occur at the next stage. (Why is this?) Notice that no splitting occurs from stage three to stage four since by that time there is only one person left unassigned. The right column in the figure shows the twelve possible seating arrangements. ●

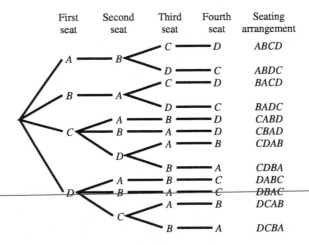

Tree diagram for concert seating

FIGURE 4

Although we have applied tree diagrams only to tasks with three or more parts, they can also be used for two-part or even simple, one-part tasks. Product tables, on the other hand, are useful only for two-part tasks.

Other Systematic Listing Methods

Product tables (for two-part tasks) and tree diagrams (for tasks of any number of parts) are useful methods for picturing and listing the possible results for given tasks. But you should feel free to create other approaches as well. To finish this section, we suggest some additional systematic ways to produce complete listings of possible results.

In Example 4, we used a product table (Table 3) to list all possible president-secretary pairs for the club $N = \{A, B, C, D, E\}$. We could also systematically construct the same list using a sort of alphabetical or left-to-right approach. First, consider the results where A is president. Any of the remaining members (B, C, D, or E) could then be secretary. That gives us the pairs AB, AC, AD, and AE. Next, assume B is president. The secretary could then be A, C, D, or E. We get the pairs BA, BC, BD, and BE. Continuing in order, we get the complete list just as in Example 4:

$$AB, \quad AC, \quad AD, \quad AE, \quad BA, \quad BC, \quad BD, \quad BE, \quad CA, \quad CB,$$
$$CD, \quad CE, \quad DA, \quad DB, \quad DC, \quad DE, \quad EA, \quad EB, \quad EC, \quad ED.$$

The **"tree diagram"** on the map came from research on the feasibility of using motor-sailers (motor-driven ships with wind-sail auxiliary power) on the North Atlantic run. At the beginning of a run, weather forecasts and computer analysis are used to choose the best of the 45 million possible routes.

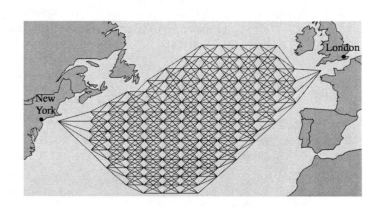

EXAMPLE 9   How many different triangles (of any size) are included in the figure shown here?

One systematic approach is to label the points as shown, begin with A, and proceed in alphabetical order to write all 3-letter combinations, then cross out the ones that are not triangles in the figure.

$$ABC, \quad ABD, \quad ABE, \quad ABF, \quad ACD, \quad ACE, \quad \sout{ACF}, \quad \sout{ADE}, \quad \sout{ADF}, \quad AEF,$$
$$\sout{BCD}, \quad BCE, \quad BCF, \quad BDE, \quad \sout{BDF}, \quad \sout{BEF}, \quad CDE, \quad \sout{CDF}, \quad CEF, \quad \sout{DEF}$$

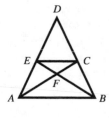

Finally, there are twelve different triangles in the figure. Why are ACB and CBF (and many others) not included in the list?

Another method might be first to identify the triangles consisting of a single region each: DEC, ECF, AEF, BCF, ABF. Then list those consisting of two regions each: AEC, BEC, ABE, ABC; and those with three regions each: ACD, BED. There are no triangles with four regions, but there is one with five: ABD. The total is again twelve. Can you think of other systematic ways of getting the same list? ●

Notice that in the first method shown in Example 9, the labeled points were considered in alphabetical order. In the second method, the single-region triangles were listed by using a top-to-bottom and left-to-right order. Using a definite system helps to ensure that we get a complete list.

The following example involves spatial visualization, which is easier for some people than for others. Remember that a systematic consideration of possibilities will help us develop insights.

EXAMPLE 10 How many distinct one-piece patterns can be constructed which will fold up to form a topless, cubical box as shown here?

Such a pattern must consist of five squares. (A closed box, one with a top, would require six.) All five squares must be attached since the pattern is to be "one-piece." Also, since we want only possibilities that are distinct, we would include, for example, only one of the following patterns.

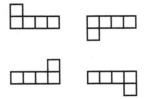

This is because any one of these four can be merely turned or flipped to form all the others. The box can be formed from this pattern by folding as shown here.

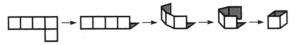

Here is one possible approach to our problem:

Is any pattern possible that has no more than two squares in a row? This would require turning after two squares. The only possibility is a zigzag pattern, the first entry in Figure 5. Next, consider patterns with exactly three squares in a row, but not four. Five such entries appear in the figure. Finally, we also show two possibilities with four squares in a row. Convince yourself that placing all five squares

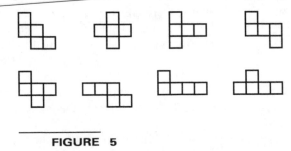

FIGURE 5

in a row will not work. The total number of distinct patterns possible is eight. (If you have trouble visualizing how the topless box is formed, you may want to actually cut out patterns and show that these eight work, and that others do not.) ●

Repetitive processes of certain types are called "iterations." In mathematical applications, a sequence of results is produced where each particular result is fed back through the process to produce the next result. An example of an iterative process is taking any whole number, multiplying its digits together to get a second whole number, then repeating the process, producing a chain of whole numbers that always eventually terminates with a single-digit number. Starting with 283, for example, we obtain

$$283 \rightarrow 48 \rightarrow 32 \rightarrow 6,$$

a chain of *length* 4, with *leading number* 283.

EXAMPLE 11   Find all possible number chains (of the type described above) which have a leading number less than 100 and terminate with 4.

The direct approach here might involve writing out the chain for each whole number from 0 through 99 and observing which ones terminate with 4. But it will be much quicker to work backwards and to employ a tree diagram (also a problem solving strategy). To begin the tree, write down the terminating number of the chain (4). Then, since 4 can only be factored as $1 \cdot 4$, $2 \cdot 2$, and $4 \cdot 1$, 4 must have come from 14, 22, or 41 as shown in Figure 6. Similar reasoning completes the tree diagram. Now the simplest chain that terminates with 4 is just 4. Reading from the tree diagram, we get ten chains altogether, one of length 1, three of length 2, two of length 3, and four of length 4:

4	$14 \rightarrow 4$	$27 \rightarrow 14 \rightarrow 4$	$39 \rightarrow 27 \rightarrow 14 \rightarrow 4$
	$22 \rightarrow 4$	$72 \rightarrow 14 \rightarrow 4$	$93 \rightarrow 27 \rightarrow 14 \rightarrow 4$
	$41 \rightarrow 4$		$89 \rightarrow 72 \rightarrow 14 \rightarrow 4$
			$98 \rightarrow 72 \rightarrow 14 \rightarrow 4$ ●

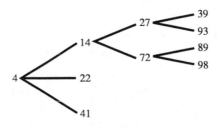

Tree diagram for number chains terminating at 4

FIGURE 6

1 EXERCISES

Refer to Examples 1 and 4, involving the club N = {Andy, Bill, Cathy, David, Evelyn}. Assuming all members are eligible, but that no one can hold more than one office, list and count the different ways the club could elect the following groups of officers.

1. a president and a treasurer

2. a president and a treasurer if the president must be a female

3. a president and a treasurer if the two officers must not be the same sex

4. a president, a secretary, and a treasurer, if the president and treasurer must be women

5. a president, a secretary, and a treasurer, if the president must be a man and the other two must be women

6. a president, a secretary, and a treasurer, if the secretary must be a woman and the other two must be men

List and count the ways club N could appoint a committee of three members under the following conditions.

7. There are no restrictions.

8. The committee must include more men than women.

Refer to Table 2 (the product table for rolling two dice). Of the 36 possibilities, determine the number for which the sum (for both dice) is the following.

9. 2	**10.** 3	**11.** 4	**12.** 5	**13.** 6	**14.** 7
15. 8	**16.** 9	**17.** 10	**18.** 11	**19.** 12	**20.** odd

21. even   22. from 6 through 8 inclusive

23. between 6 and 10   24. less than 5

25. Construct a product table showing all possible two-digit numbers using digits from the set {1, 2, 3, 4, 5, 6}.

Of the thirty-six numbers in the product table for Exercise 25, list the ones that belong to each of the following categories.

26. odd numbers   27. numbers with repeating digits   28. multiples of 6

29. prime numbers   30. triangular numbers   31. square numbers

32. Fibonacci numbers   33. powers of 2

34. Construct a tree diagram showing all possible results when three fair coins are tossed. Then list the ways of getting the following results.
    (a) at least two heads   (b) more than two heads   (c) no more than two heads
    (d) fewer than two heads

35. Extend the tree diagram of Exercise 34 for four fair coins. Then list the ways of getting the following results.
    (a) more than three tails   (b) fewer than three tails   (c) at least three tails
    (d) no more than three tails

Determine the number of triangles (of any size) in each of the following figures.

36.   **37.**   **38.**    **39.**

Determine the number of squares (of any size) in each of the following figures.

40.
41.
42.
43.

Consider only the smallest individual cubes and assume solid stacks (no gaps). Determine the number of cubes in each stack that are not visible.

44.
45.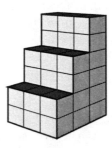

46.
47.

48. In the plane figure shown here, only movement that tends downward is allowed. Find the total number of paths from *A* to *B*.

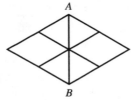

49. Find the number of paths from *A* to *B* in the figure shown here if the directions on various segments are restricted as shown.

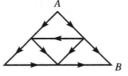

In each of Exercises 50–52, determine the number of different ways the given number can be written as the sum of two primes.

50. 30   **51.** 40   **52.** 95

53. A group of twelve strangers sat in a circle, and each one got acquainted only with the person to the left and the person to the right. Then all twelve people stood up and each one shook hands (once) with each of the others who was still a stranger. How many handshakes occurred?

54. Fifty people enter a single elimination chess tournament. (If you lose one game, you're out.) Assuming no ties occur, what is the number of games required to determine the tournament champion?

55. How many of the numbers from 10 through 100 have the sum of their digits equal to a perfect square?

56. How many three-digit numbers have the sum of their digits equal to 22?

57. How many integers between 100 and 400 contain the digit 2?

58. Jim Northington and friends are dining at the Bay Steamer Restaurant this evening, where a complete dinner consists of three items: (1) soup (clam chowder or minestrone) or salad (fresh spinach or shrimp), (2) sourdough rolls or bran muffin, and (3) entree (lasagna, lobster, or roast turkey). Jim selects his meal subject to the following restrictions. He cannot stomach more than one kind of seafood at a sitting. Also, whenever he tastes minestrone, he cannot resist having lasagna as well. And he cannot face the teasing he would receive from his companions if he were to order both spinach and bran. Use a tree diagram to determine the number of different choices Jim has.

For Exercises 59–61, refer to Example 7. How many different settings could Mollie choose in each case?

59. No restrictions apply to adjacent switches.

60. No two adjacent switches can be off *and* no two adjacent switches can be on.

61. There are five switches rather than four, and no two adjacent switches can be on.

62. Determine the number of odd, non-repeating three-digit numbers that can be written using digits from the set {0, 1, 2, 3}.

63. A line segment joins the points (8, 12) and (53, 234) in the Cartesian plane. Including its endpoints, how many lattice points does this line segment contain? (A *lattice point* is a point with integer coordinates.)

64. In the pattern shown here, dots are one unit apart horizontally and vertically. If a segment can join any two dots, how many segments can be drawn with each of the following lengths?
    (a) 1   (b) 2   (c) 3   (d) 4   (e) 5

```
· · · · ·
· · · · ·
· · · · ·
· · · · ·
· · · · ·
```

65. Uniform length matchsticks are used to build a rectangular grid as shown here. If the grid is 15 matchsticks high and 28 matchsticks wide, how many matchsticks are used?

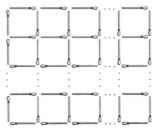

66. A square floor is to be tiled with square tiles as shown here with blue tiles on the main diagonals and red tiles everywhere else. (In all cases, both blue and red tiles must be used and the two diagonals must have a common blue tile at the center of the floor.)

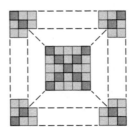

(a) If 81 blue tiles will be used, how many red tiles will be needed?

(b) For what numbers in place of 81 would this problem still be solvable?

(c) Find a formula expressing the number of red tiles required in general.

67. The text stated that number chains such as those of Example 11 always terminate with a single-digit number. This follows from the fact that adding the digits of a whole number with more than one digit always produces a sum smaller than the original number.

(a) Show that this last statement is true for any two-digit number. (*Hint:* Express the number as *tu*, where *t* is the tens digit and *u* is the units digit. Then the *value* of the number *tu* is $10t + u$.)

(b) Explain how part (a) implies that any two-digit number will eventually lead to a one-digit number.

(c) Show that adding the digits of any three-digit number will produce a sum smaller than the original number.

68. Example 10 established eight distinct patterns for topless cubical boxes. Adding a sixth square in an appropriate place on the pattern will provide a top for such a box. For example, the topless box made from the pattern

gains a top when we modify the pattern in any of the following ways:

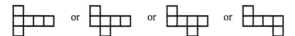

Remembering that two patterns are really the same if one can be turned or flipped to form the other, determine the total number of distinct patterns for a closed cubical box.

69. Kent Merrill and his son were among four father-and-son pairs who gathered to trade baseball cards. As each person arrived, he shook hands with anyone he had not known previously. Each person ended up making a different number of new acquaintances (0–6), except Kent and his son, who each met the same number of people. How many hands did Kent shake?

2

The Fundamental Counting Principle

In Section 1, we obtained complete lists of all possible results for various tasks. However, if the total number of possibilities is all we need to know, then an actual listing is usually unnecessary and is often very difficult or tedious to obtain, especially when the list is long. In this section, we develop ways to calculate "how many" using the *fundamental counting principle,* which is stated below.

The tree diagram in Figure 2 of the previous section can be used to illustrate the idea. It showed all possible non-repeating three-digit numbers formed from the set $\{1, 2, 3\}$. There were three stage-one branches, each of which split two ways to stage two. And each stage-two branch continued in just one way to stage three. Simply multiplying these three numbers gives the total number of possible results: $3 \cdot 2 \cdot 1 = 6$; and, the factors 3, 2, and 1 become evident without the tree diagram. We can reason that there are three possibilities for the first digit. After the first is chosen, two choices remain for the second digit. After the second is chosen, one choice remains for the third digit. This method of counting by products can be generalized as follows.

Fundamental Counting Principle

When a task consists of k separate parts, if the first part can be done in n_1 ways, the second part can be done in n_2 ways, and so on through the kth part, which can be done in n_k ways, then the total number of possible results for completing the task is given by the product

$$n_1 \cdot n_2 \cdot n_3 \ldots n_k.$$

All of the following examples utilize the fundamental counting principle. It may be helpful to set up a sequence of blanks for the various parts of the task, fill in the number of choices for each part as it is determined, and finally multiply the factors.

Richard Dedekind
(1831–1916) studied at the University of Göttingen, where he was Gauss' last student. His work was not recognized during his lifetime, but his treatment of the infinite and of what constitutes a real number are influential even today.

While on vacation in Switzerland, Dedekind met Georg Cantor. Dedekind was interested in Cantor's work on infinite sets. Perhaps because both were working in new and unusual fields of mathematics, such as number theory, and because neither received the professional attention he deserved during his lifetime, the two struck up a lasting friendship.

EXAMPLE 1   How many two-digit numbers are there in our (base ten) system of counting numbers? (While 80 is a two-digit number, 08 is not.)

The "task" is to select, or design, a two-digit number. This task consists of two parts: select the first digit and select the second digit. There are nine ways to choose the first digit (1 through 9), and then ten ways to choose the second digit (0 through 9). The total number of possibilities is $9 \cdot 10 = 90$.

In this example the second digit could have been chosen first, with ten choices possible. Then there are nine choices for the first digit. Again the total is $10 \cdot 9 = 90$. ●

EXAMPLE 2   Find the number of two-digit numbers that do not contain repeated digits (for example, 66 is not allowed).

The basic task is again to select a two-digit number, and there are two parts: select the first digit and select the second digit. But a new restriction applies—no repetition of digits. There are nine choices for the first digit (1 through 9). Then nine choices remain for the second digit, since one nonzero digit has been used and cannot be repeated, but zero is now available. The total number is $9 \cdot 9 = 81$. ●

Starting with the second digit in Example 2 would have led to trouble. After observing that there are ten choices for the second digit, it would not be possible to decide on the number of choices for the first digit, since there is no way to know whether the second digit was zero or nonzero. To avoid this kind of ambiguity, it is usually best to start with any part of the task that has any special restrictions. In Example 2, the first digit is restricted in that it cannot be zero, so consider it first.

EXAMPLE 3   In how many ways can club N of the previous section elect a president and secretary if the secretary must be a man?

Since the special restriction applies to secretary, consider that office first. There are three choices: A, B, and D. Then four choices remain for president (the two men who were not chosen as secretary, together with the two women). The total number of ways is $3 \cdot 4 = 12$. ●

EXAMPLE 4   How many four-digit numbers are there in our system of counting numbers?

The task of selecting a four-digit number has four parts. There are no restrictions implied except that the first digit must not be zero. There are $9 \cdot 10 \cdot 10 \cdot 10 = 9,000$ (or $9 \cdot 10^3 = 9,000$) possible four-digit numbers. ●

EXAMPLE 5   In some states, auto license plates have contained three letters followed by three digits. How many different licenses are possible before a new scheme is necessary?

The basic task is to design a license number consisting of three letters followed by three digits. There are six component parts to this task. Since there are no restrictions on letters or digits to be used, the fundamental counting principle shows that there are

$$26^3 \cdot 10^3 = 17{,}576{,}000$$

possible licenses. (In practice a few of the possible sequences of letters are considered undesirable and are not used.) ●

EXAMPLE 6   Mark decides to give his five remote control vehicles to his three younger brothers.

(a) In how many ways can he make the distribution?

This is a matter of distributing five objects among three recipients. Consider each of the five toys in turn. Notice that, for each one, there are three choices as to which brother will receive it. By the fundamental counting principle, the task can be completed in $3 \cdot 3 \cdot 3 \cdot 3 \cdot 3 = 3^5 = 243$ ways.

Notice that this problem is much harder if we try considering each brother in turn rather than considering the toys. The number of different *sets* of toys the first brother could be given is $2^5 = 32$ since there are 5 toys. But now the number of possibilities for the second brother cannot be easily found since the number of toys remaining is not known. Considering toys in turn was better since the choices for each successive toy did not depend on what was done with any previous toy.

(b) How many choices are there if the remote control jeep must go to brother Chris and the remote control Indy racer must go to either Chris or Scott?

In this case, two parts of the task are restricted. There is just one choice of brothers for the jeep, and just two choices for the Indy racer. The other three toys have three choices each. They can each go to any of the three brothers. The fundamental counting principle gives a total of $1 \cdot 2 \cdot 3 \cdot 3 \cdot 3 = 54$ choices. ⬢

EXAMPLE 7   Rework Example 8 of Section 1, this time using the fundamental counting principle.

Recall that Andy, Betty, Clyde, and Dawn (*A, B, C,* and *D*) are to seat themselves in a row so that *A* and *B* are side by side. Use the methods of this section and break the task into a series of three parts, each of which is simpler than the overall task.

The task is to seat four people (*A, B, C,* and *D*) in four adjacent seats (say 1, 2, 3, and 4) in such a way that *A* and *B* sit next to each other. One approach is to make three decisions as follows:

1. Which pair of seats should *A* and *B* occupy? There are *three* choices ($1 - 2, 2 - 3$, or $3 - 4$, as illustrated in the margin).
2. Which order should *A* and *B* take? There are *two* choices (*A* left of *B,* or *B* left of *A*).
3. Which order should *C* and *D* take? There are *two* choices (*C* left of *D,* or *D* left of *C,* not necessarily right next to each other).

1	2	3	4
X	X	_	_
_	X	X	_
_	_	X	X

Seats available to *A* and *B*

Once the three decisions above are made, the seating order of the four people is decided. Using the fundamental counting principle, the total number of choices is $3 \cdot 2 \cdot 2 = 12$, the same result found in the previous section. ●

Factorials

This section began with a discussion of non-repeating three-digit numbers with digits from the set {1, 2, 3}. The number of possibilities was $3 \cdot 2 \cdot 1 = 6$, in keeping with the fundamental counting principle. That product can also be thought of as the total number of distinct *arrangements* of the three digits 1, 2, and 3. Similarly, the number of distinct arrangements of four objects, say *A, B, C,* and *D,* is, by the fundamental counting principle, $4 \cdot 3 \cdot 2 \cdot 1 = 24$. Since this type of product occurs so commonly in applications, we give it a special name and symbol as follows. For any counting number *n,* the product of *all* counting numbers from *n* down through 1 is called *n* **factorial,** and is denoted *n*!.

FOR FURTHER THOUGHT

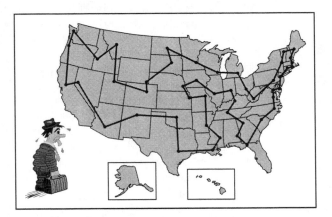

A Classic Problem   Suppose a salesperson wants to make exactly one visit to each capital city in the 48 contiguous states, starting and ending up at the same capital. What is the shortest route that would work?

The so-called "traveling salesman problem" (or TSP), in various versions, has baffled mathematicians for years. For the version stated above, there are 24!/3 possible routes to consider, and the huge size of this number is the reason the problem is difficult (even using the most powerful computers). In 1985, mathematician Shen Lin came up with the 10,628-mile route shown here, and even though he could not prove it was the shortest, he offered $100 to anyone who could find a shorter one.

In 1984, the Bell Laboratories mathematician, Narenda Karmarkar, devised a greatly improved algorithm to help solve the kinds of TSPs involving routing in the areas of transportation and communication. And in 1991, Donald L. Miller of Du Pont and Joseph R. Penky of Purdue University announced a solution to TSPs related to the efficiency of chemical and maintenance processes.

For Group Discussion

1. Within the accuracy limits of the drawing above, try to identify other routes that may be as good or better than the one shown.
2. Realistically, what factors other than *distance* might be important to the salesperson?
3. When a chemical company schedules the steps of a complex manufacturing process, what quantities might it want to minimize?

0! = 1
1! = 1
2! = 2
3! = 6
4! = 24
5! = 120
6! = 720
7! = 5,040
8! = 40,320
9! = 362,880
10! = 3,628,800

Short Table of Factorials
Their numerical value increases rapidly. The value of 100! is a number with 158 digits.

Factorial Formula

For any counting number n, the quantity n factorial is given by

$$n! = n(n-1)(n-2) \ldots 2 \cdot 1.$$

The first few factorial values are easily found by simple multiplication, but they rapidly become very large, as indicated in the margin. The use of a calculator is advised in most cases. Scientific calculators often have a factorial key ($\boxed{x!}$ or $\boxed{n!}$).

EXAMPLE 8   Evaluate the following expressions.

(a) $2! = 2 \cdot 1 = 2$ **(b)** $5! = 5 \cdot 4 \cdot 3 \cdot 2 \cdot 1 = 120$

(c) $6! = 6 \cdot 5 \cdot 4 \cdot 3 \cdot 2 \cdot 1 = 720$ **(d)** $6! - 3! = 720 - 6 = 714$

(e) $(6-3)! = 3! = 6$

(f) $\dfrac{6!}{3!} = \dfrac{6 \cdot 5 \cdot 4 \cdot \cancel{3} \cdot \cancel{2} \cdot \cancel{1}}{\cancel{3} \cdot \cancel{2} \cdot \cancel{1}} = 6 \cdot 5 \cdot 4 = 120$

(g) $\left(\dfrac{6}{3}\right)! = 2! = 2$

(h) $15! = 1.307674368 \times 10^{12}$

(i) $100! = 9.332621544 \times 10^{157}$

Notice the difference between parts (d) and (e) and between parts (f) and (g) above. Parts (h) and (i) were found on a scientific calculator. Part (h) is exact, but part (i) is accurate only to the number of significant figures shown.   ◗

So that factorials will be defined for all whole numbers, including zero, it is common to define 0! as follows.

$$0! = 1$$

(We will see later that this special definition makes other results easier to state.)

Whenever we need to know the total number of ways to *arrange* a given number of distinct objects, we can use a factorial. The fundamental counting principle would do, but factorials provide a shortcut.

Arrangements of n Objects

The total number of different ways to arrange n distinct objects is $n!$.

EXAMPLE 9 Marsha Mildred has seven essays to include in her English 1A folder. In how many different orders can she arrange them?

The number of ways to arrange seven distinct objects is $7! = 5,040$. ●

EXAMPLE 10 Whenever Laura Stowe takes her fourteen daycare children to the park, they all want to be at the front of the line. How many different ways can they be arranged?

Fourteen children can be arranged in $14! = 87,178,291,200$ different ways. ●

---

2 EXERCISES

1. Explain the fundamental counting principle in your own words.

2. Describe how factorials can be used in counting problems.

For Exercises 3 and 4, n and m are counting numbers. Do the following: (a) *Say whether or not the given statement is true in general, and* (b) *explain your answer, using specific examples.*

3. $(n + m)! = n! + m!$

4. $(n \cdot m)! = n! \cdot m!$

Evaluate each expression without using a calculator.

5. $4!$

6. $7!$

7. $\dfrac{8!}{5!}$

8. $\dfrac{16!}{14!}$

9. $\dfrac{5!}{(5-2)!}$

10. $\dfrac{6!}{(6-4)!}$

11. $\dfrac{9!}{6!(6-3)!}$

12. $\dfrac{10!}{4!(10-4)!}$

13. $\dfrac{n!}{(n-r)!}$, where $n = 7$ and $r = 4$

14. $\dfrac{n!}{r!(n-r)!}$, where $n = 12$ and $r = 4$

Evaluate each expression using a calculator. (Some answers may not be exact.)

15. $11!$

16. $17!$

17. $\dfrac{12!}{7!}$

18. $\dfrac{15!}{9!}$

19. $\dfrac{13!}{(13-3)!}$

20. $\dfrac{16!}{(16-6)!}$

21. $\dfrac{20!}{10! \cdot 10!}$

22. $\dfrac{18!}{6! \cdot 12!}$

23. $\dfrac{n!}{(n-r)!}$, where $n = 23$ and $r = 10$

24. $\dfrac{n!}{r!(n-r)!}$, where $n = 28$ and $r = 15$

A panel containing three on-off switches in a row is to be set.

25. Assuming no restrictions on individual switches, use the fundamental counting principle to find the total number of possible panel settings.

26. Assuming no restrictions, construct a tree diagram to list all the possible panel settings of Exercise 25.

27. Now assume that no two adjacent switches can both be off. Explain why the fundamental counting principle does not apply.

28. Construct a tree diagram to list all possible panel settings under the restriction of Exercise 27.

29. Table 2 in Section 1 shows that there are 36 possible outcomes when two fair dice are rolled.

How many would there be if three fair dice were rolled?

30. How many five-digit numbers are there in our system of counting numbers?

Recall the club

$N = \{\text{Andy, Bill, Cathy, David, Evelyn}\}.$

In how many ways could they do each of the following?

31. line up all five members for a photograph

32. schedule one member to work in the office on each of five different days, assuming members may work more than one day

33. select a male and a female to decorate for a party

34. select two members, one to open their next meeting and another to close it, given that Bill will not be present

In the following exercises, counting numbers are to be formed using only digits from the set $\{0, 1, 2, 3, 4\}$. *Determine the number of different possibilities for each type of number described. (Note that* 201 *is a three-digit number while* 012 *is not.)*

35. three-digit numbers

36. even four-digit numbers

37. five-digit numbers with one pair of adjacent 0s and no other repeated digits

38. four-digit numbers beginning and ending with 3 and unlimited repetitions allowed

39. five-digit multiples of five which contain exactly two 3s and exactly one 0

40. six-digit numbers containing two 0s, two 2s, and two 4s

The Bay Steamer restaurant (see Exercise 58 of Section 1) offers four choices in the soup and salad category (two soups and two salads), two choices in the bread category, and three choices in the entree category. Find the number of dinners available in each of the following cases.

41. One item is to be included from each of the three categories.

42. Only soup and entree are to be included.

Determine the number of possible ways to mark your answer sheet (with an answer for each question) for each of the following tests.

43. an eight-question true-or-false test

44. a thirty-question multiple choice test with four answer choices for each question

Glenn Russell is making up his class schedule for next semester, which must include one class from each of the four categories shown here.

Category	Choices	Number of Choices
English	Medieval Literature Composition Modern Poetry	3
Mathematics	College Algebra Trigonometry	2
Computer Information Science	Introduction to Spreadsheets Advanced Word Processing C Programming BASIC Programming	4
Sociology	Social Problems Sociology of the Middle East Aging in America Minorities in America Women in American Culture	5

For each situation in Exercises 45–50, use the table above to determine the number of different sets of classes Glenn can take.

45. All classes shown are available.

46. He is not eligible for College Algebra or for BASIC Programming.

47. All sections of Minorities in America and Women in American Culture are filled already.

48. He does not have the prerequisites for Medieval Literature, Trigonometry, or C Programming.

49. Funding has been withdrawn for three of the computer courses and for two of the Sociology courses.

50. He must complete English Composition and Trigonometry next semester to fulfill his degree requirements.

51. Sean took two pairs of shoes, four pairs of pants, and six shirts on a trip. Assuming all items are compatible, how many different outfits can he wear?

52. A music equipment outlet stocks ten different guitars, four guitar cases, six amplifiers, and three effects processors, with all items mutually compatible and all suitable for beginners. How many different complete setups could Lionel choose to start his musical career?

53. Tadishi's zip code is 95841. How many zip codes, altogether, could be formed using all of those same five digits?

54. Georgia Owen keeps four textbooks and three novels on her desk. In how many different ways can she arrange them in a row if
  (a) the textbooks must be to the left of the novels?
  (b) the novels must all be together?
  (c) no two novels should be next to each other?

Andy, Betty, Clyde, Dawn, Evan, and Felicia have reserved six seats in a row at the theater, starting at an aisle seat. (Refer to Example 7 in this section.)

55. In how many ways can they arrange themselves? (*Hint:* Divide the task into the series of six parts shown below, performed in order.)
  (a) If *A* is seated first, how many seats are available for him?
  (b) Now, how many are available for *B?*
  (c) Now, how many for *C?*
  (d) Now, how many for *D?*
  (e) Now, how many for *E?*
  (f) Now, how many for *F?*
  Now multiply together your six answers above.

56. In how many ways can they arrange themselves so that Andy and Betty will be next to each other? (*Hint:* First answer the following series of questions, assuming these parts are to be accomplished in order.)

1	2	3	4	5	6
X	X	_	_	_	_
_	X	X	_	_	_
_	_	X	X	_	_
_	_	_	X	X	_
_	_	_	_	X	X

Seats available to *A* and *B*

  (a) How many pairs of adjacent seats can *A* and *B* occupy?
  (b) Now, given the two seats for *A* and *B*, in how many orders can they be seated?
  (c) Now, how many seats are available for *C?*
  (d) Now, how many for *D?*
  (e) Now, how many for *E?*
  (f) Now, how many for *F?*

57. In how many ways can they arrange themselves if the men and women are to alternate seats and a man must sit on the aisle? (*Hint:* First answer the following series of questions.)
  (a) How many choices are there for the person to occupy the first seat, next to the aisle? (It must be a man.)
  (b) Now, how many choices of people may occupy the second seat from the aisle? (It must be a woman.)
  (c) Now, how many for the third seat? (one of the remaining men)
  (d) Now, how many for the fourth seat? (a woman)
  (e) Now, how many for the fifth seat? (a man)
  (f) Now, how many for the sixth seat? (a woman)

58. In how many ways can they arrange themselves if the men and women are to alternate with either a man or a woman on the aisle? (*Hint:* First answer the following series of questions.)

(a) How many choices of people are there for the aisle seat?

(b) Now, how many are there for the second seat? (This person may not be of the same sex as the person on the aisle.)

(c) Now, how many choices are there for the third seat?

(d) Now, how many for the fourth seat?

(e) Now, how many for the fifth seat?

(f) Now, how many for the sixth seat?

3

Permutations and Combinations

In Section 2 we introduced factorials as a way of counting the number of *arrangements* of a given set of objects. For example, the members of the club $N = \{$Andy, Bill, Cathy, David, Evelyn$\}$ can arrange themselves in a row for a photograph in $5! = 120$ different ways. Using a factorial is generally more efficient than using the fundamental counting principle. We have also used previous methods, like tree diagrams and the fundamental counting principle, to answer questions like: How many ways can club N above elect a president, a secretary, and a treasurer if no one person can hold more than one office? This again is a matter of *arrangements*. The difference is that only three, rather than all five, of the members are involved in each case. A common way to rephrase the basic question here is as follows: *How many arrangements are there of five things taken three at a time?* The answer, by the fundamental counting principle, is $5 \cdot 4 \cdot 3 = 60$. The factors begin with 5 and proceed downward, just as in a factorial product, but do not go all the way to 1. (In this example the product stops when there are three factors.) We now generalize this idea.

In the context of counting problems, arrangements are often called **permutations;** the number of permutations of n distinct things taken r at a time is written $P(n, r)$.* Since the number of objects being arranged cannot exceed the total number available, we assume for our purposes here that $r \leq n$. Applying the fundamental counting principle to arrangements of this type gives

$$P(n, r) = n(n - 1)(n - 2) \ldots [n - (r - 1)].$$

Simplification of the last factor gives the following formula.

Permutation Formula

The number of **permutations,** or *arrangements,* of n distinct things taken r at a time, where $r \leq n$, is given by

$$P(n, r) = n(n - 1)(n - 2) \ldots (n - r + 1).$$

The factors in this product begin at n and descend until the total number of factors is r. We now see that the number of ways in which club N can elect a president, a secretary, and a treasurer can be denoted $P(5, 3) = 5 \cdot 4 \cdot 3 = 60$.

---

*Alternate notations are $_nP_r$ and P_r^n.

Change Ringing, the English way of ringing church bells, combines mathematics and music. Bells are rung first in sequence, 1, 2, 3, ... Then the sequence is permuted ("changed"). On six bells, 720 different "changes" (different permutations of tone) can be rung: $P(6, 6) = 6!$.

Composers work out changes so that musically interesting and harmonious sequences occur regularly.

The church bells are swung by means of ropes attached to the wheels beside them. One ringer swings each bell, listening intently and watching the other ringers closely. If one ringer gets lost and stays lost, the rhythm of the ringing cannot be maintained; all the ringers have to stop.

A ringer can spend weeks just learning to keep a bell going and months learning to make the bell ring in exactly the right place. Errors of 1/4 sec mean that two bells are ringing at the same time. Even errors of 1/10 sec can be heard.

EXAMPLE 1 Evaluate each permutation.

(a) $P(4, 2) = 4 \cdot 3 = 12$ (Begin at 4, descend until there are two factors.)

(b) $P(5, 2) = 5 \cdot 4 = 20$ (Begin at 5, use two factors.)

(c) $P(7, 3) = 7 \cdot 6 \cdot 5 = 210$ (Begin at 7, use three factors.)

(d) $P(8, 5) = 8 \cdot 7 \cdot 6 \cdot 5 \cdot 4 = 6,720$ (Begin at 8, use five factors.)

(e) $P(5, 5) = 5 \cdot 4 \cdot 3 \cdot 2 \cdot 1 = 120$ (Begin at 5, use five factors.) ◆

Notice that $P(5, 5)$ is equal to $5!$. It is true for all whole numbers n that $P(n, n) = n!$. (This is the number of possible arrangements of n distinct objects taken all n at a time.)

Permutations, in general, can also be related to factorials in the following way. Recall that

$$P(n, r) = n(n - 1)(n - 2) \ldots (n - r + 1).$$

Extending this product all the way down to 1 gives

$$n(n - 1)(n - 2) \ldots (n - r + 1)(n - r)(n - r - 1) \ldots 2 \cdot 1.$$

Then, dividing by exactly the same factors that were introduced into the product gives

$$\frac{n(n - 1)(n - 2) \ldots (n - r + 1)(n - r)(n - r - 1) \ldots 2 \cdot 1}{(n - r)(n - r - 1) \ldots 2 \cdot 1}.$$

This quotient is equal to $n!/(n - r)!$, and since it was obtained by *multiplying and dividing* $P(n, r)$ by the same quantity, it must be equal to $P(n, r)$. This formula can always be used to evaluate permutations.

Factorial Formula for Permutations

The number of **permutations,** or *arrangements,* of n distinct things taken r at a time, where $r \leq n$, can be calculated as

$$P(n, r) = \frac{n!}{(n - r)!}.$$

If n and r are very large numbers, a calculator with a factorial key and this formula will save a lot of work when finding permutations. (Some scientific calculators will even compute permutations directly, so that you merely enter the values n and r and push the appropriate key, which may be labeled $\boxed{_nP_r}$ or $\boxed{\text{PERM}}$.)

The formula above also shows that, for any whole number n,

$$P(n, 0) = \frac{n!}{(n - 0)!} = \frac{n!}{n!} = 1.$$

In other words, the number of arrangements of n things, taken 0 at a time, is 1. This is reasonable since there is exactly one way to arrange none of the n things.

EXAMPLE 2 Use the factorial formula to evaluate each permutation.

(a) $P(7, 3) = \dfrac{7!}{(7-3)!} = \dfrac{7!}{4!} = 210$

(b) $P(10, 4) = \dfrac{10!}{(10-4)!} = \dfrac{10!}{6!} = 5,040$

(c) $P(25, 0) = \dfrac{25!}{(25-0)!} = \dfrac{25!}{25!} = 1$

(d) $P(18, 12) = \dfrac{18!}{(18-12)!} = \dfrac{18!}{6!} = 8,892,185,702,400$

Concerning part (d), most calculators will not display this many digits, so you may obtain an answer such as 8.8921857×10^{12}. ●

Permutations can be used any time we need to know the number of size-*r* arrangements that can be selected from a size-*n* set. The word *arrangement* implies an ordering, so we use permutations only in cases where the order of the items is important. Also, permutations apply only in cases where no repetition of items occurs. We summarize with the following guidelines.

Guidelines for Permutations

Permutations are applied only when
1. repetitions are not allowed, and
2. order is important.

Examples 3 and 4 involve cases that meet these guidelines.

EXAMPLE 3 How many non-repeating three-digit numbers can be written using digits from the set {3, 4, 5, 6, 7, 8}?

Repetitions are not allowed since the numbers are to be "non-repeating." (For example, 448 is not acceptable.) Also, order is important. (For example, 476 and 746 are *distinct* cases.) So we use permutations:

$$P(6, 3) = 6 \cdot 5 \cdot 4 = 120. \quad ●$$

The next example illustrates the common situation where a task involves multiple parts, and hence calls for the fundamental counting principle, but where the individual parts can be handled with permutations.

EXAMPLE 4 Suppose certain account numbers are to consist of two letters followed by four digits and then three more letters, where repetitions of letters or digits are not allowed *within* any of the three groups, but the last group of letters may contain one or both of those used in the first group. How many such accounts are possible?

The task of designing such a number consists of three parts.

1. Determine the first set of two letters.
2. Determine the set of four digits.
3. Determine the final set of three letters.

Each part requires an arrangement without repetitions, which is a permutation. Apply the fundamental counting principle and multiply together the results of the three parts.

$$P(26, 2) \cdot P(10, 4) \cdot P(26, 3) = \underbrace{26 \cdot 25}_{\text{Part 1}} \cdot \underbrace{10 \cdot 9 \cdot 8 \cdot 7}_{\text{Part 2}} \cdot \underbrace{26 \cdot 25 \cdot 24}_{\text{Part 3}}$$

$$= 650 \cdot 5{,}040 \cdot 15{,}600$$
$$= 51{,}105{,}600{,}000 \quad \bullet$$

So far in this section, we have introduced permutations in order to evaluate the number of arrangements of *n* things taken *r* at a time, where repetitions are not allowed. The order of the items was important. Recall that club $N = \{$Andy, Bill, Cathy, David, Evelyn$\}$ could elect three officers in $P(5, 3) = 60$ different ways. With three-member committees, on the other hand, order is not important. The committees *B, D, E* and *E, B, D* are no different. The possible number of committees is not the number of arrangements of size 3. Rather, it is the number of *subsets* of size 3 (since the order of listing elements in a set makes no difference).

Subsets in this new context are called **combinations.** The number of combinations of *n* things taken *r* at a time (that is, the number of size *r* subsets, given a set of size *n*) is written $C(n, r)$.*

Here is a list of all the size-3 committees (subsets) of the club (set) $N = \{A, B, C, D, E\}$:

$$\{A, B, C\}, \quad \{A, B, D\}, \quad \{A, B, E\}, \quad \{A, C, D\}, \quad \{A, C, E\},$$
$$\{A, D, E\}, \quad \{B, C, D\}, \quad \{B, C, E\}, \quad \{B, D, E\}, \quad \{C, D, E\}.$$

There are ten subsets of 3, so ten is the number of three-member committees possible. Just as with permutations, repetitions are not allowed. For example, $\{E, E, B\}$ is not a valid three-member subset, just as *EEB* is not a valid three-member arrangement.

To see how to find the number of such subsets without listing them all, notice that each size-3 subset (combination) gives rise to six size-3 arrangements (permutations). For example, the single combination *ADE* yields these six permutations:

$$A, D, E \quad D, A, E \quad E, A, D \quad A, E, D \quad D, E, A \quad E, D, A.$$

Then there·must be six times as many size-3 permutations as there are size-3 combinations, or in other words, one-sixth as many combinations as permutations. Therefore

$$C(5, 3) = \frac{P(5, 3)}{6} = \frac{5 \cdot 4 \cdot 3}{6} = 10.$$

The 6 appears in the denominator because there are six different ways to arrange a set of three things (since $3! = 3 \cdot 2 \cdot 1 = 6$). Generalizing from this example, *r* things can be arranged in *r*! different ways, so we obtain the following formula.

*Alternate notations include $_nC_r$, C_r^n, and $\binom{n}{r}$.

Combination Formula

The number of **combinations,** or *subsets,* of n distinct things taken r at a time, where $r \le n$ is given by

$$C(n, r) = \frac{P(n, r)}{r!} = \frac{n(n-1)(n-2)\ldots(n-r+1)}{r(r-1)(r-2)\ldots 2 \cdot 1}.$$

We saw earlier that permutations are expressible entirely in terms of factorials:

$$P(n, r) = \frac{n!}{(n-r)!}.$$

Using this formula, we obtain

$$C(n, r) = \frac{P(n, r)}{r!} = \frac{\dfrac{n!}{(n-r)!}}{r!} = \frac{n!}{r!(n-r)!}.$$

Factorial Formula for Combinations

The number of **combinations,** or *subsets,* of n distinct things taken r at a time, where $r \le n$, can be calculated as

$$C(n, r) = \frac{P(n, r)}{r!} = \frac{n!}{r!(n-r)!}.$$

With this result, combinations also can be computed using factorials. Using this formula together with the fact that $0! = 1$ gives, for any whole number n,

$$C(n, 0) = \frac{n!}{0!(n-0)!} = \frac{n!}{1 \cdot n!} = \frac{n!}{n!} = 1.$$

This means that there is exactly one combination of n things taken zero at a time. That is, a set of n objects has exactly one "empty" subset.

(Again, some scientific calculators provide direct computation of combinations, using a key which may be labeled $\boxed{nC_r}$ or $\boxed{\text{COMB}}$.)

The following guidelines stress that combinations have an important common property with permutations (repetitions are not allowed), as well as an important difference (order is *not* important with combinations).

Guidelines for Combinations

Combinations are applied only when
1. repetitions are not allowed, and
2. order is *not* important.

"Biliteral Cipher" (above) was invented by Francis Bacon early in the seventeenth century to code political secrets. This binary code, *a* and *b* in combinations of five, has 32 permutations. Bacon's "biformed alphabet" (bottom four rows) uses two type fonts to conceal a message in some straight text. The decoder deciphers a string of *a*'s and *b*'s, groups them by fives, then deciphers letters and words. This code was applied to Shakespeare's plays in efforts to prove Bacon the rightful author.

FOR FURTHER THOUGHT

Poker Hands In 5-card poker, played with a standard 52-card deck, 2,598,960 different hands are possible. (See Example 6.) The desirability of the various hands depends upon their relative chance of occurrence, which, in turn, depends on the number of different ways they can occur, as shown in Table 4.

TABLE 4

Event E	Description of Event E	Number of Outcomes Favorable to E
Royal flush	Ace, king, queen, jack, and 10, all of the same suit	4
Straight flush	5 cards of consecutive denominations, all in the same suit (excluding royal flush)	36
Four of a kind	4 cards of the same denomination, plus 1 additional card	624
Full house	3 cards of one denomination, plus 2 cards of a second denomination	3,744
Flush	Any 5 cards all of the same suit (excluding royal flush and straight flush)	5,108
Straight	5 cards of consecutive denominations (not all the same suit)	10,200
Three of a kind	3 cards of one denomination, plus 2 cards of two additional denominations	54,912
Two pairs	2 cards of one denomination, plus 2 cards of a second denomination, plus 1 card of a third denomination	123,552
One pair	2 cards of one denomination, plus 3 additional cards of three different denominations	1,098,240
No pair	No 2 cards of the same denomination (and not all the same suit)	1,302,540
Total		2,598,960

For Group Discussion As the table shows, a full house is a relatively rare occurrence. (Only four of a kind, straight flush, and royal flush are less likely.) To verify that there are 3,744 different full house hands possible, carry out the following steps.

1. Explain why there are $C(4, 3)$ different ways to select three aces from the deck.
2. Explain why there are $C(4, 2)$ different ways to select two 8s from the deck.
3. If "aces and 8s" (three aces and two 8s) is one *kind* of full house, show that there are $P(13, 2)$ different *kinds* of full house altogether.
4. Multiply the expressions from steps 1, 2, and 3 together. Explain why this product should give the total number of full house hands possible.

The remaining examples of this section involve cases that meet these guidelines.

EXAMPLE 5 Find the number of different subsets of size 2 in the set $\{a, b, c, d\}$. List them to check the answer.

A subset of size 2 must have two distinct elements, so repetitions are not allowed. And since the order in which the elements of a set are listed makes no difference, we see that order is not important. Use the combination formula with $n = 4$ and $r = 2$.

$$C(4, 2) = \frac{P(4, 2)}{2!} = \frac{4 \cdot 3}{2 \cdot 1} = 6$$

or

$$C(4, 2) = \frac{4!}{2!(4 - 2)!} = \frac{4!}{2!2!} = 6$$

The six subsets of size 2 are $\{a, b\}, \{a, c\}, \{a, d\}, \{b, c\}, \{b, d\}, \{c, d\}$. ◆

EXAMPLE 6 A common form of poker involves hands (sets) of five cards each, dealt from a standard deck consisting of 52 different cards (illustrated in the margin). How many different 5-card hands are possible?

A 5-card hand must contain five distinct cards, so repetitions are not allowed. Also, the order is not important since a given hand depends only on the cards it contains, and not on the order in which they were dealt or the order in which they are listed. Since order does not matter, use combinations:

$$C(52, 5) = \frac{P(52, 5)}{5!} = \frac{52 \cdot 51 \cdot 50 \cdot 49 \cdot 48}{5 \cdot 4 \cdot 3 \cdot 2 \cdot 1} = 2{,}598{,}960$$

or

$$C(52, 5) = \frac{52!}{5!(52 - 5)!} = \frac{52!}{5!47!} = 2{,}598{,}960.$$

In this case, we will refrain from listing them all. ◆

EXAMPLE 7 Melvin wants to buy ten different books but can afford only four of them. In how many ways can he make his selection?

The four books selected must be distinct (repetitions are not allowed), and also the order of the four chosen has no bearing in this case, so we use combinations:

$$C(10, 4) = \frac{P(10, 4)}{4!} = \frac{10 \cdot 9 \cdot 8 \cdot 7}{4 \cdot 3 \cdot 2 \cdot 1} = 210 \text{ ways,}$$

or

$$C(10, 4) = \frac{10!}{4!(10 - 4)!} = \frac{10!}{4!6!} = 210 \text{ ways.} ◆$$

Notice that, according to our formula for combinations,

$$C(10, 6) = \frac{10!}{6!(10 - 6)!} = \frac{10!}{6!4!} = 210,$$

which is the same as $C(10, 4)$. In fact, Exercise 62 asks you to prove the fact that, in general, for all whole numbers n and r, with $r \leq n$,

$$C(n, r) = C(n, n - r).$$

The set of 52 playing cards in the standard deck has four suits:

- ♠ spades
- ♥ hearts
- ♦ diamonds
- ♣ clubs

Ace is the unit card. Jacks, queens, and kings are "face cards." Each suit contains thirteen denominations: ace, 2, 3, . . . , 10, jack, queen, king. (In some games, ace rates above king, instead of counting as 1.)

The illustration above is from the 1560's text ***Logistica,*** by the mathematician J. Buteo. Among other topics, the book discusses the number of possible throws of four dice and the number of arrangements of the cylinders of a combination lock. Note that "combination" is a misleading name for these locks since repetitions are allowed, and, also, order makes a difference.

EXAMPLE 8 How many different three-member committees could club *N* appoint so that exactly one woman is on the committee?

Recall that *N* = {Andy, Bill, Cathy, David, Evelyn}. Two members are women; three are men. Although the question mentioned only that the committee must include exactly one woman, in order to complete the committee two men must be selected as well. Therefore the task of selecting the committee members consists of two parts:

1. Choose one woman.
2. Choose two men.

One woman can be chosen in $C(2, 1) = 2/1 = 2$ ways, and two men can be chosen in $C(3, 2) = (3 \cdot 2)/(2 \cdot 1) = 3$ ways. Using the fundamental counting principle gives $2 \cdot 3 = 6$ different committees. This number is small enough to check by listing the possibilities:

$$\{C, A, B\}, \{C, A, D\}, \{C, B, D\}, \{E, A, B\}, \{E, A, D\}, \{E, B, D\}. \quad \bullet$$

EXAMPLE 9 In the game of bridge, 13-card hands are dealt from a standard 52-card deck. How many different bridge hands are possible?

As in most all card games, the order of the cards dealt to a hand is not important, so we use combinations and evaluate with a calculator:

$$C(52, 13) = \frac{52!}{13!39!} = 635,013,559,600. \quad \bullet$$

As we have illustrated in this section, many counting problems involve selecting some of the items from a given set of items. The particular conditions of the problem will determine which specific technique to use. Since choosing the appropriate technique is critical, we offer the following guidelines.

Guidelines for Choosing a Counting Method

1. If selected items can be repeated, use the fundamental counting principle.
   Example: How many five-digit numbers are there?

$$9 \cdot 10^4 = 90,000$$

2. If selected items cannot be repeated, and order is important, use permutations.
   Example: How many ways can three of seven people line up at a ticket counter?

$$P(7, 3) = 7 \cdot 6 \cdot 5 = 210$$

3. If selected items cannot be repeated, and order is not important, use combinations.
   Example: How many ways can a committee of four be selected from a group of ten people?

$$C(10, 4) = \frac{10 \cdot 9 \cdot 8 \cdot 7}{4 \cdot 3 \cdot 2 \cdot 1} = 210$$

If a task consists of multiple parts, consider one of the methods above for each of the individual parts, and then apply the fundamental counting principle to multiply all factors. Also, remember that not all counting problems are addressed by the above guidelines. Do not feel confined by any list of methods. Use your own insights. Since permutations and combinations are easily confused, we include the following table to emphasize both the similarities and the differences between them.

Permutations	**Combinations**
Number of ways of selecting r items out of n items	
Repetitions are not allowed	
Order is important	Order is not important
Arrangements of n items taken r at a time	Subsets of n items taken r at a time
$P(n, r)$ $$= n(n-1)(n-2)\ldots(n-r+1)$$ $$= \frac{n!}{(n-r)!}$$	$C(n, r)$ $$= \frac{n(n-1)(n-2)\ldots(n-r+1)}{r(r-1)(r-2)\ldots 2 \cdot 1}$$ $$= \frac{n!}{r!(n-r)!}$$

3 EXERCISES

Evaluate each of the following expressions.

1. $P(5, 2)$ **2.** $P(8, 3)$ **3.** $P(10, 0)$ **4.** $P(12, 5)$

5. $C(7, 3)$ **6.** $C(10, 6)$ **7.** $C(8, 4)$ **8.** $C(12, 8)$

Determine the number of permutations (arrangements) of each of the following.

9. 7 things taken 4 at a time   **10.** 8 things taken 5 at a time

11. 12 things taken 3 at a time   **12.** 41 things taken 2 at a time

Determine the number of combinations (subsets) of each of the following.

13. 5 things taken 4 at a time   **14.** 9 things taken 0 at a time

15. 11 things taken 7 at a time   **16.** 14 things taken 3 at a time

Use a calculator to evaluate each of these expressions.

17. $P(26, 8)$ **18.** $C(38, 12)$

In "Super Lotto," a California state lottery game, you select six distinct numbers from the counting numbers 1 through 51, hoping that your selection will match a random list selected by lottery officials.

19. How many different sets of six numbers can you select?

20. Marja always includes her age and her husband's age as two of the numbers in her Super Lotto selections. How many ways can she complete her list of six numbers?

21. Is it possible to evaluate $P(8, 12)$? Explain.

22. Is it possible to evaluate $C(6, 15)$? Explain.

23. Explain how permutations and combinations differ.

24. Explain how factorials are related to permutations.

25. How many different ways could 1st, 2nd, and 3rd place winners occur in a race with six runners competing?

26. John Young, a contractor, builds homes of eight different models and presently has five lots to build on. In how many different ways can he place homes on these lots? Assume five different models will be built.

27. How many different five-member committees could be formed from the 100 U.S. senators?

28. If any two points determine a line, how many lines are determined by seven points in a plane, no three of which are collinear?

29. Radio stations in the United States have call letters that begin with K or W (for west or east of the Mississippi River, respectively). Some have three call letters, such as WBZ in Boston, WLS in Chicago, and KGO in San Francisco. Assuming no repetition of letters, how many three-letter sets of call letters are possible?

30. Most stations that were licensed after 1927 have four call letters starting with K or W, such as WXYZ in Detroit or KRLD in Dallas. Assuming no repetitions, how many four-letter sets are possible?

31. Subject identification numbers in a certain scientific research project consist of three letters followed by three digits and then three more letters. Assume repetitions are not allowed within any of the three groups, but letters in the first group of three may occur also in the last group of three. How many distinct identification numbers are possible?

32. How many triangles are determined by twenty points in a plane, no three of which are collinear?

33. How many ways can a sample of five CD players be selected from a shipment of twenty-four players?

34. If the shipment of Exercise 33 contains six defective players, how many of the size-five samples would not include any of the defective ones?

35. In how many ways could twenty-five people be divided into five groups containing, respectively, three, four, five, six, and seven people?

36. Larry Sifford and seven of his friends were contemplating the drive back to Denver after a long day of skiing.

(a) If they brought two vehicles, how many choices do they have as to who will do the driving?

(b) Suppose that (due to an insurance limitation) one of the vehicles can only be driven by Larry, his wife, or their son, all of whom are part of the skiing group. Now how many choices of drivers are there?

37. Each team in an eight-team basketball league is scheduled to play each other team three times. How many games will be played altogether?

38. The Coyotes, a minor league baseball team, have seven pitchers, who only pitch, and twelve other players, all of whom can play any position other than pitcher. For Saturday's game, the coach has not yet determined which nine players to use nor what the batting order will be, except that the pitcher will bat last. How many different batting orders may occur?

39. A music class of eight girls and seven boys is having a recital. If each member is to perform once, how many ways can the program be arranged in each of the following cases?

(a) The girls must all perform first.

(b) A girl must perform first and a boy must perform last.

(c) Elisa and Doug will perform first and last, respectively.

(d) The entire program will alternate between the sexes.

(e) The first, eighth, and fifteenth performers must be girls.

40. Carole has eight errands to run today, five of them pleasant, but the other three unpleasant. How many ways can she plan her day in each of the following cases?

(a) She decides to put off the unpleasant errands to another day.

(b) She is determined to complete all eight errands today.

(c) She will work up her courage by starting with *at least* two pleasant errands and then completing the rest of the eight.

(d) She will begin and end the day with pleasant errands and will accomplish only six altogether.

(e) She will succeed in all eight by facing all three unpleasant errands first.

For Exercises 41–46, refer to the standard 52-card deck pictured in the text and notice that the deck contains four aces, twelve face cards, thirteen hearts (all red), thirteen diamonds (all red), thirteen spades (all black), and thirteen clubs (all black). Of the 2,598,960 different five-card hands possible, decide how many would consist of the following cards.

41. all diamonds

42. all black cards

43. all aces

44. four clubs and one non-club

45. two face cards and three non-face cards

46. two red cards, two clubs, and a spade

47. How many different three-number "combinations" are possible on a combination lock having 40 numbers on its dial? (*Hint:* "Combination" is a misleading name for these locks since repetitions are allowed and also order makes a difference.)

48. In a 7/39 lottery, you select seven distinct numbers from the set 1 through 39, where order makes no difference. How many different ways can you make your selection?

John Young (the contractor) is to build six homes on a block in a new subdivision. Overhead expenses have forced him to limit his line to two different models, standard and deluxe. (All standard model homes are the same and all deluxe model homes are the same.)

49. How many different choices does John have in positioning the six houses if he decides to build three standard and three deluxe models?

50. If John builds only two deluxe and four standards, how many different positionings can he use?

Because of his good work, John gets a contract to build homes on three additional blocks in the subdivision, with six homes on each block. He decides to build nine deluxe homes on these three blocks; two on the first block, three on the second, and four on the third. The remaining nine homes will be standard.

51. Altogether on the three-block stretch, how many different choices does John have for positioning

the eighteen homes? (*Hint:* Consider the three blocks separately and use the fundamental counting principle.)

52. How many choices would he have if he built 2, 3, and 4 deluxe models on the three different blocks as before, but not necessarily on the first, second, and third blocks in that order?

53. (a) How many numbers can be formed using all six digits 2, 3, 4, 5, 6, and 7?

(b) Suppose all these numbers were arranged in increasing order: 234,567; 234,576; and so on. Which number would be 363rd in the list?

54. How many four-digit counting numbers are there whose digits are distinct and have a sum of 10, assuming the digit 0 is not used?

55. How many paths are possible from A to B if all motion must be to the right or downward?

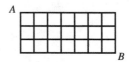

56. How many cards must be drawn (without replacement) from a standard deck of 52 to guarantee that at least two are from the same suit?

57. Libby Zeitler and her husband want to name their new baby so that her monogram (first, middle, and last initials) will be distinct letters in alphabetical order. How many different monograms could they select?

58. How many pairs of vertical angles are formed by eight distinct lines that all meet at a common point?

59. In how many ways can three men and six women be assigned to two groups so that neither group has more than six people?

60. Verify that $C(8, 3) = C(8, 5)$.

61. Verify that $C(12, 9) = C(12, 3)$.

62. Use the factorial formula for combinations to prove that in general, $C(n, r) = C(n, n - r)$.

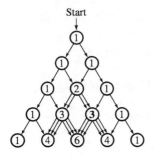

Start

FIGURE 7

4 Pascal's Triangle and the Binomial Theorem

The triangular array in Figure 7 represents what we can call "random walks" that begin at START and proceed downward according to the following rule. At each circle (branch point), a coin is tossed. If it lands heads, we go downward to the left. If it lands tails, we go downward to the right. At each point, left and right are equally likely. In each circle we have recorded the number of different routes that could bring us to that point. For example, the colored 3 can be reached as the result of three different coin-tossing sequences: *htt, tht,* and *tth.*

Another way to generate the same pattern of numbers is to begin with 1s down both diagonals and then fill in the interior entries by adding the two numbers just above a given position (to the left and right). For example, the boldface 28 in Table 5 is the result of adding 7 and 21 in the row above it.

TABLE 5 Pascal's Triangle

Row Number													Row Sum
0						1							1
1					1		1						2
2				1		2		1					4
3			1		3		3		1				8
4		1		4		6		4		1			16
5	1		5		10		10		5		1		32
6		1		6	15		20		15	6		1	64
7	1		7	21		35		35		21	7	1	128
8	1	8	**28**		56		70		56	28	8	1	256
9	1	9	36	84		126		126	84	36	9	1	512
10	1	10	45	120	210		252		210	120	45	10 1	1,024

By continuing to add pairs of numbers, we extend the array indefinitely downward, always beginning and ending each row with 1s. (The table shows just rows 0 through 10.) This unending "triangular" array of numbers is called **Pascal's triangle,** since Blaise Pascal wrote a treatise about it in 1653. There is evidence, though, that it was known as early as around 1100 and may have been studied in China or India still earlier. At any rate, the "triangle" possesses many interesting properties. In counting applications, the most useful property is that, in general, entry number r in row number n is equal to $C(n, r)$—the number of *combinations* of n things taken r at a time. This correspondence is shown (through row 7) in Table 6.

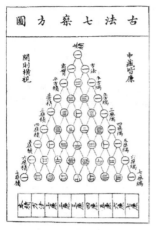

"Pascal's" triangle shown in the 1303 text, **Szu-yuen Yu-chien** (The Precious Mirror of the Four Elements) by the Chinese mathematician Chu Shih-chieh.

TABLE 6

Row Number

0	$C(0, 0)$
1	$C(1, 0)$ $C(1, 1)$
2	$C(2, 0)$ $C(2, 1)$ $C(2, 2)$
3	$C(3, 0)$ $C(3, 1)$ $C(3, 2)$ $C(3, 3)$
4	$C(4, 0)$ $C(4, 1)$ $C(4, 2)$ $C(4, 3)$ $C(4, 4)$
5	$C(5, 0)$ $C(5, 1)$ $C(5, 2)$ $C(5, 3)$ $C(5, 4)$ $C(5, 5)$
6	$C(6, 0)$ $C(6, 1)$ $C(6, 2)$ $C(6, 3)$ $C(6, 4)$ $C(6, 5)$ $C(6, 6)$
7	$C(7, 0)$ $C(7, 1)$ $C(7, 2)$ $C(7, 3)$ $C(7, 4)$ $C(7, 5)$ $C(7, 6)$ $C(7, 7)$

and so on

Having a copy of Pascal's triangle handy gives us another option for evaluating combinations. Any time we need to know the number of combinations of n things taken r at a time (that is, the number of subsets of size r in a set of size n), we can simply read entry number r of row number n. Keep in mind that the *first* row shown is *row number 0*. Also, the first entry of each row can be called entry number 0. This entry gives the number of subsets of size 0 (which is always 1 since there is only one empty set).

EXAMPLE 1   A group of ten people includes six women and four men. If five of these people are randomly selected to fill out a questionnaire, how many different samples of five people are possible?

Since this is simply a matter of selecting a subset of five from a set of ten (or combinations of ten things taken five at a time), we can read $C(10, 5)$ from row 10 of Pascal's triangle in Table 5. The answer is 252.   ●

EXAMPLE 2   Among the 252 possible samples of five people in Example 1, how many of them would consist of exactly two women and three men?

Two women can be selected from six women in $C(6, 2)$ different ways, and three men can be selected from four men in $C(4, 3)$ different ways. These combination values can be read from Pascal's triangle. Then, since the task of obtaining two women and three men requires both individual parts, the fundamental counting principle tells us to multiply the two values:

$$C(6, 2) \cdot C(4, 3) = 15 \cdot 4 = 60.   ●$$

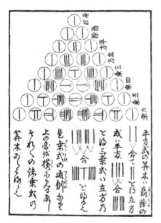

Japanese version of the triangle dates from the eighteenth century. The "stick numerals" evolved from bamboo counting pieces used on a ruled board. Possibly Omar Khayyam, twelfth-century Persian mathematician and poet, may also have divined its patterns in pursuit of algebraic solutions. (The triangle lists the coefficients of the binomial expansion.)

EXAMPLE 3   If five fair coins are tossed, in how many different ways could exactly three heads be obtained?

There are various "ways" of obtaining exactly three heads because the three heads can occur on different subsets of the coins. For example, *hhtht* and *thhth* are just two of many possibilities. When such a possibility is written down, exactly three positions are occupied by an *h*, the other two by a *t*. Each distinct way of choosing three positions from a set of five positions gives a different possibility.

(Once the three positions for *h* are determined, each of the other two positions automatically receives a *t*.) So our answer is just the number of size-three subsets of a size-five set, that is, the number of combinations of five things taken three at a time. We read this answer from row 5 of Pascal's triangle: $C(5, 3) = 10$. ●

Notice that row 5 of Pascal's triangle also provides answers to several other questions about tossing five fair coins. They are summarized in Table 7.

TABLE 7 Tossing Five Fair Coins

Number of Heads *n*	Ways of Obtaining Exactly *n* Heads	Listing
0	$C(5, 0) = 1$	ttttt
1	$C(5, 1) = 5$	htttt, thttt, tthtt, tttht, tttth
2	$C(5, 2) = 10$	hhttt, hthtt, httht, httth, thhtt, ththt, thtth, tthht, tthth, ttthh
3	$C(5, 3) = 10$	hhhtt, hhtht, hhtth, hthht, hthth, htthh, thhht, thhth, ththh, tthhh
4	$C(5, 4) = 5$	hhhht, hhhth, hhthh, hthhh, thhhh
5	$C(5, 5) = 1$	hhhhh

The Binomial Theorem

We will now look briefly at a totally different line of mathematical reasoning which also leads to Pascal's triangle, and applies it to a very important result in algebra. The "triangular" pattern of entries, it turns out, also occurs when "binomial" expressions are raised to various powers. (In algebra, any two-term expression, such as $x + y$, or $a + 2b$, or $w - 4$, is called a binomial.) The first few powers of the binomial $x + y$ are shown here, so that we can see the pattern.

$$(x + y)^0 = 1$$
$$(x + y)^1 = x + y$$
$$(x + y)^2 = x^2 + 2xy + y^2$$
$$(x + y)^3 = x^3 + 3x^2y + 3xy^2 + y^3$$
$$(x + y)^4 = x^4 + 4x^3y + 6x^2y^2 + 4xy^3 + y^4$$
$$(x + y)^5 = x^5 + 5x^4y + 10x^3y^2 + 10x^2y^3 + 5xy^4 + y^5$$

The coefficients in any one of these expansions are just the entries of one of the rows of Pascal's triangle. The expansions can be verified by direct computation, using the distributive, associative, and commutative properties of algebra. For example,

$$(x + y)^3 = (x + y) \cdot (x + y) \cdot (x + y)$$
$$= (x + y) \cdot [(x + y) \cdot (x + y)]$$
$$= (x + y) \cdot (x^2 + xy + yx + y^2)$$
$$= (x + y) \cdot (x^2 + 2xy + y^2)$$
$$= x^3 + 2x^2y + \ xy^2 + x^2y + 2xy^2 + y^3$$
$$= x^3 + 3x^2y + 3xy^2 + y^3.$$

Since the coefficients of the binomial expansions give us the rows of Pascal's triangle, they are precisely the numbers we have been referring to as *combinations* in our study of counting. (In the study of algebra, they have traditionally been referred to as **binomial coefficients,** and have been denoted differently. For example, rather than $C(n, r)$, you may see the notation $\binom{n}{r}$.) As "binomial coefficients," they can still be thought of as answering the question "How many?" if we reason as follows. In the expansion for $(x + y)^4$, how many are there of the expression x^2y^2? By looking in the appropriate entry of row 4 of Pascal's triangle, we see that the answer is 6.

Generalizing the pattern shown by the six expansions above, we obtain the important result known as the **binomial theorem** (or sometimes known as the **general binomial expansion**).

Binomial Theorem

For any positive integer n,

$$(x + y)^n = C(n, 0) \cdot x^n + C(n, 1) \cdot x^{n-1}y + C(n, 2) \cdot x^{n-2}y^2$$
$$+ C(n, 3) \cdot x^{n-3}y^3 + \ldots$$
$$+ C(n, n-1) \cdot xy^{n-1} + C(n, n) \cdot y^n,$$

or, using the factorial formula for combinations, and the fact that $C(n, 0) = C(n, n) = 1$,

$$(x + y)^n = x^n + \frac{n!}{(n-1)!1!} x^{n-1}y + \frac{n!}{(n-2)!2!} x^{n-2}y^2$$
$$+ \frac{n!}{(n-3)!3!} x^{n-3}y^3 + \ldots$$
$$+ \frac{n!}{1!(n-1)!} xy^{n-1} + y^n.$$

EXAMPLE 4 Write out the binomial expansion for $(x + y)^7$.

Reading the coefficients from row 7 of Pascal's triangle (Table 5), we obtain

$$(x + y)^7 = x^7 + 7x^6y + 21x^5y^2 + 35x^4y^3 + 35x^3y^4 + 21x^2y^5 + 7xy^6 + y^7. \quad \bullet$$

Recall that "binomial" expressions can involve terms other than x and y. The binomial theorem still applies.

EXAMPLE 5 Write out the binomial expansion for $(2a + 5)^4$.

Initially, we get coefficients from Pascal's triangle (row 4), but after all the algebra is finished the final coefficients are different numbers:

$$(2a + 5)^4 = (2a)^4 + 4(2a)^3 5 + 6(2a)^2 5^2 + 4(2a)5^3 + 5^4$$
$$= 2^4a^4 + 4(2^3a^3)5 + 6(2^2a^2)5^2 + 4(2a)5^3 + 5^4$$
$$= 16a^4 + 4 \cdot 8 \cdot a^3 \cdot 5 + 6 \cdot 4 \cdot a^2 \cdot 25 + 4 \cdot 2a \cdot 125 + 625$$
$$= 16a^4 + 160a^3 + 600a^2 + 1{,}000a + 625. \quad \bullet$$

4 EXERCISES

Read the following combination values directly from Pascal's triangle.

1. $C(4, 3)$
2. $C(5, 2)$
3. $C(6, 4)$
4. $C(7, 5)$

5. $C(8, 2)$
6. $C(9, 4)$
7. $C(9, 7)$
8. $C(10, 6)$

A committee of four Congressmen will be selected from a group of seven Democrats and three Republicans. Find the number of ways of obtaining each of the following. (See Example 2.)

9. exactly one Democrat
10. exactly two Democrats
11. exactly three Democrats
12. exactly four Democrats

Suppose eight fair coins are tossed. Find the number of ways of obtaining each of the following. (See Example 3.)

13. exactly three heads
14. exactly four heads
15. exactly five heads
16. exactly six heads

Kelly Melcher, searching for an Economics class, knows that it must be in one of nine classrooms. Since the professor does not allow people to enter after the class has begun, and there is very little time left, Kelly decides to try just four of the rooms at random.

17. How many different selections of four rooms are possible?

18. How many of the selections of Exercise 17 will fail to locate the class?

19. How many of the selections of Exercise 17 will succeed in locating the class?

20. What fraction of the possible selections will lead to "success"? (Give three decimal places.)

For a set of five elements, find the number of different subsets of each of the following sizes. (Use row 5 of Pascal's triangle to find the answers.)

21. 0
22. 1
23. 2
24. 3
25. 4
26. 5

27. How many subsets (of any size) are there for a set of five elements?

28. Find and explain the relationship between the row number and row sum in Pascal's triangle.

Over the years, many interesting patterns have been discovered in Pascal's triangle.* Exercises 29 and 30 exhibit two such patterns.

29. Name the next five numbers of the diagonal sequence indicated in the figure below. What special name applies to the numbers of this sequence?

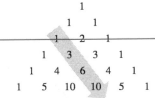

*For example, see the article "Serendipitous Discovery of Pascal's Triangle" by Francis W. Stanley in *The Mathematics Teacher*, February 1975.

30. Complete the sequence of sums on the diagonals shown in the figure below. What pattern do these sums make? What is the name of this important sequence of numbers? The presence of this sequence in the triangle apparently was not recognized by Pascal.

31. More than a century before Pascal's treatise on the "triangle" appeared, another work by the Italian mathematician Niccolo Tartaglia (1506–1559) came out and included the table of numbers shown here.

1	1	1	1	1	1
1	2	3	4	5	6
1	3	6	10	15	21
1	4	10	20	35	56
1	5	15	35	70	126
1	6	21	56	126	252
1	7	28	84	210	462
1	8	36	120	330	792

Explain the connection between Pascal's triangle and Tartaglia's "rectangle."

32. Construct another "triangle" by replacing every number in Pascal's triangle (rows **0** through **5**) by its remainder when divided by 2. What special property is shared by rows **2** and **4** of this new triangle?

33. What is the next row that would have the same property as rows **2** and **4** in Exercise 32?

34. How many even numbers are there in row number **256** of Pascal's triangle? (Do Exercises 32 and 33 first.)

Write out the binomial expansion for each of the following powers.

35. $(x + y)^6$ **36.** $(x + y)^8$ **37.** $(z + 2)^3$

38. $(w + 3)^5$ **39.** $(2a + 5b)^4$ **40.** $(3d + 5f)^4$

41. $(b - h)^7$ (*Hint:* First change $b - h$ to $b + (-h)$.)   **42.** $(2n - 4m)^5$

43. How many terms appear in the binomial expansion for $(x + y)^n$?

44. Observe the pattern in this table and fill in the blanks to discover a formula for the *r*th term (the general term) of the binomial expansion for $(x + y)^n$.

Term Number	Coefficient	Variable Part	Term
1	1	x^n	$1\,x^n$
2	$\dfrac{n!}{(n-1)!1!}$	$x^{n-1}y$	$\dfrac{n!}{(n-1)!1!}\,x^{n-1}y$
3	$\dfrac{n!}{(n-2)!2!}$	$x^{n-2}y^2$	$\dfrac{n!}{(n-2)!2!}\,x^{n-2}y^2$
4	$\dfrac{n!}{(n-3)!3!}$	$x^{n-3}y^3$	$\dfrac{n!}{(n-3)!3!}\,x^{n-3}y^3$
.	.	.	.
.	.	.	.
.	.	.	.
r	$\dfrac{n!}{(n-r+1)!(r-1)!}$	_____	_____

Use the results of Exercise 44 to find the indicated term of each of the following expansions.

45. $(x + y)^{12}$; 5th term

46. $(a + b)^{20}$; 16th term

47. Look at Table 5 and write out row 11 of Pascal's triangle.

The binomial theorem is sometimes used to approximate powers of decimal numbers that are close to some integer. For example, we can expand quantities like $3.1^{20} = (3 + .1)^{20}$, and $5.99^{18} = [6 + (-.01)]^{18}$.

Write each of the following expressions as a power of a sum or difference, and write out the first four terms only of its binomial expansion. Add those four terms and round your answer to three decimal places. Then use a scientific calculator to obtain the value of the original expression and verify that your approximation was accurate to three decimal places.

48. $(2.01)^{10}$

49. $(1.99)^8$

50. Explain why, in Exercises 48 and 49, just the first few terms of the expansion gave such good accuracy.

---

5   Counting Problems with "Not" and "Or"

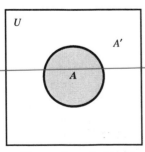

The complement of a set

FIGURE 8

When counting the number of ways that an event can occur (or that a "task" can be done), it is sometimes easier to take an indirect approach. In this section we will discuss two indirect techniques: first, the *complements principle*, where we start by counting the ways an event would *not* occur, and then the *additive principle*, where we break an event into simpler component events, and count the number of ways one component *or* another would occur.

Suppose *U* is the set of all possible results of some type and *A* is the set of all those results that satisfy a given condition. Recall from Chapter 2 that for any set *S*, the cardinal number of *S* (number of elements in *S*) is written $n(S)$, and the complement of *S* is written S'. Then Figure 8 suggests that

$$n(A) + n(A') = n(U), \qquad \text{or} \qquad n(A) = n(U) - n(A'),$$

as summarized here.

Complements Principle of Counting

If A is any set within the universal set U, then

$$n(A) = n(U) - n(A').$$

By this principle, the number of ways a certain condition can be satisfied is the total number of possible results minus the number of ways the condition would **not** be satisfied. (The arithmetic operation of *subtraction* corresponds to the set operation of *complementation* and to the logical connective of *negation,* that is "not.")

EXAMPLE 1   For the set $S = \{a, b, c, d, e, f\}$, find the number of proper subsets.

Recall that a proper subset of S is any subset with fewer than all six elements. Several subsets of different sizes would satisfy this condition. However, it is easier to consider the one subset that is not proper, namely S itself. As shown in Chapter 2, set S has a total of $2^6 = 64$ subsets. Thus, from the complements principle, the number of proper subsets is $64 - 1 = 63$. In words, the number of subsets that *are* proper is the total number of subsets minus the number of subsets that are *not* proper. ◆

Consider the tossing of three fair coins. Since each coin will land either heads (h) or tails (t), the possible results can be listed as follows.

hhh, hht, hth, thh, htt, tht, tth, ttt

(Even without the listing, we could have concluded that there would be eight possibilities. There are two possible outcomes for each coin, so the fundamental counting principle gives $2 \cdot 2 \cdot 2 = 2^3 = 8$.)

Now suppose we wanted the number of ways of obtaining *at least* one head. In this case, "at least one" means one or two or three. But rather than dealing with all three cases, we can note that "at least one" is the opposite (or complement) of "fewer than one" (which is zero). Since there is only one way to get zero heads (*ttt*), and there are a total of eight possibilities (as shown above), the complements principle gives the number of ways of getting at least one head: $8 - 1 = 7$. (The number of outcomes that include at least one head is the total number of outcomes minus the number of outcomes that do *not* include at least one head.) We find that indirect counting methods can often be applied to problems involving "at least," or "at most," or "less than," or "more than."

EXAMPLE 2   If four fair coins are tossed, in how many ways can at least one tail be obtained?

By the fundamental counting principle, $2^4 = 16$ different results are possible. Exactly one of these fails to satisfy the condition of "at least one tail" (namely, no tails, or *hhhh*). So our answer (from the complements principle) is $16 - 1 = 15$. ◆

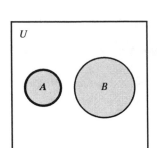

Disjoint sets

FIGURE 9

EXAMPLE 3 How many bridge hands (13 cards each) containing at least one heart are possible?

Example 9 of Section 3 showed that the total number of bridge hands possible is 635,013,559,600. The ones that do not have at least one heart are the ones formed from the 39 cards in the deck that are not hearts. So the number of hands with no hearts is

$$C(39, 13) = \frac{39!}{13!26!} = 8,122,425,444.$$

By the complements principle, the number of hands with at least one heart is

$$635,013,559,600 - 8,122,425,444 = 626,891,134,156. \quad \bullet$$

The complements formula is one way of counting indirectly. Another technique is related to Figure 9. If A and B are disjoint sets (have no elements in common), then writing the union of sets A and B as $A \cup B$ gives the principle stated here.

Special Additive Counting Principle

If A and B are disjoint sets, then

$$n(A \cup B) = n(A) + n(B).$$

(It is *special* because A and B are disjoint.) The principle states that if two conditions cannot both be satisfied together, then the number of ways that one **or** the other of them could be satisfied is found by adding the number of ways one of them could be satisfied to the number of ways the other could be satisfied. The idea is that we can sometimes analyze a set of possibilities by breaking it into a set of simpler component parts. (The arithmetic operation of *addition* corresponds to the set operation of *union* and to the logical connective of *disjunction,* that is "or.")

EXAMPLE 4 How many five-card hands consist of either all clubs or all red cards?

No hand that satisfies one of these conditions could also satisfy the other, so the two sets of possibilities (for all clubs and all red cards) are disjoint. Therefore, the special additive principle applies.

$$C(13, 5) + C(26, 5) = \frac{13 \cdot 12 \cdot 11 \cdot 10 \cdot 9}{5 \cdot 4 \cdot 3 \cdot 2 \cdot 1} + \frac{26 \cdot 25 \cdot 24 \cdot 23 \cdot 22}{5 \cdot 4 \cdot 3 \cdot 2 \cdot 1}$$
$$= 1,287 + 65,780$$
$$= 67,067 \quad \bullet$$

The special additive principle also extends to the union of three or more disjoint sets, as illustrated by the next example.

EXAMPLE 5   Terry White needs to take twelve more specific courses for a bachelors degree, including four in math, three in physics, three in computer science, and two in business. If five courses are randomly chosen from these twelve for next semester's program, how many of the possible selections would include at least two math courses?

Of all the information given here, what is important is that there are four math courses and eight other courses to choose from, and that five of them are being selected for next semester. If T denotes the set of selections that include at least two math courses, then we can write

$$T = A \cup B \cup C$$

where A = the set of selections with exactly two math courses,

                  B = the set of selections with exactly three math courses,

and C = the set of selections with exactly four math courses.

(In this case, *at least two* means exactly two **or** exactly three **or** exactly four.) The situation is illustrated in Figure 10.

By previous methods, we know that

$$n(A) = C(4, 2) \cdot C(8, 3) = 6 \cdot 56 = 336,$$
$$n(B) = C(4, 3) \cdot C(8, 2) = 4 \cdot 28 = 112,$$
and
$$n(C) = C(4, 4) \cdot C(8, 1) = 1 \cdot 8 = 8,$$

so that, by the additive principle,

$$n(T) = 336 + 112 + 8 = 456. \quad \blacklozenge$$

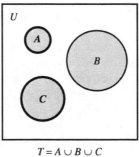

$T = A \cup B \cup C$	Nondisjoint sets
FIGURE 10	**FIGURE 11**

Figure 11 illustrates the case where two sets A and B are not disjoint, suggesting the general principle stated here.

General Additive Counting Principle

If A and B are any two sets, disjoint or not, then

$$n(A \cup B) = n(A) + n(B) - n(A \cap B).$$

(Recall that $A \cap B$ denotes the intersection of sets A and B.)

By this principle, the number of elements in $A \cup B$ is found by adding the number of elements in A and the number in B. Since this process counts the overlapping region twice, once for A and once for B, it is necessary to subtract one occurrence of the overlapping region.

EXAMPLE 6   Table 8 categorizes a diplomatic delegation of 18 Congressional members as to political party and sex. If one of the members is chosen randomly to be spokesperson for the group, in how many ways could that person be a Democrat or a woman?

TABLE 8

	Men (*M*)	Women (*W*)	Totals
Republican (*R*)	5	3	8
Democrat (*D*)	4	6	10
Totals	9	9	18

Using the general additive counting principle, we obtain

$$n(D \cup W) = n(D) + n(W) - n(D \cap W)$$
$$= 10 + 9 - 6$$
$$= 13. \quad \bullet$$

EXAMPLE 7   How many three-digit counting numbers are multiples of 2 or multiples of 5?

A multiple of 2 must end in an even digit (0, 2, 4, 6, or 8), so there are $9 \cdot 10 \cdot 5 = 450$ even three-digit counting numbers. A multiple of 5 must end in either 0 or 5, so there are $9 \cdot 10 \cdot 2 = 180$ of those. A multiple of both 2 and 5 is a multiple of 10 and must end in 0. There are $9 \cdot 10 \cdot 1 = 90$ of those, giving

$$450 + 180 - 90 = 540$$

possible three-digit numbers that are multiples of 2 or multiples of 5. $\bullet$

EXAMPLE 8   A single card is drawn from a standard 52-card deck.

(a) In how many ways could it be a heart or a king?

A single card can be both a heart and a king (the king of hearts), so use the general additive formula. There are thirteen hearts, four kings, and one card that is both a heart and a king:

$$13 + 4 - 1 = 16.$$

(b) In how many ways could the card be a club or a face card?

There are 13 clubs, 12 face cards, and 3 cards that are both clubs and face cards, giving

$$13 + 12 - 3 = 22. \quad \bullet$$

<table>
<tr><td>EXAMPLE 9</td></tr>
</table>

EXAMPLE 9 How many subsets of a 25-element set have more than three elements?

It would be a real job to count directly all subsets of size 4, 5, 6, . . . , 25. It is much easier to count those with three or fewer elements:

There is	$C(25, 0) = 1$	size-0 subset.
There are	$C(25, 1) = 25$	size-1 subsets.
There are	$C(25, 2) = 300$	size-2 subsets.
There are	$C(25, 3) = 2,300$	size-3 subsets.

Since the total number of subsets is $2^{25} = 33,554,432$ (use a calculator), the number with more than three elements must be

$$33,554,432 - (1 + 25 + 300 + 2,300) = 33,554,432 - 2,626$$
$$= 33,551,806. \quad ●$$

In Example 9, we used both the special additive formula (to get the number of subsets with no more than three elements) and the complements principle.

As you work the exercises of this section, keep in mind that indirect methods may be best, and that you may also be able to use permutations, combinations, the fundamental counting principle, or listing procedures such as product tables or tree diagrams. Also, you may want to obtain combination values, when needed, from Pascal's triangle.

---

5 EXERCISES

1. Explain why the complements principle of counting is called an "indirect" method.

2. Explain the difference between the *special* and *general* additive principles of counting.

If you toss seven fair coins, in how many ways can you obtain each of the following results?

3. at least one head ("At least one" is the complement of "none.")

4. at least two heads ("At least two" is the complement of "zero or one.")

5. at least two tails

6. at least one of each (a head and a tail)

If you roll two fair dice (say red and green), in how many ways can you obtain each of the following? (Refer to Table 2 in Section 1.)

7. a 2 on the red die

8. a sum of at least 3

9. a 4 on at least one of the dice

10. a different number on each die

Among the 635,013,559,600 possible bridge hands (13 cards each), how many contain the following cards? (The standard card deck was described in Section 3.)

11. at least one card that is not a spade (complement of "all spades")

12. cards of more than one suit (complement of "all the same suit")

13. at least one face card (complement of "no face cards")

14. at least one diamond, but not all diamonds (complement of "no diamonds or all diamonds")

How many three-digit counting numbers meet the following requirements?

15. even or a multiple of 5

16. greater than 600 or a multiple of 10

If a given set has twelve elements, how many of its subsets have the given numbers of elements?

17. at most two elements

18. at least ten elements

19. more than two elements

20. from three through nine elements

Of a group of 50 students, 30 enjoy music, 15 enjoy literature, and 10 enjoy both music and literature. How many of them enjoy the following?

21. at least one of these two subjects (general additive principle)

22. neither of these two subjects (complement of "at least one")

If a single card is drawn from a standard 52-card deck, in how many ways could it be the following? (Use the general additive principle.)

23. a club or a jack

24. a face card or a black card

25. a diamond or a face card or a denomination greater than 10 (First note that this is the same as "A diamond or a denomination greater than 10" since every face card has denomination greater than 10. Do not consider ace to be greater than 10 in this case.)

26. a heart or a queen or a red card (First note that this is the same as "A queen or a red card." Why is this true?)

Table 4 in Section 3 (For Further Thought) briefly descibed the various kinds of hands in five-card poker. A "royal flush" is a hand containing 10, jack, queen, king, and ace all in the same suit. A "straight flush" is any five consecutive denominations in a common suit. The lowest would be ace, 2, 3, 4, 5, and the highest is 9, 10, jack, queen, king. (An ace high straight flush is not referred to as a straight flush since it has the special name "royal flush.") A "straight" contains five consecutive denominations but not all of the same suit, and a "flush" is any hand with all five cards the same suit, except a royal flush or a straight flush. A "three of a kind" hand contains exactly three of one denomination, and furthermore the remaining two must be of two additional denominations. (Why is this?)

Verify each of the following. (Explain all steps of your argument.)

27. There are four ways to get a royal flush.

28. There are 36 ways to get a straight flush.

29. There are 5,108 ways to get a flush.

30. There are 10,200 ways to get a straight.

31. There are 624 ways to get four of a kind.

32. There are 54,912 ways to get three of a kind.

If three-digit numbers are formed using only digits from the set $\{0, 1, 2, 3, 4, 5, 6\}$, how many will belong to the following categories?

33. even numbers   **34.** multiples of 10

35. multiples of 100   **36.** multiples of 25

37. If license numbers consist of three letters followed by three digits, how many different licenses could be created having at least one letter or digit repeated? (*Hint:* Use the complements principle of counting.)

38. If two cards are drawn from a 52-card deck without replacement (that is, the first card is not replaced in the deck before the second card is drawn), in how many different ways is it possible to obtain a king on the first draw and a heart on the second? (*Hint:* Split this event into the two disjoint components "king of hearts and then another heart" and "non-heart king and then heart." Use the fundamental counting principle on each component, then apply the special additive principle.)

39. A committee of four faculty members will be selected from a department of twenty-five which includes professors Fontana and Spradley. In how many ways could the committee include at least one of these two professors?

Edward Roberts is planning a long-awaited driving tour, which will take him and his family on the southern route to the West Coast. Ed is interested in seeing the twelve national monuments listed here, but will have to settle for seeing just three of them since some family members are anxious to get to Disneyland.

New Mexico	Arizona	California
Gila Cliff Dwellings	Canyon de Chelly	Devils Postpile
	Organ Pipe Cactus	Joshua Tree
Petroglyph	Saguaro	Lava Beds
White Sands		Muir Woods
Aztec Ruins		Pinnacles

In how many ways could the three monuments chosen include the following?

40. sites in only one state

41. at least one site not in California

42. sites in fewer than all three states

43. sites in exactly two of the three states

44. In the figure here, a "segment" joins intersections and/or turning points. For example, the path from A straight up to C and then straight across to B consists of six segments. Altogether, how many paths are there from A to B that consist of exactly six segments?

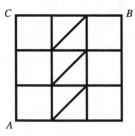

45. How many of the counting numbers 1 through 100 can be expressed as a sum of three or fewer powers of three (not necessarily distinct)? For example, 5 is such a number since $5 = 1 + 1 + 3$. (For one solution, see the October 1992 issue of *Mathematics Teacher,* page 497.)

46. Extend the general additive counting principle to three overlapping sets (as in the figure) to show that

$$n(A \cup B \cup C) = n(A) + n(B) + n(C)$$
$$- n(A \cap B) - n(A \cap C)$$
$$- n(B \cap C) + n(A \cap B \cap C).$$

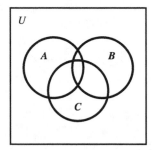

47. How many of the counting numbers 1 through 300 are *not* divisible by 2, 3, or 5? (*Hint:* Use the complements principle and the result of Exercise 46.)

48. How many three-digit counting numbers do not contain any of the digits 2, 5, 7, or 8?

49. Caralee Woods manages the shipping department of a firm that sells gold watches. If the watches can be shipped in packages of four, three, or one, in how many ways can a customer's order for fifteen watches be filled?

A Civil Air Patrol unit of fifteen members includes four officers. In how many ways can four of them be selected for a search and rescue mission in each of the following cases?

50. The search group must include at least one officer.

51. The search group must include at least two officers.

1 Counting by Systematic Listing

Use a definite system to get a complete list. (Consider possibilities from smaller to larger, in alphabetical order, from left to right, clockwise, and so on.) For multiple-part tasks, try product tables or tree diagrams.

2 The Fundamental Counting Principle

Statement of the Principle

When a task consists of k separate parts, if the first part can be done in n_1 ways, the second part can be done in n_2 ways, and so on through the kth part, which can be done in n_k ways, then the total number of possible results for completing the task is given by the product

$$n_1 \cdot n_2 \cdot n_3 \ldots n_k.$$

Factorials

For any counting number n, the quantity n factorial is given by

$$n! = n(n-1)(n-2) \ldots 2 \cdot 1.$$

Also, $0! = 1$ (by definition).

Arrangements of n Objects

The total number of different ways to arrange n distinct objects is $n!$.

3 Permutations and Combinations

$P(n, r)$ denotes the number of permutations, or arrangements, of n distinct things taken r at a time.

Permutation Formulas

$$P(n, r) = n(n-1)(n-2) \ldots (n-r+1) = \frac{n!}{(n-r)!}.$$

$C(n, r)$ denotes the number of combinations, or subsets, of n distinct things taken r at a time.

Combination Formulas

$$C(n, r) = \frac{P(n, r)}{r!} = \frac{n(n-1)(n-2) \ldots (n-r+1)}{r(r-1)(r-2) \ldots 2 \cdot 1} = \frac{n!}{r!(n-r)!}.$$

Guidelines for Choosing a Counting Method

1. If selected items *can* be repeated, use the fundamental counting principle.
2. If selected items *cannot* be repeated, and order *is* important, use permutations.
3. If selected items *cannot* be repeated, and order *is not* important, use combinations.

4 Pascal's Triangle and the Binomial Theorem

Pascal's Triangle

Row Number													Row Sum
0							1						1
1						1		1					2
2					1		2		1				4
3				1		3		3		1			8
4			1		4		6		4		1		16
5		1		5		10		10		5		1	32
6	1		6		15		20		15		6	1	64

and so on

In row n, the rth entry is $C(n, r - 1)$ and the row sum is 2^n.

Binomial Theorem

For any positive integer n,

$$(x + y)^n = C(n, 0) \cdot x^n + C(n, 1) \cdot x^{n-1}y$$
$$+ C(n, 2) \cdot x^{n-2}y^2 + C(n, 3) \cdot x^{n-3}y^3 + \ldots$$
$$+ C(n, n - 1) \cdot xy^{n-1} + C(n, n) \cdot y^n,$$

or, using the factorial formula for combinations, and the fact that $C(n, 0) = C(n, n) = 1$,

$$(x + y)^n = x^n + \frac{n!}{(n-1)!1!}x^{n-1}y + \frac{n!}{(n-2)!2!}x^{n-2}y^2$$
$$+ \frac{n!}{(n-3)!3!}x^{n-3}y^3 + \ldots$$
$$+ \frac{n!}{1!(n-1)!}xy^{n-1} + y^n.$$

5 Counting Problems with "Not" and "Or"

Complements Principle of Counting

If A is any set within the universal set U, then

$$n(A) = n(U) - n(A').$$

Special Additive Counting Principle

If A and B are disjoint sets, then

$$n(A \cup B) = n(A) + n(B).$$

General Additive Counting Principle

If A and B are any two sets, disjoint or not, then

$$n(A \cup B) = n(A) + n(B) - n(A \cap B).$$

CHAPTER TEST

If digits may be used from the set {0, 1, 2, 3, 4, 5, 6}, find the number of each of the following.

1. three-digit numbers

2. even three-digit numbers

3. three-digit numbers without repeated digits

4. three-digit multiples of five without repeated digits

5. Determine the number of triangles (of any size) in the figure shown here.

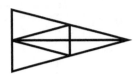

6. Construct a tree diagram showing all possible results when a fair coin is tossed four times, if the third toss must be different than the second.

7. How many non-repeating four-digit numbers have the sum of their digits equal to 30?

8. Using only digits from the set {0, 1, 2}, how many three-digit numbers can be written which have no repeated odd digits?

Evaluate the following expressions.

9. 5!

10. $\dfrac{8!}{5!}$

11. $P(12, 4)$

12. $C(7, 3)$

13. How many five-letter "words" without repeated letters are possible using the English alphabet? (Assume that any five letters make a "word.")

14. Using the Russian alphabet (which has 32 letters), and allowing repeated letters, how many five-letter "words" are possible?

If there are twelve players on a basketball team, find the number of choices the coach has in selecting each of the following.

15. four players to carry the team equipment

16. two players for guard positions and two for forward positions

17. five starters and five subs

18. a set of three or more of the players

Determine the number of possible settings for a row of four on-off switches under each of the following conditions.

19. There are no restrictions.

20. The first and fourth switches must be on.

21. The first and fourth switches must be set the same.

22. No two adjacent switches can be off.

23. No two adjacent switches can be set the same.

24. At least two switches must be on.

Four distinct letters are to be chosen from the set {A, B, C, D, E, F, G}. Determine the number of ways to obtain a subset that includes each of the following.

25. the letter D

26. both A and E

27. either A or E, but not both

28. equal numbers of vowels and consonants

29. more consonants than vowels

30. Write out and simplify the binomial expansion for $(x + 2)^5$.

31. If $C(n, r) = 495$ and $C(n, r + 1) = 220$, find the value of $C(n + 1, r + 1)$.

32. If you write down the second entry of each row of Pascal's triangle (starting with row 1), what sequence of numbers do you obtain?

33. Explain why there are $r!$ times as many permutations of n things taken r at a time as there are combinations of n things taken r at a time.

Answers to Selected Exercises

CHAPTER 1 *Sets*

1 Exercises

1. {1, 2, 3, 4}   **3.** {0, 1, 2, 3, 4, 5, 6}   **5.** {6, 7, 8, 9, 10, 11, 12, 13, 14}   **7.** {−15, −13, −11, −9, −7, −5, −3, −1}
9. {2, 4, 8, 16, 32, 64, 128, 256}   **11.** {1, 1/3, 1/9, 1/27, 1/81, 1/243}   **13.** {0, 2, 4, 6, 8, 10, 12, 14}
15. {21, 22, 23, . . .}   **17.** {Democrat, Republican}   **19.** {4, 8, 12, . . .}   **21.** {1, 1/2, 1/3, 1/4, . . .}
In Exercises 23–27, there may be other acceptable descriptions.
23. {$x \mid x$ is a rational number}   **25.** {$x \mid x$ is a movie released this year}   **27.** {$x \mid x$ is an odd counting number less
than 100}   **29.** finite   **31.** finite   **33.** infinite   **35.** infinite   **37.** 7   **39.** 500   **41.** 26   **43.** 19
45. 28   **47.** well defined   **49.** not well defined   **51.** not well defined   **53.** ∈   **55.** ∉   **57.** ∈   **59.** ∉
61. false   **63.** true   **65.** true   **67.** true   **69.** false   **71.** true   **73.** true   **75.** true   **77.** false
79. false   **81.** true   **85.** {2} and {3, 4} (Other examples are possible.)   **87.** {a, b} and {a, c} (Other examples are
possible.)   **89. (a)** {r}, {g, s}, {c, s}, {v, r}, {g, r}, {c, r}, {s, r}   **(b)** {v, g, r}, {v, c, r}, {v, s, r}, {g, c, r}, {g, s, r},
{c, s, r}

2 Exercises

1. ⊄   **3.** ⊆   **5.** ⊆   **7.** ⊄   **9.** both   **11.** ⊆   **13.** both   **15.** neither   **17.** true   **19.** false
21. true   **23.** true   **25.** true   **27.** true   **29.** true   **31.** false   **33.** false   **35.** true   **37.** false
39. 8; 7   **41.** 64; 63   **43.** 32; 31   **45.** {2, 3, 5, 7, 9, 10}   **47.** {2}   **49.** {1, 2, 3, 4, 5, 6, 7, 8, 9, 10}
51. {High cost, Entertaining, Fixed schedule, Current films, Low cost, Flexible schedule, Older films}   **53.** {High cost,
Fixed schedule, Current films}   **55.** {Low cost, Flexible schedule, Older films}   **57.** ∅   **59.** *ABCD, ABCE,
ABDE, ACDE, BCDE*   **61.** *AB, AC, AD, AE, BC, BD, BE, CD, CE, DE*   **63.** one way (none present)   **65.** They
are the same: $32 = 2^5$. The number of ways that people from a group of five can gather is the same as the number of subsets
there are of a set of five elements.   **67. (a)** 15   **(b)** 16, since it is now possible to select *no* bills.

3 Exercises

1. {a, c}   **3.** {a, b, c, d, e, f}   **5.** {a, b, c, d, e, f, g}   **7.** {b, d, f}   **9.** {d, f}   **11.** ∅   **13.** {a, b, c, e, g}
15. {a, c, e, g}   **17.** {a}   **19.** {e, g}   **21.** {d, f}   **23.** {e, g}

In Exercises 25–29, there may be other acceptable descriptions.
25. the set of all elements that either are in *A*, or are not in *B* and not in *C*   **27.** the set of all elements that are in *C* but not in *B*, or are in *A*   **29.** the set of all elements that are in *A* but not *C*, or in *B* but not *C*   **31.** $U = \{e, h, c, l, b\}$
33. $\{l, b\}$ **35.** $\{e, h, c, l, b\}$ **37.** the set of all tax returns showing business income or filed in 1994   **39.** the set of all tax returns filed in 1994 without itemized deductions   **41.** the set of all tax returns with itemized deductions or showing business income, but not selected for audit   **43.** always true   **45.** always true   **47.** not always true
49. always true   **51.** always true   **53.** (a) $\{1, 3, 5, 2\}$ (b) $\{1, 2, 3, 5\}$ (c) For any sets *X* and *Y*, $X \cup Y = Y \cup X$.
55. (a) $\{1, 3, 5, 2, 4\}$ (b) $\{1, 3, 5, 2, 4\}$ (c) For any sets *X*, *Y* and *Z*, $X \cup (Y \cup Z) = (X \cup Y) \cup Z$.   **57.** (a) $\{4\}$
(b) $\{4\}$ (c) For any sets *X* and *Y*, $(X \cup Y)' = X' \cap Y'$.   **59.** (a) $\{1, 3, 5\}$ (b) For any set *X*, $X \cup \varnothing = X$.
61. true   **63.** false   **65.** false   **67.** true   **69.** true   **71.** $A \times B = \{(2, 4), (2, 9), (8, 4), (8, 9), (12, 4),$
$(12, 9)\}$; $B \times A = \{(4, 2), (4, 8), (4, 12), (9, 2), (9, 8), (9, 12)\}$ **73.** $A \times B = \{(d, p), (d, i), (d, g), (o, p), (o, i), (o, g), (g, p),$
$(g, i), (g, g)\}$; $B \times A = \{(p, d), (p, o), (p, g), (i, d), (i, o), (i, g), (g, d), (g, o), (g, g)\}$ **75.** $n(A \times B) = 6$; $n(B \times A) = 6$
77. $n(A \times B) = 210$; $n(B \times A) = 210$ **79.** 3

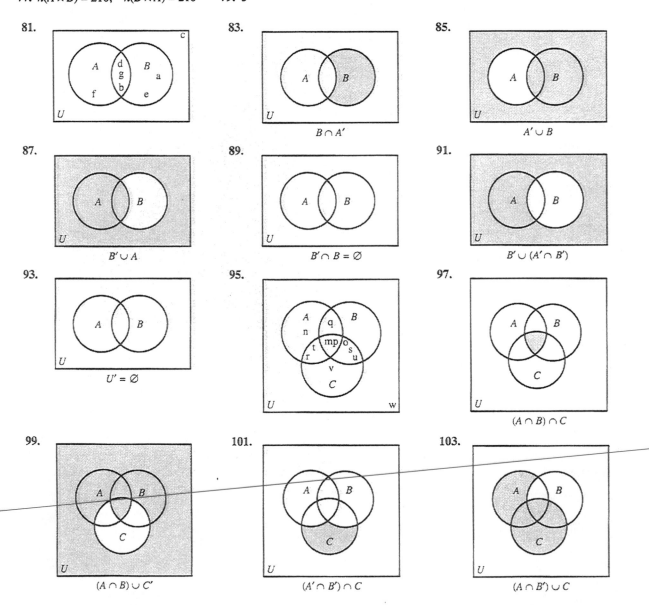

105.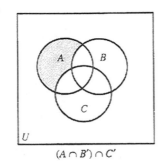
$(A \cap B') \cap C'$

107.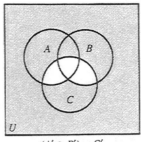
$(A' \cap B') \cup C'$

109. $A' \cap B'$ or $(A \cup B)'$ 111. $(A \cup B) \cap [(A \cap B)']$ or $(A \cup B) - (A \cap B)$ 113. $(A \cap B) \cup (A \cap C)$ or $A \cap (B \cup C)$ 115. $(A \cap B) \cap C'$ or $(A \cap B) - C$ 117. $A \cap B = \emptyset$ 119. true for *any* set A
121. $A = \emptyset$ 123. $A = \emptyset$ 125. $A = \emptyset$ 131. yellow (components: red and green); magenta (components: red and blue); cyan (components: blue and green)   135. both red and blue   137. always true   139. not always true
141. not always true   143. (a) $\{(3, 5), (3, 6), (4, 5), (4, 6)\}$

4 Exercises

1. (a) 16 (b) 32 (c) 33 (d) 45 (e) 14 (f) 26   3. (a) 0 (b) 4 (c) 3 (d) 0 (e) 6   5. (a) 37 (b) 22
(c) 50 (d) 11 (e) 25 (f) 11   7. (a) 31 (b) 24 (c) 11 (d) 45   9. (a) 9 (b) 9 (c) 20 (d) 20 (e) 27
(f) 15   11. 17   13. 16

15.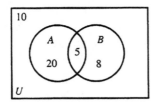

17.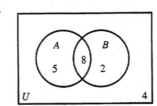

19.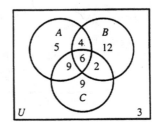

21.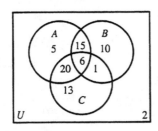

25. 4, 8, 16
27. 1, 2, 3, 4, 5, 6, 7, 8 , 9, 10, 11, 12, 13, 14, 15 (all except 16)
29. 5, 8, 13
31. (a) none (b) 52 (c) 44

5 Exercises

1. (Other correspondences are possible.)   3. (Other correspondences are possible.)   5. 11   7. 0   9. $\aleph_0$

$\{$I, II, III$\}$
$\updownarrow$ $\updownarrow$ $\updownarrow$
$\{$x, y, z$\}$

$\{$a, d, i, t, o, n$\}$
$\updownarrow$ $\updownarrow$ $\updownarrow$ $\updownarrow$ $\updownarrow$ $\updownarrow$
$\{$a, n, s, w, e, r$\}$

11. $\aleph_0$ 13. $\aleph_0$ 15. 12   17. $\aleph_0$ 19. both   21. equivalent   23. equivalent
25. $\{2, 4, 6, 8, \ldots, 2n, \ldots\}$ 27. $\{1,000,000, 2,000,000, 3,000,000, \ldots, 1,000,000n, \ldots\}$
$\updownarrow$ $\updownarrow$ $\updownarrow$ $\updownarrow$ $\updownarrow$ $\updownarrow$ $\updownarrow$ $\updownarrow$ $\updownarrow$
$\{1, 2, 3, 4, \ldots, n, \ldots\}$ $\{$ 1, 2, 3, $\ldots,$ n, $\ldots\}$
29. $\{2, 4, 8, 16, 32, \ldots, 2^n, \ldots\}$
$\updownarrow$ $\updownarrow$ $\updownarrow$ $\updownarrow$ $\updownarrow$ $\updownarrow$
$\{1, 2, 3, 4, 5, \ldots, n, \ldots\}$

31. Not always true. For example, let A = the set of counting numbers, B = the set of real numbers. **33.** Not always true. For example, A could be the set of all subsets of the set of reals. Then $n(A)$ would be an infinite number *greater* than c. **35.** **(a)** Rays emanating from point P will establish a geometric pairing of the points on the semicircle with the points on the line.

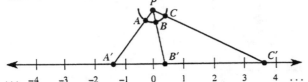

(b) The set of real numbers is infinite (having been placed in a one-to-one correspondence with a proper subset of itself).

37. $\{3, \quad 6, \quad 9, \quad 12, \quad \ldots, \quad 3n, \quad \ldots\}$
$\quad\;\; \updownarrow \quad \updownarrow \quad \updownarrow \quad \updownarrow \qquad\quad \updownarrow$
$\quad\;\; \{6, \quad 9, \quad 12, \quad 15, \quad \ldots, \quad 3n+3, \ldots\}$

39. $\{3/4, \quad 3/8, \quad 3/12, \quad 3/16, \quad \ldots, \quad 3/(4n), \quad \ldots\}$
$\quad\;\; \updownarrow \qquad \updownarrow \qquad \updownarrow \qquad \updownarrow \qquad\qquad \updownarrow$
$\quad\;\; \{3/8, \quad 3/12, \quad 3/16, \quad 3/20, \quad \ldots, \quad 3/(4n+4), \ldots\}$

41. $\{1/9, \quad 1/18, \quad 1/27, \quad \ldots, \quad 1/(9n), \quad \ldots\}$
$\quad\;\; \updownarrow \qquad \updownarrow \qquad \updownarrow \qquad\qquad \updownarrow$
$\quad\;\; \{1/18, \quad 1/27, \quad 1/36, \quad \ldots, \quad 1/(9n+9), \ldots\}$

45. $\aleph_0$ **47.** c **49.** c

Chapter 1 Test

1. $\{a, b, c, d, e\}$ **2.** $\{a, b, d\}$ **3.** $\{c, f, g, h\}$ **4.** $\{a, c\}$ **5.** true **6.** false **7.** true **8.** true
9. false **10.** true **11.** true **12.** true **13.** 8 **14.** 15

Answers may vary for Exercises 15–18.
15. the set of odd integers between -4 and 10 **16.** the set of months of the year **17.** $\{x \mid x \text{ is a negative integer}\}$
18. $\{x \mid x \text{ is a multiple of 8 between 20 and 90}\}$ **19.** $\subseteq$ **20.** neither

21.

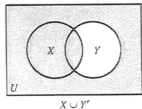

$X \cup Y'$

22.

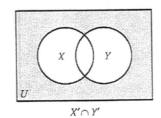

$X' \cap Y'$

23.

$(X \cup Y) - Z$

24.

$[(X \cap Y) \cup (Y \cap Z) \cup (X \cap Z)] - (X \cap Y \cap Z)$

25. {Electric razor}
26. {Adding machine, Barometer, Pendulum clock, Thermometer}
27. {Electric razor}
30. 18 **31.** 15 **32.** 20 **33.** 5

CHAPTER 2 *Logic*

1 Exercises

1. statement **3.** statement **5.** statement **7.** statement **9.** not a statement **11.** not a statement
13. statement **15.** not compound **17.** compound **19.** compound **21.** compound **23.** The flowers must

not be watered.   **25.** Some rain fell in southern California today.   **27.** At least one student present will not get another chance.   **29.** No people have all the luck.   **31.** Someone does not like Sara Lee.   **33.** $x \leq 3$ **35.** $p < 4$ **39.** She does not have blue eyes.   **41.** She has blue eyes and he is 43 years old.   **43.** She does not have blue eyes or he is 43 years old.   **45.** She does not have blue eyes or he is not 43 years old.   **47.** It is not the case that she does not have blue eyes and he is 43 years old.   **49.** $p \wedge \sim q$ **51.** $\sim p \vee q$ **53.** $\sim(p \vee q)$ or, equivalently, $\sim p \wedge \sim q$ **57.** true   **59.** true   **61.** true   **63.** false   **65.** false   **67.** C   **69.** B   **71.** A, B   **73.** A, B   **79.** against capital punishment

2 Exercises

1. It must be true.   **3.** F   **7.** T   **9.** T   **11.** F   **13.** T   **15.** T   **17.** T   **19.** a disjunction   **21.** T   **23.** T   **25.** T   **27.** T   **29.** F   **31.** T   **33.** T   **35.** T   **37.** 4   **39.** 16   **41.** 128   **43.** 6

In Exercises 45–59 and later in this chapter, we give the truth values found in the order in which they appear in the final column of the truth table, when the truth table is constructed in the format described in the section.
45. FFTF   **47.** FTTT   **49.** TTTT   **51.** FFFT   **53.** TFFF   **55.** FFFFTFFF   **57.** FTFTTTTT   **59.** TTTTTTTTTTTTFTTT   **61.** You can't pay me now and you can't pay me later.   **63.** It is not summer or there is snow.   **65.** I did not say yes or she did not say no.   **67.** $5 - 1 \neq 4$ or $9 + 12 = 7$ **69.** Neither Dasher nor Dancer will lead Santa's sleigh next Christmas.   **71.** T   **73.** F   **75.** F   **77.** T   **79.** F   **81.** T   **83.** T   **85.** inclusive disjunction   **87.** F   **89.** T   **91.** (a) Number the tubes from left to right across the top of the photograph. One sequence of balls is 1, 2, 4, 5, 8, and 11.   (b) Number the tubes from left to right. Use tubes 1, 3, 4, 5, 8, and 12.

3 Exercises

1. true   **3.** true   **5.** false   **7.** true   **11.** If it's in *USA Today*, then you can believe it.   **13.** If the person is Kathi Callahan, then her area code is 708.   **15.** If you're a soldier, then you maintain your weapon.   **17.** If it's a koala, then it doesn't live in Mississippi.   **19.** If it's an alligator, then it cannot live in these waters.   **21.** T   **23.** F   **25.** T   **27.** If I do not major in mathematics, then I pass my psychology course.   **29.** If I study in the library, then I major in mathematics and I pass my psychology course.   **31.** If I do not pass my psychology course, then I do not major in mathematics or I study in the library.   **33.** $s \rightarrow d$ **35.** $\sim d \rightarrow \sim s$ **37.** $d \vee (c \rightarrow s)$ **39.** $\sim s \rightarrow d$ **41.** T   **43.** F   **45.** T   **47.** F   **49.** T   **51.** T   **55.** TTTF   **57.** TTFT   **59.** TTTT; tautology   **61.** TFTF   **63.** TTTTTTFT   **65.** TTTTTTTTTTTTTTFT   **67.** You give your plants tender, loving care and they do not flourish.   **69.** She doesn't and he will not.   **71.** The person is a resident of Boise and is not a resident of Idaho.   **73.** You do not give your plants tender, loving care or they flourish.   **75.** She does or he will.   **77.** The person is not a resident of Boise or is a resident of Idaho.   **79.** equivalent   **81.** equivalent   **83.** equivalent   **85.** not equivalent   **87.** The truth table for both statements has final column TTTFFFFF.   **89.** true   **91.** true   **93.** false

Extension Exercises

1. $p \wedge (r \vee q)$ **3.** $q \vee [p \wedge (q \vee \sim p)]$; The statement simplifies to q.   **5.** $(\sim p \vee q) \vee (\sim p \vee \sim q)$; The statement simplifies to T.

7.

9.

11.

The statement simplifies to $(\sim p \wedge r) \wedge \sim q$.

13.

The statement simplifies to T.

15. $262.80

4 Exercises

Wording may vary in the answers to Exercises 1–9.
1. (a) If I follow, then you lead.   **(b)** If you do not lead, then I will not follow.   **(c)** If I do not follow, then you do not lead.   **3. (a)** If I were rich, then I would have a nickel for each time that happened.   **(b)** If I did not have a nickel for each time that happened, then I would not be rich.   **(c)** If I were not rich, then I would not have a nickel for each time that happened.   **5. (a)** If it contains calcium, then it's milk.   **(b)** If it's not milk, then it does not contain calcium.   **(c)** If it does not contain calcium, then it's not milk.   **7. (a)** If it gathers no moss, then it is a rolling stone.   **(b)** If it is not a rolling stone, then it gathers moss.   **(c)** If it gathers moss, then it is not a rolling stone.   **9. (a)** If there's fire, then there's smoke.   **(b)** If there's no smoke, then there's no fire.   **(c)** If there's no fire, then there's no smoke.
11. (a) $\sim q \to p$ **(b)** $\sim p \to q$ **(c)** $q \to \sim p$ **13. (a)** $\sim q \to \sim p$ **(b)** $p \to q$ **(c)** $q \to p$ **15. (a)** $(q \lor r) \to p$ **(b)** $\sim p \to (\sim q \land \sim r)$ **(c)** $(\sim q \land \sim r) \to \sim p$ **19.** If I finish studying, then I'll go to the party.
21. If $x > 0$, then $x > -1$.   **23.** If a number is a whole number, then it is an integer.   **25.** If you are in Fort Lauderdale, then you are in Florida.   **27.** If one is elected, then one is an environmentalist.   **29.** If the principal hires more teachers, then the school board approves.   **31.** If a number is an integer, then it is rational.   **33.** If pigs fly, then Rush will be a liberal.   **35.** If the figure is a parallelogram, then it is a four-sided figure with opposite sides parallel.
37. If the figure is a square, then it is a rectangle with two adjacent sides equal.   **39.** If an integer has a units digit of 0 or 5, then it is divisible by 5.   **41. (d)**   **45.** true   **47.** true   **49.** false   **51.** true   **53.** false   **55.** false
57. true   **59.** contrary   **61.** consistent   **63.** contrary   **65.** For example: That man is Arnold Parker.   That man sells books.   **67. (a)** $b \to \sim m$; $b \lor m$; $m \to b$ **(b)** FTTT   **(c)** The butler did it and the maid did it.   **(d)** TTF   **(e)** Neither did it;   TF.   **(f)** The butler did it.

5 Exercises

1. valid   **3.** invalid   **5.** invalid   **7.** valid   **9.** invalid   **11.** invalid   **13.** invalid   **15.** One possible conclusion is "All expensive things make you feel good."   **17.** invalid   **19.** valid   **21.** invalid   **23.** valid
25. invalid   **27.** invalid   **29.** valid   **33.** The boys are Dan Petry, Matt Bennington, Dave Walsh, and Barry and Billy Parker.

6 Exercises

1. valid by reasoning by transitivity   **3.** valid by modus ponens   **5.** fallacy by fallacy of the converse
7. valid by modus tollens   **9.** fallacy by fallacy of the inverse   **11.** valid by disjunctive syllogism   **13.** valid
15. invalid   **17.** invalid   **19.** invalid   **21.** valid   **23.** valid

25. Every time something squeaks, I use WD-40.
Every time I use WD-40, I go to the hardware store.
Every time something squeaks, I go to the hardware store.

27. valid   **29.** invalid   **31.** invalid   **33.** valid   **35.** valid

Answers in Exercises 39–45 may be replaced by their contrapositives.
39. If he is your son, then he cannot do logic.   **41.** If the person is a teetotaler, then the person is not a pawnbroker.
43. If it is an opium-eater, then it has no self-command.   **45.** If it is written on blue paper, then it is filed.
47. (a) $r \to p$ **(b)** $\sim r \to \sim q$ **(c)** $s \to \sim p$ **(d)** Your sons are not fit to serve on a jury.
49. (a) $s \to r$ **(b)** $p \to q$ **(c)** $q \to \sim r$ **(d)** Guinea pigs don't appreciate Beethoven.
51. (a) $p \to q$ **(b)** $\sim u \to \sim s$ **(c)** $t \to \sim r$ **(d)** $q \to s$ **(e)** $v \to p$ **(f)** $\sim r \to \sim u$ **(g)** Opium-eaters do not wear white kid gloves.

Chapter 2 Test

1. $5 + 3 \neq 9$ **2.** There is a good boy who does not deserve favour.   **3.** All people here can play this game.
4. It comes to that and I am here.   **5.** My mind is not made up or you can change it.   **6.** $\sim p \to q$ **7.** $p \vee \sim q$
8. $p \to \sim q$ **9.** It is not broken and you can fix it.   **10.** It is broken if and only if you can't fix it.   **11.** F
12. F   **13.** T   **14.** T   **15.** For a conditional statement to be false, the antecedent must be true and the consequent must be false. For a conjunction to be true, both component statements must be true.

In Exercises 17–18, we give the truth values found in the order in which they appear in the final column of the truth table, when the truth table is constructed in the format described in the chapter.
17. TFFF   **18.** TTTT (tautology)   **19.** true   **20.** true

Wording may vary in the answers to Exercises 21–25.
21. If it is a rational number, then it is a real number.   **22.** If a polygon is a rectangle, then it is a quadrilateral.
23. If a number is divisible by 6, then it is divisible by 2.   **24.** If she cries, then she is hurt.   **25. (a)** If the graph helps me understand it, then a picture paints a thousand words.   **(b)** If a picture doesn't paint a thousand words, then the graph won't help me understand it.   **(c)** If the graph doesn't help me understand it, then a picture doesn't paint a thousand words.   **26. (a)** $(q \wedge r) \to \sim p$ **(b)** $p \to (\sim q \vee \sim r)$ **(c)** $(\sim q \vee \sim r) \to p$ **27.** valid
28. (a) B   **(b)** F   **(c)** C   **(d)** B   **29.** valid   **30.** invalid

CHAPTER 3 *Numeration and Mathematical Systems*

1 Exercises

1. 2,412   **3.** 3,005,231   **5.** ????∩∩|||||| **7.** [Egyptian numerals]   **9.** [Egyptian numerals]

11. [Egyptian numerals]   **13.** [Egyptian numerals]   **15.** 246   **17.** 4,902   **19.** 六十三 [Chinese numeral]   **21.** 二千四百十六 [Chinese numeral]

23. 二百零二 to 二百二十 [Chinese numerals]   **25.** 九百六十 to 一千二百七十九 [Chinese numerals]   **27.** 392   **29.** 6,168   **31.** 22   **33.** 1,263

35. 57   **37.** 1,116   **39.** 533,000 shekels   **45.** 99,999   **47.** 3,124   **49.** $10^d - 1$ **51.** $7^d - 1$

2 Exercises

1. $(3 \times 10^1) + (7 \times 10^0)$ **3.** $(2 \times 10^3) + (8 \times 10^2) + (1 \times 10^1) + (5 \times 10^0)$ **5.** $(3 \times 10^3) + (6 \times 10^2) + (2 \times 10^1) + (8 \times 10^0)$
7. $(1 \times 10^7) + (3 \times 10^6) + (6 \times 10^5) + (0 \times 10^4) + (6 \times 10^3) + (0 \times 10^2) + (9 \times 10^1) + (0 \times 10^0)$ **9.** 73   **11.** 5,072
13. 50,602,003   **15.** 89   **17.** 32   **19.** 109   **21.** 722   **23.** 6   **25.** 207   **27.** 23   **29.** 4,536
31. [abacus diagram]   **33.** [abacus diagram]   **35.** 1,764   **37.** 28,084   **39.** 3,035,154

41. 496   **43.** 217,204   **45.** 410   **47.** 26,598

3 Exercises

1. 1, 2, 3, 4, 5, 6, 10, 11, 12, 13, 14, 15, 16, 20, 21, 22, 23, 24, 25, 26   **3.** 1, 2, 3, 4, 5, 6, 7, 8, 10, 11, 12, 13, 14, 15, 16, 17, 18, 20, 21, 22   **5.** 13_{five}; 20_{five} **7.** $B6E_{\text{sixteen}}$; $B70_{\text{sixteen}}$ **9.** 3   **11.** 11   **13.** smallest: $1,000_{\text{three}} = 27$; largest: $2,222_{\text{three}} = 80$ **15.** 14   **17.** 11   **19.** 956   **21.** 881   **23.** 28,854   **25.** 139   **27.** 5,601   **29.** 321_{five} **31.** $10,011_{\text{two}}$ **33.** 93_{sixteen} **35.** $2,131,101_{\text{five}}$ **37.** $1,001,001,010_{\text{two}}$ **39.** $102,112,101_{\text{three}}$ **41.** $111,134_{\text{six}}$ **43.** 32_{seven} **45.** $11,651_{\text{seven}}$ **47.** $11,110,111_{\text{two}}$ **49.** 467_{eight} **51.** $11,011,100_{\text{two}}$ **53.** $2D_{\text{sixteen}}$ **55.** 37_{eight} **57.** 1,427   **59.** 1011000   **61.** 1110010   **63.** CHUCK   **65.** 100111111100101101100110010111000011101110111010011   **67.** 27 and 63   **69.** pennies, nickels, and quarters   **73.** 32   **75.** no   **77.** no   **79.** no   **81.** no   **83.** no   **85.** 3,000,000   **87.** 200, 2,310

4 Exercises

1. 5   **3.** 6   **5.** row 2: 0, 6, 10;   row 3: 9, 0, 9;   row 4: 0, 4, 0, 8, 0;   row 5: 1, 9, 2, 7;   row 6: 6, 0, 0;   row 7: 4, 11, 6, 8, 3, 5;   row 8: 8, 4, 0, 0;   row 9: 6, 3, 9, 3, 9, 6, 3;   row 10: 6, 4, 0, 10, 8, 6, 4;   row 11: 10, 9, 8, 7, 6, 5, 4, 3, 2   **7.** yes   **9.** row 1: 0;   row 2: 0;   row 3: 0, 1, 2;   row 4: 0, 1, 2   **11.** yes   **13.** yes (0 is its own inverse, 1 and 4 are inverses of each other, and 2 and 3 are inverses of each other.)   **15.** yes   **17.** yes (1 is the identity element.)   **19.** 3   **21.** 4   **25.** 0700   **27.** 0000   **29.** false   **31.** true   **33.** 3   **35.** 3   **37.** 1   **39.** 10   **43.** 5   **45.** 4   **47. (a)** row 1: 0;   row 2: 2, 3, 4, 5, 6, 0, 1;   row 3: 3, 4, 5, 6, 0, 1, 2;   row 4: 4, 5, 6, 0, 1, 2, 3;   row 5: 5, 6, 0, 1, 2, 3, 4;   row 6: 6, 0, 1, 2, 3, 4, 5   **(b)** All four properties are satisfied.   **(c)** 0 is its own inverse, 1 and 6 are inverses of each other, 2 and 5 are inverses of each other, and 3 and 4 are inverses of each other.   **49. (a)** 1   **(b)** All properties are satisfied.   **(c)** 1 is its own inverse and 2 is its own inverse.   **51. (a)** row 2: 1, 3, 7;   row 3: 3, 0;   row 4: 3, 2, 1;   row 5: 6, 7, 4;   row 7: 3, 1, 6, 4;   row 8: 6, 5, 2   **(b)** no inverse property   **(c)** 1 is its own inverse, as is 8; 2 and 5 are inverses of each other, as are 4 and 7; 3 has no inverse, and 6 has no inverse.   **53.** {3, 10, 17, 24, 31, 38, . . .}   **55.** identity   **57.** 100,000   **59.** 62   **61. (a)** 365   **(b)** Friday   **63.** Chicago: July 23 and 29;   New Orleans: July 5 and August 16;   San Francisco: August 9   **65.** $-i$ **67.** i **69.** Sunday   **71.** Monday   **73.** Jan., Oct.   **75.** June   **77.** Wednesday   **79.** Monday   **81.** incorrect   **83.** 0   **85.** 9

5 Exercises

1. all properties;   1 is the identity element;   1 is its own inverse, as is 4;   2 and 3 are inverses.   **3.** commutative, associative, and identity properties; 1 is the identity element; 2, 3 and 4 have no inverses.   **5.** all properties;   1 is the identity element;   1, 3, 5, and 7 are their own inverses.   **7.** closure and commutative properties   **9.** all properties; A is the identity element; J and U are inverses; A and T are their own inverses.   **11.** a **13.** a **15.** row b: d;   row c: d, b;   row d: b, c **17.** associative, commutative, identity (U), closure

19.

	a	b	c	d
a	a	b	c	d
b	b	a	d	c
c	c	d	a	b
d	d	c	b	a

21. no   **23. (a)** true   **(b)** true   **(c)** true   **(d)** true   **25.** $a + b + c = 1$ or $a = 0$

27. (a) $a = 0$ **(b)** $a = 0$ **29.** Each side simplifies to e.   **31.** Each side simplifies to d.

33.

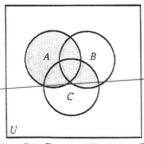

$A \cup (B \cap C) = (A \cup B) \cap (A \cup C)$

35. TTTTTFFF for each final column

6 Exercises

3. yes **5.** yes **7.** no: inverse **9.** no: closure **11.** no: inverse **13.** no: identity, inverse **15.** yes
17. yes **21.** S **23.** N **25.** M **27.** M **29.** N **31.** R **33.** T **35.** yes **37.** yes
39. all **41.** yes **43.** yes **45.** no **47.** 2 **49.** 3 **51.** 2 **53.** no: $4^1 = 4, 4^2 = 1, 4^3 = 4, 4^4 = 1$
55. yes; 3 and 5 are generators. **57.** yes; M and P are generators. **59.** cyclic group; generator $C*$
61. not a group **63.** yes **65.** no **67.** yes

Chapter 3 Test

1. ancient Egyptian; 2,536 **2.** 8,364 **3.** $(6 \times 10^4) + (0 \times 10^3) + (9 \times 10^2) + (2 \times 10^1) + (3 \times 10^0)$ **4.** 114
5. 38 **6.** 43,020 **7.** $111,010_{\text{two}}$ **8.** $24,341_{\text{five}}$ **9.** 256_{eight} **10.** $101,101,010,010_{\text{two}}$ **11.** less repetition
of symbols **12.** fewer different symbols to learn **13.** fewer digits in numerals **14.** 8 **15.** 9 **16.** 0
17. 6 **18.** 1 **19.** 0 **20.**

+	0	1	2	3	4	5
0	0	1	2	3	4	5
1	1	2	3	4	5	0
2	2	3	4	5	0	1
3	3	4	5	0	1	2
4	4	5	0	1	2	3
5	5	0	1	2	3	4

21.

×	0	1	2	3	4	5
0	0	0	0	0	0	0
1	0	1	2	3	4	5
2	0	2	4	0	2	4
3	0	3	0	3	0	3
4	0	4	2	0	4	2
5	0	5	4	3	2	1

22. $\{5, 17, 29, 41, 53, 65, \ldots\}$ **23.** $\{7, 15, 23, 31, 39, 47, \ldots\}$ **24.** 75 **26.** (a) yes (b) 0 **27.** (a) yes
28. (a) no **29.** (a) no **30.** (a) no

CHAPTER 4 *The Real Number System*

1 Exercises

1. **3.** **5.**

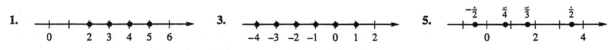

7. (a) 3, 7 (b) 0, 3, 7 (c) −9, 0, 3, 7 (d) −9, −5/4, −3/5, 0, 3, 5.9, 7 (e) $-\sqrt{7}, \sqrt{5}$ (f) All are real numbers.
9. true **11.** true **13.** false **15.** true **17.** true **19.** true **21.** (a) −5 (b) 5 **23.** (a) 6 (b) 6
27. 3; 3; 3; −3 **29.** $\{1, 2, 3, 4, 5, 6\}$ **31.** $\{12, 14, 16, 18, \ldots\}$ **33.** $\varnothing$ **35.** $\{3, -3\}$
37. $\{0, 5, 10, 15, \ldots\}$

Answers may vary in Exercises 39–43.
39. 1/2, 5/8, 1 3/4 **41.** −3 1/2, −2/3, 3/7 **43.** $\sqrt{5}, \sqrt{2}, -\sqrt{3}$ **45.** false **47.** true **49.** false **51.** true
53. true **55.** false **57.** true **59.** true **61.** 3 **63.** −7 **65.** 3 **67.** −4 **69.** yes, yes
71. no, no, yes, no, yes **73.** no, yes **75.** yes, yes, yes, no, yes **77.** no, no, yes, yes

2 Exercises

1. true **3.** false **5.** true **7.** −20 **9.** −4 **11.** −11 **13.** 9 **15.** 20 **17.** 4 **19.** 24
21. −1,296 **23.** 6 **25.** −6 **27.** 0 **29.** −6 **31.** −4 **33.** 27 **35.** 45 **37.** −2 **39.** (a), (b),
(c) **41.** commutative property of addition **43.** associative property of addition **45.** inverse property of addition
47. identity property of multiplication **49.** identity property of addition **51.** distributive property

53. closure property of addition **55. (a)** $-2, 2$ **(b)** commutative **(c)** Yes; choose $a = b$. For example, $a = b = 2$: $2 - 2 = 2 - 2$. **57. (a)** messing up your room **(b)** spending money **(c)** decreasing the volume on your portable radio **59.** identity **61.** no **65.** -81 **67.** 81 **69.** -81 **71.** -81 **73.** Any real number will satisfy the equation. **75.** 45° F **77.** 133 degrees (Fahrenheit) **79.** 34,500 ft **81.** 543 ft **83.** $-110°$ C **85.** $2,500 - (-140) = 2,640$ ft **87.** 14 ft

Extension Exercises

1. Let $A = \{a, b, c\}$ and let $B = \{d, e, f, g\}$. $A \cap B = \varnothing$ and $A \cup B = \{a, b, c, d, e, f, g\}$. $n(A) = 3$ and $n(B) = 4$, so $3 + 4 = n(A \cup B) = 7$. **3.** 4 **5.** $\{m, n, o, p, q\}$ **7.** no **9.** $\geq$ **11.** $5 = 5 + 0$ **13.** $26 = 26 \times 1$ **15.** Let $A = \{a, b, c\}$ and let $B = \{d, e, f, g, h\}$. $n(A) = 3$ and $n(B) = 5$. $\{d, e, f\}$ is a proper subset of B which is equivalent to A. Therefore, $3 < 5$.

3 Exercises

1. true **3.** true **5.** 1/3 **7.** $-3/7$

Answers will vary in Exercises 9 and 11. We give three of infinitely many possible answers.
9. 6/16, 9/24, 12/32 **11.** $-10/14, -15/21, -20/28$ **13. (a)** 1/3 **(b)** 1/4 **(c)** 2/5 **(d)** 1/3 **15.** the dots in the intersection of the triangle and the rectangle as a part of the dots in the entire figure **17. (a)** Carlton **(b)** De Palo **(c)** De Palo **(d)** Bishop **(e)** Crowe and Marshall; 1/2 **19.** 1/2 **21.** 43/48 **23.** $-5/24$ **25.** 23/56 **27.** 27/20 **29.** 5/12 **31.** 1/9 **33.** 3/2 **35.** 3/2 **37.** 23/22 **41.** 13/3 **43.** 29/10 **45.** 6 3/4 **47.** 6 1/8 **49.** -17 7/8 **51.** 3 **53.** 3/7 **55.** $-103/89$

57. $2 + \dfrac{1}{6 + \dfrac{1}{2}}$ **59.** $4 + \dfrac{1}{1 + \dfrac{1}{2 + \dfrac{1}{1 + \dfrac{1}{2}}}}$

61. 25/9 **63.** 70/29 **65.** 30 1/4 in **67.** 1/3 cup **69.** 14 7/16 tons

71. $2\left(\dfrac{10}{100}\right) + 3\left(\dfrac{10}{100}\right) = \dfrac{50}{100}$

In Exercise 73, we give only the numerical measures.
73. Monday: 1/2, 3/4, 1/2, 2 1/2, 1 1/4, 1 1/2, 1/4, 1 1/2, 1/4; Thursday: 2, 3, 2, 10, 5, 6, 1, 6, 1 **75.** 5/8 **77.** 19/30 **79.** $-3/4$ **81.** 14/19 **83.** 13/29 **85.** 5/2 **87.** It gives the rational number halfway between the two integers. **89.** .75 **91.** .1875 **93.** $.\overline{27}$ **95.** $.\overline{285714}$ **97.** 2/5 **99.** 17/20 **101.** 467/500 **103.** 8/9 **105.** 6/11 **107.** 13/30 **109.** 2 **111.** repeating **113.** terminating **115.** terminating **117. (a)** $.\overline{3}$ or .333. . . **(b)** $.\overline{6}$ or .666. . . **(c)** $.\overline{9}$ or .999. . .

4 Exercises

1. rational **3.** irrational **5.** rational **7.** rational **9.** irrational **11.** rational **13.** irrational **15. (a)** $.\overline{8}$ **(b)** irrational, rational

The number of digits shown will vary among calculator models in Exercises 17–23.
17. 6.244997998 **19.** 3.885871846 **21.** 29.73213749 **23.** 1.060660172 **25.** yes, yes **27.** no, no, yes, no, yes **29.** no, yes **31.** no, no, yes, yes **33.** The result is 3.1415929, which agrees with the first seven digits in the decimal form of π. **35. (a)** 3.1415926 **(b)** 3.141592653589 **(c)** 3.14159265358979 **37.** They are only rational *approximations* of π. **39.** $5\sqrt{2}$; 7.071067812 **41.** $5\sqrt{3}$; 8.660254038 **43.** $12\sqrt{2}$; 16.97056275 **45.** $5\sqrt{6}/6$; 2.041241452 **47.** $\sqrt{7}/2$; 1.322875656 **49.** $\sqrt{21}/3$ 1.527525232 **53.** $2\sqrt{6}$ **55.** $3\sqrt{17}$ **57.** $4\sqrt{7}$ **59.** $10\sqrt{2}$ **61.** $3\sqrt{3}$ **63.** $20\sqrt{2}$ **65. (a)** 1.414213562 **(b)** 2.645751311 **(c)** 3.633180425 **(d)** 5 **67. (a)** $\sqrt[3]{a}$ **(b)** 2.5198421 **(c)** 2.5198421 **(d)** They are the same. **(e)** They are the same.

5 Exercises

1. true   **3.** false   **5.** false   **7.** false   **9.** false   **11.** 11.315   **13.** −4.215   **15.** .8224   **17.** 47.5
19. 31.6   **21.** $61.48   **23.** $4,313.14   **25.** $35.34   **27. (a)** .031   **(b)** .035   **29.** 297
31. (a) 78.4   **(b)** 78.41   **33. (a)** .1   **(b)** .08   **35. (a)** 12.7   **(b)** 12.69   **37.** 42%   **39.** 36.5%
41. .8%   **43.** 210%   **45.** 20%   **47.** 1%   **49.** 37 1/2%   **51.** 150%   **55. (a)** 5   **(b)** 24   **(c)** 8   **(d)** .5
or 1/2   **(e)** 600   **57.** No, it is $49.50.   **59. (a)** 33 1/3%   **(b)** 25%   **(c)** 40%   **(d)** 33 1/3%   **61.** 124.8
63. 2.94   **65.** 150%   **67.** 600   **69.** 1.4%   **71. (a)**   **73. (c)**   **75.** $533   **77.** 11.8%   **79.** 180%
81. 16.1%   **83.** 2,243   **85. (a)** 15.6%   **(b)** 50%   **87.** $4.50   **89.** $.75   **91. (a)** 3; 2; 5   **(b)** 5; 5

Extension Exercises

1. $12i$ **3.** $-15i$ **5.** $i\sqrt{3}$ **7.** $5i\sqrt{3}$ **9.** −5   **11.** −18   **13.** −40   **15.** $\sqrt{2}$ **17.** $3i$ **19.** 6
23. 1   **25.** −1   **27.** $-i$ **29.** i

Chapter 4 Test

1. (a) 10   **(b)** 0, 10   **(c)** −8, 0, 10   **(d)** −8, −4/3, −.6, 0, 3.9, 10   **(e)** $-\sqrt{6}, \sqrt{2}$ **(f)** All are real numbers.
3. {1, 2, 3}   **4.** Answers may vary. Three examples are 1/2, 3/4, 5/6.   **5.** true   **6. (a)** 1   **(b)** 3   **(c)** 10
7. $(7 + 7)/(7 - 7)$ is undefined.   **8. (a)** E   **(b)** A   **(c)** B   **(d)** D   **(e)** F   **(f)** C   **9.** 20°   **10. (d)**
11. (a) Hickman   **(b)** Camp and Levinson   **(c)** Hickman   **(d)** Cooper and Cornett; 2/5   **12.** 11/16   **13.** 57/160
14. − 2/5   **15.** 3/2   **16.** 8 23/24 hours   **17.** .45   **18.** .41$\overline{6}$ **19.** 18/25   **20.** 58/99   **21. (a)** irrational
(b) rational   **(c)** rational   **(d)** rational   **(e)** irrational   **22. (a)** $5\sqrt{6}$ **(b)** 12.247448714   **23. (a)** $\dfrac{13\sqrt{7}}{7}$
(b) 4.913538149   **24. (a)** $-32\sqrt{2}$ **(b)** − 45.254834   **26.** 13.81   **27.** −.315   **28.** 38.7
29. −24.3   **30. (a)** 9.04   **(b)** 9.045   **31.** 16.65   **32.** 101.5   **33.** 400%   **34. (c)**   **35.** 12.1%
36. 26 2/3%   **37.** 66 2/3%   **38.** true   **39.** false   **40.** true

CHAPTER 5   *Counting Methods*

1 Exercises

1. *AB, AC, AD, AE, BA, BC, BD, BE, CA, CB, CD, CE, DA, DB, DC, DE, EA, EB, EC, ED*; 20 ways   **3.** *AC, AE, BC,*
BE, CA, CB, CD, DC, DE, EA, EB, ED; 12 ways   **5.** *ACE, AEC, BCE, BEC, DCE, DEC*; 6 ways   **7.** *ABC, ABD,*
ABE, ACD, ACE, ADE, BCD, BCE, BDE, CDE; 10 ways   **9.** 1   **11.** 3   **13.** 5   **15.** 5   **17.** 3   **19.** 1
21. 18   **23.** 15   **25.**   **27.** 11, 22, 33, 44, 55, 66

	1	2	3	4	5	6
1	11	12	13	14	15	16
2	21	22	23	24	25	26
3	31	32	33	34	35	36
4	41	42	43	44	45	46
5	51	52	53	54	55	56
6	61	62	63	64	65	66

29. 11, 13, 23, 31, 41, 43, 53, 61   **31.** 16, 25, 36, 64   **33.** 16, 32, 64

35.

| First coin | Second coin | Third coin | Fourth coin | Result |

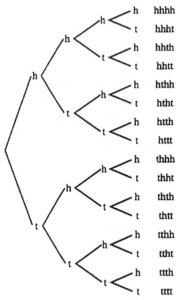

(a) tttt (b) hhhh, hhht, hhth, hhtt, hthh, htht, htth, thhh, thht, thth, tthh (c) httt, thtt, ttht, ttth, tttt
(d) hhhh, hhht, hhth, hhtt, hthh, htht, htth, httt, thhh, thht, thth, thtt, tthh, ttht, ttth **37.** 16 **39.** 44 **41.** 17
43. 72 **45.** 12 **47.** 10 **49.** 6 **51.** 3 **53.** 54 **55.** 18 **57.** 138 **59.** 16 **61.** 13 **63.** 4
65. 883 **69.** 3

2 Exercises

3. (a) no **5.** 24 **7.** 336 **9.** 20 **11.** 84 **13.** 840 **15.** 39,916,800 **17.** 95,040 **19.** 1,716
21. 184,756 **23.** $4.151586701 \times 10^{12}$ **25.** $2 \cdot 2 \cdot 2 = 8$ **29.** 216 **31.** $5! = 120$ **33.** $3 \cdot 2 = 6$
35. $4 \cdot 5^2 = 100$ **37.** $3 \cdot 4 \cdot 3 \cdot 2 = 72$ **39.** $6 \cdot 3^2 \cdot 1 = 54$ **41.** $4 \cdot 2 \cdot 3 = 24$ **43.** $2^8 = 256$
45. $3 \cdot 2 \cdot 4 \cdot 5 = 120$ **47.** $3 \cdot 2 \cdot 4 \cdot 3 = 72$ **49.** $3 \cdot 2 \cdot 1 \cdot 3 = 18$ **51.** $2 \cdot 4 \cdot 6 = 48$ **53.** $5! = 120$
55. (a) 6 **(b)** 5 **(c)** 4 **(d)** 3 **(e)** 2 **(f)** 1; $6 \cdot 5 \cdot 4 \cdot 3 \cdot 2 \cdot 1 = 720$ **57. (a)** 3 **(b)** 3 **(c)** 2 **(d)** 2 **(e)** 1
(f) 1; $3 \cdot 3 \cdot 2 \cdot 2 \cdot 1 \cdot 1 = 36$

3 Exercises

1. 20 **3.** 1 **5.** 35 **7.** 70 **9.** 840 **11.** 1,320 **13.** 5 **15.** 330 **17.** 62,990,928,000
19. $C(51, 6) = 18,009,460$ **25.** $P(6, 3) = 120$ **27.** $C(100, 5) = 75,287,520$ **29.** $2 \cdot P(25, 2) = 1,200$
31. $P(26, 3) \cdot P(10, 3) \cdot P(26, 3) = 175,219,200,000$ **33.** $C(24, 5) = 42,504$ **35.** $C(25, 3) \cdot C(22, 4) \cdot C(18, 5) \cdot$
$C(13, 6) = 2.47365374256 \times 10^{14}$ **37.** $\dfrac{8 \cdot 21}{2} = 84$ **39. (a)** $8! \cdot 7! = 203,212,800$ **(b)** $8 \cdot 7 \cdot 13! = 348,713,164,800$
(c) $13! = 6,227,020,800$ **(d)** $8! \cdot 7! = 203,212,800$ **(e)** $8 \cdot 7 \cdot 6 \cdot 12! = 160,944,537,600$ **41.** $C(13, 5) = 1,287$

43. 0 (impossible)   **45.** $C(12, 2) \cdot C(40, 3) = 652,080$ **47.** $40^3 = 64,000$ **49.** $C(6, 3) = 20$
51. $C(6, 2) \cdot C(6, 3) \cdot C(6, 4) = 4,500$ **53. (a)** $6! = 720$ **(b)** 523,647   **55.** $C(10, 3) = 120$ **57.** $C(24, 2) = 300$
59. $C(9, 3) + C(9, 4) = 210$ **61.** Each is equal to 220.

4 Exercises

1. 4   **3.** 15   **5.** 28   **7.** 36   **9.** $C(7, 1) \cdot C(3, 3) = 7$ **11.** $C(7, 3) \cdot C(3, 1) = 105$ **13.** $C(8, 3) = 56$
15. $C(8, 5) = 56$ **17.** $C(9, 4) = 126$ **19.** 56   **21.** 1   **23.** 10   **25.** 5   **27.** 32   **29.** $\ldots, 15, 21, 28,$
$36, 45, \ldots$; these are the triangular numbers.   **31.** The rows of Tartaglia's rectangle correspond to the diagonals of
Pascal's triangle.   **33.** row 8   **35.** $x^6 + 6x^5y + 15x^4y^2 + 20x^3y^3 + 15x^2y^4 + 6xy^5 + y^6$ **37.** $z^3 + 6z^2 + 12z + 8$
39. $16a^4 + 160a^3b + 600a^2b^2 + 1,000ab^3 + 625b^4$ **41.** $b^7 - 7b^6h + 21b^5h^2 - 35b^4h^3 + 35b^3h^4 - 21b^2h^5 + 7bh^6 - h^7$

43. $n + 1$ **45.** $n = 12, r = 5$: $\dfrac{12!}{8!4!}x^8y^4 = 495x^8y^4$ **47.** 1   11   55   165   330   462   462   330   165   55   11   1

49. $[2 + (-.01)]^8 = 2^8 + 8 \cdot 2^7(-.01) + 28 \cdot 2^6(-.01)^2 + 56 \cdot 2^5(-.01)^3 + \ldots$
$$= 256 - 10.24 + .1792 - .001792 + \ldots$$
$$= 245.937408$$
$$\approx 245.937$$

Calculator:
$$(1.99)^8 = 245.937419155 \ldots$$
$$\approx 245.937 \text{ (same answer to three places)}$$

5 Exercises

3. $2^7 - 1 = 127$ **5.** 120   **7.** 6   **9.** $6 + 6 - 1 = 11$ **11.** $635,013,559,600 - 1 = 635,013,559,599$
13. $635,013,559,600 - C(40, 13) = 622,980,336,720$ **15.** $9 \cdot 10 \cdot 6 = 540$ **17.** $C(12, 0) + C(12, 1) + C(12, 2) = 79$
19. $2^{12} - 79 = 4,017$ **21.** $30 + 15 - 10 = 35$ **23.** $13 + 4 - 1 = 16$ **25.** $13 + 12 - 3 = 22$ **33.** $6 \cdot 7 \cdot 4 = 168$
35. $6 \cdot 1 \cdot 1 = 6$ **37.** $26^3 \cdot 10^3 - P(26, 3) \cdot P(10, 3) = 6,344,000$ **39.** $C(25, 4) - C(23, 4) = 3,795$
41. $C(12, 3) - C(5, 3) = 210$ **43.** $C(12, 3) - (15 + 60) = 145$ **45.** 40   **47.** $300 - (150 + 100 + 60 - 50 - 30 -$
$20 + 10) = 80$ **49.** 15   **51.** $C(15, 4) - [C(11, 4) + C(11, 3) \cdot C(4, 1)] = 375$

Chapter 5 Test

1. $6 \cdot 7 \cdot 7 = 294$ **2.** $6 \cdot 7 \cdot 4 = 168$ **3.** $6 \cdot 6 \cdot 5 = 180$ **4.** $6 \cdot 5 \cdot 1 = 30$ end in 0; $5 \cdot 5 \cdot 1 = 25$ end in 5;
$30 + 25 = 55$ **5.** 13   **6.**   **7.** $4! = 24$ **8.** 12   **9.** 120   **10.** 336

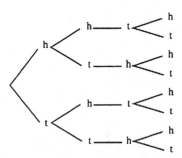

First   Second   Third   Fourth
toss   toss   toss   toss

11. 11,880   **12.** 35   **13.** $P(26, 5) = 7,893,600$ **14.** $32^5 = 33,554,432$ **15.** $C(12, 4) = 495$ **16.** $C(12, 2) \cdot$
$C(10, 2) = 2,970$ **17.** $C(12, 5) \cdot C(7, 5) = 16,632$ **18.** $2^{12} - [C(12, 0) + C(12, 1) + C(12, 2)] = 4,017$
19. $2^4 = 16$ **20.** $2^2 = 4$ **21.** $2 \cdot 2^2 = 8$ **22.** 8   **23.** 2   **24.** $16 - (1 + 4) = 11$ **25.** $C(6, 3) = 20$
26. $C(5, 2) = 10$ **27.** $2 \cdot C(5, 3) = 20$ **28.** $C(5, 2) = 10$ **29.** $C(5, 4) + C(2, 1) \cdot C(5, 3) = 25$
30. $x^5 + 10x^4 + 40x^3 + 80x^2 + 80x + 32$ **31.** $495 + 220 = 715$ **32.** the counting numbers

Index